OXFORD MEDIEVAL TEXTS

GENERAL EDITORS

C. N. L. BROOKE   D. E. GREENWAY

M. WINTERBOTTOM

BEDE'S
ECCLESIASTICAL HISTORY
OF THE ENGLISH PEOPLE

Bede's
Ecclesiastical History of the English People
A Historical Commentary

J. M. WALLACE-HADRILL

CLARENDON PRESS · OXFORD

OXFORD
UNIVERSITY PRESS

Great Clarendon Street, Oxford OX2 6DP

Oxford University Press is a department of the University of Oxford.
It furthers the University's objective of excellence in research, scholarship,
and education by publishing worldwide in

Oxford New York

Athens Auckland Bangkok Bogotá Buenos Aires Cape Town
Chennai Dar es Salaam Delhi Florence Hong Kong Istanbul Karachi
Kolkata Kuala Lumpur Madrid Melbourne Mexico City Mumbai Nairobi
Paris São Paulo Shanghai Singapore Taipei Tokyo Toronto Warsaw

with associated companies in Berlin Ibadan

Oxford is a registered trade mark of Oxford University Press
in the UK and in certain other countries

Published in the United States
by Oxford University Press Inc., New York

ISBN 0-19-822269-6 (Hbk)
ISBN 0-19-822174-6 (Pbk)

Printed in Great Britain by
Biddles Short Run Books
King's Lynn

GENERAL EDITORS' NOTE

Over many years the late Professor Michael Wallace-Hadrill acted as adviser to the general editors of this series, and we owe a deep debt to his wisdom and support among the Delegates of the Press. The first of his Oxford colleges, Corpus Christi, where he was an undergraduate and honorary fellow, gave him an early link with Charles Plummer; and when we consulted him (with Sir Roger Mynors' ready support) on the revision of the edition of Bede's *Historia Ecclesiastica*, we did not turn to him in vain. In the event he decided to follow Plummer's example and provide a second volume of commentary, leaving the edition of Colgrave and Mynors untouched. At his death the commentary was complete, though not finally revised and still in a state which he regarded as provisional. His family have generously allowed us to publish it as he left it, and we and all scholars who study Bede owe much to them for their help and understanding, and especially to Mrs Anne Wallace-Hadrill, his widow, to Andrew Wallace-Hadrill, his son, and to Andrew's wife Jo, who typed the manuscript.

In accordance with the author's wish, Thomas Charles-Edwards has seen it through the Press. This has involved an immense amount of detailed checking, in which he has been greatly aided by David Dumville and Clive Burgess. All who use and profit from this book owe them deep gratitude. He and the general editors have made the minor corrections which were needed, which were astonishingly few, and in this he has been generously helped by Patrick Wormald, whose penetrating eye has also surveyed the text of the commentary: the addenda, which incorporate some additions to the commentary from the most recent literature, and a few notes on difficult points of interpretation, are the joint work of Wormald and Charles-Edwards—to both we offer warmest thanks; some of the addenda incorporate observations made by David Dumville, Paul Meyvaert, and Robert Markus, to whom we are very grateful; to Charles-Edwards also for the bibliography and index,

and for all he has done as editor of this book; and to Sir Richard
Southern for his wise and friendly counsel. All that is missing is
the introduction, which remained unwritten; in its place we have
set the author's own account of the other great commentator on
whose work his own was founded, Charles Plummer. This first
appeared in Michael Wallace-Hadrill's collected essays, *Early
Medieval History* (Oxford, Basil Blackwell, 1975), 76–95, and in
Famulus Christi, ed. G. Bonner (London, SPCK, 1976), 366–85,
and we are grateful to the publishers for their concurrence to its
reprinting here.

This commentary was written as a companion volume to the
edition and translation by Bertram Colgrave and Sir Roger
Mynors, published in OMT in 1969. When it first appeared it
was immediately apparent that Mynors's introduction on the
history of the text was a major contribution to scholarship, and
that his text—though it differed little from Plummer's, owing to
the textual accuracy which the early scribes must have learnt
from Bede himself—was almost immaculate. But Colgrave's
notes made no pretence to match the ample commentary of
Charles Plummer, in the second volume of his edition of 1896.
Wallace-Hadrill once suggests a correction to Mynors' text,
following J. O. Prestwich (p. 121); at various points he corrects
Colgrave's translation and replaces his notes. But for the most
part he assumes knowledge of Colgrave's notes on biblical
sources and on persons and the like, and builds his own
commentary in his terse and lapidary style, richly charged with
point and meaning, so familiar to all students of the early middle
ages. Reference is by page and line of the OMT Latin text, and
by book and chapter. In the margin of the OMT text may be
found the pages of Plummer's text, and these pages were also
noted in Plummer's commentary: by comparison of these the
references in this book to Plummer may be readily identified—
for at all points he watched Plummer's comments with an
attentive eye; and the student of the present commentary will
recall that there is still a rich harvest to be gathered from
Plummer himself—for no modern commentator could repeat the
mass of detail (not always, it must be confessed, immediately
relevant to Bede's text) which Plummer deployed, any more
than Wallace-Hadrill would have thought of imitating Plummer's 'amplifying style'. He once spoke as if a revised Plummer

would be larger than the original (p. xviii below); but an attentive reader who compares the two will readily understand why it has not proved so.

It is a singular privilege to welcome to the Series this book, in which one of the most notable medievalists of our day paid tribute to his noble predecessors.

C.N.L.B.
D.E.G.
M.W.

CONTENTS

ABBREVIATIONS

AA SS	*Acta Sanctorum* (Bollandists).
AA SS Ben.	*Acta Sanctorum Ordinis S. Benedicti*, ed. L. d'Achery and J. Mabillon.
Anal. Boll.	*Analecta Bollandiana.*
The Anglo-Saxons	*The Anglo-Saxons*, ed. J. Campbell (Oxford, 1982).
ASC	*Anglo-Saxon Chronicle.*
ASE	*Anglo-Saxon England*, ed. P. Clemoes (Cambridge, 1972–).
Stenton, *ASE*	F. M. Stenton, *Anglo-Saxon England*, 3rd edn. (Oxford, 1971).
BJRL	*Bulletin of the John Rylands Library.*
BLTW	*Bede, His Life, Times and Writings: Essays in Commemoration of the Twelfth Century of his Death*, ed. A. Hamilton Thompson (Oxford, 1935).
CCSL	*Corpus Christianorum, Series Latina* (Turnhout).
Celt and Saxon	*Celt and Saxon: Studies in the Early British Border*, ed. N. K. Chadwick (Cambridge, 1963).
Christianity in Britain	*Christianity in Britain, 300–700*, ed. M. W. Barley and R. P. C. Hanson (Leicester, 1968).
Chron. Maj.	Bede, *Chronica Maiora.*
CLA	E. A. Lowe, *Codices Latini Antiquiores: A Palaeographical Guide to Latin Manuscripts*

	Prior to the Ninth Century (11 vols. and suppl.; Oxford, 1934-71).
CS	W. de Gray Birch, *Cartularium Saxonicum* (3 vols. and index; London, 1885-99).
CSEL	*Corpus Scriptorum Ecclesiasticorum Latinorum* (Vienna).
DA	*Deutsches Archiv für Erforschung des Mittelalters.*
De Excidio	Gildas, *De Excidio Britanniae.*
EHD i	*English Historical Documents*, i, ed. D. Whitelock (London, 1955).
EHR	*English Historical Review.*
England before the Conquest	*England before the Conquest. Studies in Primary Sources presented to Dorothy Whitelock*, ed. P. Clemoes and K. Hughes (Cambridge, 1971).
EPNS	English Place Name Society.
Famulus Christi	*Famulus Christi. Essays in Commemoration of the Thirteenth Centenary of the Birth of the Venerable Bede*, ed. G. Bonner (London, 1976).
Fm. S.	*Frühmittelalterliche Studien.*
HE	*Historia Ecclesiastica.*
Hist.	(Gregory of Tours) *Libri Historiarum Decem.*
Ideal and Reality	*Ideal and Reality in Frankish and Anglo-Saxon Society: Studies presented to J. M. Wallace-Hadrill*, ed. P. Wormald with D. Bullough and R. Collins (Oxford, 1983).
JEH	*Journal of Ecclesiastical History.*
JRS	*Journal of Roman Studies.*
JTS	*Journal of Theological Studies.*

Lib. Pont.	*Liber Pontificalis.*
MGH	*Monumenta Germaniae Historica:*
AA	*Auctores Antiquissimi*
Epp.	*Epistolae*
SRM	*Scriptores Rerum Merovingicarum*
SRG	*Scriptores Rerum Germanicarum*
SS	*Scriptores.*
OCT	Oxford Classical Texts.
OMT	Oxford Medieval Texts.
PBA	*Proceedings of the British Academy*
PG	*Patrologia Graeca*, ed. J.-P. Migne.
PL	*Patrologia Latina*, ed. J.-P. Migne.
Plummer	*Baedae Opera Historica*, ed. C. Plummer (2 vols.; Oxford, 1896).
RB	*Revue Bénédictine.*
RuFF	W. Levison, *Aus rheinischer und fränkischer Frühzeit* (Düsseldorf, 1948).
Saints, Scholars	*Saints, Scholars and Heroes: Studies in Medieval Culture in Honour of Charles W. Jones*, ed. M. H. King and W. M. Stevens (2 vols.; Collegeville, Minn., 1979).
Sawyer	P. H. Sawyer, *Anglo-Saxon Charters: An Annotated List and Bibliography* (Royal Historical Society Guides and Handbooks, 8; London, 1968).
SC	*Sources chrétiennes* (Paris).
Spoleto	*Settimane di studio del Centro italiano di studi*

sull'alto medioevo (Spoleto,
1953–).

Studies in Early British History   *Studies in Early British History*,
ed. N. K. Chadwick
(Cambridge, 1954).

The Writing of History   *The Writing of History in the*
Middle Ages: Essays presented to
Richard William Southern, ed.
R. H. C. Davis and J. M.
Wallace-Hadrill (Oxford,
1981).

BEDE AND PLUMMER[*]

There is in Corpus Christi College, Oxford, a large pen and ink cartoon, dated 1905. It shows the Fellows of the College processing to High Table. This they do above the caption *Nos miseri et egentes homines* (the first words of the College Grace before dinner). The only one of them who could be thought to look even remotely *miser et egens*—he was in fact a sumptuous host—happens to be the antepenultimate in the queue. It is Charles Plummer: a frail, stooping little figure, with a determined face, a high brow, a strong nose, and a jutting black beard. A firm but reticent man, one might guess, who would not wish posterity to know more about him than could be inferred from his published writings. Nor are we likely now to know more than will be found in the final pages of R. W. Chambers' lecture on Bede,[1] and in the British Academy memoir by P. S. Allen, Sir Frank Stenton, and R. I. Best,[2] a trio that in itself is striking witness to Plummer's scholarly range. He does not appear in the *DNB*. However, anyone who has lived at all long with Plummer's edition of and commentary on Bede's *Ecclesiastical History*[3]—I say nothing of his other writings—will be clear that it tells him a good deal about Plummer, and about how Plummer conceived of his task. For there is nothing impersonal about a good commentary: it is the work of one man's mind, with all the selection, rejection, and emphases that this implies. To comment on Bede is not merely to lighten dark places: it is to make a statement about Bede. The purpose of this paper is to discuss some aspects of the statement Plummer made.

Much turns on the fact—and it did not escape Sir Frank Stenton—that Plummer was a humane man. He was interested

---

[*] A paper delivered at a conference held in Durham in September 1973 to celebrate the twelfth centenary of Bede's birth. Reprinted with permission from J. M. Wallace-Hadrill, *Early Medieval History* (Oxford, Basil Blackwell, 1975).

[1] *PBA* 22 (1936), 29–30.

[2] *PBA* 15 (1929), 463–76.

[3] *Baedae Historia Ecclesiastica Gentis Anglorum: Venerabilis Baedae Opera Historica* (2 vols.; Oxford, 1896).

in people, not in society, and had no marked taste for the technical adjuncts of Anglo-Saxon history, though he was not unaware of them. In this he was strangely unlike his Corpus tutor, Sir Samuel Dill, who saw the early European scene in terms of societies, groups, and cliques, usually in decay. They can by no means be said to have cross-fertilized one another. But Plummer's humanity, heart-warming as it is, caused him to some extent to identify himself with Bede. One could almost say that Bede becomes Plummer; becomes, that is to say, rather like a nineteenth-century scholar and divine. 'A somewhat prolonged study of Bede's work', he confesses, 'has produced in my mind such a personal feeling towards their author, that I am well content that some trace of my own personal feelings and circumstances should remain in what I have written about him.'[4] And again: 'It is no light privilege to have been for so long a time in constant communion with one of the saintliest characters ever produced by the Church of Christ in this island.'[5] Bede's character, in so far as we can see it, was indeed attractive; and Plummer was not the first to have found it so. Stubbs had already fallen to its charm, and so too Bright; and the writings of these two scholars were congenial to Plummer in a marked way. The fact remains that Bede was no don.

I must not go further without acknowledging the great range of Plummer's equipment as a commentator; great, and in some ways, astonishing; for his work was completed in 1896. Subsequent technical advances in knowledge should not blind us to this. In the first place, he was aware to a unique degree that Bede as historian could not be appreciated outside the sum total of his writings. He saw that chronology was basic to Bede's thinking. Poole,[6] Levison,[7] Jones,[8] and others[9] have taken the matter further than Plummer, but Plummer was the pioneer. He had an intimate knowledge of Bede's exegetical work, bad though the editions were that he had to use. Repeatedly he will cite a

[4] Plummer, i, p. iii.
[5] Plummer, i, p. v.
[6] *Studies in Chronology and History* (Oxford, 1934).
[7] *England and the Continent in the Eighth Century* (Oxford, 1946).
[8] *Bedae Opera de Temporibus* (Cambridge, Mass., 1943).
[9] e.g. Kenneth Harrison, 'The *Annus Domini* in Some Early Charters', *Journal of the Society of Archivists*, 4 (1973): 'Early Wessex Annals in the Anglo-Saxon Chronicle', *EHR* 86 (1971), 527-33.

passage of biblical commentary that throws light on Bede's history; and he can look beyond Bede to Gregory the Great and other masters in that field. Soaked in all Bede's writings, he had a grasp of the writer's style—which nobody, since, has shown any keenness to investigate. For example, he notes Bede's use of *peto* construed with a double accusative,[10] of *vel* and *sive*,[11] of the infinitive of purpose,[12] of *bene venisti* in the sense of 'bien-venu',[13] and the stylistic difficulty of the chapters on St Æthelburh.[14] He was keenly alive to the changing senses of technical words as well as to the possibility of textual corruption. I wish he had examined Bede's borrowings from Canterbury (to which he drew attention) from the stylistic point of view. Not only with St Æthelburh but with the Life of Fursa (and others) Plummer can show how Bede treats a source, even on occasion obscuring its sense.[15] He can also spot difficulties in the division of books and chapters and knows that later additions can throw out the balance of the narrative. He is keenly alive to Celtic sources, and reasonably so to Scandinavian, following to some extent where Rhys and York Powell led him. (I am uncertain when he became friendly with Vigfússon.) What he says about the Irish can plainly be corrected and expanded, but no one could accuse him of dismissing the Celtic world as a fringe to the Anglo-Saxon. He envisages the whole Anglo-Celtic scene. Often he reminds us that Bede was the first in a progression of English historians: what Bede writes he will compare with the corresponding passage in the Old English translation of the *Ecclesiastical History*, in the Anglo-Saxon Chronicle, in William of Malmesbury, or Florence of Worcester. A future commentator on Bede's *History* might feel less generously disposed, but he would also miss something. Plummer's citations from Browning and Tennyson, Kingsley and Rossetti, Froissart and Dante, do not, as H. A. L. Fisher observed in his review of Plummer, 'materially advance our knowledge of Bede';[16] but they came to him naturally. He saw—and this was real insight—that Bede's Anglo-

[10] Plummer, ii. 98 (II. 12).
[11] Plummer, ii. 82 (II. 4).
[12] Plummer, ii. 124 (III. 2).
[13] Plummer, ii. 219 (IV. 9).
[14] Plummer, ii. 218 (IV. 7-10).
[15] Plummer, ii. 169-760 (III. 19).
[16] *EHR* 12 (1897), 339.

Saxons showed no community of political sentiment; no more than Bede himself did Plummer see Alfred and Athelstan on the horizon. He was not to be taken in by J. R. Green. The dawning unity he did see was ecclesiastical, though a scholar who appreciated, as he did, the slowness of the movement of the Early Church away from Judaic practices[17] was unlikely to overestimate the speed of ecclesiastical development anywhere at any time. His commentary contains a wealth of what may be called special notes on technical subjects. Apart from the famous excursus on the Easter question, there are long notes on subjects as varied as the rite of baptism, church music, exorcism, symbolism, monophysitism, visions, and poetry. A note on *Ad* in place-names shows him painstakingly at work on a subject not at all near his heart.[18] Not many cared for place-names in 1896. Finally, he could use charter-evidence where it was relevant. All this I say in praise of Plummer, and could say more. His commentary was and is a masterpiece. A revised edition of it—if indeed one should ever revise a masterpiece—would in many ways be a blessing. There is so much more (for example, in the field of archaeology) that now has to be taken into account. It would be a bulkier volume than Plummer's, since apart from the incorporation of the results of Bedan research over the last seventy years, not much of Plummer's own solid researches could be discarded. Nevertheless, Plummer's approach to Bede's objectives in the *Ecclesiastical History* may not in all respects be that of historians who will soon be writing about Bede.

Of Plummer's personal identification with Bede I have said almost enough. He believed that Bede was the same type of 'saintly scholar-priest' as R. W. Church and H. P. Liddon.[19] These were very considerable men. None the less, Bede was something more than a saintly scholar-priest. His learning was a route to objectives that scarcely put us in mind of the Victorian scholar, however enlightened.

One such objective was Bede's intention to write ecclesiastical history. *Historia Ecclesiastica* can be translated 'History of the Church'; and this, at its lowest level, is what it is. Thus we may

---

[17] Plummer, ii. 190 (III. 25).
[18] Plummer, ii. 103-4. See now R. Forsberg, 'On OE *ād* in English Placenames', *Namn och Bygd*, 58 (1971), 20-82.
[19] Plummer, i., p. lxxix.

speak of Bede's 'History of the Church of the English', meaning
the story of the foundations consequent upon St Augustine's
mission, Theodore's reorganization, and so on: a story of
bishoprics and to a lesser extent of monasteries. At this level it
was entirely relevant to include Arculf's description of the Holy
Places in Palestine.[20] Levison remarked that Bede, like Rufinus,
planned much of his history in terms of episcopal succession,
while not breaking down his material into continuous blocks of
diocesan history in the manner of William of Malmesbury.[21]
Within this framework the deeds of kings could be exhibited as
conducive or detrimental to the well-being of the Church. But
there was another level and a subtler sense of ecclesiastical
history, familiar since the time of Eusebius: history, that is, as a
record of salvation,[22] the proof of God's providence at work. The
English past could be presented in this way. Both senses are
plainly operative with Bede, conditioning what he said, how he
said it, and what he did not say. Plummer was not fully aware of
this deeper sense, possibly because he had little interest in
Bede's forebears and near-contemporaries in the art of writing
ecclesiastical history. He sees Bede as the father of English
historiography, not as heir to an ancient, if only spasmodically
practised, tradition in European historiography. Levison, a
master of continental sources, did better than this, but even he
was apt to confuse the techniques of writing (notably of
chronology and hagiography) with the purposes. Let me give an
example of what I mean. Bede's treatment of Romano-British
history presents, in one sense, very little of a problem. We know
most of his sources and can be tempted to see his account as
little more than a medley. It is there to introduce our island
story, completed with some geography and a selection of
interesting local detail. This is roughly how Plummer sees it. But
in fact Bede has taken from Orosius and others rather more than
a selection of material useful to this end. His Romano-British
history also exhibits a great preliminary: national disaster in
the face of divine displeasure; for the Romano-British had had
their own ecclesiastical history, and it was a bleak one. Gildas
was right: how could such a people prosper? They started off

---

[20] *HE* v. 16.
[21] 'Bede as Historian', *BLTW*, p. 143.
[22] See R. W. Hanning, *The Vision of History in Early Britain* (Columbia, 1966), ch. 3.

well enough; the curious tale of Lucius and their conversion shows that Bede accepted that a proper beginning for Christianity in Britain was by papal mandate to a king. And they continued on their Christian course under Diocletian's persecution, bound to Christendom at large in martyrdom. He concludes: *Denique etiam Brittaniam tum plurima confessionis Deo devotae gloria sublimavit*,[23] and goes on to his long account of the martyrdom of St Alban, hailed by Venantius as 'faithful Britain's child', as Bede notes. Alban thus decisively links Britain to the great church tradition of martyrdom, and through martyrdom to miracles. Next comes Arianism, which Plummer, following Bright, thought unduly emphasized, though a people's reaction to heresy is a very natural issue in ecclesiastical history. And after Arianism, Pelagianism,[24] and the terrible moral decline consequent upon the withdrawal of the Romans, the guardians of religion as well as of frontiers. Bede's reconstruction raises many problems. On one, Bede's ready acceptance of Gildas' picture of British luxury and vice, unchecked by God's warnings in the form of plague, Plummer makes no comment; indeed, no real collation of any kind of the views of Bede and Gildas. So we reach God's final judgement—the Saxons. These fourteen Romano-British chapters are in one sense 'political' history, but they are also Bede's interpretation of the British and their Roman involvement within the framework of ecclesiastical history. Here, as always, what Bede took from his sources was not allowed to lie inert. It became *his* history.

Let me turn to another major issue in the *Ecclesiastical History*: the conversion of the Anglo-Saxons. Bede does not consider it necessary to explain what paganism was. Whatever he knew or could know (and it was far more than we know) seemed irrelevant; and if we add to his chance references to paganism in stories involving conversion whatever can be had from later literary sources, archaeology, and place-names, we still know rather less about Anglo-Saxon paganism than about the paganism of St Boniface's Germans. Why is the content of paganism irrelevant to Bede? It did not seem so to Paul the

[23] *HE* I. 6 (p. 28, pp. 8–9).
[24] See J. N. L. Myres, 'Pelagius and the End of Roman Rule in Britain', *Journal of Roman Studies*, 50 (1960), 21–36; and Peter Brown, 'Pelagius and his Supporters', *JTS* NS 19 (1968), 93–114.

Deacon, whose Lombards were remorselessly pagan. The answer lies in the purposes of ecclesiastical history. Speaking generally, the ecclesiastical historian conceived of the content of paganism, and especially of Germanic paganism, unseriously. There was no need to define its objectives, still less to distinguish its facets. It might indeed be tenaciously held, for which reason its adherents had had to be humoured or eased over the hurdle of conversion; but theologically it afforded no springboard into Christianity. However barbarous and bloody, its mere innocence protected it from serious consideration. Theologically at least, the pagan Germans seemed to offer western Christianity an unresisting field for missionary work. If Bede had been writing a history of the English people, as distinct from their ecclesiastical history, he could scarcely have avoided some treatment of their paganism as part and parcel of their life, not only past but present. As it was, he could and did avoid it. Gregory of Tours, who also wrote ecclesiastical history, also avoided it for the Franks. Plummer might perhaps have been more explicit on this point. It is right that we should know at least that Germanic paganisms were warband-religions and kin-religions, whereas Christianity was neither; and moreover, that pagan cultus as practised by warriors shared ethical concepts with the warrior's fighting-creed, from which indeed the Church borrowed some meaning-laden words when it faced the task of expressing Christian doctrine in the vernacular. Coifi's naïve equation of pagan honour and success with Christian salvation was the reaction of a high priest whose congregation was a royal court of warriors.[25] Plummer was, of course, alive to the fact of paganism. In his notes to Book I, chapter 30, he considers at some length the approach of missionaries to it. However, this is not quite the same as considering what it was that missionaries were approaching. How did missionaries deal with paganism? Plummer is able to marshal a number of examples from papal correspondence, reports of English missionaries abroad, the

[25] This has been thoroughly investigated by D. H. Green, *The Carolingian Lord* (Cambridge, 1965), esp. chapter ix. However, I do not share the view, held by many, that paganism had no ethical content. Paganism is our word for a range of religious experience among the Germanic peoples that reached from Woden-worship at one extreme to that of sticks and stones at the other. How can one divorce paganism from the ethic of the warband, or how deny ethical content to the religious beliefs of peasants?

council of Ratisbon, Theodore's Penitential, and so on. There is more, but his assortment is a fair one. Moreover, he can point to Bede on conversion in other contexts: in his exposition of the Acts of the Apostles and in *De Temporum Ratione*. He knows that Christianity was 'contaminated' by paganism—in other words, that there was a degree of 'religious syncretism'—and that conversion was a slow business. But he does not ask whether the slowness, or indeed relapses, were in any way due to the nature of paganism itself. It was enough that paganism should yield to the demonstration of Christianity in action: first, the demonstration that victories in battle proved the power of the Christian god, and secondly that the teaching of Christianity was irrefutable. Teaching, indeed, was very much in Bede's mind: Æthelberht was taught and Edwin was taught, just as Clovis had once been. They were open to instruction. This in itself tells us something about paganism, as well as of the Christian attitude to conversion. Bede is clear that the conversion of the Anglo-Saxons had been mainly a matter of persuasion and teaching, not of compulsion. Was it still so in his own day—in Germany, for example? It had been Coifi, not Paulinus, who had desecrated the pagan shrine at Goodmanham;[26] by contrast, it was Willibrord and Boniface, not renegade high-priests, who went for the pagan shrines of the continental Germans. But the tradition of persuasion was a respectable one. The young Augustine of Hippo had been no friend of coercion[27] nor, to judge from his popular sermons, had Caesarius been. Bishop Daniel, too, was all for a reasoned presentation of Christianity,[28] which did take some account of the facts of paganism. The conversion of the countryside—and not only of the countryside—was still a living issue in Bede's time. We must suppose that Christianity was presented to village communities in something of the spirit of St Pirmin's *Scarapsus*; in brief, it was a matter of simple teaching, of weaning rustics from pagan junketings and offerings, from soothsayers, medicine men, and so forth. Certainly it cannot have been presented to them as the religion of victory, so efficacious with kings, nor as the religion of

---

[26] *HE* ii. 13 (p. 184, l. 24–p. 186, l. 2).
[27] Cf. Ep. 22. 5. Also R. A. Markus, *Saeculum: History and Society in the Theology of St Augustine* (Cambridge, 1970), 140.
[28] *Die Briefen des Heiligen Bonifatius und Lullus*, ed.M. Tangl (Berlin, 1955), No. 23.

penitence, appropriate to substantial folk with uneasy con-
sciences, some of whom were not above enjoying *Ingeld* in their
monasteries. Bede, then, looked back on the history of the
conversion and decided that the content of paganism was better
ignored, whether in the raw state or as in part subsumed into
current Christian practice. But heresy was quite another matter,
and understandably worried him much more than did paganism.
The conversion of heretics and schismatics could indeed be a
matter of coercion; and here, too, Bede had Augustine of Hippo
behind him. Into this context falls Bede's obsession with the
issue of the date of Easter. You will recall Plummer's words: 'we
cannot help feeling that the question occupies a place in Bede's
mind out of all proportion to its real importance ... but the
holiest men have their limitations'.[29] In other words, Bede
overdid Whitby. But our business is surely to decide why the
date of Easter assumed the proportions it did assume in his
mind. Two consecutive Easters at one royal court were no doubt
embarrassing to King Oswiu and his entourage but can hardly
have moved Bede so greatly, over half a century later. Nor will it
quite do to claim that a master in chronology would have been
shocked by untidy thinking about dates, whenever it occurred. It
is not even enough that Bede's view of Petrine primacy was
engaged (and it may be observed in passing that it was Peter the
doorkeeper, not Peter the bishop of Rome, for whom Oswiu
opted). A deeper reason may lie in Bede's view of the unity of the
Church, a portion of whose history he was writing. Unity of
discipline, as of doctrine, were for Bede a condition of survival
for the Church; even the well-loved Celtic clergy were rightly
sacrificed to its claims. For Bede—and I do not think that
Plummer quite saw this—knew the western Church for what it
was: a confederation of churches, often fissile, divergent,
ignorant, and passionately local.

I come to another major preoccupation of Bede's *History* on
which Plummer has much to say, *more suo*. Miracles are widely
distributed through the *History*. Levison, too, had much to say of
Bede's miracle-stories, to the extent, indeed, of deciding that
hagiography, like chronology, was a backbone of the whole
undertaking.[30] In other words, Bede grew out of these technical

[29] Plummer, i. pp. xl, xli.
[30] 'Bede as Historian' (see n. 21 above).

studies into something bigger. One could add biblical commentary as a study at least as important on Bede's journey to history. However, Levison does fill out Plummer's picture by showing how Bede used hagiography and what of it was available to him. Following Karl Werner[31] he drew attention to certain hagiographers whose work influenced Bede—for example, Venantius Fortunatus; and particularly he emphasized Bede's debt to Gregory's *Dialogues*. This was a real service. But fundamentally Levison was not saying anything very different from what Plummer had already said. It amounts to this: Bede, a man of his times, must be expected to record miracles; we should be thankful that they so often include interesting historical fact and not bother ourselves about their role in an otherwise carefully thought-out history, for they do not really affect the rest of the matter. Yet it is not so clear why they were relevant, nor what canons of criticism apply to miracle-stories that do not apply to the remainder of the *History*.

Bede's miracle-stories make varying demands on modern credulity. Some can be explained as possible on grounds of normal experience; some are impossible on the same ground; some are partly possible. How they are vouched for is a separate issue. In what sense Bede himself accepted them is an important question. Dr Hunter Blair has written that Bede included miracles in his *History* because 'it was part of the function of history to record what ordinary people believed'.[32] This is certainly what Bede thought, and St Jerome and others thought the same. But there is a further consideration. Bede, for these purposes, was himself an ordinary person, since he too accepted the miracles he recorded. Plummer also may occasionally have done so,[33] though on the other hand he accepted that Herebald's riding accident could be rationally accounted for. 'In the story as told by Bede', he comments, 'there is nothing distinctly miraculous.'[34] Nor is there. For some of the miracles attributed to St Cuthbert a rational explanation is possible; for example, the cure of the young man with a diseased eyelid,[35] or Bede's own

---

[31] *Beda der Ehrwürdige und seine Zeit* (Vienna, 1881), 104.
[32] *The World of Bede* (London, 1970), 303.
[33] See his comments on St Cuthbert, Plummer, ii. 271 and i, pp. lxix–lxv.
[34] Plummer, i. 277.
[35] *HE* iv. 32.

recovery, referred to elsewhere, from a tongue complaint.[36] St Cuthbert shared with St Martin the ability to look after his own, and to this I shall return. I shall not be the only one present who has heard how St Cuthbert shrouded his city in impenetrable fog on the night when German bombers were detailed to destroy it. Take another sort of miracle: Dryhthelm's vision.[37] How much of it was really Dryhthelm's? Bede calls it a *miraculum memorabile* but adds that it was *antiquorum simile*. It followed a well-known pattern and was undoubtedly the better for it. But what are we to say of a partly possible miracle-story such as that of Imma?[38] Let me remind you of it. At the battle of the Trent, a Northumbrian thegn named Imma was struck down. On regaining consciousness he bandaged his wounds and made off, only to be taken prisoner by a Mercian, to whom he represented himself as a peasant. He made a good recovery and was then shackled to prevent his escape; but his fetters fell off, not once but several times. His captor, discovering that he was in fact a thegn, and moreover suspecting him of using pagan *litteras solutorias*, sold him to a Frisian in London. The fetters continued to fall off. So he was allowed to ransom himself through the good offices of King Hlothere of Kent. Thence he returned to Northumbria and visited his brother, who was abbot of Tunnacaestir. The abbot revealed that he had been saying masses for him, believing him to be dead. The falling-off of the fetters had generally coincided with the celebration of a mass. Bede is clear about the moral: masses are efficacious for the deliverance of the souls of dead kinsmen—and, he could have added, for the bodies of live kinsmen, too. What was Bede's source? 'This story was told me by some of those who heard it from the very man to whom these things happened; therefore since I had so clear an account of the incident, I thought that it should undoubtedly be inserted into this *History*.' How are we to comment on this? The story is overwhelmingly circumstantial: no one will question that Imma actually had the adventure that is described. We might go on to speculate that in reality the Mercian sold him to the Frisian because he would fetch a good price, and the Frisian accepted his ransom because the Kentish king was prepared to find it, thus yielding him a quicker and better return than he might

---

[36] *Bedas metrische Vita sancti Cuthberti*, ed. Werner Jaager (Leipzig, 1935), 57.
[37] *HE* v. 12.   [38] Ibid. IV. 22.

have obtained by selling him as a slave abroad. We may explain things thus, or in other ways. But what of the fetters so repeatedly falling off? They were presumably suggested by a Petrine parallel.[39] Someone, perhaps Imma himself or his brother, had recast the adventure as a miracle-story. Yet to Bede no part of the story is less reliable than any other part, and the miracle is the point of it, the only thing that makes it worth recording. I instance this particular story because of the combination of what we readily accept with what we tacitly reject, or accept only at a different level. There are, of course, other miracle-stories in Bede, and countless more in other writings of the period, that raise the same issue. Their narrators are living in a world where the miraculous can at once be interwoven into accounts of happenings and accepted on the same terms. I suppose that Bede was perfectly aware of this, and I therefore think that we should look carefully at the reasons behind his interweaving of the two strands of a story such as that of Imma. For it is the same mind and the same pen that report both and blend them into a narrative of ecclesiastical history. Plummer does not give us much assistance here. I do not of course mean that Bede falsified facts but only that we should consider with some care our own interpretation of what, in such a context, Bede thought facts were for; or, put another way, be sure of the level at which we choose to appreciate his history. He was phenomenally 'factual' for a man who lived in a world of invention that could perpetrate straightforward forgery, with the best of intentions. Consider his world. Scarcely more than a century after Bede's death we have the greatest of all medieval forgeries—Pseudo-Isidore—and that was not the first. What is remarkable in the forgers is the conjunction of forgery with high religious sense, though no theologian gave any justification for it. It seemed to them to be an inspired action to reveal God's purpose by providing in writing what ought to have existed but did not. Bede was no forger, but he does bring the same high religious sense to his history—I mean, his history as opposed to the facts out of which it is constructed. What this signifies for the historian could be further explored.[40]

[39] Acts 12: 7. See also Gregory of Tours, *Hist.* x. 6 and elsewhere.

[40] See H. Fuhrmann, *Einfluss und Verbreitung der pseudoisidorischen Fälschungen*, vol. I (Stuttgart, 1972), ch. I.

To take another instance: how should we comment on the
story of the healing of the wife of the gesith named Puch?[41] She
suffered for weeks from a severe illness. According to Bede's
informant (Abbot Berhthun, who was present), Bishop John sent
some holy water to the woman, which she drank and washed in,
and at once rose from her bed, cured, and served the company at
dinner. 'In this', Bede concludes, 'she imitated the mother-in-law
of St Peter.'[42] Indeed she did. Plummer notes that very similar
stories are told of St Cuthbert and draws attention to Bede's
comments on relevant biblical passages. Colgrave adds a note on
the building of *Eigenkirchen*, which has some relevance to the
story. And that is all. Now it so happens that Bede, while
avoiding a direct statement, is fairly clear about one aspect of the
role of miracles in ecclesiastical history. They are *signa*,[43] signs of
God's intervention in the affairs of men, demonstrating the
sanctity of his chosen servants. At a time when martyrdom was
rarely available as the route to sanctity, the working of miracles
was a fair substitute. A miracle, then, at any time, and whether
performed before or after death, was irrefutable evidence of
something very special: God's power to override the normal
course of nature for a particular purpose. This had been the
lesson of Gregory's *Dialogues*, the burden of which was that, as in
biblical times and since, so still God continued to intervene
miraculously in the life of Italy. It was not lost on Bede. Plummer
observed that Bede's other writings contain clues to his view of
miracles; as, for instance, that miracles were relative to a certain
state in the development of the Church, that the cessation of
miracles should be attributed in part to man's sin, and that some
men are permitted by divine intervention to recover part of this
lost heritage;[44] in short, that God was and is always prepared to
intervene miraculously. Such interventions are characteristic of
the life of the Church, having a cumulative force. Beyond that,
they reveal and prove the presence of saints. One could say that
Bede's Church functioned at more than one level. It was at one
and the same time a *signum*, a spiritual manifestation of God's

---

[41] *HE* v. 4.
[42] Matt. 8: 14-15.
[43] e.g. 'signa miraculorum usque hodie narrari' (*HE* III. 8) and 'in hoc etenim
monasterio plura virtutum sunt signa patrata' (IV. 7).
[44] Plummer, i, p. lxv.

business, and a *res*, a visible institution, a human instrument if not an instrument of the state. Dr Markus has ably discussed this duality in relation to St Augustine.[45] It applies also to Bede. One is always aware of Bede's Church as an institution of men and women, meetings and buildings, and especially as a bishops' Church. He describes the Church at this level in a cool, even detached, manner. It is evidently a *res*. The Church at the higher level is principally revealed for him in the lives of its saints; and here there could be little room for detachment. What he really feels about it is revealed in his treatment of St Æthelthryth. He starts with an account of her life;[46] of her perpetual virginity through two marriages, her entry into religion, her austerities, her death, and the discovery of her uncorrupt body sixteen years later, including the witness of the physician who had treated her. The chapter ends with a brief reference to miracles associated with her coffin, and with a note on Ely. Bede then inserts a hymn on the saint which he had composed many years before. He does this, he says, 'imitating the method of holy scripture in which many songs are inserted into the history'.[47] There is, then, a biblical analogy; but it is not the reason for the insertion. Nor is the reason instructional, since the hymn contains no information on the saint that is not already in the preceding chapter. In a learned note on serpentine elegiacs, in which the hymn is written, Plummer mentions other practitioners of the art: Ovid, Martial, Sedulius (whose work was known to Bede), and Paul the Deacon. The hymn is also alphabetic, and for this too Plummer cites other examples. The subject is virginity. It also attracted Avitus and then Aldhelm, whose poem Bede is not known to have seen, and, earlier, Venantius Fortunatus, whose work he certainly did see. Plummer confines himself to noting that the virgins commemorated by Bede are also commemorated by Aldhelm, except for Euphemia, and suggests that the metre would be improved if Bede had substituted Eugenia (also known to Aldhelm).[48] He notes, too, that both Euphemia and Eugenia

---

[45] *Saeculum*, ch. 7, esp. p. 185.

[46] *HE* iv. 19.

[47] *HE* iv. 20. Plummer provides some biblical analogies, ii. 241.

[48] Despite his long note on St Aldhelm ii. 308, Plummer was not interested in the content of his thought but, like others, was obsessed with his style—which Bede accepted, however.

occur in Venantius' *De Virginitate*. But there is more to it than
that. Venantius' poem is the greatest of the early medieval
statements about virginity. Its subject is not the nun's vocation
but the visionary world that virginity conjures up, where the
bride of Christ sees the heavens opened and dreams of her union
with Christ. For the poet it is an ecstasy of song and light,
flashing gems and brilliant flowers; a vision that points straight
to medieval mysticism. Now this goes a good deal further than
Bede. Moreover, Venantius' poem is much longer and the metre
is different. Yet it has something fundamental in common with
Bede's poem. Incidentally, there are linguistic parallels. For
example, both writers use the verb *beare*, rare (except as *beatus*)
in classical and early medieval Latin; and they use it once only, in
these poems.[49] It is true that it is also used by St Augustine and
by Sedulius and, very rarely, elsewhere; but the coincidence of its
use in two poems on the same subject is striking. Similarly, both
writers use the word *hydrus* once only,[50] and this, too, is a rare
word. But to return to what is fundamental, Bede sees virginity
as Venantius saw it. What, Bede asks, has a great lady to do with
earthly marriage who has Christ for her groom? Is she not
affianced to the Lamb in heaven? Does she not court him with
new songs on her harp in heaven? This is precisely Venantius'
approach, tender and imaginative, if less erotic; altogether, one
would say, inappropriate to any historical narrative. Yet there it
is. The reason once again is that Bede is writing ecclesiastical
history. It is no more irrelevant to Bede the historian to hymn
virginity in Latin than it was to report that Caedmon praised
God in the vernacular. But there is this difference: Bede merely
reports the miracle of Caedmon, whereas his song to virginity is
his personal contribution. And it is a contribution to history,
Bede's spiritual justification for what he describes more prosai-
cally on other occasions: namely, the highest calling of a royal
lady, which is either not to marry, or, if married, to remain virgin;
it was best to enter the service of God as Christ's spouse. It
seems to have implications that invite comment.

Any Church bent on the conversion of a Germanic people to
Catholicism faced the problem of what it called evil spirits. Their

---

[49] *HE* IV. 20, l. 25 of poem; Venantius, *Vita Martini* II. 376 (*MGH AA* 4; i. 326).
[50] Bede, ibid., 12 lines from end; Venantius, *Carmina* VIII. 3. 330 (*MGH AA* 4; i. 190).

activity was never denied; they were everywhere. Not for
nothing did Germanic burials continue to be furnished with
amulets, charms, phylacteries, and talismans, long after formal
conversion had taken place. Indeed, I have the strong impression
that in western Europe generally those in authority were much
more worried by attention paid to evil spirits, in high places and
low, in the ninth century than in Bede's century and earlier.[51]
Pagans had their ways of dealing with such spirits. The Church
for its part had always practised exorcism. We have in the
Ecclesiastical History a very instructive case.[52] A man, Bede tells
us, was possessed by an evil spirit: *subito a diabolo arreptus*. The
correct procedure was followed. A priest was summoned, who
pronounced the exorcisms provided for such an occasion.
Indeed, he worked hard at it; but nothing happened. Bede
expresses no surprise. Gregory of Tours provides a comparable
instance.[53] He says that a woman possessed by a spirit of
prophecy made a good living out of proclaiming the where-
abouts of thieves and what they had done with their loot, to the
extent that people thought there was something divine about
her. The bishop had her arrested, diagnosed an evil spirit and
conducted an exorcism. Again, nothing happened. The woman
made off to another part of the country. And again, Gregory
expresses no surprise. I think it would equally not have surprised
Caesarius, who often preached to his people of Arles about evil
spirits, nor yet Martin of Braga. It was possible for exorcism not
to work, and this was a serious matter at a time when the
Church had to demonstrate the efficacy of its procedures to a
semi-pagan population. But Bede has more to say, for the failure
of exorcism occurs in the course of a story that makes a different
point, since it provides a substitute for exorcism. The man with
the evil spirit was cured by something different: the mere
presence of some soil that had been moistened by the water
used to wash the bones of the saintly Oswald; in other words, a
miracle was performed by a saint. In itself, this was nothing out
of the way. What is remarkable is the juxtaposition of the
efficacy of an English saint and the failure of the traditional

---

[51] See P. Riché, 'La Magie à l'époque carolingienne', *Académie des Inscriptions et Belles-
Lettres, comptes rendus* (Paris, 1973), 127–38.

[52] *HE* III. 11.

[53] *Hist.* VII. 44, ed. Krusch and Levison, p. 364.

method of expelling an evil spirit. Plummer has an excellent note on exorcism, so far as it goes. He points out that there was more than one kind of exorcism and can cite Isidore, Theodore's Penitential, and Bede's own works, including a curious personal reminiscence from his commentary on St Luke.[54] What he misses is the significance of the juxtaposition. I suppose he did so because, though he saw well enough that Bede's age was one of transition from paganism to Christianity, he was less impressed by the extent of the Church's own reactions to what the Germanic mind could take. The Christianity of the missionary Anglo-Saxon Church was experimental' in important respects. Bede here reveals one of these respects.

Bede's book was an ecclesiastical history of the whole English people but it is not without a local slant. Like Plummer, Bede was a Bernician. Perhaps even more, he was a Northumbrian. The slant was not such as to worry Canterbury, which had to some extent inspired the work and contributed to it a little more extensively than Plummer thought, though it cannot on this account be said to have been written for Canterbury. However, a copy, *ad transscribendum*, may well have reached Canterbury within a year of its completion.[55] One might expect the Canterbury material to be handled in a way satisfactory to Canterbury, and doubtless it was. As for the rest, it had to satisfy a critical audience nearer home. We may ask, then, what sort of picture of Northumbrian history Bede created, and also ask what Plummer made of it. Despite his 'innumerable witnesses' to the Northumbrian past, Bede's account is selective and purposive. Modern scholarship has deepened our knowledge of this past and revealed something of what Bede does not record. As to what he does record, it seems to me that he means to emphasize the unity or at least the entity of Northumbria and to say no more than is necessary about the distinct traditions and rivalries of Bernicia and Deira, which he shows were real enough. His royal heroes were expansionists, men who not only controlled both parts of Northumbria but pushed her influence yet further afield. The division that seemed more critical to him was between Northumbria and Southumbria.

---

[54] Luke 8: 30. Ed. Hurst (*CCSL* 120), 184.
[55] Bede to Albinus, Plummer, i. 3.

There is a religious side to this unsteady process of Northumbrian unification. It may be that we, and possibly Plummer, make too neat a distinction between Celtic Bernicia and Roman Deira. Wilfrid himself, Roman as he was, had much of the Celtic ascetic in him and was trained in a severe monastic tradition; and it is Bede, not Eddius, who gives us the epitaph of the *magnus praesul*, ending with a prayer that his flock might tread the same path.[56] On the evidence of the *History*, Bede was not as anti-Wilfrid as Plummer was. Bede's reservations about Wilfrid were less about the moral aspects of his life and rule than about his disruptive relations with kings and others: bishops and kings could not afford to live on a hostile basis. We all know that Bede venerated Aidan for his moral qualities; and these so captivated Plummer that he may have overestimated his importance, which was not lasting. The man who did have a future was St Cuthbert. He brings together not merely Lindisfarne and Rome in his career but Bernicia and Deira in his cult. Plummer had remarkably little to say about him, however much he might be attracted to the story of Cuthbert and Herbert of Derwentwater. Plummer's text makes it perfectly clear that Bede is drawing on his own version of Cuthbert's Life, itself based on an earlier anonymous Life. But it was left to Bertram Colgrave to indicate something of the literary background to the Lives as a whole.[57] In particular he showed that the Anonymous and Bede, and possibly Cuthbert himself, were indebted, whether directly or indirectly I am uncertain, to the Life of St Martin by Sulpicius Severus. (There is so much of Sulpicius in Venantius' Life of St Martin that it may be from Venantius that the material was derived.) At all events my strong impression is that both the Anonymous and Bede had access to that material, and that Bede used it more extensively than the Anonymous.[58] The debt was in fact greater than Colgrave recognized. Of course, Cuthbert may actually have been like St Martin, though I doubt it. Nevertheless, the literary figure of Cuthbert seems fairly closely modelled on that of St Martin, the greatest patron saint in western Europe, St Peter excepted; patron most notably of the Merovingian dynasty since its beginnings under Clovis, and so of the Franks as a new

---

[56] *HE* v. 19.
[57] *Two Lives of St Cuthbert* (Cambridge, 1940), 11–12.
[58] It should be noted that Bede also used Paulinus of Périgueux on St Martin.

people. The national hero of the Franks was the ascetic monk-bishop *par exellence*. Cuthbert, then, is cast in something of this mould. More specifically he is cast in Martin's role as miracle-working protector. Was Cuthbert designed to do for the Northumbrians what Martin did for the Franks? Was Lindisfarne to be Northumbria's Tours? It is no accident that Bede ends Book IV with a long account of the career and death of Cuthbert in 687 but yet includes the saint's translation in 698 and his miracles. Cuthbert in this respect shares a distinction with Gregory the Great, the account of whom marks the division between Books I and II.[59] There were several routes by which Northumbria could have acquired a copy or copies of Sulpicius. One—and I suspect not the most likely—was direct from Ireland. Professor Brown has recently discussed one manuscript-link between Ireland and Lindisfarne.[60] It was real enough, but rather circuitous. Another link would be with Francia direct, which may, of course, be another way of saying with Ireland indirect. If we need to look for particular inter-mediaries we might think of Willibrord or Wilfrid, both of whom were well aware of St Martin, or possibly the Church of St Ninian, *Ad Candidam Casam*. Eddius himself seems to have known and used Sulpicius' Life.[61] Nor is it at all unlikely that Lindisfarne had a copy of Jonas' Life of St Columbanus, itself influenced by Martin. But this is not the occasion to pursue these questions in detail. The fact remains that Bede's Cuthbert is a recognizable type of monk-bishop of ascetic stamp with a potential role in the making of a people. Whether or not Cuthbert modelled himself on St Martin, his career could be described in words that often come from Sulpicius.

Finally, and in no pejorative sense, Plummer's approach to the continent is insular. Where Bede points directly to the continent Plummer will follow and will often find material to illuminate what Bede has said; and even occasionally when he does not: as, for example, when Plummer spots a Frankish parallel to Redwald's polytheism in Gregory of Tours or draws attention to Childebert I's *carta* abolishing idolatry. But the fact is that it was no part of Bede's plan to correlate the closely parallel develop-

[59] As Levison pointed out, 'Bede as Historian', *BLTW*, p. 142.
[60] 'Northumbria and the Book of Kells', *ASE* 1 (1972), 219–46.
[61] H. Moonen, *Eddius Stephanus, Het Leven van Sint Wilfrid* (1946), 12–16.

ment of the English and Frankish Churches. We have to do that for ourselves, and ought to do it.[62] Plummer would have claimed no deep familiarity with continental history—even that of the Franks, England's closest neighbour—and did not move easily in continental sources. Therefore he did not see Anglo-Saxon history as part of a whole, a closeknit history of the western Germanic kingdoms. One may instance his treatment of law, of feud, of kingship, of war, of monasticism, and of cultural matters generally. An example of how much more clearly Bede might be understood when one places his *History* in a wider continental context is in the matter of the burial of kings and queens. Bede's Christian rulers were laid to rest in a number of very different churches, of which St Augustine's Canterbury, York minster, and Whitby are only the most famous; different in their foundations, dedications, relics, organization, and wealth. What caused royal kindreds to lay their dead in one kind of church rather than another? Were they dynastic or 'national' mausoleums? Was it important to be buried near bishops? Of how many saints would a king seek the patronage, and why is he sometimes apparently deliberately not buried near their relics? What significance have architectural differences between basilicas? These and related questions, all raised by Bede's text, can only be answered when we take a wider view, that embraces the royal sanctuaries and burial-places at Paris, Tours, Soissons, Orleans, Pavia, Monza, Ravenna, and ultimately Constantinople (to mention, again, only the most famous).[63] Ecclesiastical history is bad at observing national frontiers. Plummer's Anglo-Saxons were thus more isolated from their brethen than they needed to be, or in fact were.

Plummer's commentary was nobly conceived and beautifully executed. It should not surprise us that he relates Bede to William of Malmesbury and Dean Liddon, rather than to Gregory of Tours and Eusebius; that he looks to the continent to explain this or that event in the Anglo-Saxon kingdoms, but

---

[62] I agree with James Campbell, 'The First Century of Christianity in England', *Ampleforth Journal*, 76 (1971), 16 ff., that this is one of the respects in which Bede's reticence is misleading.

[63] A basic instrument for this work is now K. H. Krüger, *Königsgrabkirchen der Franken, Angelsachsen und Langobarden bis zur Mitte des 8. Jahrhunderts* (Münstersche Mittelalter-Schriften, 4; Munich, 1971).

without any real awareness that they live one life; that he sees the miraculous in terms of beguiling stories, not in terms of the most dramatic example of God's patronage through the saints of a troubled society; that he sees paganism as immoral barbarism, not as an elaborate propitiation of the spiritual world, and that he sees ecclesiastical history as an account of an institution, not as an arrangement of past events in terms of Providence. Such an approach was natural to an English scholar of his generation; it dates his work in some respects but does not vitiate it. Ecclesiastical history was a very special craft. To evaluate it, to be sure of the rules and to appreciate its objectives, we shall continue to need all the help that Plummer and scholars of his calibre can give us.[64]

[64] In preparing this paper I have been conscious of the debt I owe to my research pupils for discussion of this or related matters, in particular to Mr Patrick Wormald, Mr Alfred Smyth, Miss Clare Stancliffe, and Mr Alan Thacker, and I thank them.

COMMENTARY

Note: Asterisks (*) indicate passages on which further comment may be found in the Addenda.

PRAEFATIO

p. 2, l. 1. Gloriosissimo . . . Ceoluulfo. This prefatory letter is not strictly a dedication but a submission to King Ceolwulf, though a wider readership is already envisaged. Abbot Albinus must have had a copy at about the same time (Plummer, i. 3, for text). As to content, the letter owes something to prefatory material known to Bede from earlier writings, not all historical. From other prefaces it differs markedly (cf. Isidore's prologue to his *Gothic History*, probably unknown to Bede; and Orosius' dedication of his *History* to Augustine, which Bede certainly did know). It comes a little nearer to the general preface of Gregory of Tours to his *History*, which, for all its brevity, at least makes the point that Gregory meant 'to hand down the memory of the past to future generations, not leaving untold the conflicts of the wicked and those who lived righteously'. Gregory does not here cite his sources, though his continuator, Fredegar, does so in his own prologue. Bede could have known both texts. They were sometimes transmitted as one collection. Nearer still comes the preface of Eusebius to his *Ecclesiastical History*, where he says something of the plan of his work, of the reason for its composition, and in general terms of the existence of source-material. With this preface in Latin translation Bede was familiar. That of Gildas to his *De Excidio*, with which again Bede was familiar, has nothing in common with Bede's preface. Their objectives were distinct. In the end, Bede's preface is very much his own; and with it he sends the whole *History* to a king who had already read it and now, at his request, has it back in revised and completed form for copying (perhaps at Lindisfarne?). The contents therefore have the personal approval of Ceolwulf, as Gregory's *History* clearly did not have the approval of any king: only King Gunthramn might have read it with any satisfaction. But other kings than Ceolwulf had received dedicatory prefaces; as King Mir of the Sueves, to whom Martin of Braga sent his *Formula Vitae Honestae*, and King Sisebut of the Visigoths, to whom Isidore sent his *De Natura Rerum* (the latter known to Bede). To approach a Germanic king with a work of learning was thus not unusual. But Bede's work is history that comes very near the experience and memories of Ceolwulf himself. There is no evidence that Bede had met the king but the terms in which he addresses him suggest to me that he might have done so.

No special significance need be seen in Bede's use of *gloriosissimus*. His employment of this and comparable terms (e.g. *christianissimus*, *potentissimus*) is usually loose. On early medieval usage in such matters see H. Wolfram, *Intitulatio*, i (1967), *passim*, and H. J. Diesner, 'Fragen', p. 7 n. 17.*

p. 2. l. 3. **Historiam ... ecclesiasticam.** Bede's book is ecclesiastical history and not any other kind; nor is it a chronicle, though it rests upon his own. He knows he stands in a tradition of which Eusebius was the great originator and Orosius and Gregory of Tours were practitioners in their different ways. Above all, Bede's principal exemplar was the Bible, equally ecclesiastical history (see Judith McClure, 'Bede's Old Testament Kings', *Ideal and Reality*, pp. 76–98, and R. Kottje, *Studien zum Einfluss des Alten Testamentes auf Recht und Liturgie des frühen Mittelalters*, 2nd edn., 1970). His story concerns the transmission of Christianity and the mission of the Universal Church to the Anglo-Saxon settlers in a former province of the Roman Empire. But it is not Church history in any narrow sense. Like Eusebius, Bede views the fate of man under God's providence. To do this, it was necessary to say much about the structure of the English churches, of the work of their bishops, and of the reactions of kings. What we should call the political aspect of the story was thus basic but was strictly conditioned by its place in the unfolding tale of the divine plan. Kings, whether Christian or pagan, were worldly instruments in God's hands. History is *historia sacra*. (Well explained by P. Hunter Blair, *Bede's Ecclesias-*

tical History of the English Nation and its Importance Today (Jarrow Lecture, 1959); by R. Markus, 'Church History and Early Christian Historians'; and by Roger Ray, 'Bede, the Exegete, as Historian', *Famulus Christi*, pp. 125-40.) Equally important within the divine plan were the lives of holy men and the evidence of the miraculous—itself a literary genre in which Bede was already an expert. W. Levison has shown, in his 'Bede as Historian', *BLTW*, pp. 111-51, how Bede's skills as chronographer, hagiographer, and exegete come together in his *History*. Yet they are not in themselves his *History*, which is a creation apart from them and above them.

p. 2, ll. 6-15. **satisque studium ... accenditur.** Bede praises Ceolwulf for his interest in the words and deeds of famous men of their race as well as for his attention to the Scriptures, and at the same time defines his own programme: to make a contribution to moral edification through close attention to the Scriptures and by presenting ancestral history as in some sort a collection of *exempla* for present use. (See G. Tugène, 'L'Hist. "eccl."', pp. 152-3.)

p. 2, l. 15. **Quod ipsum ... deprehendens.** Ceolwulf looks for ethical lessons, the stuff of hagiography, rather than for 'facts' from annals. (See C. W. Jones, *Medievalia et Humanistica*, 4 (1946), 31.)

p. 2, ll. 16-17. **te regendis ... auctoritas.** Ceolwulf rules by divine authority. His contemporaries on the continent would claim the same and Bede acknowledges it. But he does not mean that Ceolwulf owes his kingship to any clerical participation at his inauguration: all kings rule by God's permission, though if they rule ill they will be known as tyrants. (See my *Early Germanic Kingship in England and on the Continent* (1971), ch. IV, and H. Vollrath-Reichelt, *Königsgedanke und Königtum bei den Angelsachsen* (1971), 21-9.)

p. 2, ll. 18-21. **Vt autem ... curabo.** Bede here follows the prologue of Gregory the Great's *Dialogues* (ed. A. de Vogüé, *SC* 260 (1979), 16): 'sed ut dubitationis occasionem legentibus subtraham, per singula quae describo, quibus mihi haec auctoribus sint comperta manifesto.' But it is not only the king's mind that must be put at rest but also the minds of other readers and hearers. It is significant that thus early in his *History* Bede acknowledges his debt to the writings of Pope Gregory I. Alan Thacker, 'Bede's Ideal of Reform', *Ideal and Reality*, pp. 135 ff., draws attention to Bede's appreciation of the relationship between Gregory's commentaries and his hagiography.

p. 4, l. 1. **monimentis litterarum.** What written records would Albinus find at Canterbury? One may agree with Kenneth Harrison that 'it is very probable that an episcopal list formed part of the material, although not giving many particulars for the earliest days of the see' ('The Synod of Whitby and the Beginning of the Christian Era in England', *Yorkshire Archaeological Journal*, 45 (1973), 112). Another possibility would be Easter Tables with marginal notes on events of interest to Canterbury. Bede goes on to say that he has not recorded everything that has reached him, and this should always be borne in mind.

p. 4, ll. 5-6. **Nothelmus postea Romam ueniens.** For what Nothhelm did, and did not, bring back, see note on I. 27.

p. 4, ll. 11-13. **A principio ... didicimus.** It is not clear when precisely Bede would place the acceptance of Christianity by the *gens Anglorum*, nor whom he means. But it is clear that his sources up to this point are written, not from *seniorum traditione*.

pp. 4, l. 13-16, l. 4. **Exinde autem ... successio sacerdotalis extiterit ...** Compare this with Eusebius, *HE* I. I, pref., and Rufinus, *HE* I. I. Bede means to follow his predecessors by using the apostolic succession of bishops as a groundwork for his *History*. See L. W. Barnard, 'Bede and Eusebius as Church Historians', *Famulus Christi*, p. 107, and Levison, 'Bede as Historian', *BLTW*, 142 ff.

p. 4, ll. 18-19. **necnon et Orientalium Anglorum.** Bede's likely sources for East Anglian events are examined by D. Whitelock,

'The Pre-Viking Age Church in East Anglia', *ASE* 1 (1972), 2 ff.
These include, first, Albinus himself, then earlier writings and
traditions unspecified, and finally the otherwise unrecorded
Abbot Esi.

p. 6, ll. 19–21. **uera lex historiae ... studuimus.** This may be a
general justification or it may refer only to what Bede has just
been saying about his account of Bishop Cuthbert. In either case
it is a crux much commented upon. Bede's source for the phrase
was St Jerome, *Adversus Helvidium de Mariae Virginitate Perpetua*
(*PL* 23, col. 187 c) and he had already used it in his commentary
on Luke 2 (ed. D. Hurst, p. 67, l. 1910), as Plummer of course
saw. C. W. Jones first recognized St Jerome in the *HE* context
(*Saints' Lives and Chronicles in Early England* (1947), 83) and goes
on to say that Bede's 'is not a plea for literal truth, but for a truth
which denies the literal statement or uses the literal statement
to achieve an image in which the literal statement is itself
incongruous'. Here, and indeed elsewhere when 'uera lex' is not
specifically mentioned, Bede is justifying the introduction of
common belief or common report ('fama uulgante'). He does not
mean rustic tittle-tattle. He means that which would be generally acceptable (e.g. by religious communities) from whatever
kind of source. 'Though he feels the need to submit to the
normal "law" of history in cases where a full control of the
evidence is not possible, Bede nowhere identifies himself with
the [*opinio*] *vulgi*, but rather with the *docti* or *eruditi*'
(P. Meyvaert, 'Bede the Scholar', *Famulus Christi*, p. 67). It is not,
then, the nature of the evidence but the quality of its transmission that is in question. The truth of 'facts' had to be accommodated to the higher truth of the programme of Providence, so
reaching *historica fides*, which a wide audience could accept and
understand. In other words, Bede's understanding of the *uera lex*
was a narrative that would not seem strange to those circles
from which his information derived. The matter is well investigated by Roger Ray, 'Bede, the Exegete, as Historian', *Famulus
Christi*, pp. 131 ff. I do not see why Jones, and less decisively
M. L. W. Laistner, *Thought and Letters in Western Europe*, 2nd edn.
(1957) 166, think that a history thus designed as edification ('ad
instructionem') cannot stand in the direct line of descent from
Eusebius.*

p. 6, l. 28. **incolis.** A curious word to choose. Does Bede mean the inhabitants of Britain as a whole? Or does he mean the inhabitants of those places he has particularly in mind (religious houses and those who serve churches)? The latter seems acceptable provided that one does not suppose that such communities were cut off from intercourse with the surrounding secular world.

Book I

p. 8, ll. 1–2. 1, *capitula*. **Haec continentur ... gentis Anglorum.** This should be translated 'These are the contents of the first book of the ecclesiastical history of the English people', and not '... of the history of the Church of the English people'.

p. 14, l. 1. 1. 1. **Britannia.** Plummer describes the first twenty-two chapters of this book as 'in the nature of an introduction to Bede's main subject'. But they are more than that. They are a vital and highly contrived prelude. Their subject is Britain in what has been called her pre-Fall state, the Fall itself, and its immediate consequences. Their position in the *History* has been clarified by Calvin B. Kendall, 'Imitation and the Venerable Bede's *Historia Ecclesiastica*', *Saints, Scholars*, i. 161–90. Bede starts with a geographical evocation derived from well-known sources but what is in his mind is the paradisal setting at the beginning of Genesis. It is, by *imitatio*, a creation scene, indicative of the abundance, richness, and variety of animate and inanimate nature in Britain and Ireland; and these contrast sharply with natural descriptions elsewhere in the *History*. What matters therefore is what Bede adds to his sources; and what he adds is impressionistic, not the result of personal observation.

p. 14. ll. 6–7. 1. 1. **quadragies ... conpleat.** This means 3,600 miles and not 4,875 miles.

p. 14, l. 26. 1. 1. **fontes calidos.** Bath? 'This passage has no known classical source and it sounds very like "Nennius" ' description' (Campbell, *The Anglo-Saxons*, p. 41; cf. *Historia Brittonum*, ch. 67, ed. Mommsen, *MGH AA* 13. 213). 'Nennius' however is an early ninth-century collection made in Wales, though this does not prevent Bede from having had access to early material later used in the collection. D. Dumville, '"Nennius" and the *Historia Brittonum*', *Studia Celtica*, 10–11 (1975–6), 78–95, has shown that the attribution of the work to Nennius is no earlier than the mid-eleventh century. For an evaluation of 'Nennius' see Robert W. Hanning, *The Vision of History in Early Britain* (1966), ch. IV, and Wendy Davies, *Wales in the Early Middle Ages* (1982), 205–6.*

p. 16, ll. 3–4. I. 1. **aeris . . . gagatem.** 'Ores of copper, iron, lead and silver were plentiful, and there was an abundance of jet. Bede does not say whether the ores were being worked in his day, nor does he mention tin, gold or coal.' (P. Hunter Blair, *The World of Bede* (1970), 11). He is likely enough to have known about jet at Whitby.

p. 16, ll. 9–20. I. 1. **lucidas aestate noctes . . . conpleat horas.** There is more to this than dependence on the second book of Pliny's *Natural History*. Bede was himself aware of equinoctial hours. On the possibilities for calculation in Bede's Northumbria, see Kenneth Harrison, 'Easter Cycles and the Equinox in the British Isles', *ASE* 7 (1978), 4 ff.

p. 16, l. 21. I. 1. **iuxta numerum librorum.** Five languages in Britain; five books of the *lex divina* (the Pentateuch); therefore five books of the *Ecclesiastical History*? This is a better explanation, if one is required, than to suppose that Bede saw the ten books of Gregory of Tours' *History* and divided by two.*

p. 16, ll. 22–6. I. 1. **quinque gentium linguis . . . facta communis.** Bede insists that though he is to be concerned with one place, Brittania, he must consider the effects of four ethnic groups (English, British, Irish, and Picts) who seek one and the same truth and knowledge in their own languages. However, they are united by common use of a fifth language, Latin, which they know from study of the Scriptures. This is not evidence that anything resembling the Latin of Roman Britain had survived to the eighth century. Plummer is doubtless right to say that Bede is speaking of languages employed in the service of religion rather than of nations; but languages in this sense certainly do imply ethnic groups. A. C. Thomas writes: 'I suspect the four languages, English, British (P-Celtic), "Scottish" or Primitive Irish, and Pictish, are listed in (to Bede) order of decreasing intelligibility' ('The Evidence from North Britain', *Christianity in Britain*, p. 119). I do not see why.*

p. 16, ll. 26–7. I. I. **Brettones ... de tractu Armoricano.** Bede reports a legend with the necessary caution. Plummer's account of the shrinkage of the *tractus* to modern Brittany leaves out of consideration the exodus of British to the same area from south-western Britain in face of the Anglo-Saxon advance. The legend is a typical origin-story; cf. Gregory of Tours on Frankish origins (*Hist.* II. 9, p. 57, 'tradunt enim multi', and, more extravagantly, Fredegar, *Chron.* III. 2, 'de Francorum origine', ed. Krusch, p. 93).

p. 16, l. 30. I. I. **Pictorum de Scythia.** Again, Bede sees this as legend; one that people believe and which should therefore be reported. It is possible that he or his sources confused Scythia with Scandia. F. T. Wainwright concludes that 'he seems to have got the story ultimately from an Irish source, and his version of it in turn influenced later Irish scribes. At best it represents a tradition current among the Irish, and perhaps also among the Picts' (*The Problem of the Picts* (1955), 10). Jordanes, historian of the Goths, also confused Scythians with other peoples (see J. Svennung, *Jordanes und Scandia* (1967), 217–23); but Bede did not read Jordanes. However, the possibility remains that the legend is neither specifically Irish nor Pictish: 'probably Isidore of Seville provided the name of the Scythians, but if there already existed a pseudo-etymology it was surely of the "*Scotti* from Scythia" nature; "*Picti* from Scythia" must be an invention for the purposes of Bede's source, to explain the Picts in terms of the *Scotti*' (Archibald Duncan, 'Bede, Iona, and the Picts', pp. 3 ff.).*

p. 18, l. 2. I. I. **Hiberniam peruenisse.** The whole passage concerning the Picts' arrival in Ireland and their settlement in northern Britain on certain conditions is Bede's version of a legend from an ultimately Irish source. The historical facts are matters for debate: see Duncan, 'Bede, Iona, and the Picts', pp. 3 ff.; D. P. Kirby, '... per universas Pictorum provincias', *Famulus Christi*, pp. 286 ff.; and Alfred P. Smyth, *Warlords and Holy Men* (1984), 60-1, where the point is made that Bede is not describing matrilinear succession as such but a custom in use in his own day that involved female succession in exceptional circumstances; and it is therefore a mixture of Irish legend with contemporary Pictish practice. But what matters here is that the story that reaches Bede satisfies his requirements as an explanation of the presence of Picts in Scotland as well as being generally acceptable to those (in Dalriada?) from whom he derived it. Moreover, he dramatizes it by the use of *oratio recta*.

p. 18, ll. 29-30. i. i. **Hibernia ... Brittaniae praestat.** Bede takes his cue from Isidore (*Etymol.* XIV. vi. 6) as Plummer recognized: 'Scotia idem et Hibernia proxima Brittaniae insula, spatio terrarum angustior, sed situ fecundior', and Isidore goes on to the legend about snakes. One might conclude, with Mayr-Harting, *The Coming of Christianity*, p. 50, that 'Bede's passage is evidently a witty parody of this sort of nonsense', inserted to persuade the reader that he knew how to entertain before getting on to the serious stuff. But even if one does not, Mayr-Harting is clearly right to suspect that 'the appearance of naiveté here is very deceptive indeed'. Kendall, 'Imitation', p. 181, pursues a more promising path by linking the descriptions of Britain and Ireland as companion-pieces in an evocation of Paradise: 'it is the Promised Land which prefigures the redemption of the world ... An island abounding with milk and honey is meant to evoke the land God promised to the people of Moses ... Since a serpent caused man's (spiritual) death (Gen: iii), it is fitting that there are no snakes or reptiles in the land that prefigures the promise of eternal life'. Bede does not elucidate the allegorical significance of these 'signs', as he might have done in a learned commentary: his readers must take them at the level appropriate to each.

p. 20, l. 2. i. i. **rasa folia codicum.** C. W. Jones, *Saints' Lives*, pp. 88-9, commenting on the miraculous power of an emulsion of dust, originating in the Gospels, observes: 'The fact that this story consistently recurs in the border lands suggests its popularity in the Celtic Church. We are therefore not surprised to find Bede applying the same story to the effective power of Irish books, though such a story would not appear in his nonhagiological works.' It can hardly mean that Irish books were so numerous that Bede thought one might as well emulsify a few. In fact, he takes it seriously and says that he had seen the cure happen with his own eyes. Strictly, then, this was no miracle, which, for Bede, should be instantaneous in its effect according to P. Meyvaert, 'Bede the Scholar', *Famulus Christi*, p. 55. However, Bede does add that the cures happened 'protinus'.

p. 20, ll. 15-16. 1. 2. **usque ad Gaium Iulium Caesarem.** Compare Bede's treatment of ten Roman emperors—he is only interested in those with British connections—with that of 'Nennius'' seven. This at least suggests that Bede's seven 'Bretwaldas' owed nothing, as a mystical number, to any Roman precedent, nor to any Celtic tradition.

p. 20, ll. 16-17. 1. 2. **anno ab Vrbe condita sescentesimo nonagesimo tertio.** Bede promptly transforms this date into an incarnational date, doing so again in chapters 3 and 11. 'Always a theologian, Bede would not desert the Bible; and for the reckoning of time his allegiance was now transferred from the Old Testament to the New. There is indeed a remarkable contrast between the jumbled chronicle and an air of order and simplicity which pervades the *Historia* ... thereafter, except for the Indiction, the ancient forms of reckoning are never referred to. Bede evidently decided for a clean break with the past ... (Harrison, *Framework*, p. 77). Is it possible that this transference plays a more significant part in Bede's mind than chronological clarification? He now places the whole course of historical development in Britain under the aegis of Christ. On the equation used by Bede to translate Roman years of St Jerome's tradition into AD terms, see M. Miller, 'Bede's Roman Dates', *Classica et Medievalia*, 31 (1970), 240. It is unknown whether Bede was the first in Britain to attempt this chronological translation, thus following the example of Dionysius Exiguus in his Easter Tables in the sixth century (cf. P. Hunter Blair, 'The Historical Writings of Bede', *Spoleto*, 17 (1970), 206 ff.). The dedication stone of Bede's own church at Jarrow has no AD dating; but the date is early—685. For some comparable church dedications see my *Bede's Europe* (Jarrow Lecture, 1962), reprinted in *Early Medieval History* (1975), 60-1, and John Higgitt, 'The Dedication Inscription at Jarrow and its Context', *Antiquaries Journal*, 59 (1979), 348ff. Did Jarrow use a basic *dedicatio* formula of continental origin?

p. 24, l. 5. I. 3. **quae in Actibus Apostolorum.** This is Bede's own addition to his source and emphasizes the New Testament link.

p. 24, ll. 12-13. I. 3. **Succedens autem Claudio.** Bede clearly approves of Claudius' intervention in Britain. Nero on the other hand 'nihil omnino in re militari ausus est', with disastrous results for the Empire and Britain. As elsewhere, Bede favours military action of the right sort.

p. 24, l. 15. I. 3. **illic capta.** L. D. Reynolds draws attention to the reversal of Eutropius's words (*capta illic*) and suggests that Bede had access to what was, or was to become, the B tradition of the text: 'The Northumbrian tradition may well pre-date, and have no connection with, our extant manuscript groups' (*Texts and Transmission: A Survey of the Latin Classics* (1983), 161-2).

p. 24, l. 23. I. 4. **susceptamque fidem Brittani.** No doubt it is true that Bede derived the Lucius legend from the *Liber Pontificalis* but his gloss on the text—'et mox effectum . . . in pace servabant'— suggests that he had some other source for his statement that the Britons, and not only Lucius, were converted and practised their Christianity in peace till the reign of Diocletian. Moreover, British Christianity was in Bede's eyes properly launched by papal mandate to a king. There is at least archaeological evidence of the practice of Christianity in Romano-British villas by the fourth century. Charles Thomas, *Christianity in Roman Britain to AD 500* (1981), provides useful maps and plates.

p. 26, ll. 2-3. I. 5. **non muro . . . sed uallo.** This distinction is ultimately from Vegetius. C. E. Stevens, 'Gildas Sapiens', *EHR* 56 (1941), 353ff., examines Gildas' treatment of Romano-British relations, which differs from Bede's. Bede's rationalization of the construction of the northern Roman walls does not pass the test of modern scholarship but does help to explain subsequent events as he saw them. In other words, this is not a piece of unnecessary antiquarianism.

p. 26, l. 10. I. 5. **apud Eboracum.** The transition from Roman to Anglo-Saxon York is sketched by Rosemary Cramp, *Anglian and Viking York* (Borthwick Papers, 33; 1967).*

p. 28, ll. 8–9. I. 6. **Denique ... sublimauit.** Orosius continues to provide the background for Roman control of Britain in the troubled years of the late third century; but the purpose of the chapter lies in the last sentence: Diocletian's persecution of Christians, here as elsewhere, leads to burning of churches, outlawry, and martyrdom, so that Britain too earns the special glory of faithful witness. Gregory of Tours, describing a later persecution in Gaul which recalls that of Diocletian, also records the burning of churches and the killing of clergy but without drawing attention to the permanent gain to society of martyrdom (*Hist.* IV. 47). Bede's final sentence leads naturally to the following long chapter.

p. 28, l. 10. I. 7. **Siquidem in ea passus est sanctus Albanus.** This story, in part at least legend, is of great significance to Bede. He does not take it from Gildas, who reports it in a different way, but from a later version of the *Passio Albani*, which places the martyrdom at Verulamium. It was also referred to, as Bede knew, by Venantius Fortunatus, and is attested in the *Acta Martyrum* and Constantius' *Vita Germani*. Bede may be wrong, if logical, in associating the martyrdom with Diocletian's persecution: it may have been earlier. (See W. H. C. Frend, 'The Christianization of Roman Britain', *Christianity in Britain*, p. 38). But Verulamium is an acceptable site for the martyrdom, and Bede is himself evidence for a cult of St Alban at Verulamium that stretched back long before his own time. C. E. Stevens, 'Gildas Sapiens', *EHR* 56 (1941), 373, seems unduly sceptical. Campbell, who draws attention to the existence of similar problems and possibilities of martyrdom elsewhere in Europe, writes: 'The case for continuity is strengthened by the situation of the later abbey of St Alban's—outside Roman Verulamium, where an extra-mural cemetery, and so St Alban's tomb, could well have been ... St Alban's could have been within an area not conquered from the Britons till the 570s' ('The First Christian Kings', *The Anglo-Saxons*, ed. Campbell, p. 51). It is of some significance that, as Stenton noted, 'along the course of Watling Street, *Verolamium* is the only Romano-British name which survived, even in part, between London and north Warwickshire' (*Preparatory*, p. 256). Bede's lesson is clear: martyrdom leads to miracles, which in this case links the Christianity of Britain with that of the Anglo-Saxons.*

p. 34, ll. 24-5. i. 8. **basilicas sanctorum ... passim propalant.** With this quotation Bede emphasizes what relief from persecution entails: rebuilding of churches but also the building of shrines to martyrs. They were tokens of victory. This tells us nothing of the actual size of Christian communities in Britain towards the end of the third century. Perhaps Christianity was no more prestigious than any other eastern mystery cult. But at least Christians could build and avoid persecution. What has come through to a time of peace is the cult of martyrs: and this, a matter of firm orthodoxy to Bede, is the necessary prelude to the appearance of unorthodoxy in the form of heresy. For evidence of church-building in Late Roman Britain see Charles Thomas, *Christianity in Roman Britain*, ch. 7. However, 'it is not of itself an overwhelmingly sound inference that there *were* churches in the last century of Roman Britain, simply because Gildas and after him Bede thought, and said, that there had been. It is a presumption' (p. 146).

p. 34, l. 28. i. 8. **Arrianae uaesaniae.** Plummer, following Bright, and others following both, have judged Bede to have put too much emphasis on Arianism in Britain, though Plummer justly adds that 'noui semper aliquid' (p. 36, l. 1) 'seems to hint at the existence of various heresies in Britain'. To this can also be added the evidence of flourishing paganism of several types (on which Frend, 'Christianization of Roman Britain', *Christianity in Britain*, pp. 33 ff.). However, Bede's point is not the quantity of heresy but its quality. It offers a general threat to orthodoxy throughout the western world and is serious wherever it occurs. Gregory of Tours had been equally convinced of this and, like Bede, has been accused of exaggeration. Both, looking back

through their sources and looking at their own times, dreaded
doctrinal deviation and schism; and both stood within good
patristic tradition. Bede had already seen Arianism prefigured in
the Pale Horse of the Apocalypse (*Explan. Apoc.* I. 6; *PL* 93, col.
147 C and D) and had warned that those who separated themselves from the unity of the Catholic Church would have their
place with the goats at the left hand of Christ on the Day of
Judgement (*In Cant.* v; *PL* 91, col. 1183B). On this see Gerald
Bonner, 'Bede and Medieval Civilization', *ASE* 2 (1973), 73.*

p. 36, l. 5. I. 8. **Constantinum filium.** A reader of Eusebius, Bede
is fully aware of the significance of Constantine the Great for the
history of Christianity (cf. p. 112, ll. 10–18; I. 32). It is a measure
of his control of material that he is content here to limit himself
to what is relevant to Britain, which he finds in Eusebius. For a
general survey of Constantine's role in early medieval thought
see Eugen Ewig, 'Das Bild Constantins des Grossen in den
ersten Jahrhunderten des abendländischen Mittelalters', *Historisches Jahrbuch*, 75 (1956), 1–46, reprinted in *Spätantikes und
fränkisches Gallien* (1976), i. 72–113.

p. 36, l. 19. I. 9. **Maximus ... strenuus et probus.** As Plummer
noted, Gildas gives him a very different character and brands
him as the principal *tyrannus*, whose actions left Britain
defenceless against disaster. For his career see Sheppard Frere,
Brittania (1978), 404–6 (with correction by David N. Dumville,
'Sub-Roman Britain, History and Legend', *History*, NS, 62 (1977),
179 ff.). Gildas ignores Constantine III, another British usurper,
after his account of Maximus, and does so because Constantine
would have been irrelevant to his account of the northern wars
in the late fourth and early fifth centuries, not because he had
not read Orosius. M. Miller has attempted to demonstrate this,
'Bede's Use of Gildas', *EHR* 90 (1975), 241–61. Bede 'corrects'
Gildas' narrative, thus possibly producing some chronological
distortion, and does so because of his concern with dates and
the need he feels to reconcile his sources. See note on I. 12. On
the difficulties involved in interpreting Gildas's text and
chronology—and they partly defeated Bede—see David N.
Dumville, 'The Chronology of *De Excidio Britanniae*, Book I', in

Gildas: New Approaches, ed. M. Lapidge and D. Dumville (1984), 61-84.*

p. 38, l. 3. I. 10. **Pelagius Bretto.** It is impossible to estimate the grip of Pelagianism within the British churches and equally impossible to deny its presence. For Bede, however, it was enough that 'the faith of the Fathers was as his own and their enemies were to be regarded as his' (Bonner, 'Bede and Medieval Civilization', *ASE* 2 (1973), 74). Frend, 'The Christianization of Roman Britain', *Christianity in Britain*, pp. 44-5, makes a good case for taking British Pelagianism seriously though he may follow too closely the arguments of J. N. L. Myres,'Pelagius and the End of Roman Rule in Britain', *JRS* 50 (1960), 21-36, over-dependent as they are on a special interpretation of the word *gratia*. For a different interpretation see Peter Brown, 'Pelagius and his Supporters: Aims and Environment', *JTS* NS 19 (1968), 93-114. Bede's point is that though Augustine and others had effectively demolished the heresy, there were yet those in Britain who compounded their folly by resistance to rebuke and rebuttal. It was an instance of the obstinacy of British churchmen. Gildas mentions neither Pelagianism nor the consequential visits of Germanus, presumably because they had little to do with the northern situation that concerned him.*

p. 38, ll. 21-2. I. 11. **ante biennium ... facta est.** How did Bede know about Alaric? His account which to some extent corroborates that of Procopius (which he did not know) 'would appear to suggest the existence of a Western tradition recording the emergence of an independent Britain *ca* 410' (Ian Wood, 'The End of Roman Britain: Continental Evidence and Parallels', *Gildas: New Approaches*, ed. M. Lapidge and D. Dumville, p. 2).

p. 40, l. 6. I. 11. **Fracta est autem Roma.** Leaving his text of Orosius, Bede makes his own summary of the Roman occupation of Britain, and does so with a hint of regret. Cities, bridges, lighthouses, and roads still remained in southern Britain to remind the English of the Roman past of the island. He says nothing of religion though we know that ecclesiastical links with Gaul were maintained and Pelagianism continued to be active.

p. 40, l. 15. I. 12. **Exin Brittania.** Chapters 12 to 16, along with
22, constitute Bede's statement on early British history and are
firmly based on Gildas' *De Excidio.* He had already used Gildas
for his British entries in his *Chronica Majora* incorporated in *De
Temporum Ratione*, completed some six years before the *HE*; but
this was not a connected narrative of British or any other
history, and the entries were scanty. Bede's treatment of the
same material in *HE* is altogether fuller and is differently
conceived; and it suggests that he had now come to have greater
respect for Gildas even if he reorders Gildas' chronology in
certain respects and incorporates other material. He omits
details of internal British history, makes stylistic changes, and,
more importantly, some interpretative changes. We are thus left
with three distinct approaches: (1) Gildas, (2) *Chron. Maj.*, and
(3) *HE.* The development is well investigated by M. Miller,
'Bede's Use of Gildas', *EHR* 90 (1975), 241–6. For a more
sceptical appraisal of Gildas see Patrick Sims-Williams, 'Gildas
and the Anglo-Saxons', *Cambridge Medieval Celtic Studies*, 6
(1983), 1–30, and see also Thomas, *Christianity in Roman Britain*,
pp. 247–52. There are useful comments on the differing
historical approaches of Gildas and Bede in Robert W. Hanning,
The Vision of History in Early Britain, chs. 2 and 3.

p. 40, l. 15. I. 12. **in parte Brettonum.** This addition shows that
Bede here took Gildas' 'Brittania' to mean territory inhabited by
Britons, thus excluding Pictish territory. Bede's normal sense of
'Brittania', as ll. 21–2 ('quod extra Brittaniam'), embraces the
whole island, though he seems in the same sentence to under-
stand only British-occupied territory by 'Brittaniae terras'.

p. 40, l. 20. I. 12. **Scottorum a circio, Pictorum ab aquilone.**
'When Bede wrote that the Clyde had formed the frontier
between the British of Strathclyde and (formerly) the Picts, by
Bede's day the *Scotti*, on the West, and that the Forth was a
similar division between the Picts and, by Bede's day, the Angles,
on the East, he must have been repeating traditional information of great age, known to everyone in North Britain' (A. C.
Thomas, 'The Evidence from North Britain', *Christianity in
Britain*, p. 106, who also considers likely settlements of Picts
around Tayside and in Fife.)*

p. 40, l. 26. i. 12. **urbem Giudi.** Possibly Inveresk but also possibly Stirling (Kenneth Jackson—following Angus Graham—'On the Northern British Section in Nennius', *Celt and Saxon*, pp. 36-7). Bede's eight British *urbes* are considered by James Campbell, 'Bede's Words for Places', *Names, Words*, pp. 35 ff. By explaining that the two great firths are dominated by Giudi and Dumbarton, he clearly takes Gildas to mean (though not necessarily rightly) that the Scots were in 'Cowal and beyond' while the Picts were in 'Fife and beyond' (Miller, 'Bede's Use of Gildas', p. 243).*

p. 42, ll. 6-7. i. 12. **murum ... cespitibus construentes.** Bede accepts Gildas' dating of the turf wall, which must be rejected on archaeological grounds. It was in fact the Antonine turf wall built between AD 140 and 142, and therefore not by Severus. Did Gildas know of post-Roman earthworks of comparable length? For the archaeology of the Antonine wall see Sheppard Frere, *Brittania* (1978), pp. 166 ff. Bede, following Gildas, did not know that it was built after, and not before, Hadrian's wall to the south. The reasons for Gildas' mistakes are discussed by Miller, 'Bede's Use of Gildas', p. 245. But the dating of the Antonine wall earlier than Hadrian's made sense of their accounts of the Pictish incursions into Northern Britain, and they had no evidence to the contrary. Indeed, the only written source that could have given them the true date of the walls was the *Scriptores Historiae Augustae*. Since the British frontier was withdrawn from the Forth-Clyde to the Tyne–Solway line, as Gildas knew it was, a natural inference would be that the southerly wall was built after the northerly.

p. 42, ll. 8-9. i. 12. **inter duo freta.** That is, the wall between Kinneil and Dumbarton; and he knows that parts of it are still visible. He presumably refers to the stone wall that in part replaced it within fifteen years.

p. 42, ll. 24-5. i. 12. **Rursum mittitur legio ... tempore autumni.** These words are additions to Gildas. They do not sound like Bede's inferences and may derive from glosses on Gildas. Alternatively, Bede may have had an additional source of written information unknown to us.

p. 44, ll. 3-4. I. 12. **ubi et Seuerus ... fecerat.** It is true that Severus had reconstructed Hadrian's wall. Orosius records that Severus built a fosse and a rampart, but it is unlikely that Gildas had read Orosius. See E. A. Thompson, 'Gildas and the History of Britain', *Britannia*, 10 (1979), 209-11. Bede on the other hand had read both Orosius and Jerome, and was thus able to add the Severan *vallum*, extra military details, and a date in the reign of Honorius. Surviving inscriptions prove that work on Hadrian's wall was undertaken both by British cities and by at least one private person, and this supports 'sumtu publico priuatoque' (Stevens, 'Gildas Sapiens', *EHR* 56 (1941), 359).*

p. 44, l. 7. I. 12. **octo pedes latum et** XII **altum.** This detail is not a gratuitous addition to show that Bede knew his wall. It is concrete evidence of his admiration for the enduring quality of *Romanitas*.

p. 44, l. 28. I. 13. **Anno ... CCCCXXIII.** Bede provides a date. This short chapter, a skilful fusion of Gildas, Prosper's chronicle, and Marcellinus Comes, slightly changed the shorter account in *Chron. Maj.*, and is designed to bring a Roman mission to the Irish and a refusal of help to the British from imperial forces on the continent.

p. 46, l. 1. I. 13. **anno imperii octauo Palladius.** As Miller points out ('Bede's Use of Gildas', p. 246), Bede departs from his *Chron. Maj.* dating to place Palladius' mission after the beginning of the third phase of the Pictish wars, immediately preceding Aetius' third consulship, perhaps because he 'has continued the narrative of the Pictish wars up to Aetius' year before he turns to Roman affairs; and it may consequently be that he entered Palladius among the Roman events rather than that he intended any change of relative dating'. Reasoned accounts of the successive missions to Ireland of Palladius and Patrick (not mentioned by Bede in *HE*) are: L. Bieler, 'St Patrick and the British Church', *Christianity in Britain*, pp. 125 ff., F. J. Byrne, *Irish Kings and High Kings* (1973), 78 ff.; for early Christianity in Munster see D. A. Binchy, *Celtic and Anglo-Saxon Kingship* (1970), 40-1. For Bede, what is important is the papal initiative in sending a bishop to the Irish already 'in Christum credentes'.*

p. 46, l. 4. i. 13. **Aetius uir inlustris.** So Bede interprets Gildas' Agitius. K. H. Jackson's opinion is that 'there is no philological difficulty over Agitius = Aetius' (*Antiquity*, 47 (1973), 81). I do not understand the argument for 'perpetual consulship' in sub-Roman Britain advanced by J. R. Morris, 'Pelagian Literature', *JTS* NS 16 (1965), 39 ff. Bede goes on to explain Aetius' refusal of help by drawing attention to the Hunnic menace.*

p. 46, ll. 8–9. i. 13. **Repellunt barbari ... ad barbaros.** Whatever Gildas understood by these *barbari* (and he may not have known), there is no reason to think that Bede meant more than Picts and *Scotti*. It is true that by this time Saxons may have been involved in early incursions, whether independently of the Picts or in concert with them (cf. Stevens, 'Gildas Sapiens', esp. p. 362, and Harrison, *Framework*, pp. 22 ff.). But Bede knows nothing of that. I also see no reason why Gildas should have derived his copy of the British letter to Aetius from the work of Renatus Frigeridus (lost, apart from some extracts in Gregory of Tours' *History*).

p. 46, ll. 16–17. i. 13. **Quin et hisdem temporibus fames.** Bede clearly associates the famine and plague at Constantinople with those in Britain which he goes on to report at the beginning of his next chapter. On the plague see M. Todd, '*Famosa Pestis* and Britain in the Fifth Century', *Britannia*, 8 (1977), 319–25.

p. 46, l. 22. i. 14. **Interea Brettones.** Gildas' account of the Pictish wars ends in his summary in chapter 21, and 'interea' introduces his readers to the Saxon wars. In *Chron. Maj.* Bede replaces *interea* with *mox*, whereas here in *HE* he returns to *interea* and gives a longer account. Whatever Gildas meant by *interea* Bede clearly understood something very like *mox*.*

p. 46, ll. 25–6. i. 14. **potius confidentes ... cessabat, auxilium.** Bede paraphrases Gildas, making it even clearer that human aid had already failed: it is God who moves historical events. The point is well made by Claudio Leonardi, 'Il venerabile Beda e la cultura del secolo VIII', *Spoleto*, 20 (1973), 637. I do not see that we have any grounds for deciding that Gildas was here thinking of North Britain rather than the south-east, though E. A.

Thompson firmly rejects the latter ('Gildas and the History of
Britain', *Britannia*, 10 (1979), 214 ff.) on the ground that mention
by the Chronicler of AD 452 of early Saxon attacks on Britain will
have reference to south-east Britain, not the north, and therefore would not interest Gildas. Bede at all events seems from the
context to be thinking of the north. His Saxons are firmly
relegated to the end of the chapter.

p. 48, ll. 22–3. I. 14. **initum ... agendum.** From this point to the
end of the chapter Bede changes Gildas' text in important
respects. Either he is putting his own interpretation of Gildas'
vaguer account or he has another source at his disposal; perhaps
a glossed text of Gildas or, more likely, an account derived from
Canterbury. The Saxons come by invitation and he names
Gildas' *superbus tyrannus*. There is no call to dismiss this, as does
A. W. Wade-Evans, as 'pure invention' (*The Emergence of England
and Wales*, 2nd edn. (1959), 37), at least by Bede. That the Saxons
had in fact been settling in Britain for a long time is certain from
archaeological evidence—see J. N. L. Myres, *Anglo-Saxon Pottery
and the Settlement of England* (1969), and Sonia Chadwick Hawkes
(with G. C. Dunning), 'Soldiers and Settlers in Britain, Fourth to
Fifth Century', *Medieval Archaeology*, 5 (1961)—but it does not
follow that Bede or Canterbury knew this.

p. 48, ll. 25–6. I. 14. **cum suo rege Uurtigerno.** In *Chron. Maj.*
Bede names him Vertigernus, using the Celtic form, perhaps
from a glossed text of Gildas. His change here, on the authority
of K. H. Jackson, 'perhaps represents the Primitive Anglo-Saxon
form, and if so must be from an earlier written source' (*Language
and History in Early Britain* (1953), 273; see also D. N. Dumville,
'A New Chronicle-Fragment', *EHR* 88 (1973), 313 n. 5).
Between the years 725 and 731 Bede clearly obtained access to
an Anglo-Saxon Latin text. From what follows it would be a fair
assumption that this text reached him from Canterbury. Who
was this Vortigern (as we have called him since Geoffrey of
Monmouth's time) with his council? He may have been an
independent sub-Roman kinglet after the fashion of Syagrius in
Gaul as recounted by Gregory of Tours (*Hist.* II. 27) or an 'all-
powerful prefect of a military emperor' (J. R. Morris, 'The
Literary Evidence', *Christianity in Britain*, p. 58); but at least he

could employ *foederati* from abroad and had a council to advise him. D. N. Dumville discusses the history of Vortigern in his Welsh form (Gwrtheyrn) in 'Sub-Roman Britain: History and Legend', *History*, 62 (1977), 183 ff. 'Nennius' has a fuller account of the *adventus Saxonum* but is heavily overloaded with legend and adds nothing of substance to Bede. 'It is possible—it may be preferable, and in the particular case of "Arthur" it is *desirable*— to construct models of fifth-century Britain devoid of individual names altogether' (Thomas, *Christianity in Roman Britain*, p. 245). Bede thought otherwise: there must be leaders, and leaders must have names. Wendy Davies, *Wales in the Early Middle Ages* (1982), 94 ff., discusses Vortigern and his kingdom.*

p. 48, ll. 27-9. I. 14. **Quod Domini ... probauit.** Bede ends the chapter with the point that matters: it was God's will that brought the Saxons to Britain so that punishment should fall on the British 'inprobos'.

p. 48, l. 30-p. 50, l. 1. I. 15. **Anno ... Tunc.** This means that Bede places the origin of the Kentish settlement between the years 450 and 457. It may be an approximation but he means it to be as exact as he can for what to him (and to Canterbury) was a vital moment.*

p. 50, ll. 1-3. I. 15. **Anglorum siue Saxonum ... in orientali parte.** I cannot account for this qualification but see no difficulty in the first contingent arriving in three boats. Gildas may have intended Northumbria by *in orientali parte* since this would afford the protection the British required against the Picts; but it is not clear that Bede took it in that way. Nor have we any knowledge of the extent of Vortigern's authority. We do not know that he controlled northern England any more than we know that he ruled from Wales to Kent. E. A. Thompson, 'Gildas and the History of Britain', p. 217, seems unduly positive. If Bede understood Kent or East Anglia he is not brushing aside the archaeological evidence available to us of earlier English settlements in the north-east; he simply knew nothing about it. Nor would he have known of the Kentish settlement without written information from Canterbury. However, as Stevens points out ('Gildas Sapiens', p. 368), there may be some truth in 'Nennius''

report that Hengist had kinsmen in the north who could have
moved south to Kent after their victory: thus in Stevens' view
'one tradition covered the exploits of two united but originally
distinct bodies whose leaders were kinsmen'. But this is pure
conjecture.

p. 50, l. 10. I. 15. **donantibus Brittanis.** Bede dispenses with the
technical terms of settlement employed here by Gildas, possibly
not understanding them. Gildas knew how federates were
settled.

p. 50, l. 15. I. 15. **Saxonibus, Anglis, Iutis.** This much-discussed
distinction stands up fairly well to modern archaeological
evidence, even when we include parties of Frisians, Franks, and
others among the earliest settlers. The Franks cannot have been
a significant element at this stage, despite the arguments of
Vera I. Evison, *The Fifth-Century Invasions South of the Thames*
(1965). See Myres' review, *EHR* 81 (1966), 340 ff., and that of
Sonia Hawkes in *Antiquity*, 40 (1966), 322–3. Place-name study
also tends to support Bede (see Stenton, *Preparatory*, pp. 118 ff.,
366 ff.). Myres regards this whole passage as a later insertion by
Bede, not I think very convincingly (though compare v. 9 on the
Frisians, a passage noted by Gibbon, *Decline and Fall*, ed. J. B.
Bury (1909), iv. 157–8 and n. 37). Campbell, 'The Lost Centuries', *The Anglo-Saxons*, pp. 29, 30, agrees with Myres. Plainly it
will have been part of the information from Canterbury that
gave him the Kentish story and made possible a framework for
his *History*. However, Myres accepts that Bede's view of the
distinctness of his three peoples, their continental homes, and
their settlement-areas in Britain is in general supported by
archaeology ('The Angles, the Saxons and the Jutes', *PBA* 56
(1970), 145–74). It is unclear why Tugène holds ('L'Hist. "eccl."',
p. 132) that Bede was uninterested in Anglo-Saxon origins, even
if he is less full in this regard than was Isidore on the Goths. See
a good summary by Patrick Wormald, 'Bede, the *Bretwaldas* and
the Origins of the *Gens Anglorum*', *Ideal and Reality*, p. 100.*

p. 50, ll. 21–2. I. 15. **Angulus … desertus.** Archaeology supports
this statement. Contact had therefore been kept, 'usque hodie',
between Bede's informants and the English homelands.

p. 50, l. 25. I. 15. **ad Boream Humbri.** Bede's appreciation of geographical factors was born not of observation but of biblical study. Judith McClure instances his account of the Jordan as a political boundary ('Bede's Old Testament Kings', *Ideal and Reality*, p. 83; *Nomina Locorum*, s.v. *Iordanes* (*CCSL* 119; 1962), ed. D. Hurst, p. 282), and this may have struck Bede as a precedent for the Humber.

p. 50, ll. 26–7. I. 15. **Duces fuisse perhibentur ... Hengist et Horsa.** Bede reports Kentish tradition about the Jutish arrival— and treats it as tradition. Even if he had received comparable reports of English arrivals elsewhere, this one would still have struck him as of paramount importance since in Kent was Canterbury and to Canterbury came Augustine. Miller considers that the Kentish claim was dynastic propaganda originally intended to distinguish the two leaders as 'the first Woden-born to arrive'; they were royal, thus emphasizing the seniority of Kent ('Bede's Use of Gildas', p. 254). Whether or not this was so, by the time of Albinus and Bede it would have been a matter of prestige rather than of history. The pagan tradition had been translated into a Christian context. Bede could see Kent as an ancient political unit and, exceptionally, give it a territorial designation—*Cantia*. One authentic Kentish charter of 689 (*CS* 73) speaks of *rex Cantiae* (see E. John, *Orbis Britanniae* (1966), p. 4). Bede does not say that he considered Woden a god; indeed, Harrison questions whether he did ('Woden', *Famulus Christi*, pp. 351 ff.); yet other royal families also claimed descent from Woden, and it is difficult to believe that Bede did not see a god in him, whatever he may have understood by a pagan god (which may well have approximated to what his correspondent Bishop Daniel understood when he wrote to St Boniface). Bede's 'Hengist' may conceivably be the Jute commemorated in the Finnsburh saga, in which case he will have been 'one of the great mercenaries and exiles of the migration period' (Mayr-Harting, *Coming of Christianity*, p. 14). But even if he is not, I see no reason to question his historicity, as does J. E. Turville-Petre, 'Hengist and Horsa', *Saga-Book of the Viking Society*, 14/iv (1956–7) mainly on the ground that the two brothers bore cult names and so would have been equine deities whose cults had been fostered by the heathen priests of Kent. Continental analogies do not really help here except in so far as Germanic mercenaries were customarily employed to defend Roman *civitates*; and this, for Bede, is why under God's providence they were summoned to Kent; a Roman *civitas* with its territory grows under its Jutish kings into Augustine's Canterbury.*

p. 52, l. 4. I. 15. **inito ... foedere cum Pictis.** Thompson, 'Gildas', p. 218, thinks Bede had no authority for this. It was not in Gildas, who said nothing of any Pictish-Saxon alliance that marked the end of the Roman-Saxon *foedus* that was to protect North Britain from the Picts. 'It is not necessary on this point to appeal to Bede's Kentish source, for his Saxon-Pictish alliance seems to be a direct result of Bede's attempt to bring Germanus' Alleluia battle into place in his historical narrative (Miller, 'Bede's Use of Gildas', p. 255). It is not necessary but it is possible. As to the Saxon excuse for revolt (inadequate *annonae*, which, whether meant technically or not, may well have been true, considering their increasing numbers) one could instance parallels on the continent (e.g. Odovacer in Italy). Bede did not invent this, whatever his reasons for inserting it. For some parallels for the treatment of Germanic *foederati* on the continent, see P. Sims-Williams, 'Gildas and the Anglo-Saxons', *Cambridge Medieval Celtic Studies*, 6 (1983), 28–9; they are notably various.

p. 52, ll. 11–14. I. 15. **iustas de sceleribus ... iusto Iudice.** Effectively from Gildas but altered. The Old Testament is invoked, as so often (here, 4 Kings [2 Kings] 25: 9–10). It is the first time that divine sanction is invoked to account for English ravages among the British. It is not simply a reminder of an Old Testament parallel but, for Bede, an historical instance of God's retribution at work in modern times precisely as it had worked in the history of Israel. (See Tugène, 'L'Hist. "eccl."', p. 153.)

p. 52, l. 15. I. 15. **ciuitates ... depopulans.** Though he does not say so, the implication for Bede must have been that the English engaged in the north now turned south, if they were to ravage cities from east to west; and they ravaged 'nullo prohibente', which is more than Gildas reported but a fair inference. The passage may be rhetorical; Bede could have known from the evidence of place-names alone that the British population survived the first onrush; but God's vengeance cannot be painted in muted colours. It was so ordained, 'iusto Iudice'. Gildas plainly had been shocked.

p. 52, ll. 22-4. I. 15. **fame confecti ... seruitium.** This is as good an explanation for the persistence of the British population as we are likely to have.

p. 52, l. 25. I. 15. **alii transmarinas regiones.** Bede accepts Gildas' judgement that it was only in face of the English menace, not the Pictish, that the earliest British migration to the continent (and Ireland?) occurred. There are four explicit references to Britons in Gaul at precisely this time. They are discussed by Thompson, 'Gildas', pp. 221 f.*

p. 52, l. 29. I. 16. **domum reuersus est.** We cannot tell what 'home' the 'exercitus' returned to. It may have been an island or islands near the coast (Thanet?) as Colgrave suggests, but it is more likely to have been further north—say, East Anglia or Northumbria. The word is in Gildas: Bede repeats it and makes no guess. Neither writer can have supposed that the 'exercitus' went back to the continent.*

p. 54, l. 1. I. 16. **duce Ambrosio Aureliano.** Gildas calls Ambrosius a Roman, not a Briton. He appears in 'Nennius' as an opponent, and possibly a relation, of Vortigern (Stevens, 'Gildas Sapiens', p. 367) and may conceivably have been active on the continent as well as in Britain (Campbell, *The Anglo-Saxons*, p. 37). Bede now follows Gildas more closely than he had in *Chron. Maj.* but clearly had difficulty with the text and wished to give the sentence recording the date for the decisive battle between Ambrosius and the English a fresh interpretation (Miller, 'Bede's Use of Gildas', p. 259). The battle took place 44 years after the *Aduentus*: that is, for Bede, between 494 and 501 (see the note on p. 48, l. 30–p. 50, l. 1). Gildas would have placed it *c.* 500.*

p. 54, l. 6. I. 16. **Badonici montis.** The site remains unidentified. E. T. Leeds felt convinced it was near Bath (*Antiq. Journ.* 13

(1933), 233 and n.) and Finberg seems to agree, but it is unlikely
to have been Bath on linguistic grounds. It could have been
further east, as at Badbury Hill above the Vale of White Horse or
Badbury near Swindon. It depends in part on the direction from
which one supposes the English advanced. The best we can say
is that Badon was somewhere in the west. Stenton makes no
guess. Gildas might have had the information to be more explicit
but Bede did not. It was not the site of the battle that interested
him. The interpretation of G. H. Wheeler, 'Gildas De Excidio
Britanniae, Chapter 26', *EHR* 41 (1926), 498, of Gildas' 'ut novi'
is not accepted by Michael Winterbottom, *Gildas* (1978), 28,
who translates, 'That was the year of my birth; as I know, one
month of the forty-fourth year since then has already passed'.
Neither Gildas nor Bede implies that English penetration and
settlement ceased after the great battle.*

p. 54, ll. 10–11. I. 17. **Ante paucos ... per Agricolam.** Bede now
puts aside Gildas and turns first briefly to Prosper and then to
Constantius' Life of St Germanus. The space he devotes to
Germanus is some measure of the importance he attached to his
visits (only one of which was noticed in *Chron. Maj.*). He is
apparently dating Agricola, not Germanus, to AD 429, and the
visit of Germanus and Lupus to the time of the Saxon–Pictish
pact (Miller, 'Bede's Use of Gildas', p. 255). Germanus' second
visit with Severus is now included—both visits seemingly in the
early 450s, presumably because Constantius records a Saxon–
Pictish raid. The dates now preferred are 429 and 435–44 (at
latest). Bede's long excursus on Germanus and British Pelagianism is more than a piece of history he felt he could not omit. He
was acquainted with some Pelagian literature (perhaps deriving
from Ireland) and refutes the Pelagian Julian of Eclana
(Aeclanum) in his commentary on the Song of Songs. Germanus'
way of dealing with a major heresy in Britain was a lesson for all
time: the defence of orthodoxy demands constant vigilance and
determined action. Ian Wood ('The End of Roman Britain',
p. 14) reminds us that Constantius' Life of St Germanus was
written from a Frankish, not an Anglo-Saxon, viewpoint, though
it goes too far to suggest that it is primarily an allegorical
account. It is certainly true that St Germanus' visits 'suggest that
Britain was still subject to the Roman Church if not to the

Emperor and that papal policy was being pursued with confidence on the fringes of the world'.

p. 54, l. 19. I. 17. **Germanus Autisidorensis.** Good modern studies of Germanus and his world are included in *Saint Germain d'Auxerre et son temps* (Auxerre, 1950), which should be read in conjunction with the edition and translation by René Borius, *Constance de Lyon: vie de Saint Germain d'Auxerre* (*SC* 112; 1965). On possible early connections between Auxerre and Ireland see K. Hughes, *The Church in Early Irish Society* (1966), 70. Germanus may have taught St Patrick at Auxerre according to Ludwig Bieler, 'St Patrick and the British Church', *Christianity in Britain*, pp. 125-6. Bishop Victricius of Rouen seems to have visited Britain about 395 (N. K. Chadwick, 'Intellectual Contacts between Britain and Gaul in the Fifth Century', *Studies in Early British History* (1954), 221) and did so at the request of the Gallic Church, which would make him a kind of predecessor of Germanus. It is at least clear that the churches in Britain and Gaul were still sufficiently in touch in the earlier fifth century to collaborate to combat Pelagianism, the latest recorded contact being the council of Arles in 455. There is no reason to suppose that this had anything to do with the arrival of mercenary companies of Franks in southern Britain. Germanus' death can plausibly be dated to 31 July 446 (Ralph W. Mathisen, *Anal. Boll.* 99 (1981), 151-9).*

p. 56, l. 25. I. 17. **conspicui diuitiis.** Myres must be right to see this as evidence that, in Constantius' view at least, the British Pelagians were people of substance and no mere peasants, though it would not follow that 'the movement had attained such political authority in Britain as to be thought a serious menace to the orthodox regime in Gaul' ('Pelagius and the End of Roman Rule in Britain', *JRS* 50 (1960), 34). Bede adds emphasis to the religious motive inspiring the mission and will not have missed the parallel between the missionaries' preaching in the countryside and the pressing needs of his own day. Moreover, the debate with the Pelagians had a very different outcome from that between Augustine and the British clergy.

p. 58, l. 12, l. 18. **tribuniciae potestatis.** Stevens, 'Gildas Sapiens', p. 364, is no doubt right that Constantius' contemporaries would have understood this rank: 'he is a thoroughly appropriate figure in a background of provisionally independent British *civitates*'. More to the point, Britain (as opposed to Ireland) was still Roman from the ecclesiastical point of view; and it was this latter point that Bede would have grasped. There follows the miracle of the healing of a blind girl, with its deliberate reminiscence of New Testament miracles.

p. 58, ll. 28–9. l. 18. **beatum Albanum ... petierunt.** Recent excavations to the south of the present abbey have failed to cast light on the sight of the saint's tomb. Germanus adds relics to the tomb (see Frend, *JEH* 30 (1979), 140). Germanus is not claimed to have discovered Alban's relics but to have added to them (Stevens, 'Gildas Sapiens', p. 373). It is of interest that 'there is a much higher proportion of foreign than native saints in the (Anglo-Saxon) relic lists' (D. W. Rollason, 'Lists of Saints' Resting-Places in Anglo-Saxon England', *ASE* 7 (1978), 81).

p. 60, l. 17. l. 19. **Sed ut Dei potentia.** It is God who performs miracles through the persons of his saints. This traditional Christian teaching would have been reinforced for Bede by his reading of Gregory's *Dialogues*.

p. 64, ll. 5–6. l. 20. **Triumphant pontifices hostibus.** Bede's attention is not focused on the political and military implications of the Alleluia victory as recounted by Constantius; indeed, he even manages to obscure the battle somewhat further by substituting *mediis* for Constantius' *editis*, as Plummer noted. His interest is centred on a document of spirituality: the British, many converted *en masse*, witness, without actively intervening, a victory of God at Easter through the person of Germanus. The bishop himself appears as a fairly new type, the pastor who is a leader and a man of action. The type is also found in the *Vita Martini* and the *Vita Ambrosii*, neither far distant in date of composition. A foreshadowing of St Wilfrid may not have occurred to Bede while writing Book I. The two visiting bishops had conquered through *merita propria* as well as through the intercession of St Alban.

p. 64, ll. 8-12. I. 20. **Composita ... carina restituit.** Bede somewhat alters the passage as found in Constantius, where the victorious bishops prepare to return home 'quippe qui uicissent Pelagianistas et Saxones' (ed. Borius, p. 158). This he omits (assuming it to have been in his text), leaving the Pelagians to the next chapter and perhaps not wishing to emphasize the discomfiture of the Saxons.

p. 64, l. 13. I. 21. **Nec multo interposito tempore.** Bede is dissatisfied with Constantius' *interea* and substitutes a phrase suggestive of a more definite passage of time between the departure of Germanus and the renaissance of Pelagianism. There is no reason to question the return of Germanus on a second visit, on which see Thompson, 'Gildas and the History of Britain', pp. 214-15. For a defence of Bede's identification of Germanus' companion Severus with Severus of Trier (and not Severus of Vence) see E. Ewig, *Trier im Merowingerreich* (1954), 41-2 n. 150. Constantius mentions no see for Severus. It is unclear where Bede got his extra information. It is not borrowed from the Life of Lupus of Troyes, which draws on Bede, but is likely to derive from an account written soon after Severus' promotion to Trier ('tunc ... ordinatus').

p. 64, ll. 23-4. I. 21. **Elafius ... primus.** A local king? Stevens, 'Gildas Sapiens', p. 365, sees him as a 'first man of Britain'. Grosjean detects a correspondence between Elafius and Elesa, father of Cerdic of Wessex, which would throw light on the *regio* (*Anal. Boll.* 75 (1957), 179 and n. 1). This is unconvincing.*

p. 66, l. 15, p. 67, l. 17. I. 21. **ad mediterranea.** Bede understands 'the Midlands', not the 'marchlands'.

p. 66, ll. 18-26. I. 21. **Itaque conpositis ... concidit regnum.** The last paragraph of the chapter draws on Marcellinus (Levison, *BLTW*, p. 135). Bede is clear that his *Aduentus Saxonum* co-incides with the assassination of Valentinian in 455 and the end of the Western Empire (whatever he may have understood by 'concidit'). 'He was certainly not aware of the peculiar and very definite ideological background of the view, which he took over from the sixth-century chronicle he was using at this point

[Marcellinus], that the Western Empire had fallen' (R. A. Markus, *Bede and the Tradition of Ecclesiastical Historiography* (Jarrow Lecture, 1975), 4). It was enough for Bede that the Empire would now play no part in the story of Britain and the Anglo-Saxons.*

p. 66, ll. 27–8. I. 22. **Interea ... bellis.** Bede reverts for the last time to Gildas. Whether or not they were right in seeing a cessation of attacks from abroad for a period after the Alleluia victory, it is worth noting, as Plummer does, that the Anglo-Saxon Chronicle 'assuredly gives no countenance to the view that there was any cessation in the attacks of the Saxons after 493. It records their unresting advance during the sixth century'.

p. 68, ll. 6–7. I. 22. **historicus eorum Gildas.** 'Gildas is cited only once (I, 22), not as a source, but as a repository of further details omitted by Bede, whose frankness about his informants in the dedicatory epistle is thus shown to be selective' (A. A. M. Duncan, 'Bede, Iona, and the Picts', *The Writing of History*, p. 1).*

p. 68, ll. 7–12. I. 22. **ut numquam ... destinauit.** Whatever in general Bede felt about the British, as opposed to the Irish, he seized this opportunity to record what to him was their real crime: they failed to convert the English, which by implication they could have done (see T. Charles-Edwards, 'Bede, the Irish and the Britons', *Celtica*, 15 (1983), 42 ff.). But this was God's doing. Conversion was reserved for *digniores praecones*, the missionaries to be sent from Rome. It seems likely enough that British clergy would be in no hurry to convert their oppressors though it is unclear how Bede knew this—it is more than an inference on his part. On Gildas' evidence, indeed, one may doubt whether the clergy were in a position to convert anyone. It will be noted, however, that up to this point Bede's account of the British has not been wholly black. They had their ups and downs, and for all their moral turpitude, they remained Christian and had responded positively to the threat of heresy. Bede's comment here marks one of the basic transitions in *HE*.*

p. 68, ll. 13–15. I. 23. **Siquidem ... Gregorius.** According to Plummer, 'with this chapter begins the real subject of Bede's

work ... to which the preceding chapters have been introduc-
tory'. Though true in a sense, the preceding chapters are vital to
the story because they place the English in their British context,
both physical and religious. On I. 23-33, Bede's account of the
Gregorian mission and the beginnings of Christianity in Kent,
see P. Meyvaert, *Bede and Gregory the Great* (Jarrow Lecture,
1964), 8 ff. Here, if anywhere, is a mainspring of *HE* in the shape
of material communicated to Bede by Canterbury through
Nothhelm. Without it, *HE* in the form in which we have it
would have been inconceivable. It was this that impelled Bede to
look with a fresh eye at Romano-British sources and to collect
material from other parts of the country. His earlier writings
reveal that Bede, like Aldhelm and the Anonymous of Whitby,
had long held Gregory in veneration. I. 23-33 comprise narrative
sections interspersed with quotations from Gregory's letters, the
latter preponderating. The narrative material seems mostly to
have reached Bede on Nothhelm's first journey north, and the
letters (with the exception of the Gregorian *Responsa*) some time
later, on the second journey. Bede's text as we now have it may
well have been revised in the narrative sections as a result of the
arrival of the letters (though not all of those that he received
need have been inserted). An example of probable change is the
substitution of the Gregorian mission to England in two stages
in place of the one-stage mission that appears in *Chron. Maj.*
(completed 725). Another change may have been the episcopal
consecration of Augustine. Meyvaert concludes that 'Bede's first
draft of the Gregorian mission in the *HE* may have been much
closer to the account in the Whitby Life of Gregory than his final
version, the only one we now possess, might lead us at first sight
to suspect.' On Canterbury sources see also C. W. Jones, *Saints'
Lives*, pp. 46-7.

p. 68, ll. 26-8. I. 23. **Augustinum ... disposuerat.** Bede's account
of Augustine's consecration is an instance of his ability to make
deductions from the material available. He would have had no
problem if he had known Gregory's letter to Eulogius of
Alexandria, dated July 598, which clearly states that Augustine
was consecrated by the bishops of Germania before he reached
Britain. Bede presumably started from the tradition also
reported in the Whitby Life that Gregory himself consecrated

Augustine before despatching him from Rome. The statement here that Augustine was to be consecrated in Gaul if received by the English, and further (I. 27) that he returned to Arles for consecration, must be a later deduction derived from the Gregorian letters; for the letter cited in this chapter shows that Augustine finally left Rome in 596 as an abbot, not a bishop. By 601, however, he clearly was a bishop, and Bede thus assumes that he must have returned from Britain to Gaul for consecration before 601. Arles seemed the natural place to go, in view of the letter in the following chapter, even if he got the name of the bishop wrong.

p. 70, ll. 29–30. I. 24. **quem necesse … festinet.** There is no reason to doubt that the substantial help that Gregory foresaw would be required of the Gallic bishops by his missionaries was in fact forthcoming. It re-established the link between the Church in Britain and the continent, if not with the British.

pp. 72–8. I. 25, 26. It will be noted that no documents are cited in chapters 25 and 26. The account of the missionaries' arrival in Kent may still have been transmitted to Bede in writing, but in either event must be the account current in Canterbury c. 700.

p. 72, ll. 12–13. I. 25. **rex Aedilberct … potentissimus.** The tradition had survived that the king exercised some sort of overlordship as far north as the Humber. This may have been known to Gregory, who would also be influenced by the king's known connections with Francia. Æthelberht's marriage with Bertha, whenever it took place, may well have constituted an alliance that placed the Kentish dynasty in a position of political dependence on the Merovingians. So at least Gregory supposed when he wrote to the Frankish kings Theuderic and Theudebert in July 596, commending Augustine to their care (*Reg.* VI. 49). See my *Early Germanic Kingship*, p. 25, for further treatment of this point. This does not, however, imply that the Kentish Jutes were Franks but only that they were in close contact with them. English settlements along the Frankish coastline are well evidenced and it may be, as Campbell observes, that 'The Channel was not necessarily the most important of the boundaries [Augustine] crossed; so far as religion and culture went the crucial divide was further south' ('The First Century of Christianity in Britain', *Ampleforth Journal*, 76 (1971), 17). It is remarkable that Bertha's Frankish chaplain—I do not see what else to call him—was a bishop. Does this imply that his Merovingian masters intended him to convert Kent and add it to the Frankish Church? If so, it proved too much for Æthelberht. Bede however does not suggest that Liudhard had a mission he proved unable to further.*

p. 72, l. 16. i. 25. **Tanatos insula.** Bede here, as elsewhere, avoids discussion of English paganism. However, Albinus and Nothhelm may not have reported to him that Thanet had been a centre of the worship of Thunor among the Jutes. For an interesting discussion of the significance of *Thunores hlæw* in Thanet see Stenton, *Preparatory*, pp. 293-4. This adds point to Æthelberht's refusal to meet Augustine in any building.

p. 72, ll. 16-18. i. 25. **id est ... sexcentarum.** Bede's hides have been much discussed. Though his qualifier, 'iuxta consuetudinem aestimationis', leaves the proportions of his compound unclear, his expression appears to combine population (in households) with productive area. He does not say how the English measured 'family'. See W. Goffart, 'From Roman Taxation to Mediaeval Seigneurie', *Speculum*, 47 (1972), 166; also Charles-Edwards, 'Kinship, Status and the Origins of the Hide', *Past and Present*, 56 (1972), 4 ff.; and Campbell's review of J. Morris, *Age of Arthur*, in *Studia Hibernica* 15 (1975), 182 ff. No doubt the hide varied from region to region but since we know that Thanet comprised 600 hides, and we know the area of the island, it should be possible to estimate the size of the hide in East Kent in Bede's day.

p. 72, l. 23. i. 25. **interpretes.** These were Frankish interpreters for the missionaries, not for the Jutes. Considering the Frankish presence at Æthelberht's court, it is unnecessary to suppose that the court did not understand Frankish. Early Kentish vernacular was not derived from Frankish. No doubt there were Franks at court who spoke that vernacular. What the passage suggests, if it does not absolutely prove it, is that Bede had knowledge of Gregory's letters in *Reg.* VI. 49 and 57, where reference is made to Frankish interpreters (noted by Charles-Edwards, 'Bede, the Irish and the Britons', *Celtica*, 15 (1983), 44 n. 8).

p. 72, l. 29–p. 74, l. 4. I. 25. **Nam et antea ... licentiam haberet.** The marriage of Æthelberht and Bertha raises problems as to date as well as to its political and religious implications. Bede seems to be unclear. If, as he states, the king died in 616 after a reign of 56 years, and if Gregory of Tours is right that he was not yet king when he married some time after 562, there is a chronological incompatibility, as Plummer saw. Further, Bede thinks that the king's conversion took place after Augustine's arrival in 597, but yet 21 years before the king's death, i.e. in 595. Was he converted before Augustine's arrival? Ian Wood concludes that if Gregory of Tours is right, 'Aethelberht married Bertha some time before 581, that he succeeded to the throne around 590, and that he expressed interest in christianity, even if he was not actually converted, in 595' (*The Merovingian North Sea* (1983), 16). There is much to be said, on the analogy of Clovis himself, for a long period of toleration, conversion, and finally baptism. If the king were already tolerant of Christianity before Augustine's arrival, we must suppose that Canterbury tradition was unwilling to recall what might detract from Gregory's achievement, and also that little had been done towards converting the Kentish people from their paganism before 597. Certainly Gregory had expected Bertha to have been more active in this respect: she had softened up her husband but no more. See A. Lohaus, *Die Merowinger und England* (Münchener Beiträge zur Mediävistik und Renaissance-Forschung; 1974), 8 ff., and Harrison, *Framework*, pp. 121 ff. (who retains the date 560 for the king's accession, partly because Bede states that he received Bertha 'a parentibus', and her father died in 567; but the word means kindred, not parents). The arguments for and against Æthelberht's baptism in the early years of Augustine's mission are summarized by Mayr-Harting, *Coming of Christianity*, pp. 266–9.

p. 74, ll. 5–6. I. 25. **Post dies ... colloquium.** The hopes of Augustine and Gregory for the king are best discussed under I. 30 and II. 3–6, where it is clear that Bede wishes to emphasize the personal role of the Christian overlord.

p. 74, l. 11. I. 25. **imaginem Domini ... depictam.** Paul
Meyvaert, 'Bede and the Church Paintings at Wearmouth-
Jarrow', *ASE* 8 (1979), 68, examines this passage, where Bede
alludes to a panel painted with an image of Christ brought from
Rome to England, and draws attention to his justification for the
use of images in his commentary on the Temple of Solomon
written shortly before 731 (*De Templo*, ii, *CCSL* 119 A, pp. 212–
13). Meyvaert associates this with Nothhelm's visit: 'it is very
possible that Nothhelm also brought news from Rome of the
iconoclastic movement which was just beginning to develop in
the east'. Bede would have had in mind the panel paintings at
Wearmouth-Jarrow to which he refers in *Historia Abbatum*
(Plummer, i. 369, 373). We must thus place Bede among the
western defenders of images as venerable objects of instruction,
not of worship.

p. 74, ll. 15–18. I. 25. **Pulchra sunt ... seruaui.** Despite Gregory's
view (I. 31) that English souls are drawn by 'exteriora miracula',
the Canterbury tradition was that Augustine had performed no
miracles at this point but had aimed at interior conviction—what
struck Æthelberht as 'pulchra ... uerba et promissa'. See
Leonardi, 'Il venerabile Beda', *Spoleto*, 20 (1973), 638.

p. 74, ll. 24–7. I. 25. **Dedit ergo ... non abstulit.** On the early
settlement of the missionaries in Canterbury see Margaret
Deanesly, 'The Familia at Christchurch, Canterbury, 597–832',
Essays in Medieval History presented to Thomas Frederick Tout (1925),
7, and J. Armitage Robinson, 'The Early Community at Christ
Church, Canterbury', *JTS* 27 (1926), 231–3 (who sees Christ
Church as staffed by secular clergy while the monastery outside
the walls was reserved for the Roman monks). As in II. 3 Bede
means 'capital' by *metropolis*, the centre of authority if not of
population; in other words, the king's principal *palatium*.
Campbell, *The Anglo-Saxons*, p. 39, compares sixth-century
Canterbury and York, for both of which archaeological evidence
is sparse. London was equally a *metropolis* for Bede, if arguably
not a capital, though Gregory originally envisaged an archbishopric there. In fact, Canterbury proved no very convenient
site for an archbishop. We have no evidence that any Church
council was ever summoned to Canterbury in this period. On

Augustine's settlement within Canterbury and Æthelberht's donations to Christ Church, see Brooks, *Early History*, ch. 2, who also assesses the archaeological evidence for settlement in Canterbury over this period.

p. 74, l. 30–p. 76, l. 2. i. 25. **Deprecamur te . . . Alleluia.** This 'can hardly be regarded as historical although editors and commentators have treated it as such' (D. A. Bullough, 'Alcuin and the Kingdom of Heaven', in *Carolingian Essays*, ed. Uta-Renate Blumenthal, p. 6 n. 14). This antiphon is from the rogation litany and would only have reached Rome in the time of Leo III (795–816).

p. 76, ll. 3–4. i. 26. **coeperunt . . . imitari.** That Augustine's followers lived under a rule is certain. Both he and Gregory were well acquainted with St Benedict's Rule and were influenced by it, but it does not follow that the Canterbury monks were exclusively devoted to it or to any other identifiable rule. Had they been known as followers of St Benedict, Bede would surely have recorded it. What he does record is the attractiveness of their simple communal life and the limited effect ('crediderunt nonnulli') of their teaching on the people of Kent. The pagan reaction under Æthelberht's successor explains Bede's 'nonnulli'.*

p. 76, ll. 12–15. i. 26. **Erat autem . . . incolerent.** Bede surely means what he says: the dedication to St Martin of the church used by Bertha and the missionaries was an original dedication of 'Roman' times, by which may be understood the first half of the fifth century. I agree with Myres (*EHR* 70 (1955), 92–3) that 'contacts with Sulpicius and his circle make it virtually certain that the Christian communities of southern Britain visited by Victricius [c.395] were in possession of all the materials required for developing a cult of St Martin by the early years of the fifth century'. This implies that, following Frankish usage, relics of the saint would have been placed in the church (on which see Lohaus, *Die Merowinger und England*, pp. 13, 112). However, though the Franks were the likeliest importers of the Martinian cult, they were not the only possibility. The present church, incorporating what may be a Roman Christian building, is perhaps partly a rebuilding of Bertha's time. I am not persuaded by P. A. Wilson, 'The Cult of St Martin in the British Isles', *Innes Review*, 19 (1968), 129-43, that Liudhard was the likely founder of St Martin's Canterbury. After the final stages of Æthelberht's conversion, i.e. his baptism, the missionaries were allowed to build and restore churches elsewhere in Canterbury and outside. Christ Church itself, according to Bede (I. 33), had been built by Roman Christians and was 'recovered' ('recuperauit') by Augustine and Æthelberht. Traces of an aisled building, apparently Romano-British, were found in 1973 immediately to the south of the cathedral. Bede's view, as transmitted to him from Canterbury, is thus not implausible (Brooks, *Early History*, p. 50). It looks therefore as if Canterbury had been a centre of Christian cultus, possibly as early as the fourth century. If there is one matter on which Bede would have implicitly relied on his Canterbury informants it must have been the early history of the Canterbury churches. They may have made mistakes. If they did, the mistakes should not be attributed to Bede. Thomas, *Christianity in Roman Britain*, pp. 170-4, favours the view that St Pancras' rather than St Martin's was the Roman church used by Bertha and Liudhard. If Canterbury traditions had become confused by Bede's time the responsibility cannot be laid at his door.

p.76, l. 26. I. 26. **ut nullum ... ad Christianismum.** Plummer rightly points out that this may not represent the facts (cf. p. 150, ll. 27-9. II. 5). Certainly it was unusual that Germanic kings should exercise no compulsion to conversion. Clovis showed no such weakness, once he himself was convinced; neither did Bishop Avitus of Vienne, who informed the Burgundian king, Gundobad, that, just as he does not ask his people's opinion when summoning them to the host, so equally they should accept baptism when he had decided to do so. Even allowing for the strength of Kentish paganism, the passage sounds more in conformity with Bede's own thinking (cf. commentary on Ezra 7: 13, cited by Plummer: ed. Hurst (*CCSL* 119 A; 1969), p. 312, ll. 996-1001) than with what may actually have occurred.

p. 78. I. 27. The Gregorian letters that constitute chapters 27-32 form an exceptional block of material that looks somewhat out of proportion in a work that observes proportion. Is it included out of veneration for Pope Gregory? Or is it to be seen as practical guidance for the churches of Bede's readers? Or does it simply constitute the great demonstration of Rome's loving care for the English? In the last case it would be both exemplary and historical, and thus worthy of full quotation. The letters in chapters 28–32 will have reached Bede in the second batch of correspondence supplied by Canterbury through Nothhelm and were then inserted in *HE* in their present position. An exception is chapter 27. Basic recent studies of the material are: Markus, 'The Chronology of the Gregorian Mission', *JEH* 14 (1963), 16–30; 'Gregory the Great and a Papal Missionary Strategy', *Studies in Church History*, 6 (1970), 29–38; and P. Meyvaert, 'The Registrum of Gregory the Great and Bede', *RB* 80 (1970), 162–6, and 'Bede's Text of the *Libellus Responsionum* of Gregory the Great to Augustine of Canterbury', *England before the Conquest*, pp. 15–33, which disposes of the arguments of Dom Suso Brechter, *Die Quellen zur Angelsachsenmission Gregors des Grossen* (1941), 11–111, that the whole *Libellus* (here chapter 27) was forged by Nothhelm. Bede has already used a text of the *Libellus* in 721, in his prose Life of St Cuthbert, and perhaps in his sermons. After long study of the history of the transmission of the *Libellus*, Meyvaert concludes that Bede's version probably derived from a penitential collection associated with Theodore, having no necessary connection with Nothhelm though it may have done with Canterbury. It was of inferior quality (Bede knew another version but decided not to correct his text from it) but it 'must have been a document that was part of his plan for the *History* from the start'. But when was 'the start'? We can hardly place it before Bede's earliest contact with Albinus. At all events, he quoted the *Libellus* in full, unlike the Gregorian letters that follow in *HE* as completed in 731; and he did not tamper with his text, corrupt though he knew it to be. See also D. A. Bullough, 'Roman Books and Carolingian *Renovatio*', *Studies in Church History*, 14 (1977), 25, on the form of the *Responsio* version in *HE*.

p. 78, l. 7. i. 27. **Interea ... uenit Arelas.** Even if Augustine did not return to Arles or elsewhere in Gaul for consecration (see note on p. 68, ll. 26–8. i. 23), there is no reason why he should not have visited Gaulish bishops for consultation. Gregory never refers to Augustine as archbishop of Canterbury, but despite Gregory's original intentions for London there can be no serious doubt that Augustine had his see in, and operated from, Canterbury, not London. For Bede he was *episcopus Cantuariorum ecclesiae*. Brechter argued ('Zur Bekehrungsgeschichte der Anglelsachsen', *Spoleto*, 14 (1967), 205-6, and cf. pp. 501-3) that Augustine's see was at London, that his successor as metropolitan was Mellitus, not Laurence, and that Canterbury only became the metropolitan see after London and Rochester were abandoned during the pagan reaction. In short, Bede and his informants practised a deception. Brooks, *Early History*, pp. 11-14, exposes the weaknesses of this argument.

p. 78, ll. 10-11. I. 27. **Laurentium ... monachum.** 'As far as surviving sources are concerned only two can be cited in which the names of Peter and Laurence occur together; they are Gregory's letter to Queen Bertha, King Æthelberht's consort, and the *Libellus* preface ... At present I would be inclined to consider it possible that Bede knew and used both the letter and the *Libellus* preface' (Meyvaert, *England before the Conquest*, pp. 30-1).

p. 80, ll. 28-30. I. 27. **Cum una ... Galliarum tenetur?** As Meyvaert points out, 'Diversity within Unity', *Heythrop Journal*, 4 (1963), 143, Augustine would have found the Gallican liturgy in use by Liudhard in Bertha's circle at Canterbury and may not have thought it prudent to change established custom. Hence his question. We cannot tell whether these opening words are 'a quotation from Augustine's letter or a summary by Gregory himself to indicate the matter with which he intends to deal'; nor is the answer provided by reading *aliter* for *altera*, as Meyvaert shows, since Bede was very familiar with Gregory's preferred usages. Meyvaert concludes: 'St Gregory the Great emerges from his writings as one who, in a particular way, cherished the theme of "diversity within unity" in the Church. Diversity he believed to be present on all levels not excluding that of liturgical ritual; what made this diversity into a unity was the bond of one Faith and one Charity'. Never does he criticize any church for not following the liturgical usages of Rome. It is worth noting that the pope showed a similar liberality in matters of ritual in replying to a Spanish question about baptism: 'In una fide nil officit sanctae ecclesiae consuetudo diversa' (*Reg.* I. 41).

p. 82, ll. 5–6. I. 27. **in fasciculum collecta.** Meyvaert, 'Diversity in Unity', p. 145, shows how the origin *vasculo* became corrupted to *fasciculum*, and *mensam* to *mentes.* 'The whole tenor of the *responsum* is that a certain diversity of things is good . . . this idea often evoked the image of food with Gregory the Great.' Bede's version is certainly a less telling one (*England before the Conquest,* p. 29 n. 3).

p. 82, l. 8. I. 27. **de ecclesia furtu.** Gregory characteristically prefaces his answer with a short homily on the justification for punishment generally. Plummer says what is necessary about divergences in punishment for church theft as between this answer, Æthelberht's laws, and Theodore's Penitential, the last two requiring more than simple restitution. Gregory was plainly aware that more was sometimes asked for. If the laws accurately reflect the practice at Æthelberht's court, the reason for his twelvefold restitution may have been 'that at the beginning stringent measures of protection were thought to be needed for the newcomers, surrounded as they were by pagans' attracted by the valuable objects used in Christian worship (Mayr-Harting, *Coming of Christianity,* p. 270).

p. 82, l. 26. I. 27. **duo germani fratres.** A celebrated instance of the two royal brothers marrying two sisters, well reported by Gregory of Tours, was the marriage of the Frankish king Chilperic I to the Visigoth princess Galswintha and of his brother Sigibert I to her sister Brunechildis (*Hist.* IV. 27, 28)— with disastrous results, as recorded in verse by Venantius Fortunatus (esp. in his poem *De Gelesuintha* (*MGH AA* 4) i. 136 ff.).

p. 84, ll. 1–3. I. 27. **ad quotam generationem ... copulari coniugio.** This *responsum* is generally accepted as an interpolation that does not appear in the oldest MSS of the *Libellus.* A version was sent from Rome to Canterbury, yet neither place was responsible for the diffusion of the text: 'it is northern Italy

(with its ancient Lombard kingdom) which appears to occupy a
key role in the transmission. Since the Lombards were a
Germanic people there would be no problem to explain how the
responsum on marriage came to be interpolated there' (Meyvaert,
England before the Conquest, pp. 29-30 n. 4). But interpolated by
whom? The issue of prohibited degrees of marriage is naturally
as relevant to the English as to the Lombards. It was largely
upon the inauthenticity of this *responsum* that Brechter formed
his view that the whole *Libellus* was a forgery (see *Die Quellen*,
pp. 74-81). For a more general discussion of the Church and the
marriage bond, see my *Frankish Church*, pp. 403-11.

p. 86, ll. 6-8. I. 27. **Si longinquitas ... episcopus ordinari.** The
first archbishop of Canterbury whose consecration meets the
terms set out by Gregory was Tatwine, consecrated in 731 by
Daniel of Winchester and three other bishops. However, Dom
Brechter was on weak ground in arguing that Gregory's
recommendation could only relate to the circumstances of 731,
and thus be no recommendation of his. Gregory's parallel with
'coniugia in mundo' is interesting in view of the uncertainties of
the Church of his day about the nature of marriage and the
appropriate rites. He seems to be contrasting a purely secular
event with a spiritual consecration in which 'homo Deo
coniungitur'.

p. 86, ll. 28-9. I. 27. **Qualiter debemus ... episcopis agere?**
Assuming that 'all the bishops of Britain' are understood by
Gregory as meaning or including the Celtic bishops, and as
subject henceforth to Augustine's jurisdiction, 'this was principally aimed at assuring an harmonious functioning of the
Church, and in no way implied a desire to supplant Celtic usages
by Roman practice. A Gregory the Great must never be
confused with a Gregory VII, and on the issues at stake Bede's
mind was probably closer to the latter than to the former'
(Meyvaert, *Bede and Gregory the Great* (Jarrow Lecture, 1964), 18).
As to the bishops of Gaul, Augustine is warned off interference
in any jurisdictional sense but is clearly expected to find himself
in Gaul from time to time. He can only deal with erring Gallic
bishops by persuasion, thus correcting them 'bona ... opera
eorum imitationi monstrando'. This is among the many

occasions when Bede, like Gregory himself, urges the value of exemplary imitation. (See Kendall, *Saints, Scholars*, i. 169 ff.)

p. 88, ll. 29–32. i. 27. **Hoc non ambigo ... firmari.** This long and charitable answer to a series of questions involving natural sexual functions suggests that Augustine, as a Roman monk, had had no experience of pastoral practice. It also appears that Gregory had discussed such problems with Augustine, who now needs written confirmation of what he had been told. To Bede and his readers Gregory's disquisition will have been an invaluable practical guide, though in some respects English practice will have developed over the intervening period of nearly a century and half.

p. 98, l. 15. i. 27. **Si post inlusionem ...** Meyvaert discusses textual variants in the last *responsum* in *England before the Conquest*, pp. 20, 26 n. 3, 29.

p. 102, ll. 14–16. i. 28. **Epistulam ... dederat.** Bede attempts to clear up the difficulty created by i. 24 and 27 in the references to Etherius, though in fact Vergilius was not Etherius' successor. It is interesting that Bede's text of the letter is not that sent by Gregory to Arles but the one sent to Tours and Marseilles. There is no reason to think that Bede knew this. Bede 'knew the name Etherius from Gregory's letter (*Ep.* vi. 50 = *H.E.* i. 24) commending Augustine to this bishop. As the name of the bishop's see does not occur in the protocol of the letter, he had no easily accessible documentary source to identify it; and, for some reason unknown to us, he thought it was Arles.' He could have got at the facts from Gregory of Tours but 'one can only assume that in the absence of the wonderful indexes of the *MGH* edition Bede could not easily track down names and places which he could not quite remember' (Markus, 'The Chronology of the Gregorian Mission to England', *JEH* 14 (1963), 28 n. 2).

p. 104, ll. 1–12. i. 29. **Praeterea ... iste est textus.** This is one of the two letters of Gregory to Augustine brought back from Rome in 601 by the reinforcement of the mission headed by Mellitus. Two further letters addressed to Æthelberht and

Bertha help us to glimpse the pope's missionary policy. Yet other letters were addressed to those concerned with the mission or on its route north. In I. 29 the pope 'outlined his well-known plan for the division of the island, on the lines of the Roman administrative geography but without any relation to the political actualities of the sixth or seventh centuries, into ecclesiastical provinces and dioceses' (Markus, 'Gregory the Great and a Papal Missionary Strategy', p. 33). The significance of the grant of the *pallium* is best explained by W. Levison, *England and the Continent*, p. 21: 'A new diocese can be constituted without papal intervention (though the Pope may be asked to confirm the new see), but not an ecclesiastical province, because the metropolitan must receive the pallium from Rome.'

p. 104, ll. 4-5. I. 29. **Mellitus . . . Rufinianus.** Bede had originally thought that there was only one mission to Britain, as recorded by him, without explicit date, in *Chron. Maj.* (relying on *Lib. Pont.*). This lists Mellitus, Augustine, and John by name. The Whitby Life of Gregory does the same. The arrival of the Gregorian letters showed him his mistake: there were two missions, that of Augustine in 596-7, and that of Mellitus in 601. Bede also connects the names of Laurence and Peter with the first group, however he may have learnt the names. It is not clear why he now includes Paulinus, Justus, and Rufinianus in the party of 601. They are not mentioned in surviving Gregorian letters (Meyvaert, *Bede and Gregory the Great*, p.11).

p. 104, l. 9. I. 29. **codices plurimos.** We do not know what these books were. They are likely to have included sacramentaries among other liturgical texts, on which see the summary of Mayr-Harting, *Coming of Christianity*, appendix II ('Roman Sacramentaries in England, 597-747'). They may also have included charters of land grants, though with less certainty (see Pierre Chaplais, 'Who introduced Charters into England? The Case for Augustine', *Journ. Soc. Archivists*, 3 (1965-9). Patrick Wormald, in the course of an excellent survey of early English charters, concludes that 'as it emerges into the historian's view, the Anglo-Saxon charter was neither Italian nor Frankish nor Celtic but simply *sui generis*', *Bede and the Conversion of England: The Charter Evidence* (Jarrow Lecture, 1984), 14). One book long associated with Augustine is now Corpus Christi College Cambridge 286, a sixth-century MS of the Gospels, formerly owned by St Augustine's Canterbury. 'There is nothing improbable in this tradition' (Francis Wormald, *Collected Writings* (1984), i. 13–35. See also E. A. Lowe, *CLA* ii, 2nd edn. (1973), No. 126, and suppl. bibliog., p. 56). I see no reason why they should not also have included some secular (e.g. grammatical) books for elementary instruction. Whatever they were, Bede associates them with the second, not the first, group of missionaries. However, Augustine must have brought some books with him, and as Plummer noted, King Alfred thought that a copy of Gregory's *Pastoral Care* was among them.

p. 104, l. 24. I. 29. **Ad Eburacam uero ciuitatem.** Gregory may not have known much about Anglo-Saxon Britain but he plainly saw that his organization there must be based on what had been important sites in Roman times. London was one such and York another. Continental metropolitan sees were equally sited in Roman *civitates*. It is possible that he thought he was reviving antique sees in Britain. See Rosemary Cramp, *Anglian and Viking York* (Borthwick Papers, 33; 1967), p. 4. He was aware that there were still British bishops since he goes on to place them under Augustine's jurisdiction; but it is not only they but 'all the bishops of Britain' who are covered by 'quatinus ... pertingant' (p. 106, ll. 9–12).

p. 106, ll. 25–8. I. 30. **fana idolorum ... ponantur.** Markus, 'Gregory the Great and a Papal Missionary Strategy', pp. 29–38, places this famous letter in the general context of the pope's coercive strategy for missions. It marks a change of policy since he had instructed King Æthelberht only a month earlier to destroy pagan shrines and, in the opinion of Markus, is due to his dawning realization that the king was making slow headway against paganism and needed to be accommodated as far as possible. Markus also suggests how Bede came to receive and preserve the letters to Æthelberht and Mellitus in the wrong order: I. 32 (to Æthelberht) should precede I. 30 (to Mellitus). Clare Stancliffe, 'Kings Who Opted Out', *Ideal and Reality*, p. 160, shows how Augustine must have depended on Æthelberht.

However, the fact remains that Gregory says that he had been thinking over the matter for a long time. Was it that he at last appreciated that Æthelberht was more than king of Kent and would exercise progressively less coercive authority over religious practices the greater the distance from Canterbury? As for sacrifices, another case of compromise is recorded by Gregory of Tours (*MGH SRM* 1/ii, *Liber in Gloria Confessorum*, ch. 2, pp. 749-50), involving a bishop. There is some evidence for the conversion of pagan temples into churches, e.g. at Yeavering (see Martin Biddle, 'Archaeology and the Beginnings of English Society', *England before the Conquest*, p. 405).

p. 108, l. 27. I. 31. **magna miracula.** Bede cites only that portion of Gregory's letter to Augustine that expresses his own view of the role of the miraculous, to which he adheres throughout *HE*. Miracles have nothing to do with national glory but only with his concept of a Chosen People, chosen not for their merits but for their place in God's plan of salvation. (See Tugène, 'L'Hist. "eccl."', pp. 150ff.) Still less do they provide Augustine with cause for pride. 'Bede included enough of the letter to show that his attitude was like Gregory's in that they did not deny the possibility of miracles but would stoutly contend that they are extrinsic to Christianity and valueless in relation to works. But he shortened the letter in such a way as to remove that emphasis in his *History*, where the dominant view is hagiological' (C. W. Jones, *Saints' Lives*, p. 89). 'Perhaps it was because of the pope's admonition that Augustine should not glory in them that no record of any of his miracles survived—except that one which he was "compelled by absolute necessity" to work in order to prove his case against the British' (Mayr-Harting, *Coming of Christianity*, p. 75). Gregory (and Bede) are merely cautious about miracles as evidence of sanctity. In contrast, the strict followers of Cassian had denied altogether that a holy man could be recognized by his miracles (see Owen Chadwick, *John Cassian*, 2nd edn. (1968), 51, 100).

p. 112, ll. 1-9. I. 32. **gloriose fili ... in gentibus.** The point may be that the king had been insufficiently active in spreading the faith in Kent and beyond; nor had his queen encouraged him. But what the pope provides is almost a standard exhortation to convert, suppress, overthrow, terrify, and correct that has no exclusive reference to English needs. Therefore the overthrowing of pagan buildings and shrines, soon to be countermanded, is part of a more general policy. It is clear that the king is already a baptized Christian in 601. Bede would have taken the royal duty of *correctio* literally (cf. I. 10, III. 30, v. 14). Peoples were not the less *subjecti* because they were Christian. Hans-Joachim Diesner, 'Fragen der Macht- und Herrschaftsstruktur bei Beda', *Akad. d. Wissen., Mainz*, 8 (1980), 26, discusses the passage.

p. 112, l. 10. I. 32. **Sic etenim Constantinus.** If nothing else did, this letter alone should show that Æthelberht, like Constantine, was already a Christian in the eyes of Gregory and Bede. (See Markus, 'The Chronology', pp. 21–2.) Constantine, the prototype, will be the king's model for a royal convert who prospered. No subsequent emperor attracted Bede as a model for Christian rule. (See my *Bede's Europe* (Jarrow Lecture, 1962), reprinted in *Early Medieval History* (1975), 70.) The cult of Constantine is admirably presented by E. Ewig, 'Das Bild Constantins des Grossen in den ersten Jahrhunderten des abendländischen Mittelalters', *Hist. Jahrb.* 75 (1956), 1–46, reprinted in *Spätantikes und fränkisches Gallien* (1976), 72–113. Constantine's association with the papacy will have appeared vital to Bede, though Bede himself died before the culmination of the cult and its Roman connection in the famous Roman forgery based on older material known as the Donation of Constantine (ed. H. Fuhrmann, *MGH Fontes Iuris Gemanici Antiqui in usum Schol.* 10; 1968). As Plummer notes, Gregory wrote to Queen Bertha as well as to the king, but he does not reproduce the letter and presumably did not know it at the time.

p. 112, l. 23. I. 32. **libenter audite.** Æthelberht is to listen to his bishop as his mediator with God. The same advice is frequently urged on Germanic kings. Failure to listen leads to disaster in this world and non-acceptance in the next. On the other hand, obedience to bishops brings worldly prosperity as well as acceptance in the kingdom of heaven. Bede never tires of pointing the moral.

p. 112, ll. 33–4. I. 32. **praesentis mundi iam terminus iuxta est.**
See the interesting discussion on the end of the world and its
presages by Gerald Bonner, *Saint Bede in the Tradition of Western
Apocalyptic Commentary* (Jarrow Lecture, 1966), 11 ff.

p. 114, ll. 16–18. I. 32. **Data die ... indictione** IIII. Harrison,
Framework, pp. 39–40, examines this method of dating to
demonstrate how the date cannot be in doubt: 22 June 601.

p. 114, l. 24. I. 33. **Fecit autem et monasterium.** To the Taylors'
long discussion of the architecture of St Augustine's Canterbury
(cited in Colgrave and Mynors) should be added that of K. H.
Krüger, *Königsgrabkirchen* (1971), 264–89. The purpose of the
burial of kings and their bishops in close proximity was grasped
by R. H. Hodgkin, *A History of the Anglo-Saxons*, 3rd edn.(1952),
273: 'We see, moreover, that even at Canterbury Augustine's
efforts were specially directed to the work of building a
mausoleum where the souls of the king and queen, with their
bodies in proximity to those of the holy men, might be defended
alike from heathen spirits and from Christian demons.' Together
they will be protected from evil spirits and together they will rise
to eternal life. Bede provides several examples of the dedication
of churches to SS Peter and Paul, thus emphasizing the English
link with Rome (*HE* I. 33; II. 14; III. 6, 24, 25; IV. 3; V. 19, 21).

p. 116, l. 7. I. 34. **His temporibus.** It is possible, as C. W. Jones
argues (*Saints' Lives*, pp. 34–5), that this chapter is a later
insertion. Further, 'I suggest that only the first two words of this
first part (*his temporibus*) are Bede's and that otherwise it is a
transcribed notation of an English ecclesiastical writer who was
writing hagiology, looking back some distance at the event.' He
then suggests that we have Bede again with the mention of
Degsastan—'celeberrimo' to him because not far from Jarrow;
'whereas it is barely mentioned in the Irish annals and not
mentioned at all in the Welsh'. Degsa's stone, moreover, will be a
local monument. I do not see the need for most of this and prefer
Plummer's explanation: 'Bede no doubt wished to prepare the
way for the connection of Ethelfrid with the fulfilment of
Augustine's prophecy in ii. 2'; in which case there is no need to
regard the chapter as a later insertion. An annal could have

provided Bede with the basic material and there is no call to postulate, with Colgrave, 'some lost heroic poem celebrating the deeds of Æthelfrith'. That Saul should have suggested himself to Bede (Gen. 49: 27) is in no way surprising (see my *Early Germanic Kingship*, pp. 76–8). Tugène, 'L'Hist. "eccl."', pp. 162 ff., explains that the allusion to Benjamin rests upon an accepted interpretation of Genesis that is applied to St Paul: the wolf that devours in the morning by persecuting Christians distributes his prey in the evening by preaching the Gospel to the Gentiles. Æthelfrith's people were to behave in the same way. The whole chapter thus prepares the missionary role of the English and is no mere exaltation of military power. Unhappily Bede's own commentary on Genesis is incomplete and does not reach as far as 49: 27. Nora Chadwick, *Celt and Saxon*, p. 178, sees the chapter as 'part of his cautionary story; and we may perhaps attribute to this general purpose of emphasizing the retribution on the recalcitrant Britons his detailed portrait of their enemy Æthelfrith'. This is true in a sense as shown by Judith McClure, *Ideal and Reality*, p. 87. For a less generous estimate than Stenton's of Æthelfrith's conquests, see Alfred P. Smyth, *Warlords and Holy Men* (1984), 23–4 and 30, and for early Anglian graves in Bernicia (few but rich) Leslie Alcock, 'Quantity or Quality', *Angles, Saxons and Jutes* (1981), 168–86. Duncan, *The Writing of History*, pp. 16 ff., sees some confusion in Bede's sources between the battles of Degsastan and Chester.

Book II

p. 122, ll. 1–4. II. 1. **His temporibus ... papa Gregorius ... defunctus est.** This famous sketch of the life of Gregory the Great is more than a summary of facts culled from well-known sources. It embodies Bede's view of the ideal episcopal career, such as was seldom seen in his own day in England. Gregory was at once the contemplative, the ascetic *doctor* capable of expounding the mysteries of the Bible, and the man of action, the *pastor*. What mattered was the union of the active and contemplative lives. Bede dismisses Gregory's claim that pastoral labours interfered with his contemplative life. (See

C. Leonardi, 'Il venerabile Beda e la cultura del secolo VIII', *Spoleto*, 20 (1973), 633.) Apostle as he was to the English nation, his missionary labours were conducted through others: as great, and more direct, was the example of his life and the consequent effect of his life upon the entire Church. Thus Bede presents Gregory as the episcopal ideal of which Augustine, Aidan, and Cuthbert were, in their different ways, to be reflections. See Alan Thacker, 'Bede's Ideal of Reform', *Ideal and Reality*, pp. 143 ff. Paul Meyvaert discusses the picture of Gregory (at one point designated 'Augustine') on fo. 26ᵛ of the Leningrad MS, in 'Bede and Gregory the Great', pp. 3-4, and also points out that Bede here departs from his common practice of entering an account of a saint in the year of his death. He prefers a strict chronological sequence and places his biography of Gregory at the beginning of a book in which he later refers to events which antedate Gregory's death. This can only be to ensure that Gregory has special prominence. Contrast the account of the beginning of Gregory's reign in Gregory of Tours, *Hist.* x. 1 (the historian died in 594, i.e. only four years after the pope's accession, but laid down his pen *c.* 591).

p. 122, ll. 10-11. II. I. **nostram gentem ... fecit ecclesiam.** This making of the Church of England is seen by Bede as something else: the making of the English people. It was a radical transformation of scattered groups into an ecclesiastical people. He makes the same point in his commentary on the Song of Songs: the Church is composed of 'omnibus iustorum populis' (*CCSL* 119 B (1983), 309-10), and so too does Isidore in *Sententiae*, 3. 49. 3: 'membra quippe Christi fideles sunt populi'. Looked at another way, Bede is saying that Rome operates not only through local churches but directly over the whole community of Christian peoples. (See Tugène, 'L'Hist. "eccl."', pp. 136 ff.) It is Christianity that gives a people a national identity, itself swallowed up in the greater identity of the entire *populus Christianus*.

p. 126, l. 1-p. 128, l. 22. II. I. **Nam hortati ... praesumtione respirabat.** Much has been written on Gregory's literary work and its bearing on his pontificate. One recent and thoughtful guide is Claude Dagens, *Saint Grégoire le Grand: culture et expéri-ence chrétiennes* (1977).

p. 128, ll. 24-6. II. I. **Nam alii quidam pontifices ... uacabat.** Bede's contrast between the popes who built and adorned churches and Gregory, who did not, is scarcely borne out by Gregory's biography in the *Lib. Pont.*, which records his gifts to St Peter's. This Bede certainly knew, as he must also have known that the nature of the *Lib. Pont.* precluded its compilers from recording much more than similar benefactions by Gregory's predecessors. In short, Bede omits what does not contribute to the picture of the pope he wished to present to his readers; and that picture is a piece of hagiography, and not biography in our sense.

p. 130, l. 14. II. I. **Ecce lingua Brittaniae.** On Gregory's imagery of the mouth of Britain and the proud ocean, derived from Late Antique conventions of personification of territory or nation, and so transmitted to Bede, see George Henderson, *Bede and the Visual Arts* (Jarrow Lecture, 1980), 10. The lesson to be drawn was that the fear of God can bring peace to a people where the sword fails. Britain is pacified by her missionaries, though the effect of their words was fear. Bede goes on to allow, with Gregory, that Augustine brought about conversion not only by words but also by miracles (on which see C. W. Jones, *Saint's Lives*, p. 89).

p. 130, ll. 32-3. II. I. **in ipsa missarum ... superadiecit.** Gregory's addition to the canon was not borrowed, as Colgrave thought, from the *Lib. Pont.* 'since the *Liber* does not quote the added petitions in full' (D. A. Bullough, 'Roman Books and Carolingian *Renovatio*', *Studies in Church History*, 14 (1977), 27). Meyvaert notes (*Bede and Gregory the Great*, p. 7) that Bede 'does not connect the pope's name in any way directly with church music or plain-song', despite Gregory's subsequent reputation in this field.

p. 132, ll. 3-4. II. I. **in tumba ipsius epitaphium.** As Levison saw (*BLTW*, p. 140), this forms part of a class of texts that 'manifest Bede's aim to tell a documented story'. Eusebius had shown how. Bede may of course have cited it less because it was a 'document' than because it was a summary in elegiac couplets of a saint's merits. Other sepulchral inscriptions that Bede records are Wilfrid (v. 19), Augustine (II. 3), Theodore (v. 8), and Cædwalla of Wessex (v. 7). As evidence that Bede may have had access to a corpus of Roman inscriptions, Levison notes that 'the *sylloge* of Cambridge ... supplemented from a Canterbury MS ... ends just in Bede's time with the epitaph of Pope John VII (707).'*

p. 132, l. 21. II. 1. **Nec silentio praetereunda opinio.** Bede finishes the chapter with a story that had no immediate connection with the conversion. He inserts it 'because the story was widely believed by the faithful in Northumbria, not necessarily because he himself believed the event to have happened' (P. Hunter Blair, 'The Historical Writings of Bede', *Spoleto*, 17 (1970), 202). Both the beginning and end of the story, as Bede tells it, suggest that he wanted his readers to understand that it was traditional and generally accepted. He thus places it in a category that would be understood. As to its historicity, he is still in the realm of hagiography, and it may be irrelevant whether or not he considered it to be 'fact'; but at least he is quite sure that the story ought to be related.

p. 132, l. 27. II. 1. **uidisse ... pueros.** Dom Brechter argues with some force (*Die Quellen*, pp. 120–38) that Gregory's interest in the possible conversion of the English had no connection with this allegedly late Northumbrian legend known to Bede and the Anonymous of Whitby but resulted from his contact with English slaves purchased by his agent in Gaul (*Reg.* VI. 10). But why should he have instructed his agent to make such a purchase if he were not already thinking of a mission? Markus shows that there is at least as good reason for trusting Bede's account as for trusting in the argument for a late Northumbrian legend that had nothing to do with the pope's interest in a mission ('The Chronology', *JEH* 14 (1963), 29–30).

p. 134, l. 2. II. 1. **angelicam habent faciem.** Compare a Frankish description of a queen from the *Vita Balthildis*: 'Et cum esset ex genere Saxonum, forma corporis grata ac subtilissima et aspectu decora, vultu hilaris et incessu gravis' (*MGH SRM* 2. 483).

p. 134, l. 7. II. 1. **Aelle diceretur.** '. . . neither here nor elsewhere does Bede state that Ælle was Edwin's father. Since all later sources are unanimous on this point, Bede's silence is probably not to be taken as meaning that he did not agree, but that either by chance or otherwise he simply does not state the fact' (M. Miller, 'The Dates of Deira', *ASE* 8 (1979), 37). The chance could be that the fact formed no part of the story as it reached him and might even suggest that it reached him in written form? It reached him 'ab antiquis', 'from those of former times', not necessarily 'from our ancestors'.

p. 134, l. 22. II. 2. **Interea Augustinus.** I agree with Plummer that the matter of this chapter probably falls after the reception of Gregory's *Responsa* and that 'it is most unsafe to argue from the order of Bede's chapters that it must have been after the battle of Degsastan' (cf. I. 34). No doubt this lengthy account of Augustine's failure to secure collaboration from the British Church in the conversion of the English reflects Bede's sympathies but it should be remembered that its substance, and presumably also its words, come from Canterbury. It was Canterbury in the first place that needed to record its justification of Augustine's failure (and Æthelberht's) to win over the British. This still seemed a momentous matter over a century after Augustine's time. The story does not seem to me to put Augustine in an unfavourable light or to necessitate a non-Canterbury, let alone a British, source for any part of the chapter. Mayr-Harting, *Coming of Christianity*, p. 72, disagrees. Parts of the chapter, notably the second meeting and the battle of Chester, may indeed be British (= Welsh) in origin (see Duncan, *The Writing of History*, p. 17) but Bede's source can still be Canterbury.

p. 134, ll. 22–5. II. 2. **adiutorio usus Aedilbercti . . . in confinio.** I do not see, as do Plummer and Eric John (*Orbis Britanniae* (1966), 15), that this need imply that the king had some authority over the British. What it does imply is that the king's protection covered Augustine as far as the Hwiccian–West Saxon border. The meeting did not take place in British territory.

p. 134, ll. 27-8. II. 2. **communem euangelizandi gentibus.** The British shortcoming that matters most at this stage is failure to preach to the heathen (i.e. the English). As Charles-Edwards puts it: 'Bede thus associates *pax catholica* and the *communis labor euangelizandi gentibus*: the Britons refused both' ('Bede, the Irish and the Britons', p. 44). The Irish, on the other hand, did not refuse to preach to the *gentes*, and the distinction is important to Bede. It does not follow that 'the failure of the Britons to preach to the English may have seemed all the more sinful to Bede because his own English contemporaries were failing to preach to their own people' (Charles-Edwards, ibid.).

p. 136, l. 17. II. 2. **flectit genua sua.** Is Bede here following his source or adding a gloss of his own? The use of the same image in *HE* v. 1 might suggest the latter. However, the intention to see a repetition of New Testament events in recent times is not peculiar to Bede, though characteristic of him. See Tugène, 'L'Hist. "eccl."', pp. 157-8.

p. 136, ll. 26-7. II. 2. VII **Brettonum episcopi.** Bede is concerned not with whether these bishops were diocesans, a matter on which he was possibly as ignorant as we are, but with their number, the traditional seven, 'ut perhibent'. Plummer's note is precise. It is of interest that the British representatives, apparently persuaded by Augustine, should still have desired a larger gathering to confirm wide-reaching changes. The difference between the British and the missionaries now centred not on preaching but on the dates for celebrating Easter and the sacrament of baptism. It is thought likely that the British permitted parts of the sacrament to be performed by priests and even deacons as well as by bishops; and this to Augustine would have been wholly uncanonical. (See Thomas, *Christianity in Roman Britain*, p. 209.)

p. 138, l. 2. II. 2. **Dinoot abbas.** The form of this name suggests to Jackson, *Language and History*, p. 295, that Bede's source was not oral Welsh but a contemporary English document. 'This is a valuable piece of evidence on the date of the source for the story of Augustine's Oak'. And not only the date.*

p. 138, ll. 4–5. II. 2. **apud eos anchoreticam ... solebat.** Nora
Chadwick, *Studies in the Early British Church*, p. 13, and others
think that Bede, brought up in 'the atmosphere of Old Melrose
and Lindisfarne, with their ancient Celtic traditions', would have
felt instinctive sympathy with a Church that taught humility
through a hermit. Perhaps he did. But his was a bishops' Church
and a bishops' *History*. I do not detect much sympathy for the
British Church in this passage and certainly no feeling that
Augustine had been taught a lesson. On the contrary, Augustine
was wrongly rejected, with very serious consequences which
Bede proceeds to relate.

p. 140, l. 3. II. 2. **si pacem ... bellum.** Bede is not primarily
interested in a battle of real political moment but only in its
religious significance as the fulfilment of Augustine's prophecy.
The prayers of the monks of Bangor were inefficacious against
Æthelfrith at Chester: 'sicque completum est presagium sancti
pontificis Augustini' (ll. 33–4), though Augustine himself had
been long dead. Bede's circumstantial details (e.g. Brocmail) do
indeed hint at oral tradition, as Harrison points out (*Framework*,
p. 132), but this may already have reached written form by
Bede's time and been preserved anywhere in England. It seems
idle to speculate whether his immediate source was Northumbrian, Mercian, or indeed Kentish. Could he have had at his
disposal an early collection of English battle-stories? (See C. E.
Wright, *The Cultivation of Saga in Anglo-Saxon England* (1939), 32–
3.) Nora Chadwick studies the sources for Bede's account of the
battle of Chester in *Celt and Saxon*, pp. 167–8.*

p. 142, l. 3. II. 3. **Anno ... DCIIII.** C. W. Jones, *Saints' Lives*, p. 165,
considers this 'the first clear indication of a Dionysiac annal
created in England', though Harrison, *Framework*, p. 97, thinks it
'more likely the figure is based on an episcopal list, and the
balance of evidence is in favour of Dionysiac tables being
brought back by Wilfrid from Rome in 657–8'. This seems to
leave open the nature of Bede's source.

p. 142, l. 21. II. 3. **rex Aedilberct ... fecit.** Bede, clearly using
Canterbury material, lays stress on the king's *potestas*. He builds
the church at Rochester (as also at London) but the dedication

will be Augustine's responsibility. On St Andrew, seen as the missionary *par excellence*, see Campbell, *The Anglo-Saxons*, p. 89. On the king's 'dona multa', including 'territoria ac possessiones', to the churches under his control, see Brooks, *The Early History*, pp. 100 ff.

p. 142, ll. 25-6. II. 3. **Defunctus est ... et positum corpus.** On the temporary burial of 'pater Augustinus' outside the Church of the Apostles (later St Augustine's) and its subsequent removal to its permanent resting-place in the north *porticus* of the Church, see H. M. Taylor, *ASE* I (1972), 263 n., in addition to Taylor and Taylor, *Anglo-Saxon Architecture* (1965), i. 135-89. The early archbishops were all buried outside the walls of Canterbury, as prescribed by Roman Law. The change to burial within the walls at Christ Church came with Archbishop Cuthbert (d. 760). Bede (and Albinus) considered that the early archbishops in their *porticus* lay outside the church. The canonical regulation that burials should take place outside seems to have been less clear in Theodore's Penitential (see P. W. Finsterwalder, *Die Canones Theodori Cantuariensis und ihre Überlieferungsformen* (1929), 274; and A. Lohaus, *Die Merowinger und England* (1974), 116).

p. 144, ll. 16-17. II. 4. **status ecclesiae tam rudis.** Bede understood what Augustine feared about the immediate future of his fragile Church when he appointed Laurence as his successor. It was not that pagan reaction might swamp its structure but that the purity of its teaching might be shattered by deviant doctrine and practice. Thus the new archbishop saw his mission in terms of exhortation and good works. In the same spirit he turned to the British and Irish, and turned with little success. Papal support seems not, at this stage, to have done much to bolster the authority of Canterbury.

p. 144, l. 23. II. 4. **ad profectum debiti culminis.** Levison, *England and the Continent*, p. 183, cites this among other phrases in *HE* as evidence that Bede was drawn upon by the forgers of King Æthelberht's charters. This is entirely possible. Another possibility is that Bede and the forgers were drawing on the same written account at Canterbury. That Bede was following his Canterbury source rather closely in this chapter is suggested by his informing us of what he had already reported in an earlier chapter: that Ireland is an island close to Britain. See also Pierre Chaplais, 'Who introduced Charters into England? The case for St Augustine', *Journ. Soc. Archivists*, 3 (1965-9), 526-42.

p. 146, l. 11. II. 4. **Dominis carissimis.** This letter to the Irish clergy is the only surviving Latin text from Canterbury that certainly belongs to the early missionary period. The Laws of Æthelberht were recorded in Old English. See T. J. Brown, 'An Historical Introduction to the Use of Classical Latin Authors in the British Isles from the Fifth to the Eleventh Century', *Spoleto*, 22 (1975), 252. Duncan, *The Writing of History*, pp. 36-7, comments on Bede's incomplete understanding of the Irish Church as betrayed in three letters to Ireland (of which this is one) from which he gave selections. 'The beginning of a petulant letter from Laurence ... to the Irish Church, about Irish discourtesy, described by Bede as an exhortation to keep Catholic peace and unity; he does not say that the letter referred to Easter, which was scarcely an issue outside Gaul in 610, and Laurence's reported disquiet over Irish paschal customs is merely Bede's disquiet (II. 4). This letter was sent to Ireland, for Laurence and his colleagues are named in the Stowe Missal; Bede therefore received its text from an Irish source.' I feel less sure that paschal customs were not an issue outside Gaul in 610 and not at all sure that Bede's text of the letter came to him from Ireland.

p. 146, ll. 20-2. II. 4. **Columbanum abbatem ... didicimus.** In what way had Laurence learned from Columbanus about the Irish *conuersatio*? Columbanus died in 615 at Bobbio, having passed through Britain from Ireland on his way to Gaul in 591 or a little earlier. (His dates are not easy to establish: see G. S. M. Walker (ed.), *Sancti Columbani Opera* (1957), pp. xff.) This is the only reference in *HE* to the great missionary. Nothing is known of his journey through Britain. If he travelled via Canterbury no record of it survived and there is no reason why Queen Bertha and Liudhard should have welcomed him. A journey by a westerly route and a longer sea-crossing would seem possible if, as has been proposed, he founded a community in Brittany on his route into Gaul. It seems to me likely that he did travel through Brittany and did pick up followers there. One of these, Potentinus, certainly founded a monastery at Coutances at a later date.*

p. 148, ll. 1-2. II. 4. **anno octauo ... indictione** XIII. 'Throughout the *Historia* we discover the indiction only in official documents, with one exception and that in a papal context. As a historian Bede could not be expected to approve this arbitrary and ambiguous form of reckoning, and such was his influence in promoting the Christian era that we shall find the indiction soon losing the primacy, or virtual monopoly, it had once enjoyed' (Harrison, *ASE* 2 (1973), 58-9). See the same author (*Framework*, p. 95) on Bede's attempt to equate events with imperial years, which he considers more successful than did Plummer: 'Bede's chronology for the first half of the seventh century seems to rest on good foundations'.

p. 148, l. 8. II. 4. **Hic est Bonifatius.** Bede will not have known the famous letter (No. 5) from Columbanus to Boniface IV. (Text in Walker, *S. Columb. Op.*, pp. 36-56; discussed by M. Winterbottom, 'Columbanus and Gildas', *Vigiliae Christianae*, 30 (1976), 310-17.) Bede ends the chapter with a reference to the gift of the Pantheon from the Emperor Phocas to Pope Boniface not because it echoes Gregory I's change of mind about the use of pagan temples but because it represents a triumph of Christianity in Rome itself.

p. 148, l. 15. II. 5. **Anno ... DCXVI.** On the difficulties encountered here by Bede's chronology see Harrison, *Framework*, p. 79, and D. P. Kirby, 'Bede and Northumbrian Chronology', *EHR* 78 (1963), especially p. 521. What matters to Bede is that Æthelberht is dead and that this is the point to summarize his achievement in the light of what was to follow.

p. 148, ll. 19-22. II. 5. **Qui tertius ... imperauit.** Bede's list of Bretwaldas (to use a convenient but non-Bedan term) has provoked much literature, from Plummer's time to the present. Apart altogether from questions of accuracy, one needs to ask what the list meant to Bede. Plummer put the essential point thus: 'It is safe to say that [the list] indicates no definite constitution, but only a *de facto* hegemony'; and so Bede saw it. It was a list and no more. As to *imperium*, Charles-Edwards writes ('Bede, the Irish and the Britons', p. 46): '*Imperium* is not contrasted by Bede with *regnum*, but with *tyrannis*: no doubt behind the list, in II.5, of the seven great kings who enjoyed an *imperium* there lies, largely hidden, some early English notion of hegemony, but this has been heavily overlaid by Roman ideas of *imperium* and *tyrannis* in the Christian form found in Gildas . . .'. E. John, *Orbis Britanniae*, pp. 8 ff., sees more than this in Bede's *imperium*, I suspect wrongly; and so do Hanna Vollrath-Reichelt, *Königsgedanke und Königtum bei den Angelsachsen* (1971), 95–110, and others. D. A. Binchy, *Celtic and Anglo-Saxon Kingship* (1970), removes any possibility of a Bretwalda's powers being influenced by those (largely imaginary) of early Irish high-kings, though F. J. Byrne, *Irish Kings and High-Kings* (1973), 259, is less sceptical. It is likely enough that Canterbury grasped the potential of Bretwaldas as instruments of conversion but it does not follow that this explains the power they won and wielded. Arnold Angenendt, *Kaiserherrschaft und Königstaufe* (1984), 181–96, surveys the evidence but reaches conclusions that might have surprised Bede.

p. 148, l. 22. II. 5. **sed primus ... caeli regna conscendit.** This famous chapter, which contains so much of political interest, is in fact about the pagan reaction following the deaths of Æthelberht and Sæberht. Bede's list of overkings or Bretwaldas occurs in a context of Canterbury material and has Kentish sensitivities. I should imagine that the list reached Bede from Canterbury and was not put together by himself from assorted scraps of information. It was Canterbury that had the liveliest interest in the whole territory subjected to Augustine by Pope Gregory and in part represented by the list.

p. 148, ll. 22–7. II. 5. **Nam primus ... obtenuit.** The effective power of the first four Bretwaldas in Bede's list may have been less extensive in fact than he seems to imply, but this need not have worried him. Ian Wood, *The Merovingian North Sea* (1983), 13–14, faces the implications of Merovingian interest in these early rulers: 'Perhaps the early names in Bede's list are names remembered in Canterbury as kings acknowledged by the

Merovingians and subsequently misinterpreted.' I agree that
they were remembered in Canterbury. Is it possible that Bede's
list of seven names—and I see no evidence that he ever meant to
add more—were those who interested Archbishop Theodore
soon after his arrival at Canterbury? It is characteristic of Bede to
record both forms of Caelin's name, as he would have found
them in the record before him. He can have had no other reason.
The ramifications of Caelin–Ceaulin may be pursued in D. P.
Kirby, 'Problems of Early West Saxon History', *EHR* 80 (1965),
especially p. 24.*

p. 148, ll. 26-7. II. 5. **quartus Reduald ... obtenuit.** This should
be translated not as by Colgrave but as: 'fourthly, Redwald, king
of the East Angles, obtained [it], and during the lifetime of
Æthelberht he offered the same [Æthelberht] the *ducatus* over
his own people'. So Vollrath-Reichelt, *Königsgedanke*, p. 83. It
accurately translates Bede's words and makes sense of them.
Brooks, *The Early History*, p. 63, writes that Redwald 'continued
to recognize [Æthelberht's] authority until the Kentish king's
death'. Does Bede understand that Æthelberht was permitted by
Redwald to enjoy the *ducatus* over the East Anglian people? See
Wormald, *Ideal and Reality*, p. 106. This makes more sense than
Vollrath-Reichelt's view that Redwald offered Æthelberht the
ducatus over the Kentish people, which Æthelberht already
enjoyed. Whatever the *ducatus*—and it has a military flavour—
the sentence suggests a friendly relationship between the two
kings, if not initially. It may equally hint that Kent enjoyed a
special status. If this had been due to the authority of the Church
of Canterbury Bede would have been likely to say so. Both
Æthelberht and Redwald were in close touch with Francia and
therefore a reasonable explanation would be that the settlement
between them owed something to Merovingian pressure. Bede
would be less interested to record this, if he knew it. What
neither king did was to make much provision for the con-
tinuance of Christianity in his own dynasty.*

p. 148, ll. 28-9. II. 5. **quintus Aeduini ... maiore potentia.** Ever
careful of words, Bede could not say more plainly that the great
extension of Edwin's authority was a series of acts of force that
owed nothing to any authority inherent in overlordship. Indeed,

if Bede had been writing in the vernacular he might have avoided the Old Northumbrian equivalent of Bretwalda and preferred Hythwalda (plunder-lord), which survived in a place-name (on which see Stenton, *Preparatory*, p. 277).

p. 150, ll. 8–10. II. 5. **atque in porticu … sepultus.** There was no cult of the king before the eleventh century. The only type of royal saint recognized in early Anglo-Saxon England was the martyr, or one who could be represented as such. Æthelberht is placed among 'Les saints rois confesseurs' by R. Folz, *Les Saints Rois du moyen âge en Occident* (VIe–XIIIe *siècles*) (1984), 72. The Anglo-Saxons play a large part in the development of the cultus of kings regarded as martyrs; but the origins of the cultus lie in Francia (ibid., p. 221).

p. 150, ll. 11–12. II. 5. **decreta … iuxta exempla Romanorum.** Bede singles out this from among the *bona* conferred by Æthelberht on his own people because it afforded protection to the Church. Only the first clause of Æthelberht's laws refers to the Church, but then in a striking manner. One can suppose that a new and richly endowed community of foreigners might stand in need of special protection. But what is meant by 'exempla Romanorum'? There is no trace of Roman Law in Æthelberht's *decreta* but there is a general resemblance to Germanic law-codes, whether Frankish or Gothic. *Exempla* is plural. One might have expected *exemplaria*. On the other hand, Bede does not write *exemplum*. By *exempla* he could have understood that exemplars of continental law had been brought to Canterbury by the missionaries or by Bertha's Frankish following; not for slavish copying but as models of codification proper to a Christian king. Committing the customs of Kent to writing can only have been the work of clergy and the fact that they were so committed in the vernacular rather than in Latin suggests that they were meant to be widely appreciated as a collection. Their application would be another matter. Lohaus, *Die Merowinger und England*, pp. 16–24, says what can be said about the indebtedness of Æthelberht's laws to *Lex Salica*. Charles-Edwards, while not denying the Kentish debt to continental law-codes, writes: 'I suggest that Bede was thinking more generally of Gildas' *edicta* of the *reges Romanorum*, imposed on Britain though only accepted on the surface because of incapacity to resist by war. Ethelbert is restoring the authority of written law disrupted by British rebellion against Roman and legitimate *imperatores*' ('Bede, the Irish and the Britons', pp. 48–9); but this interpretation does not fit the context very easily. If, further, the king saw fit to promulgate laws with the help of his clergy, is it not likely that he would also protect his gifts to churches in the written form of charters with which they were already familiar? Certainly no authentic Kentish charters of the period survive, but a reasonable case for such charters has been argued by Pierre Chaplais in 'The Origin and Authenticity of the Royal Anglo-Saxon Diploma' (*Journal Soc. Archivists*, 3 (1965–9) and 'Who introduced Charters into England? The Case for Augustine', ibid.). For a general and careful survey see Anton Scharer, *Die angelsächsische Königsurkunde im 7. und 8. Jahrhundert* (1982). My own views are set out more fully in *Early Germanic Kingship in England and on the Continent* (1971), ch. 2.

p. 150, ll. 17–21. II. 5. **Erat autem ... retulimus.** This early genealogy has come under fire but is well defended by Harrison, *Framework*, p. 123. There is no good reason why it should not go back to the sixth century. It might have been compiled, as Harrison suggested, in a letter, 'to assure Bertha's family of Ethelberht's eligibility' but was in any event passed on by Albinus to Bede as authentic. It might equally have seemed proper to Æthelberht to append such material to his laws. The Lombard King Rothari (in 643, slightly later than Æthelberht) began his enormous law-code of 388 chapters with both a regnal list and his own genealogy: 'utilem prospeximus propter futuris temporis memoriam, nomina regum antecessorum nostrorum ... in hoc membranum adnotari iussimus' (*Die Gesetze der Langobarden*, ed. F. Beyerle, 2nd edn. (1962), 16). Further to the Kentish genealogy cf. I. 15.

p. 150, l. 26. II. 5. **uxorem patris haberet.** To marry one's father's widow was sound Germanic practice. Bede's objection is on religious grounds. Assuming that Eadbald was the son of Bertha, his bride would have been Æthelberht's second wife, name unknown. He later married Ymme (a pet-name for one beginning

Irmin- or Ermin-), daughter of a Frankish king, though this is not recorded by Bede.

p. 150, ll. 27-9. II. 5. **Quo utroque scelere ... susceperant.** Bede fully understood that conversion depended on the king and that it could be purely nominal, conditioned 'uel fauore uel timore regio'.

p. 152, ll. 3-4. II. 5. **tres suos filios ... reliquit.** On the practices of royal inheritance—the eldest son, the most suitable kinsman, or division among sons—see Charles-Edwards, 'Kinship, Status and the Origins of the Hide', *Past and Present*, 56 (1972), 29. The story is clearly part of Mellitus' account of his London experiences as preserved in Kent: 'uenit Cantiam' (l. 24). The planned return to Rome included all three bishops (Canterbury, London, and Rochester) though Bede gives no information on the pagan reaction in Rochester diocese as distinct from Kent as a whole. Two of them go to Gaul to await developments, probably as guests of the Frankish bishops. The subsequent defeat of the pagan kings by the Gewisse seems not to affect the paganism of the former missionary area.*

p. 154, ll. 9-10. II. 6. **apparuit ... apostolorum princeps.** Proceeding with the tale of the rejected missionaries, preserved at Canterbury, Bede describes the miracle that causes Laurence to remain at his post. It is St Peter who saves the day. Equally to the point are two references to Gregory the Great's teaching. They would have been known to Bede but just as certainly to Laurence and his two colleagues. In his *Dialogues*, II. 3 (ed. A. de Vogüé and P. Antin, ii. 140-8) Gregory relates how St Benedict retreated from a monastery of which he was abbot when the monks, finding him too strict, tried to poison him. Did he act rightly? Yes, says Gregory: 'uir itaque sanctus propter quem custodiendum staret, qui omnes unanimiter se persequentes cerneret?' The second reference concerns the miracle of Mellitus and the fire at Canterbury, recounted in II. 7. Here again one of the missionaries must have recalled a very similar miracle performed by Bishop Marcellinus of Ancona (also gout-ridden), recorded in *Dialogues*, I. 6 (ibid., pp. 62-4): 'it was this kind of thing, and its effects on people's lives, which swayed them to accept or lapse from the Christian faith' (Mayr-Harting, *Coming of Christianity*, p. 76, with an excellent discussion). Neither Canterbury nor Bede would seem to condemn the missionaries for what looks like pusillanimity. They had faced the test of recurrent paganism in the spirit of Gregory. Laurence's vision of St Peter includes a reference to Christ as king: 'ipse cum Christo coronandus', and Bede had made clear in his exegesis (e.g. Psalm 26) that he saw Christ as *rex et sacerdos*. The importance of this to Bede is brought out by Arnold Angenendt, 'Rex et Sacerdos: Zur Genese der Königssalbung', in *Tradition als historische Kraft* (1982), 104.

p. 154, ll. 25-6. II. 6. **suscepit fidem Christi.** Some Frankish pressure on Eadbald to accept Christianity is not unlikely: his mother and his second wife were Franks. Bede knew from a regnal list that he died in 640, but only the Salzburg annals record that the day of his death was 20 January. Harrison, 'The Synod of Whitby and the Beginning of the Christian Era' (*Yorks. Arch. Journ.* 45 (1973), 111), observes that 'such a chequered career would hardly qualify him for a place in an ecclesiastical calendar, and it was his son who banned the worship of idols'; but, given his Frankish connections and the number of English princesses in Frankish monasteries (including Eadbald's granddaughter, Earcongota), 'it would not be surprising if the day and month of his death had been written on the fly-leaf of a gospel book or preserved in some similar way'. The conversion of Eadbald, not with his father but after his father's death, is the first of several instances recorded by Bede when all members of the royal house are not converted at the same time as the king. It seems deliberate and may have been a form of insurance that in case of pagan reaction a suitable member of the royal house should still be available to assume the kingship. The matter is well investigated by Arnold Angenendt, *Kaiserherrschaft und Königstaufe* (1984), 178-81.

p. 154, l. 33. II. 6. **Non enim ... regni potestas.** This has been taken to be a reference to Æthelberht's special authority as Bretwalda, taken over by Redwald and not by Eadbald. If so, it is oblique. When Bede wished to make a point he did so with clarity. He was plainly uninterested in what vexes modern historians. On the other hand, the royal power that Eadbald lacked was the power to restore a bishop against the wishes of his pagan people; and this does not seem to have much bearing on the problem of a Bretwalda's authority, at least in the context of London.

p. 156, l. 14. II. 7. **scripta exhortatoria.** Bede gives the texts of three letters from Pope Boniface V to England and may have known more. But he has no text of the 'scripta exhortatoria' to Mellitus and Justus. One assumes that they were letters of encouragement to hard-pressed missionaries. (See Hunter-Blair, 'The Letters of Pope Boniface V and the Mission of Paulinus to Northumbria', *England before the Conquest*, p. 7). Bede's view is that Mellitus more than held his own and attributes his success-ful fire-miracle to what he had already achieved by prayer and preaching, so protecting his people from 'tempestates potesta-tum aeriarum' (p. 158, ll. 8–9). The whole passage plays skilfully with the motif of fire in such a way as to suggest Bede himself at work upon drier facts in his Canterbury material.

p. 158, l. 17. II. 8. **Cui statim ... Justus.** Hunter Blair, *England before the Conquest*, p. 10, rightly urges that chapters 8–13 should be taken as a group. I agree with him, as against Plummer, that the change from 'uos' and 'uester' in the earlier part of the letter to 'tu' and 'tuus' in the later part hardly implies the running-together of two originally distinct letters. Bede inserts the letter to demonstrate by what authority Justus consecrated Romanus to Rochester.

p. 160, ll. 9–10. II. 8. **Susceptis ... Adulualdi regis.** Was this a scribal mistake for 'Eadbaldi regis'? The manuscript evidence favours Adulwald, an otherwise unknown king. Hunter Blair, *England before the Conquest*, p. 8, thinks that he will have been a ruler in western Kent, converted by Justus when bishop of Rochester. It is true that the two names are distinct and that Bede would have known this. Whatever he may have suspected, he would not have altered the form of a name recorded in a papal letter. The king is not said to have been converted by Justus, whose contribution was to guide his soul to the assurance of true conversion and a state of real faith. This rather points to

Justus having completed the good work for Eadbald. Reference to the king causes the pope to reflect on the wider issue of conversion: from the king, his people and their neighbours should follow, as a logical step in a process, 'uniuersalis gentium confessio' (ll. 18-19). This is a consummation constantly in Bede's mind. (See Tugène, 'L'Hist. "eccl."', pp. 144, 161.)*

p. 162, l. 1. II. 9. **Quo tempore ... Nordanhymbrorum.** This chapter bristles with chronological problems. They are tackled by e.g. Hunter Blair, *England before the Conquest*, pp. 10-13, and by D. P. Kirby, 'Bede and Northumbrian Chronology', *EHR* 78 (1963), 514-27. Kirby concludes that Edwin's marriage and Paulinus' move north happened in 618-19, Paulinus was consecrated in 626 and Edwin was converted in 628. The Roman mission was at work in Northumbria from 618 to 634, not from 625 to 633. Bede's difficulty was that he was using two different kinds of source, written and oral. The former one can suppose to have been based on Paulinus' recollections recorded at Canterbury, the latter perhaps derived from Whitby traditions (notably Edwin's experiences at Redwald's court). The opening words of the chapter do not leave the impression that he was using a Northumbrian source. The hero of the chapter is surely not Edwin but Paulinus? A different account of the conversion of Northumbria is provided by 'Nennius', who alleges that Edwin was baptized by Rhun, son of Urien, of the royal dynasty of the northern British kingdom of Rheged. There may be something in this, but if it is to be taken seriously then Bede's account must be wrong; and this seems broadly impossible, given the letters of Pope Honorius. One may accept the presence of Rhun at Edwin's court since it sorts well enough with the king's relations with the British. There may have been preparatory British efforts at conversion there; but in the end one must accept Bede's account of Paulinus' mission. (See Campbell, 'Bede', in *Latin Historians*, ed. T. A. Dorey (1966), 166, 181.) It passed the scrutiny of King Ceolfrith. If Bede had ever heard the British version I suspect he would have paused to rebut it.*

p. 162, ll. 4-6. II. 9. **Cui uidelicet regi ... creuerat imperii.** Bede may have been concerned that Edwin's power increased before conversion. That it was an augury, on account so to say, was a neat way out of the difficulty. McClure, *Ideal and Reality*, draws attention to parallels between Edwin's power and what Bede found in the Old Testament: 'Like the Hebrew editors of the Acts of Solomon, he added to his description of the peace and prosperity which were the result of Edwin's victories what he claimed was a current proverb ... Similar conditions obtained under the powerful King Solomon' (p. 88). She refers to 1 Kings 4: 21, 24–5. On the connection between conversion and victory in the field, there is much of value in D. H. Green, *The Carolingian Lord* (1965): 'evidence as to the way in which warfare could be subjected to a christian interpretation and thus (indirectly) give rise to a different conception of christianity itself is provided by the occasions, reported by Bede, where an Anglo-Saxon king is won over to christianity in circumstances very reminiscent of those in which Constantine and Clovis were finally convinced of the power of the new God' (p. 297). This is one such occasion; and indeed there are remarkable similarities between Bede's story of Edwin's conversion and Gregory of Tours' account of the conversion of Clovis (*Hist.* II. 29–31).

p. 162, l. 8. II. 9. **Quin et Meuanias insulas.** Bede may be right about Edwin's conquest of Anglesey and Man. Chadwick, *Celt and Saxon*, pp. 184–5, places it in the general context of the struggles between Northumbria and the British, of which the battle of Chester was no isolated event: 'It was a war of potential extermination.' F. J. Byrne, *Irish Kings and High-Kings*, p. 112, seems prepared to accept the conquest of Man 'but by the end of the century the island had been occupied by expelled British princes who took to raiding the Ulster and Leinster coasts'.*

p. 162, ll. 9–13. II. 9. **quarum prior ... tenet.** On Bede's hides, about which much has been written, there are wise words in Stenton, *Latin Charters of the Anglo-Saxon Period* (1955), 73.

p. 162, l. 17. II. 9. **Tatae uocabatur.** On pet-names see Stenton, *Preparatory*, pp. 92, 95. I take it that Bede found this detail in his Canterbury material since it concerns Æthelberht's daughter, Æthelburh, who after Edwin's death retreated to the Kentish monastery of Lyminge, founded for her by her brother Eadbald. It was one of the earliest Kentish double-monasteries, no doubt established on Frankish models (see S. E. Rigold, 'The "Double Minsters" of Kent and their Analogies', *Journ. Brit. Arch. Assoc.* 31 (1968), 31 ff.).

p. 164, l. 3. II. 9. **quasi comes.** The Old English Bede translates *comes* as *gesith*; and this, according to H. R. Loyn, is an 'exception to the rule' that a 'clear distinction seems to be made between a *comes* who is a companion of some higher authority, and a *comes* who is a land-owner. The former is called a *gefera*, the latter *gesith*.' Here, however, '*gesith* is used to describe a *comes* who is a simple companion, but even in this instance he is not a member of a *comitatus*' (Loyn, 'Gesiths and Thegns in Anglo-Saxon England from the Seventh to the Tenth Century', *EHR* 70 (1955), 534). But the context is difficult. I think Bede means that Paulinus accompanied Æthelburh as a Christian witness to her secular marriage. We proceed at once to a story involving a *comes* who was far from *quasi*.*

p. 164, ll. 4–7. II. 9. **sed ipse potius … Christo.** Just as Bede's Gregory (II. 1) aimed to make 'nostram gentem' a Church of Christ, so now Bede's Paulinus hopes to makes Edwin's 'gentem' a pure virgin espoused to one husband, Christ. This presupposes some fusion of the concepts of national and spiritual identity. (See Tugène, 'L'Hist. "eccl."', p. 136.)

p. 164, ll. 7–13. II. 9. **Cumque in prouinciam … gloriae Christi.** As Bede records the tradition, Paulinus' beginnings (it was hardly a mission) in Northumbria were beset with difficulties as great as Augustine had met with in Kent. His immediate task was to protect the queen and her entourage. His attempts to convert 'aliquos … de paganis' clearly met with no success. If there were British Christians at Edwin's court, they gave no help to Paulinus and Bede learnt nothing of them from Canterbury.

p. 164, ll. 14–28. II. 9. **Anno autem sequente … peremit.** The story is related by Bede as a step on the way to Edwin's conversion. 'Bede's narrative gives only a hint of the electric atmosphere which a *scop* in the Northumbrian royal hall might have conjured up around the incident. None the less it is the true stuff of heroic saga' (Mayr-Harting, *Coming of Christianity*,

p. 224). This may be so, and the profusion of proper names adds weight to the interpretation. On the other hand, it may be no more than Paulinus' clear recollection as later recounted in Canterbury. Bede does not suggest that the attempted assassination had any religious motivation. Vivid descriptions of assassinations are not uncommon in Gregory of Tours.

p. 166, ll. 7–19. II. 9. **Quo tempore curatus ... tractabat.** Bede does not pretend that Edwin's punitive expedition against the West Saxons was other than retribution against assassins. It had nothing to do with Paulinus. The king is afterwards moved to consider Christianity more seriously and to take advice, but not yet to be converted. However, his queen's entourage even before the campaign included a baptized daughter—and eleven others, baptized with her. Plummer notes that version E of the *Chronicle* reverses Bede's order by placing the campaign before Eanfled's baptism. I see no reason to depart from Bede's order.

p. 166, ll. 20–1. II. 10. **Quo tempore ... forma.** This, and the accompanying letter from Pope Boniface V to Queen Æthelburh (II. 11) were presumably copies taken by Paulinus himself, to whom indeed they must have been sent in the first place. They plainly demand skilled interpretation. On the difficulties in dating them see Kirby, 'Bede and Northumbrian Chronology', *EHR* 78 (1963), 522, though of their genuineness there can be no doubt. 'We can say only that the two letters were written some time during Boniface's tenure of the papacy, i.e. between 619 and 25 October 625. Whether Bede knew this last date is uncertain' (Hunter Blair, *England before the Conquest*, p. 9).

p. 166, ll. 24–5. II. 10. **Viro glorioso ... Dei.** On the rubrics here and in II. 11 see Levison *BLTW* 139 n. 2, and Meyvaert, *RB* 80 (1970) 162 ff., who writes: 'The most likely explanation for the differences in presentation between the larger and smaller groups [sc. of papal letters recorded by Bede] is that Bede obtained them from different sources. We do not know through what channel the two letters of Boniface V ... reached him, but it seems likely that the copies he received were already provided with their special titles, which he transcribed into the History. Bede made no attempt to supply the farewell and date formulae, which were lacking in these letters, from other sources' (p. 163). He also notes (p. 163 n. 2) that 'these copies may derive ultimately from the originals kept in England'. Is it unlikely that the copies, if not the originals, were preserved at Canterbury but kept distinct from the larger group of papal letters, being derived from Paulinus? There are possible corruptions or unexpected difficulties in the text which Plummer did not miss. I follow Colgrave and Mynors here. But these too may suggest an unusually complicated pattern of transmission: Rome—Paulinus—Canterbury—Bede?

p. 168, l. 1. II. 10. **omnibus praecepit gentibus praedicari.** Rome's duty to convert all peoples remains paramount, as it does to Bede. Furthermore, all rulers, whether Christian or pagan, are subjected to the same God, 'quia eius dispositione omnium praelatio regnorum conceditur'. Bede will have recalled Psalm 46: 9 'Regnabit Deus super gentes', and it is often to be understood with him that *gentes* are heathen. This same doctrine, that kings owe their authority directly to God, was not overlooked in the following centuries when Christian inauguration ceremonies could be interpreted as the bestowal of authority on kings by their consecrators.

p. 168, l. 19. II. 10. **Quae enim ... Audubaldi regis.** The assumption remains that this is Eadbald of Kent. See Kirby, *EHR* 78 (1963), 522.

p. 168, ll. 33-5. II. 10. **Quanta autem ... insinuant.** The pope's view of the idols in human form he supposes Edwin to worship is, if naïve, at least direct and challenging. Nothing is said of the way in which Paulinus will approach his task of conversion, though the bishop may have received some such directive as Bishop Daniel of Winchester, in the next century, sent to St Boniface (*Die Briefe des heiligen Bonifatius und Lullus*, ed. M. Tangl, No. 23, pp. 38-41; tr. Emerton, pp. 48-50). Note that St Peter is already seen as 'protectoris uestri' (p. 170, l. 35).

p. 172, l. 1. II. 11. **Ad coniugem ... Aedilbergam.** It does not necessarily follow that this letter reached Northumbria in the same package as that to Edwin but at least Paulinus must have

kept them together. It was not Bede who first did so. As with
Bertha, so with Æthelburh: neither seems to have made any
progress with the conversion of her husband, let alone his
people. What Pope Boniface stresses is the nature of Christian
marriage. He is not concerned with any marriage rite (indeed, he
acknowledges that they are already married in the secular sense)
but with the defiled nature of a union where one spouse is
Christian and the other pagan. Only when Edwin has been
converted can 'you ... thereby enjoy the rights of marriage in
undefiled union'. This can still have been an issue in Bede's day. I
consider the problems of the Church and marriage in *The
Frankish Church* (1983), ch. XVI. ii.

p. 174, ll. 12-16. II. 11. **quatinus ... fidelem.** The pope sees the
conversion of the Northumbrians as a realization of events
announced in the Bible. By converting Edwin, Æthelburh will be
fulfilling the testimony of St Paul: 'the unbelieving husband shall
be saved by the believing wife' (1 Cor. 7: 14, 16). See Tugène,
'L'Hist. "eccl."', p. 161.

p. 174, ll. 32-3. II. 11. **pectine eboreum inauratum.** Mayr-
Harting, *Coming of Christianity*, p. 126, has a brief but useful
survey of presents reaching England from the East. Apropos the
comb, 'we do not have to imagine travels between Britain and
Egypt.' Certainly not. The comb came from Rome. There is a
fuller discussion of combs by Peter Lasko in *The Relics of Saint
Cuthbert*, ed. C. F. Battiscombe (1956), 336-55.

p. 174, l. 35-p. 182, l. 5. II. 12. **Haec quidem ... esse participem.**
This famous story of Edwin's vision at Redwald's court is, in the
opinion of F. Graus, 'absolut nicht kirchlich' (*Volk, Herrscher und
Heiliger im Reich der Merowinger* (1965), 417), and it would be
generally accepted that it belongs to the category of popular,
and specifically Northumbrian, tradition; Northumbrian because
the Anonymous of Whitby also has it in a shortened form (*The
Earliest Life of Gregory the Great*, ed. Colgrave (1968), ch. 16).
However, Plummer notes that 'perhaps the analogy of St Paul
and Ananias in Acts ix, 10 ff. may have been present to Bede's
mind', and George Henderson (*Bede and the Visual Arts* (Jarrow
Lecture, 1980), 4) thinks that 'we may suspect that the atmos-

phere of the Psalms hangs heavily over his [Bede's] account of
the exiled Edwin at the court of Rædwald, promised by a
mysterious visitor a secure heritage like David's and menaced
like David by "bloody men" whose "right hand is full of bribes"'.
If the story has any foundation in fact it must ultimately derive
from Edwin himself. The fact that Paulinus is not identified by
Bede as the ghostly visitor (whereas he is by the Anonymous)
might suggest that Bede's version derives from Paulinus himself.
The political overtones of the story of Edwin's victory and
conversion (on which see Mayr-Harting, *Coming of Christianity*,
pp. 66ff.) do not concern Bede whose mind is fixed on an
'oraculum caeleste' (p. 174, l. 36), God's use of a vision as an aid
in the conversion of a king whose earthly power was won as a
pagan; or rather, whose pagan victory was as much God's doing
as was his subsequent conversion.

p. 182, ll. 6-13. II. 13. **Quibus auditis ... cultus uideretur.** The
meeting in Edwin's hall is the conclusion of the conversion-
story: whatever was the source of one was also the source of the
other. W. von den Steinen, *Chlodwigs Übergang zum Christentum:
eine quellenkritische Studie* (1968), 47, notes interesting parallels
between Bede's account of Edwin's conversion and Gregory of
Tours' account of Clovis' conversion. Clare Stancliffe, 'Kings and
Conversion', *Fm. S.* 14 (1980), 71ff., usefully compares Edwin's
conversion with that of the Swedish King Olaf. On the hall, see
II. 14.

p. 182, l. 14. II. 13. **Cui primus ... Coifi.** Despite this glimpse into
the mind of a pagan high-priest, Bede has no time for the
content of paganism and indeed may have known little about it.
The point was that Coifi and not Paulinus desecrated the pagan
shrine. Plummer finds it 'disappointing' that Bede applies the
words *uerba prudentia* to Coifi's speech, with its stress on
material benefits; yet such benefits were equally a first-fruit of
conversion in Bede's eyes. Did Bede receive the account in *oratio
recta*? The Latin reads like his own.

p. 182, l. 26-p. 184, l. 11. II. 13. **Cuius suasioni ... sequenda
uidetur.** Another of Edwin's *optimates* takes a broader view than
Coifi: Christianity will be worth trying if it explains man's role in

the wider context of life before and after death. Paganism merely concerns itself with our present life, the characteristic of which is brevity. He does not think that Coifi is mistaken about the present life but only that its duration—a mere sparrow's flight through a hall—is a span of time too short for consideration. A pagan of Edwin's day is likely enough to have had a view of his ancestors' fate after death; but that was no part of the story that reached Bede. Gregory Nazianzen in the fourth century had also been struck by the likeness of human life to the flight of a passing bird (*Oratio VII. In Laudem Caesarii Fratris*, ch. 19: *PG* 35, col. 77 CD). He and his readers will have been even more familiar with the sparrow-imagery in Psalm 83 (84). Donald K. Fry, 'The Art of Bede: Edwin's Council', *Saints, Scholars*, i (1979), thinks that Edwin's great men may have been half-way to conversion before the meeeting in the hall and already familiar with the Psalms: 'and we now perhaps have a pagan speech controlled in its imagery by a Christian psalm' (p. 203). I doubt this; but it does reinforce the point that the speech as Bede gives it is a sophisticated confection.

p. 184, ll. 24–7. II. 13. **Cumque a praefato ... Ego.** Compare Sulpicius Severus, *Vita Martini*, ch. 15: 'ita praedicatione sancta gentiles animos mitigabat ut ... ipsi sua templa subuerterent' (ed. J. Fontaine (*SC* 133; 1967), 286). A second, later, parallel is in *Vita Lebuini Antiqua*, ch. 6 (*MGH SS* 30, 2): 'concionator quidam Buto nomine conscendens truncum arboris sic clamabat omnibus ...'.

p. 184, ll. 35–6. II. 13. **iniecta in eo lancea.** 'The action of the pagan priest Coifi in flinging his spear into the temple ... is a small but highly significant pointer to the cult of Woden and the knowledge of his mythology at that time' (Mayr-Harting, *Coming of Christianity*, p. 26). Bede himself would scarcely have known this.

p. 186, l. 4. II. 13. **uocatur hodie Godmunddingaham.** 'The seat of worship in Edwin's reign was called *Godmundingaham*; the interpretation "enclosure of the godmundings" suggests a group of priests' (J. E. Turville-Petre, 'Hengest and Horsa', *Saga-Book of the Viking Society*, 14 (1953–7), 283). Why? Godmund is a good

...version in Kent and subsequent establishment of a
...r in his pagan temple left him a practising pagan,
Bretwalda at that. He had obviously been under
...his wife and 'quibusdam peruersis doctoribus' to
...t he was not hostile to Christianity and not unique
...on to keep his options open. (See S. C. Hawkes in
...xons, ed. Campbell, p. 48, for example.) It is clear
...glian paganism was strong enough to resist conver-
...ssible that the dual-purpose temple was the brave
defeated Christian at a serious form of religious
but Bede does not give Redwald the benefit of the
...e H. J. Diesner, 'Inkarnationsjahre, "Militia Christi"
...che Königsporträts bei Beda Venerabilis', *Mittella-*
...ahrbuch, 16 (1981), 22.) Plummer draws attention to a
...witness to syncretism reported by Gregory of Tours
...3). Bede's mind turns to the Samaritans, whose dualism
...e) clarifies Redwald's situation (see Bede's comment on
...1-2, ed. D. Hurst, *CCSL* 119 A, p. 281, and the remarks
...malley, *Spoleto*, 10 (1963), 632 ff.). D. Whitelock, *ASE* 1
...2-3, suggests that Bede owed his information about
...d to contacts between the royal families of East Anglia
...rthumbria: Hereswith, kinswoman of Edwin, married
...c of East Anglia and was mother of King Aldwulf, who
...n Redwald's pagan *arula* when he was a boy. This is
...nough, though it is unclear why the diminutive *arula*
...be contemptuous: Redwald meant the pagan altar to be
...ominent than his Christian altar. The possibility exists
...ede owed this piece of family history to King Ceolwulf
...f. If there was an intermediary it could have been Whitby,
...ouse of Hereswith's sister Hild; or Lastingham. See
...on's comment on Plummer's attempt to unravel the
...lties of East Anglian relationships (reprinted in *Prepara-*
...pp. 394-402). If it be accepted that the magnificent ship-
...ument or grave of Sutton Hoo commemorates Redwald,
...his son Eorpwald is the likeliest builder. Religious syncre-
...might be admitted there too, with its baptismal spoons and
...ls and the great gold buckle that could have been a Christian
...quary. However, the dominant message of Sutton Hoo seems
...olutely non-Christian; that is, if it has a message: it would
...haps be better to regard it as specifically neither Christian

proper name. Does 'hodie' suggest that this was a replacement for an older name? The site has not yet been located, despite Plummer's 'Goodmanham, near Market Weighton', and EPNS 14 (East Riding), 230.

p. 186, l. 7. II. 14. **cum cunctis ... nobilibus.** This, if accurate, must have been the result of royal pressure rather than conviction, for otherwise it is difficult to explain the pagan reaction on Edwin's death. It does not necessarily follow from Bede's text that the king's sons by Quoenberga were baptized at a later date, as his children by Æthelburh evidently were. See Angenendt, *Kaiserherrschaft und Königstaufe*, p. 178. Why does Bede add the number of years since the coming of the English to Britain? It suggests some sort of annalistic record, and since the contents of the chapter must chiefly rest on Paulinus's account as related at Canterbury, that record presumably belonged to Canterbury. However, Harrison (*Framework*, p. 89) remarks that 'Edwin's baptism ... represents the kind of information that could be transmitted by word of mouth, too notable an event to be forgotten'. I do not find it easy to envisage a group of clergy reciting dates to each other.

p. 186, l. 12. II. 14. **in ecclesia sancti Petri apostoli.** Recent excavations at York Minster have not revealed the site of Edwin's church, first of wood and later of stone. 'Up to the time of writing (1977) we do not know exactly where this church stood' (Rosalind Hill and Christopher Brooke, in *A History of York Minster* (1977), ed. G. E. Aylmer and Reginald Cant, p. 5). I do not know why K. H. Krüger, *Königsgrabkirchen*, p. 291, states that 'vermutlich erhob sie sich unmittelbar westlich vor der heutige Kathedrale' but his discussion of York (pp. 290-9) is valuable. See also H. M. and J. Taylor, *Anglo-Saxon Architecture*, ii. 703 ff. Parts of this chapter are clearly post-Paulinus and Bede may owe them to Bishop Egbert or his clergy. Since Eddius mentions no crypt at York in the seventh century, it is possible that 'Edwin's stone church did not carry deep foundations and was completely obliterated by later buildings on the site' (Hill and Brooke, p. 6). Thomas, *Early Christian Archaeology*, pp. 74-5, adds that 'among the Northumbrian Angles the transition to a stone technique, which actually began in the latter part of the seventh century, was really due to continental and Mediterranean influence, not to what might be taking place in Ireland or in the far north-west'.

p. 186, l. 29. II. 14. **Baptizati ... alii liberi.** Bede's account of Edwin's family (II. 9, 14, 20; III. 1, 6, 14, 24) is scattered but full. However, there are omissions, and it looks as if Bede's informants, or Bede himself, were only interested in those members who were Christians. Miller suggests ('The Dates of Deira', *ASE* 8 (1979), 37–9) that his information came from Gilling, a specifically dynastic house in which his own abbot, Ceolfrith, had begun his life in religion. Another possibility was Whitby. Miller points out that no other genealogy of the period includes children who died in childhood, whose only claim to inclusion was that they were baptized. C. W. Jones, *Saints' Lives*, p. 47, conjectures that Northumbria kept a pre-Christian regnal list; and further, that 'Paulinus made annalistic notations on the Paschal tables from the time of the conversion (ii, 9 and 14), and they were continued by James the Deacon, himself a computist (iii, 1), so that there is some continuous history despite the apparent ejection of the Roman Church.' Stenton, *Preparatory*, p. 280 n. 3, notes that Edwin named his youngest son Wuscfrea after his own great-grandfather, who lived far back in the sixth century.

p. 188, l. 6. II. 14. **Adgefrin.** This complex of royal buildings, presumably no longer in use in Bede's day, has been investigated by Brian Hope-Taylor (*Yeavering: An Anglo-British Centre of Early Northumbria*, 1977) who argues that its beginnings were British. 'Votadinian work', says Leslie Alcock (*Angles, Saxons and Jutes*, p. 179). Its nearness (20 miles) to Bamburgh makes it less likely that it was ever Edwin's principal *uilla regalis*, though he may still have held important meetings there. The largest of its halls was certainly a major achievement in carpentry and could accommodate over 300 people. Campbell, *The Anglo-Saxons*, pp. 56–8, has an excellent summary of Yeavering's possible dates and uses. Among much else it included 'what may have been a pagan temple later converted to Christian use, and what may have been a small Christian church. The halls take us straight to the world of *Beowulf*.' Martin Biddle agrees that we should count

Yeavering among the h[...] use (*England before the C*[...] identifies the wooden str[...] of *Anglo-Saxon Stone Scul*[...] miles away, was Yeaverin[...] P. V. Addyman, *ASE* 1 (1[...] Bede's account is that crow[...] which was thus not confin[...] Paulinus for 36 days. Who bu[...] fact?

p. 188, ll. 13–23. II. 14. **in prou**[...] information will at least in par[...] wulf. As Yeavering was replace[...] was replaced by a *uilla regalis* i[...] strategic importance of Catte[...] Alfred P. Smyth, *Warlords and*[...] menting on Bede's use of *uicus* t[...] writes (*Names, Words and Graves*,[...] places from which crowds descend[...] avoids *villa* or *vicus* because Yeaver[...] as *villam regiam* and he does not mea[...] to it from *villae* in the sense that it w[...] flocked from *uiculis et locis*. In view of[...] *Campodunum* and *Loidis* I do not se[...] *Campodunum* can have been in Lee[...] Church in Anglo-Saxon Towns', p. 1[...] *Campodunum* near Dewsbury. Other A[...] excavated included Old Windsor and C[...] knowledge of such sites is considerably [...] of comparable continental sites. For Brit[...] with Wales see I. Ll. Foster, 'The Emer[...] *historic and Early Wales*, ed. I. Ll. Foster an[...] 217, 228.

p. 188, ll. 24–7. II. 15. **Tantum autem ... sus**[...] to East Anglia and Eorpwald because his co[...] the 'persuasion' of his more powerful neighbo[...] of the same story. Eorpwald had not been [...] lifetime of his father, Redwald, and Bede leave[...]

Redwald's co[...] Christian alta[...] and a pagan[...] pressure fro[...] remain so. Y[...] in his decisi[...] The Anglo-S[...] that East A[...] sion and po[...] effort of a[...] syncretism[...] doubt. (Se[...] und anglis[...] *teinisches J*[...] Visigothic[...] (*Hist.* v. 4[...] (and mor[...] 1 Ezra 4:[...] of Beryl [...] (1972), [...] Eorpwal[...] and No[...] Æthelri[...] had se[...] likely [...] should[...] less p[...] that B[...] himse[...] the [...] Stent[...] diffic[...] tory,[...] mon[...] ther[...] tism[...] bo[...] rel[...] res[...] pe[...]

nor pagan. Speculation about the nature and purpose of Sutton Hoo will continue for many years yet. In the meantime, reference should be made to the massive work of Rupert Bruce-Mitford (with contributions by others), *The Sutton Hoo Ship-Burial*, i (1975) and ii (1978), and iii, parts 1 and 2 (1983), and to the illuminating summary by Campbell in *The Anglo-Saxons*, pp. 32-3. Further excavations at the site are in progress. The fact remains that Sutton Hoo was unknown to Bede; and, had it been known, would have struck him as repellent and irrelevant.*

p. 190, ll. 11-12. II. 15. **filius Tytili ... appellant.** This brief genealogy explains why the members of the East Anglian dynasty are still known as Wuffingas to Bede's contemporaries. For further information see Stenton, 'The East Anglian Kings of the Seventh Century', reprinted in *Preparatory*, pp. 394-402, and R. R. Clarke, *East Anglia* (1960), 138 ff.

p. 190, ll. 13-19. II. 15. **Verum Eorpuald ... curauit.** Wuffing connections with their homeland, Sweden, seem to have been less active than those they enjoyed with Francia. Hence Redwald named a son Sigeberht, which in its Frankish form was favoured by the Merovingians. Eorpwald was assassinated because he was a Christian: there was no other way of dismissing an unwanted king. Bede expresses the highest regard for the learned Sigeberht, who had been converted while an exile in 'Gallia' (presumably Francia); but this stems not from his being a Frankish convert but from his success in winning over East Anglia to Christianity. I cannot agree with Lohaus, *Die Merowinger und England*, p. 29, that Sigeberht's conversion is likely to indicate a more positive Merovingian attitude to conversion in England. Ian Wood, *The Merovingian North Sea*, p. 14, has useful words on the succession to Redwald, though it seems implausible that Sigeberht was 'as likely to be the man associated with Sutton Hoo as Redwald'.*

p. 190, ll. 20-3. II. 15. **Felix episcopus ... nationi Anglorum.** Bede has another account of Sigeberht and Felix in III. 18. He knows that Felix was a Burgundian, not a Frank, but this would not differentiate him in a religious sense. However, it does mean that he came from a part of Francia where the Columbanic

revival of Christianity had a strong hold. He reaches East Anglia
with a commission from Canterbury. Once again Bede emphasizes the role of Canterbury in the work of conversion over the
whole Anglo-Saxon area. Brooks, *Early History*, p. 65, is reluctant
to allow much credit to Felix, let alone Canterbury, and suggests
that 'Sigebert's contacts at the Frankish court of King
Dagobert I, or perhaps with the missionary centres of Columbanian monasticism, were the source of Felix's mission, rather than
any initiative from Canterbury'. I agree that the main impulse to
conversion came from Sigeberht himself, for this is what Bede
says: Felix supported him as a preacher.*

p. 190, l. 29. II. 15. **in ciuitate Dommoc.** We do not know for
certain that this was Dunwich. The Old English Bede renders it
Dommucceastre, possibly translating Bede's *ciuitas* by the suffix.
Campbell, in *Names, Words and Graves*, p. 34, draws a parallel
with Bede's treatment of Dorchester (*Dorcic, Dorciccaestrae*). S.E.
Rigold prefers to site 'Dommoc' at Walton Castle, Felixstowe
(*Journ. Brit. Arch. Assoc.*[3] 24 (1961), 55–9), but D. Whitelock, *ASE*
1 (1972), 4 and n. 2, inclines to Dunwich, with good reason. At
all events, it was at 'Dommoc' that Felix 'accepit ... sedem',
placed there presumably by Archbishop Honorius, and there he
taught for seventeen years.*

p. 190, l. 32. II. 16. **Praedicabat ... Lindissi.** Proceeding with his
dossier on Paulinus, Bede reaches Lindsey and the building by
Paulinus of a church at Lincoln, doubtless with the encouragement of his convert, the 'reeve' Blæcca; but he adds a local detail,
presumably from Deda of Partney: the walls of the church still
stood and the place attracted those seeking miraculous cures.
Campbell, *The Anglo-Saxons*, p. 54, provisionally identifies the
site of the church with the earliest (seventh-century) phase of the
Church of St Paul in the Bail. It stands in what was the courtyard
of the Roman forum. Stenton, *Preparatory*, p. 133, points out that
Bede throws no light on the boundaries of Lindsey and from him
we can only infer that Lincoln, Bardney, Barrow on Humber, and
Partney lay within them. Why should he have said more? Bede's
Lindocolina, an intermediate British form between *Lindum
Colonia* and Anglo-Saxon *Lindcylene* (Stenton, *Preparatory*,
p. 264), strongly suggests that, whatever had happened in the

surrounding countryside, Lincoln itself had remained in continuous occupation. See also Jackson, *Language and History*, p. 258.

p. 192, ll. 7-9. II. 16. **In qua ecclesia ... dicemus.** This fits in uncomfortably between sections of local information. It is a high point in Paulinus' career. Perhaps Bede's first draft included a longer account of the consecration of Archbishop Honorius, which he later incorporated at a more suitable point (II. 18). It took place at Lincoln, some time between 627 and 631.

p. 192, l. 15. II. 16. **qui etiam effigiem ... Paulini.** This vivid sketch of Paulinus' appearance is not entirely without parallels: e.g. Agnellus' descriptions of the archbishops of Ravenna derived, as he says, from portraits taken from the life (*MGH SS Rerum Langobardicarum*, pp. 297, 348). This was a century after Bede, and so too was Einhard's influential portrait of Charlemagne (*Vita Karoli Magni*, ch. 22), not necessarily untrue because heavily dependent on Suetonius' portraits of the Roman emperors. There is no reason to doubt that Bede's is a genuine sketch of what Paulinus actually looked like. The Roman Paulinus must have looked very different from the Angles he was baptizing, and this would have struck Deda's informant. However, some parts of the description may have become stylized in biblical language: e.g. 'terribilis aspectu' (l. 18) echoes the king in Esther 15: 9. More important, does Bede have in mind John baptizing in the Jordan (Matt. 3: 4-6)? This at least would explain his decision to include, at such length uniquely, a personal description of another baptizer. Bede has no such description of any of the five abbots of Monkwearmouth-Jarrow whom he knew, beyond recording that Eosterwine was 'honestus aspectu' (Plummer, i. 372), though he does rather better with King Oswine in *HE* III. 14. I assume that neither Deda nor Bede would have known the splendid description of St Paul in the Apocryphal Acts of Paul 2: 3 (tr. M. R. James, *The Apocryphal New Testament* (1924), 273). We should finally remember Jarrow's interest in portraiture of another kind: Gregory the Great in the Leningrad MS of *HE*, and Ezra–Cassiodorus in the Codex Amiatinus.

p. 192, ll. 19-20. ii. 16. **ac nobilem in Christo.** 'Great reputation
... with Christ' (Colgrave) is no translation of 'nobilem in
Christo'. I would translate 'A man at once zealous and noble
through Christ and in the Church'. Plummer sees that there is a
reference here to James's subsequent heroism in remaining at
his post.

p. 192, ll. 21-30. ii. 16. **Tanta autem ... amoris uellet.** This
recollection of Edwin's power 'in Britannia' and of the peace it
engendered appears entirely secular. However, to Bede, it is a
consequence of his conversion. McClure, *Ideal and Reality*, p. 88,
draws attention to the conditions obtaining under Solomon
(3 Kings [1 Kings] 4: 21, 24-5). When it came to such descriptions, including battles, Bede's mind was influenced by what he
had read in the Books of Samuel and Kings. The peace that
followed Edwin's victories could be capped with a proverb about
a mother travelling in safety with her child; similarly, Solomon's
peace (the fruit of David's conquests) permitted all to live in
security, 'each man under his vine and his fig tree'.

p. 192, ll. 30-5. ii. 16. **Tantum uero ... ferri solebat.** This
somewhat idealized description of a warrior-king at peace
recalls others of the same period: e.g. the Visigoth Liuvigild (see
K. F. Stroheker, *Germanentum und Spätantike* (1965), 134-91) and
the Lombard Agilulf (see Diesner, 'Inkarnationsjahre', p. 26). For
sub-Roman bowls of a type that could resemble Bede's 'aereos
caucos' see Cramp, *Anglian and Viking York*, pp. 5-6. Vegetius,
from whom alone Bede could have obtained *tufa*, may in fact
have written not *tufae* but *rufae*, according to M. Deanesly,
'Roman Traditionalist Influences among the Anglo-Saxons',
EHR 58 (1943), 139. As for the English *thuuf*, '*Tufa* may be a
ghost word but Old English *thuf* can only be real—designating a
standard perhaps like the iron standard of the Sutton Hoo ship
burial' (Crépin, *Famulus Christi*, p. 176). This now seems rather
less likely. If, on the other hand, the Sutton Hoo standard was a
kind of *tufa*, Edwin might have seen one like it at Redwald's
court during his exile. (See Bruce-Mitford, *The Sutton-Hoo Ship-
Burial: A Handbook*, 2nd edn. (1972), 21.) Following his usual
practice, Bede finds an appropriate Latin equivalent for his Old
English *thuuf*: *tufa* is what 'the Romans' *now* call that type of

standard. He is not saying that the standard had been in continuous use in Britain since Roman times, still less that it was the prerogative of a Bretwalda. It seems unlikely that this detailed information about Edwin's war-banners and peace-standards would have survived as popular hearsay. For that matter, the banner in *Beowulf* is not 'popular'.

p. 194, ll. 1-7. II. 17. **Quo tempore ... iste est ordo.** This letter is not dated by Bede but is likely to have been written, as Plummer saw, at the same time as the letter (II. 18) to Archbishop Honorius, dated 11 June, 7th indiction (634). The pope did not know that Edwin had already been slain in battle. If Edwin fell in October 633, it may well have been that the pope had not heard of it eight months later. Possible reasons for the delay (as it looks to us) are discussed by Susan Wood, 'Bede's Northumbrian Dates again', *EHR* 98 (1983), 290-1. See also Harrison, *Framework*, p. 58. Kirby, 'Bede and Northumbrian Chronology', *EHR* 78 (1963), 523, argues that Edwin fell in October 634, not 633; but hardly persuasively.

p. 194, ll. 12-14. II. 17. **Sic enim ... creditis.** A firm papal statement, heartily accepted by Bede, that earthly kings are only kings on condition that they have faith in the kingship of God. We do not know how completely this would have been accepted by a converted king, unless indeed he believed that he owed his crown to his conversion.

p. 194, ll. 24-6. II. 17. **Praedicatoris igitur ... habetote.** Could Edwin read the works of Pope Gregory? And which works? Neither Plummer nor Colgrave offers a comment. A reading to Edwin, perhaps in translation, of the *Pastoral Care* seems a possibility. This at least would have afforded him an insight into the qualities required of any Christian ruler, lay or ecclesiastical. It might well have fallen within the duties of Paulinus. For Bede in particular this advice of Pope Honorius was irrefutable evidence of the continuing grip of Gregory on the English mission nearly forty years after Augustine's arrival.

p. 194, ll. 32-5. II. 17. **et duo pallia ... subrogare.** The pope establishes an arrangement that was to last: a metropolitan-elect will be consecrated by the surviving metropolitan. Brooks notes (*Early History*, p. 390), that 'English pontificals beginning with that of St Dunstan (Paris, Bibliothèque Nationale Lat. MS 943) include a passage specifically referring to this arrangement'. There was both a practical and a personal reason for the arrangement, as the pope makes clear.

p. 196, ll. 4–6. II. 18. **Haec inter Iustus ... electus.** The day and month of Justus' death, but not the year, are recorded by Bede. As Wood remarks (*EHR* 98 (1983), 291–2), 'this may be as early as 627 and cannot be later than 631, because Bishop Felix came to the East Angles then or earlier, and in Honorius' time as archbishop. Paulinus' presence in Lincoln thus falls well within Bede's dates for Edwin's reign.'

p. 196, ll. 25–6. II. 18. **sectantemque magistri ... regulam.** Like Edwin, Archbishop Honorius is reminded that Gregory the Great remains *magister* and *caput* of the entire English Church and specifically of its leaders, lay and ecclesiastical. One would scarcely infer from the tone of the letter that what Gregory had begun still had a long way to go; longer in fact than the pope envisaged, since he already professed to see in the growth of the English Church the realization of 'the promises spoken by Our Lord' in Matt. 11: 28 and 25: 21 (see Tugène, 'L'Hist. "eccl."', p. 161).

p. 198, l. 4. II. 18. **Et tam iuxta ... regum.** If the kings of Northumbria and Kent in fact co-operated in requesting this papal arrangement for future consecrations to Canterbury and York, it suggests a closer link between Canterbury and Paulinus than is commonly allowed.

p. 198, l. 21. II. 18. **id est ... DCXXXIIII.** The first to point out that these words were Bede's addition to the papal dating clause was Levison, *BLTW*, p. 148 n. 3.

p. 198, l. 22. II. 19. **Misit idem papa ... genti Scottorum.** Honorius' letter is not provided by and was presumably not available to Bede. What he does provide is excerpts from the later (640) letter of the pope-elect, John IV, which perhaps

included material from Pope Honorius' letter. Bede omits the
passage in the letter that gave detailed paschal arguments,
substituting the paraphrase 'Exposita autem ... epistula
subdunt' (p. 200, ll. 23-4). In fact there was a connection
between paschal unorthodoxy and Pelagianism, as is shown by
Ceolfrith's letter to King Naiton (v. 21). An explanation of the
Roman curia's mistaken view of the Irish position is advanced by
Ó Cróinín, '"New Heresy for Old": Pelagianism in Ireland and
the Papal Letter of 640', *Speculum* 60 (1985), 505-16. Harrison,
Framework, pp. 59 ff. and Duncan, *The Writing of History*, pp. 37 ff.,
have different approaches to the difficult matters contained in
this chapter. Neither asks why it appears in *HE* where it does.
The answer must be that it followed the letter of the Pope
Honorius to Archbishop Honorius in the Canterbury dossier of
papal letters. Whatever Bede may have known about Irish and
British practices in the days of Paulinus, or later, there can be no
doubt that the issues raised by Pope John were of the greatest
importance to him. H. E. J. Cowdrey puts it well: these issues
'carried deep and grave implications, and ... upon their resolu-
tion depended the unity, peace and harmony of the church.
They raised questions of authority and jurisdiction: ... a
deliberate refusal [sc. of correct paschal observance] amounted
to a withholding of the obedience that was due from all
Christians to St Peter' ('Bede and the "English People"', p. 510).
The charge of Pelagianism, however unjustified it may in fact
have been, may have seemed even more momentous in Bede's
eyes. His biblical commentaries frequently refer to the heresy as
of present moment. The whole of Book I of his commentary on
the Song of Songs is a diatribe against Julian of Aeclanum,
Pelagius' chief supporter (Laistner, *Thought and Letters*, 2nd edn.
(1957), 160). Harrison, *Framework*, p. 61, defends Bede against
Poole's charge that he doctored John's letter and draws attention to Rome's own change of opinion about Easter dates. In a
letter to me of 22 March 1983 Harrison withdraws his previous
statement (*Framework*, p. 61) claiming that Poole charged Bede
with 'doctoring' his source, preferring to say that Bede 'sup-
pressed this amateurish piece from the Curia, having set out the
rules in his own scholarly fashion before quoting the letter ...
Anyhow we now know the papacy was supporting *luna xv* in
640'.*

p. 202, ll. 10–19. II. 20. **At uero Eduini . . . interemtus.** With the killing of Edwin and the collapse of Christian Northumbria Bede brings Book II to a close. It is also the close of Paulinus' career in Northumbria; for the rest of his life he will live as an exile caring for the see of Rochester. We may take it, then, that much of the chapter may derive from Paulinus' reporting to Canterbury on Edwin's last days.

p. 202, ll. 12–13. II. 20. **Caedualla rex Brettonum.** To Bede it is clear that the great rebellion against Edwin is led by Cadwallon and supported by Penda. Charles-Edwards ('Bede, the Irish and the Britons', pp. 45–6) comments: 'Cadwallon is important to Bede; indeed it is important to him that Cadwallon is a Briton; but there is no evidence that Bede denounced Cadwallon merely as a Briton and as an effective enemy of the Northumbrians . . . his triumph closes the story of the Gregorian missionaries in Book II and his defeat opens the way to Oswald's hegemony and the *episcopatus Scottorum* in Book III.' Cadwallon, a true *tyrannus*, stands contrasted with the Christian *imperium* of Edwin and Oswald. Bede is not interested in the political background of the alliance against Edwin (and it had justification) but in the outcome of a battle fatal to the Christian Edwin and disastrous for Roman Christianity in Northumbria. It was Cadwallon, the British Christian, and not Penda, the pagan Mercian, who wreaked vengeance on the defeated Northumbrians. Cadwallon from the Welsh aspect is considered by Wendy Davies, *Wales in the Early Middle Ages* (1982), 92, 113. She points out (p. 113) that the fostering of Edwin by Cadfan, Cadwallon's father, is a matter of 'later tradition'.

p. 202, ll. 13–14. II. 20. **Penda uiro strenuissimo.** 'Most energetic' will not do as a translation. In Bede's context, as in many Frankish, *strenuitas* is an aspect of *utilitas* and refers specifically to martial prowess. I would translate: 'a man exceptionally gifted as a warrior'. The word is discussed by J. P. Bodmer, *Der Krieger der Merowingerzeit und seine Welt* (1957), 55 ff., and in my *Long-Haired Kings*, p. 62. For an imaginative discussion of Penda's rise to power see H. P. R. Finberg, *The Early Charters of the West Midlands* (1961), ch. VII ('The Princes of the Hwicce'), and Stenton, *Preparatory*, p. 360.

p. 202, ll. 16–18. ii. 20. **occisus est . . . xl et viii.** Efforts have been made to move the date of the battle of Hatfield Chase from Bede's clear 633 to 632 or 634, but Harrison (*ASE* 2 (1973), 57) gives reasons for retaining 633, and likewise 642, the date of Oswald's death; otherwise 'we must suppose Bede wrong; and wrong not about an event distant in time and place, but also about the fate of Oswald, a Northumbrian hero, the martyr-king whose death, translation and miracles occupy six chapters of the book' (namely, iii. 9–13; iv. 14). Further, there is no manuscript evidence for emending the date.

p. 204, l. 7. ii. 20. **Adlatum est . . . Eburacum.** I see no difficulty in Bede's report here that Edwin's head reached York, and later (iii. 24) that his body was buried at Whitby (confirmed by the Anonymous Life of Gregory). One would expect decapitation and the exposure of the body on the battlefield as a sign of vengeance taken; and that head and body should somehow reach different destinations is not implausible.*

p. 204, ll. 12–18. ii. 20. **nisi in fuga . . . filii eius.** This detailed record of the flight of Æthelburh with Edwin's children, together with church treasure, can only derive from Paulinus himself; that is, from Canterbury. Albinus was familiar with the golden cross and chalice—'the English counterpart, one assumes, of the contemporary goldsmith's work of St Eligius in France' (Henderson (Jarrow Lecture, 1980), pp. 4–5).

p. 204, l. 19. ii. 20. **Daegbercto . . . amicus illius.** King Dagobert may have been Æthelburh's friend but he was something more: her kinsman and natural protector; and that is what 'amicus' means, as Bede knew. She presumably sent the children to take refuge with Dagobert at Paris. There is no mention of their coming in the *Gesta Dagoberti* (cf. pp. 413–19 of Krusch's edition, *MGH SRM* 2, covering the years 635–9, from Oswald's accession to the death of Dagobert). It was a family matter, not a political one.

p. 204, ll. 32–3. ii. 20. **pallium . . . reliquit.** The symbol of Paulinus' authority was personal to him and remained at his death in his church of Rochester. It does not go to Canterbury and cannot go to York.

p. 206, ll. 1–10. II. 20. **Iacobum diaconum ... secutus est.** Bede closes the chapter and the book with a recollection of James the Deacon that must come from northern tradition. Perhaps he overestimates James' success in the continuing work of conversion but at least it is clear that he was not interfered with. The church music that he taught is hardly a matter of conjecture: nothing is known about it. James, who lived to Bede's time, is a man of whom one might expect some personal description at this point. But, unlike Paulinus, he did not suggest any biblical parallel to Bede and merited no more than an affectionate reference. C. W. Jones, *Saints' Lives*, p. 35, suggests that Paulinus and James kept annals in Northumbria, but Harrison, *Framework*, p. 97, comments that in describing the work of James 'it would have been uncharacteristic of Bede to omit the mention of annals, had they been known to him, either at that point or in his Preface'.

BOOK III

p. 208, ll. 1–2. III. **Haec continentur ... Anglorum.** With Book III one can feel Bede moving into a more familiar world, if at one remove. In thirty chapters he covers the ecclesiastical events of little more than thirty years, from the death of Edwin to the appointment of Theodore; and the scene is predominantly Northumbrian, or Northumbrian-influenced. He is now able to cite the witness of men he knew, and does so several times. His framework is regnal but the story is largely episcopal and Celtic.

p. 212, ll. 1–2. III. 1. **suscepit pro illo regnum Deirorum.** For a reconstruction of Bede's approach to early Northumbrian chronology see M. Miller, 'The Dates of Deira', *ASE* 8 (1979), 35–61: 'Bede's assembly of statements is interesting as a whole, for it seems to amount to an experiment in the Christianization of a genre of secular learning, the royal pedigree' (p. 38).

p. 212, ll. 5-6. III. 1. **nam in has duas ... diuisa erat.** Though there was never any love lost between Deirans and Bernicians, Bede's 'history is created on the premiss that the Northumbrians were a *gens* and that Deira and Bernicia were merely *provinciae* ... He appears to have believed in an original unity of Northumbria, subsequently divided ... and then re-united in the seventh century ... Yet the very term, Northumbrian, is, as far as one can see, a creation of Bede's' (Charles-Edwards, 'Bede, the Irish and the Britons', p. 49).*

p. 212, ll. 9-10. III. 1. **cum magna nobilium iuuentute.** Æthelfrith's sons with their young retainers are converted while in exile, by the Irish; the older ones, married and landed, remained on their estates and were presumably the core of the pagan reaction. Bede does not attribute the apostasy of Eanfrith of Bernicia or of Osric of Deira to Cadwallon; despite their apostasy, Cadwallon still kills them at the earliest opportunity. One can see that Cadwallon's action was 'impia manu' but why did Bede consider it 'iusta ultione' (ll. 17-18)? J. E. Cross ('The Ethic of War in Old English', in *England before the Conquest*, p. 277) sees here 'a neat piece of sophistry ... The punishment of backsliders from Christianity was obviously a just reason for war, but the agent of God's vengeance was a pagan'. Since when was Cadwallon a pagan? For a 'not totally unintelligible' Welsh poem on Cadwallon, apparently written before his death in 633, see I. Ll. Foster, in *Prehistoric and Early Wales*, pp. 230-1. Bede has a clear idea of how a 'rex uictor' should behave: Cadwallon was merely a 'tyrannus'.*

p. 214, ll. 5-8. III. 1. **Vnde cunctis ... adsignaretur.** No doubt this is evidence for the keeping of early king-lists (Kirby, *EHR* 78 (1963), 515) though Bede does not precisely state 'that there were men whose task it was to reckon the reigns of the Northumbrian kings'. Hunter Blair ('The *Moore Memoranda* on Northumbrian History', in *The Early Cultures of North-West Europe*, p. 248) is right to stress that what had impressed Bede and his contemporaries was 'what was felt to be a stain upon the early history of the Church in Northumbria'. It was an ecclesiastical issue. 'Cunctis ... computantibus' seems to imply a concerted decision by Northumbrian religious houses. However, it might mean no more than that Bede 'possessed or had seen both James' [sc. the Deacon's] Easter-table with marginalia, and a king-list (with regnal years) noted in one of his Irish manuscripts, identical in that both made Oswald the immediate successor of Edwin, as does the Moore Memorandum written in 737' (Miller, 'Bede's Roman dates', *Classica et Mediaevalia*, 31 (1970), 251). The omission of the apostates' reigns may be reminiscent of Roman *damnatio memoriae* but I doubt if Bede knew about this, even though names were erased from public inscriptions. See also: (1) Susan Wood, *EHR* 98 (1983), 295, 'the actual period of Cadwallon's ravaging, as related by Bede, has to be a twelvemonth, running from late 633, but the *idea* of the "unlucky year" was perhaps focused on the disastrous campaigning season of 634 in which both kings fell' (Colgrave's translation obscures the meaning); (2) Harrison, *ASE* 2 (1973), 57; and (3) Miller, *ASE* 8 (1979), 56.

p. 214, l. 7. III. 1. **Osualdi uiri Deo dilecti.** Whatever Oswald's reputation may have owed to Bede, the king-martyr was not his unaided creation. See R. Folz, 'Saint Oswald roi de Northumbrie, étude d'hagiographie royale', *Anal. Boll.* 98 (1980), 49–74, and *Les Saints Rois du moyen âge en occident* (vi^e–xiiie siècles) (1984), 46–8; also Peter Clemoes, *The Cult of St Oswald on the Continent* (Jarrow Lecture, 1983). What Bede does is to provide a series of chapters bearing witness to Oswald's Christian virtues and thaumaturgical power and completes these with a moral portrait of the hero that seems to be inspired by the treatise *De Duodecim Abusivis Saeculi* of Pseudo-Cyprian. However, the point was that Oswald was a king (see my *Early Germanic Kingship*, pp. 83 ff.). It is likely enough that his followers saw him in a rather different light.

p. 214, ll. 14–15. III. 2. **signum sanctae crucis erexit.** On wooden crosses as prototypes for free-standing stone crosses see Thomas, *Early Christian Archaeology*, p. 123. 'Like the emperor Constantine before him, Oswald was identified with devotion to the cross' (Clemoes, Jarrow Lecture, p. 3); and more than that, consciously owed his victory against odds to divine aid. The story, including the passage in *oratio recta*, must be directly obtained by Bede from the monks of Hexham, guardians of the cult.

p. 214, ll. 24-5. III. 2. **quia iusta ... suscepimus.** This is unlikely to mean that 'we are fighting in a just cause for the preservation of our whole race'. I should prefer, 'we fight a just war for the salvation of our people'. The cause is religious, and victory is won through faith. It is Oswald's faith that is rewarded by miracles at the site of the cross. How far this account tallies with what actually happened cannot be asked or answered. It certainly places a royal victory within a historical context that began with Constantine and included Clovis. Cramp, *Northumbrian Sculpture* (Jarrow Lecture, 1965), 4-5, draws attention to a Jarrow inscription reconstructed by Levison as 'in hoc singulari [sig]no vita redditur mundo'. 'The first four words are identical with Rufinus' recasting of the inscription placed, according to Eusebius' *Ecclesiastical History* IX, 9, on a statue commemorating Constantine's vision of the cross which the Emperor then used as a standard of victory'. Bede was familiar with the text of Eusebius-Rufinus. See also Cramp, *Corpus*, i/1. 112-13. From Rufinus's continuation he would equally be familiar with the description of the final victory of the Emperor Theodosius I after fasting and prayer to God: 'sed ubi verae religionis fretus auxilio Theodosius ...' (*PL* 21, cols. 539-40). Note Rufinus's use of *tyrannus*, *barbari*, and *pagani*.

p. 216, ll. 3-5. III. 2. **Vocatur locus ... nomen accepit.** Bede supposes that the place-name Hefenfeld was older than the battle that took place there; in other words, that the name foretold the event.

p. 216, ll. 17-21. III. 2. **quia nullum ... statueret.** Bede has already provided evidence that this was very unlikely to be true. But he was now using a different source and stuck to his texts—in this case, orally or not, from Hexham. What this means is that in the Hexham tradition Bernician Christianity begins with Oswald's cross. On the etymology of Bede's Bernicia see Jackson, *Language and History*, pp. 70-5.

p. 216, l. 24, III. 2. **Hagustaldensis ecclesiae.** On Wilfrid's church at Hexham see Mayr-Harting, *Coming of Christianity*, p. 158, and E. Gilbert in D. P. Kirby (ed.), *Saint Wilfrid at Hexham* (1974). K. Jackson discusses the place-name *Hagustaldesham* and its Welsh counterpart in the *Annales Cambriae*, s.a. 631, in *Celt and Saxon*, p. 34: we should reject the explanation of Welsh *Cantscaul* given by Plummer (following Skene) as 'battle within the wall' in favour of 'the enclosure of the young warrior' (*cant* + *scaul*). This is probably itself the result of an error by which the Welsh annalist or his source mistook *ham* for *hamm*: the English name *Hagustaldesham* means 'the village of the young warrior'. C. W. Jones, *Saints' Lives*, p. 212 n. 4, suggests that Bede's source for his account of the annual pilgrimage of the monks of Hexham to Hefenfeld was Bardney: possibly, but why not Hexham?

p. 218, l. 13. III. 3. **misit ad maiores natu Scottorum.** It is true, as A. C. Thomas points out, *Early Christian Archaeology*, p. 132 n. 1, that Bede does not expressly mention Iona; but it may reasonably be inferred.

p. 218, l. 14. III. 3. **cum his qui ... militibus.** Presumably they belonged to the 'magna nobilium iuuentus' of III. 1.

p. 218, l. 18. III. 3. **accepit ... Aidanum.** D. A. Bullough ('Hagiography as Patriotism', *Hagiographie, cultures et sociétés, IVe–XIIe siècles* (1981), 346) makes an interesting comparison between Bede's treatment of Aidan and Alcuin's, some fifty years later. I do not think that Bede views Aidan as a fundamentally wrong-headed man with redeeming virtues but as a man who in all respects but one was an admirable bishop. There is no general contrast intended between the Roman and the Irish ideals.

p. 218, ll. 27–9. III. 3. **Porro gentes Scottorum ... didicerunt.** Harrison, *Framework*, p. 59, comments: 'This statement may be true in a general sense ... but Bede seems to have been mistaken in thinking that conformity had spread quite so soon among all the monastic *paruchiae* of the south, where a Victorian chronology can be traced as late as 655.*

p. 218, ll. 30–1. III. 3. **rex locum sedis ... tribuit.** The earlier lay-out has disappeared but it is likely that Aidan's monastery, as well as his choice of locality, was modelled on the mother-house of Iona. (See Thomas, *Early Christian Archaeology*, pp. 37–8.) A further consideration was Lindisfarne's closeness to Bamburgh, Oswald's *urbs regia*, for Oswald was not only Aidan's patron but also his interpreter. On the early Irish churches and monasteries founded in Northumbria by Aidan and his followers see Bullough, 'The Missions to the English and Picts and their Heritage', in *Die Iren und Europa im früheren Mittelalter*, ed. H. Löwe (1982), i. 86–7. There is a good discussion of Aidan's missionary career in Mayr-Harting, *Coming of Christianity*, pp. 94–9. Though Aidan was both bishop and monk, he acted in Northumbria only as bishop and not as abbot of Lindisfarne, and in this respect departed from the custom of Iona. His English career, as Bede makes plain, was exclusively episcopal. Bede had more to say about this division of responsibility in his Prose Life of St Cuthbert (*Two Lives of St Cuthbert*, ed. Colgrave (1940), 206–8). See also K. Hughes, *The Church in Early Irish Society* (1966), 83, and A. Hamilton Thompson, 'Northumbrian Monas-ticism', *BLTW*, p. 73.

p. 220, ll. 28–9. III. 4. **Siquidem anno ... quinto.** Bede is definite about the date here, though in v. 24 (p. 562, ll. 23–4) 'he distinctly implies that Iona was founded after this preaching to the northern Picts, which appears to be a mistake; the figure was got by subtracting 150 years from AD 715 [see p. 224, ll. 11–13], when the Iona monks decided to abandon the Celtic-84 [year paschal cycle] ... adopting Roman customs next year; and Bede might have been prudent to add *circiter* or *plus minus*, as was often his habit' (Harrison, *Framework*, p. 100 n. 3). It remains unclear whether Bede had a source independent of Iona for III. 4; what he certainly did not use was Adomnán's Life of St Columba. On the difficulties involved here see Bullough, 'Columba, Adomnan and the Achievement of Iona', *SHR* 43 (1964), 116–17.[*]

p. 222, ll. 1–2. III. 4. **septentrionalium Pictorum.** There seems no good reason to doubt Bede's division of the Picts into northern and southern groups. See Wainwright, *The Problem of the Picts*

(1955), 21. There is little point in speculating about Bede's sources for Pictish history, and no particular reason why one such should have been Trumwine, once bishop at Abercorn (so Thomas, in *Christianity in Britain*, pp. 105-6).

p. 222, ll. 6-8. III. 4. **Nynia episcopo ... edoctus.** Bede, by whose time Nynia's territory was in Northumbrian hands, seems to contrast the mission of Columba to the northern Picts with that of Nynia to the southerners. Nynia was 'Roman' to Bede, though whether he actually visited Rome is questioned (I think unnecessarily). It may be that he was bishop over a later Roman settlement in the area: his name is British. The dedication to St Martin hardly helps us to date him though I see no particular reason why he should not have acquired Martinian relics fairly soon after Martin's death in 397. Further, if Nynia built a stone church in honour of St Martin he was doing precisely what Sulpicius Severus said he, Sulpicius, did in southern Gaul. For a general treatment of the evidence see Thomas, *Christianity in Roman Britain*, ch. 11. While it is unknown what material about Nynia was available to Bede, there seems no special reason why Levison should doubt that he had any written source (*BLTW*, p. 138 n. 2). Oral information could of course have come from Pehthelm, bishop of Whithorn, or from King Nechtan's messengers to Ceolfrith of Jarrow. (See K. Hughes, *Early Christianity in Pictland* (Jarrow Lecture, 1970), 2.) It depends on how detailed one supposes oral information, not specifically prepared, was likely to be.

p. 222. l. 14. III. 4. **Venit ... Columba.** Bede reverts to the real business of the chapter, which is not Nynia but Columba. Hughes (Jarrow Lecture, 1970, p. 2) points out how very unusual it was that the Irish should send an evangelizing mission to the Picts; normally, evangelization was the result of pilgrimage, not its motivation. 'Either Columba was quite different from other Irish "exiles for Christ", or Bede's informants were reading history backwards from a Pictish standpoint.' The latter seems likelier, and indeed there is nothing to suggest that Columba's mission in Pictland was as successful as Bede's information indicated.

p. 222, ll. 20–2. III. 4. **sepultus est . . . adiit.** Bede dates Columba's arrival in several ways: the accession of Justin II in 565 (from the imperial *fasti*), the ninth year of King Bridei of the Picts, and 32 years before Columba's death at the age of 77. This last is derived from the Iona obit through an intermediary (Duncan, *The Writing of History*, pp. 6–7). 'Bede's ultimate source was annals now represented by the Irish annals but it is neither needful nor desirable to assume more than one mediating informant' (ibid., p. 19).

p. 222, ll. 22–4. III. 4. **priusquam Brittaniam . . . cognominatur.** Adomnán places the foundation of Durrow after, not before, that of Iona. Duncan, preferring Adomnán, writes: 'I suggest that Bede's source told of the foundation of Durrow *prius* (i.e. before his death), and that Bede misunderstood the reference. If I am correct, then Bede's informant knew at least the substance of the matter as recorded in Adomnán' (*The Writing of History*, p. 19 n.). On the other hand, Bede may be right.

p. 222, ll. 24–8. III. 4. **Ex quo . . . principatum teneret.** What does Bede understand by this *principatus* of Iona over its foundations in Brittania and Hibernia? He uses the word nowhere else in *HE*. It might be his own word to explain a, to him, highly unusual arrangement (see Bullough, 'Missions to the English', p. 90) or a word he took from his Iona-derived source. The latter seems more probable since, as Duncan says (*The Writing of History*, p. 10), '*princeps* is used in Irish sources (annalistic and in canon law) consistently of the abbot, *principatus* of his authority'. See also Angenendt, *Kaiserherrschaft*, p. 191, on the implications of this for Oswald and Oswiu. We should probably not accept a new paragraph after 'principatum teneret'. Unlike Duncan, I do not see 'something like a paragraph break' in Leningrad MS, fo. 51 *b*, though he too would abolish the paragraph.*

p. 222, l. 29–p. 224, l. 3. III. 4. **Habere autem . . . et monachus.** Bede understands that the priest-abbots of Iona were such only because of the example of Columba. K. Hughes, *Church in Early Irish Society*, p. 63, has a good example (from Adomnán) of the obedience of a Celtic bishop to his priest-abbot. 'Prouincia' can hardly be translated 'kingdom' since several were involved. The meaning is the whole monastic diocese or *paruchia* over which Iona ruled.*

p. 224, ll. 3–4. III. 4. **de cuius uita ... haberi.** Bede states clearly that he has heard of written records of Columba's life kept by Iona but has not seen them.

p. 224, l. 7. III. 4. **dubios circulos sequentes.** It now seems possible that Bede obtained his Irish computistical material from southern Ireland, perhaps by way of Malmesbury, rather than from Iona. The matter is thoroughly investigated by D. Ó Cróinín, 'The Irish Provenance of Bede's Computus', *Peritia*, 2 (1983), 229–47. It is quite clear what Bede means by 'dubios circulos': he is referring to the 84-year cycles, the weakness of which he and others were fully capable of fathoming (Harrison, *ASE* 7 (1978), 7).

p. 224, ll. 14–15. III. 4. **reuerentissimo ... Ecgbercto.** This is the first appearance of Egbert in *HE*. As has been long appreciated, he is important for several reasons to Bede, who may see his conversion of Iona to the canonical Easter as too exclusively the reason for his journey to Iona. It is uncertain that his Irish home was Mayo, though Duncan, following Mrs Chadwick, argues forcefully for it (*The Writing of History*, pp. 23 ff.); but if Mayo it was, we have to reject Bede's attribution of the foundation of the house to Colmán (see K. Hughes, *England before the Conquest*, p. 53). I think it is not possible but certain that Bede's *sacerdos* should be translated as 'bishop'. Duncan (p. 14) makes the interesting suggestion that Egbert took to Iona the use of the year of the Incarnation as a method of dating, arising from the use of the Dionysiac Easter cycle: 'may it not be that this adoption by Iona suggested or encouraged the idea that a history might be written whose framework was the era of the Incarnation?' (See also Harrison, *Framework*, chs. 3–5.) Duncan concludes: 'If the conversion of Iona brought the seed (in the *Chronica Majora*) of historical dating by the year of the Incarnation, the flowering of that seed (the *HE*) was, I suggest, brought about by the news of the death of Egbert in 729' (*The Writing of History*, p. 41). I do not see the connection.*

p. 226, ll. 1-2. III. 5. **Ab hac ... Aidan.** This makes it clear that what Bede had already reported about Columba and Iona was a necessary preface to Aidan's mission to the Northumbrians.

p. 226, ll. 4-7. III. 5. **Vnde inter alia ... ipse docebat.** This and what follows is no doubt a just estimate of how Aidan saw his mission and it suggests at several points—particularly fearlessness towards the great—the behaviour of another Celtic missionary, Columbanus, and much earlier, St Martin. It is also not far removed from the teaching of Gregory the Great, with which Bede was more familiar. The *Cura Pastoralis* comes to mind. In other words, though Bede is contrasting Celtic missionary behaviour with the 'segnitia' of his own day (on which his letter to Egbert of York is a commentary), he is not contrasting it with that of the great Roman missionaries he has already discussed. He wishes to see 'industria', not 'segnitia' (l. 18), as it was practised in the Celtic, the Roman, and the biblical times of major missionary endeavour. His comments on this in *De Templo* are discussed by Mayr-Harting (Jarrow Lecture, 1976, p. 22).

p. 226, l. 10. III. 5. **urbana et rustica loca.** The distinction, as Campbell points out ('The Church in Anglo-Saxon Towns', p. 121), is 'not so much one between town and country, as between important local centres of the kind where minsters were built and ordinary places'. The Church in England 'could not be an urban church but, as it developed under the aegis of kings, so its pattern of authority echoed theirs and where the *villa regis*, the royal *tun*, was, there, more often than not, the minster was; and there, often enough, in later centuries a real town grew up'.

p. 226, l. 31. III. 5. **Nullam potentibus saeculi pecuniam.** Contrast St Wilfrid's gift to his monasteries 'ut cum muneribus regum et episcoporum amicitiam perpetrare potuerint' (Eddius, ed. Colgrave, p. 136). However, this was not quite the same as the customary gift-exchange, of which there are many examples in Gregory of Tours, the letters of St Boniface, and elsewhere. For a continental version of Aidan, though no Celt, see Gregory of Tours on Bishop Salvius of Albi (*Hist.* VII. 1): 'Fuit autem magnae sanctitatis minimaeque cupiditatis, aurum numquam habere volens. Nam, si coactus accepisset, protinus pauperibus erogabat.'

p. 228, ll. 27–8. III. 5. **gratia discretionis ... inbutus.** Plummer rightly refers to Bede's commentary on Luke 22: 35–6 (now ed. D. Hurst, *CCSL* 120, p. 383). Bullough, 'Missions to the English', p. 86 n. 18, comments: 'I have failed to find any pre-Bedan writer ... who claims *discretio* as "the mother of all virtues", or indeed any writer before the twelfth century who singles it out as a virtue.' Bede also uses the word in *HE* II. 1, in a Gregorian context. On Pope Gregory's use of *discretio* see Claude Dagens, *Saint Grégoire le Grand; culture et expérience chrétiennes* (1977), 117–24. Gregory was himself heir to a long tradition, of which Cassian in his Conferences was a notable instance, and St Benedict also an heir. To them all, *discretio* was certainly a virtue—and among monastic virtues, even the greatest—if not precisely classified as *uirtutum mater* in any list of virtues.

p. 230, ll. 3–5. III. 6. **sed et regna ... consecutus est.** There seems to be no good reason for questioning Bede's report of the extent of Oswald's power, even if it gains no solid support from Adomnán's 'totius Brittanniae imperator a Deo ordinatus' (*Vita S. Columbae*, I. 1; ed. A. O. and M. O. Anderson, p. 200). This last is judged 'rhetorical' by D. A. Binchy, *Celtic and Anglo-Saxon Kingship* (1970), 38, but only as a title, not as indicative of wide authority. Bede goes on to make his real point: it was God, through Aidan, who granted Oswald his great increase in power. He cannot have meant that the entire British Isles were subject to Oswald; one exception, uncomfortably near home, was Penda. The fact remained that Oswald's authority, because it was Christian, took no account of language barriers.*

p. 230, ll. 9–10. III. 6. **pauperibus ... largus fuit.** The powerful ruler who cares for the poor appears also in Isidore's description of the Visigoth Swinthila (*Historia Gothorum*, ed. Mommsen, *MGH AA* 11, ch. 64), which Bede did not know. Campbell, 'The Church in Anglo-Saxon Towns', p. 122, gives other examples of Anglo-Saxon provision for the poor. There are equally Frankish instances of royal poor-relief. (See my *Long-Haired Kings*, pp. 217ff.). It may be significant that Oswald's munificence did not occur on any ordinary day: it was Easter Day. Certainly Bede is portraying Oswald as an exemplary king but I doubt if the image in his mind was specifically monastic, as Mayr-Harting suggests, *Coming of Christianity*, p. 255.

p. 230, ll. 24-5. III. 6. **in urbe regia . . . cognominatur.** As Stenton observes (*Preparatory*, pp. 73, 317) Bamburgh—*Bebbanburg* in the Alfredian translation—is the earliest recorded place-name containing a woman's name. It betrays Bede's concern to record in *HE* 'the kind of detail he had compiled for Israelite sites in the *Nomina Locorum*: the names by which each settlement were known, in which language and with what etymology . . .' (McClure, *Ideal and Reality*, p. 95).

p. 230, ll. 28-32. III. 6. **Huius industria . . . et regni.** Bede stresses the natural unity of the Northumbrians: they are a *gens*, Deira and Bernicia are *prouinciae*. 'He used a king-list which extended the single line of Northumbrian kings back into the past beyond the period at which Deira and Bernicia became united as a single kingdom' (Charles-Edwards, 'Bede, the Irish and the Britons', p. 49; see comment on III. 1, p. 212, ll. 5-6). Strictly Edwin was not Oswald's *praecessor*, nor was Oswald his *heres*. The relationship was in fact, as Bede shows, one of feud between the Deiran and Bernician royal families. 'It is essential for Bede's view of Oswald's *imperium* that it should originate in legitimate, or at least appropriate, succession, not in rebellion. Cadwallon's *tyrannis* originated in rebellion against Edwin; Oswald's *imperium* must be different' (ibid., p. 51).

p. 232, ll. 1-2. III. 7. **Eo tempore . . . uocabantur.** The connection in Bede's mind between the preceding chapters and Wessex appears to be Oswald. He had no firm dates for Wessex or for Birinus. His information about Wessex will have come in part from Bishop Daniel, but also from Canterbury and Acca (C. W. Jones, *Saints' Lives*, pp. 48-9, and D. P. Kirby, 'Problems of Early West Saxon History', *EHR* 80 (1965), 11). If ill-informed, he is not uninterested in the West Saxon church; what he records is sufficient illustration of how Christianity reached Wessex and how the West Saxon kings reacted to their bishops. Harrison,

Framework, p. 64, suggests that Birinus may have brought Dionysiac tables with him from Italy to Wessex: Easter tables 'are likely to be found at this time in the luggage of a missionary bishop'. However, neither these nor any West Saxon proto-chronicle or early set of annals, such as may lie behind the well-informed ASC (ibid., p. 135), would seriously have affected Bede's picture had he known them. On West Saxon annals see Stenton, *Preparatory*, pp. 119 ff.

p. 232, ll. 6-8. III. 7. **Vnde et iussu ... gradum.** Birinus is consecrated on the pope's orders by Asterius of Milan, not by Canterbury. Nor does Bede record any intervention by Canterbury in the subsequent appointments of Agilbert and Wine, though Leuthere was consecrated at Canterbury. Brooks, *Early History*, pp. 65 ff., sees this as further evidence of Canterbury's 'impotence' at the time. Perhaps, rather, it is evidence of the isolation of Wessex from Kent, an isolation greater than that of Wessex from Ireland or Francia.

p. 232, ll. 13-20. III. 7. **contigit tunc ... sedem episcopalem.** This is the first occasion, according to Bede, when a king of the Bretwalda-class acts as godfather to another king in that other king's territory. Bede does not say that Oswald acted thus because of his kingly status, nor does he trouble to specify why Oswald should have found himself in Wessex, though his marriage to Cyneburh is surely explanation enough. It seemed sufficient that Oswald was 'uictoriosissimus', and he was that because he was 'sanctissimus'.*

p. 232, ll. 18-19. III. 7. **Donauerunt ... ambo reges.** Why should both kings give Birinus his see at Dorchester with suitable endowment? Plummer thought that the Bretwalda was merely confirming the act of the West Saxon king; but this is not what Bede says. Wormald's explanation is attractive: 'Oswald made use of some of the land that would have come to him from his wife' (personal communication).*

p. 232, ll. 26-8. III. 7. **filius eius Coinualch ... rennuit.** It looks as if Cynegisl had left Cenwalh unbaptized when he might have insisted on it, perhaps to ensure the succession of his family in the event of a pagan reaction. Once king, Cenwalh remained a pagan and lost his kingdom. Bede does not hide the reason for Penda's intervention but implies that if you lose the heavenly kingdom you lose your earthly kingdom as well.

p. 234, ll. 7-8. III. 7. **uenit in prouinciam ... Agilberctus.** Agilbert's 'Roman' sympathies suggest that his Irish years had been spent in the south, and his subsequent association with Wilfrid may indicate that the Frankish and Anglo-Saxon groups in southern Ireland were closely connected (Ó Cróinín, 'Irish Provenance', p. 245). His links were with the heirs of Columbanus, not Columba, and it is of interest that Jouarre, Chelles, and Faremoutiers lay close together, east of Paris (Campbell, 'First Century', pp. 20 ff., discusses the connections). Agilbert ended his life at Jouarre, the family monastery, and there he was buried (see the Marquise de Maillé, *Les Cryptes de Jouarre* (1971), 195-220, for a discussion of his important tomb; and Campbell, *The Anglo-Saxons*, p. 46, for an illustration). I think that T. J. Brown, *Spoleto*, 22 (1975), 252 ff., underestimates Frankish influence on English ecclesiastical development and see no basis for his view that 'it may well have been the Frankish Bishop Agilbert, not the only one of his race to visit Ireland, who brought Irish teachers to Malmesbury when he became bishop of the West Saxons'. On the other hand, Lohaus, *Die Merowinger*, p. 52, may overestimate the Frankish contribution. Agilbert reached Wessex from Ireland, not Francia, and his mission was 'sponte', not 'direkt von Gallien aus'. Nor can one reasonably connect Agilbert with the church dues to be rendered at Martinmas in the Laws of Ine of Wessex, ch. 4 (ibid., p. 46).

p. 234, ll. 14-15. III. 7. **Tandem rex ... barbarae loquellae.** Finberg's speculation (*Early Charters of Wessex*, p. 215) is attractive: 'This sounds very much like the Winchester gossip of a subsequent generation. In reality, it was the Mercian invasion and its territorial consequences which broke up the original diocese, and would have done so even if Agilbert had been the supreme linguist of all time. His accent and vocabulary were not in fact so poor as to deter the king from inviting him back some years later and welcoming another Frank, the bishop's nephew Leuthere, as an acceptable substitute when Agilbert elected to remain in Paris.' Whether or not this is the right explanation, Bede's source is likely to have been Bishop Daniel. Biddle's view is that 'the only reason for Cenwalh's foundation of a church in Winchester seems to be that it too was attached to a pre-existing royal establishment within the walls of a Roman town' (*England before the Conquest*, p. 396) and he goes on to draw attention to 'Frankish adaptation to Roman towns in the Rhineland'. This indeed may explain the choice of Winchester, once a division of the original diocese had been decided on. On linguistic barriers to conversion see Crépin, 'Bede and the Vernacular', *Famulus Christi*, pp. 176 ff.

p. 234, l. 17. III. 7. **ipsum in Gallia ordinatum.** See Grosjean, *Anal. Boll.* 78 (1960), 269.

p. 234, l. 25. III. 7. **emit pretio ab eo.** Bede does not often draw attention to episcopal wealth, preferring to stress the good example of poor bishops (Campbell, 'First Century', p. 14). Wine, consecrated in Gaul, would have been familiar with the Frankish practice of buying and selling ecclesiastical preferment. We do not know that he proved a bad bishop. Wulfhere's reign is analysed by Stenton, 'The Supremacy of the Mercian Kings', *Preparatory*, pp. 48 ff. Bede is not concerned with the reasons why Wine found himself bishop of Winchester, only to be deprived of the see and to be forced to take refuge with Wulfhere. It explained why the West Saxons had no bishop 'tempore non pauco', and why, as he goes on to say, Cenwalh suffered heavy losses: a kingdom without a bishop is justly deprived of divine protection. The whole passage, however, still more strongly suggests that a bishop could not do without a king. Further to Leuthere, Sims-Williams, 'Continental Influence at Bath Monastery in the Seventh Century', *ASE* 4 (1975), 4 ff., and Chaplais, 'The Origin and Authenticity of the Royal Anglo-Saxon Diploma', *Journ. Soc. Archivists*, 3 (1965–9), 55, with evidence of Frankish influence. It was Leuthere who conferred the monastery of Malmesbury on Aldhelm (Levison, *England and the Continent*, p. 226), and in fact more is known from charter-evidence of early monastic foundations in Wessex than Bede knew or recorded.*

p. 236, ll. 16-17. III. 7. **ex synodica sanctione.** I feel little confidence that Bede or his source meant 'no more than a meeting of the king and his counsellors' (Colgrave). Plummer, more cautious, opts for 'a formal synod'. It is possible that it was Theodore who determined that Leuthere should rule 'solus', without a colleague elsewhere; in which case the synodal permission refers to Canterbury.

p. 236, l. 25. III. 8. **Cuius filia Earcongotae.** Bede turns to the question of what happened to royal ladies devoted to religion (i.e. to virginity) and does so in a Kentish–East Anglian context. They are sent to the northern Frankish monasteries, notably Chelles and Faremoutiers, both of which were deeply indebted to an Anglo-Saxon, the Frankish queen Balthildis, and to St Columbanus. (See Prinz, *Frühes Mönchtum*, p. 175). Balthildis' cultural connections are well brought out by Hayo Vierck, 'La "Chemise de Sainte-Balthilde" à Chelles et l'influence byzantine sur l'art de court mérovingien au VIIe siècle', *Centénaire de l'abbé Cochet, 1975; Actes du colloque international d'archéologie* (Rouen, 1978). Bede does not dwell on the implications of Anglo-Frankish connections nor cite other evidence that might have been available (e.g. Frankish associations with B●th Abbey, on which see Sims-Williams, *ASE* 4 (1975), 1 ff.). The Life of the Abbess Bertila of Chelles (*c.* 658-705) records the contrary flow: *Saxoniae reges* sent to her for teachers and for such as might establish monasteries for monks and nuns. Relics and many books were sent with them (*MGH SRM* 6, 106-7). Bede is content to set the scene for the main story of his chapter, which is about royal virginity, not Anglo-Frankish relations. He may have had access to some general account of the proliferation of Frankish Columbanic houses, such as Jonas' Life of St Columbanus.*

p. 238, ll. 11-14. III. 8. **Huius autem uirginis ... sufficiat.** There seems to be a change of style at this point from the annalistic to the hagiographical (noted by C. W. Jones, *Medievalia et Humanistica*, 4 (1946), 33 and n. 10). In part this is imposed on Bede by the matter itself but it is also likely that he had some written account to work on.

p. 238, l. 23, III. 8. **aureum illud nomisma.** Bede, or more likely his Frankish source, thinks of a Byzantine *nomisma*, not of a Roman *solidus*. Paul Antin interprets this as a symbolic reference to the biblical text (Matt. 22: 15–22; Mark 12: 13–17; Luke 20: 20–6), 'render unto Caesar the things that are Caesar's, and unto God the things that are God's' ('Aureum illud nomisma . . . de Cantia', *Journéees internationales d'études mérovingiennes* (1953), 11). I prefer to take it more literally: Eorcongota was required by the angels to pay back the coin with which she was 'bought' on her entry into religion, perhaps on the analogy of St Germanus and St Genovefa (*Vita S. Genovefae*, AA SS Jan. i. 138).

p. 240, l. 21. III. 9. **Osuald Christianissimus rex.** For Bede the significance of Oswald's death is that a Christian warrior-king may not be victorious in battle but there will be rich compensations. The king is active for good after his death. If he fell at Oswestry he had clearly been the aggressor, but that made no difference. It is probable that Bede obtained much of his material about Oswald from Bishop Acca and the church of Hexham, though he does not say so here; and for III. 13 and IV. 14 it is certain. The slant of the information is Bernician, not Deiran. See Kirby, 'Bede's Native Sources for the *Historia Ecclesiastica*', *BJRL* 48 (1965–6), 350. However, the thrust and arrangement of the material will be Bede's own.

p. 240, l. 24. III. 9. **Siquidem, ut supra docuimus.** cf. III. 1.

p. 240, l. 27–p. 242, l. 4. III. 9. **Quo completo . . . mensis Augusti.** If Maserfelth was in fact Oswestry, Finberg (*Lucerna*, p. 73) may be right in supposing that Oswald was engaged on a preventative but unsuccessful campaign to split the coalition between Mercians and Welsh. Further to the implications of the battle for the Welsh, see K. Jackson, *Celt and Saxon*, p. 39, and P. Hunter Blair, *Studies in Early British History*, p. 163.

p. 242, ll. 5–18. III. 9. **Cuius quanta fides . . . satis duximus.** The paragraph is clearly a gloss on the two miracle-stories that are to follow. Moreover, these stories, 'quae a maioribus audiuimus' (ll. 17–18), are an instance where Bede's information certainly comes by word of mouth. It does not follow that they have not been recast by him into a suitable hagiographical form. Folz notes (*Anal. Boll.* 98 (1980), 50) that his picture of royal virtues is inspired 'dans une certaine mesure par le traité *De duodecim abusivis saeculi*'. Bede's 'ubi pro patria dimicans' (ll. 6–7) may echo Gildas' 'dimicare pro patria' (6. 2; *MGH AA* 13. 30; ed. Winterbottom, p. 91), but which 'patria' does Bede mean? Is it Northumbria or is it Oswald's 'patria aeterna'? Alcuin opts for Northumbria (ed. Godman, p. 30). For a valuable general discussion see Ernst Kantorowicz, '*Pro Patria Mori* in Medieval Political Thought', *Selected Studies* (1965), 308–24.

p. 244, l. 6. III. 10. **Eodem tempore.** Bede means what he says: 'at this same time', not 'about this time'. The story follows on from the miracles of the previous chapter. McClure, *Ideal and Reality*, p. 86 n. 56, lists Bede's phrases indicating the passage of time (III. 18, 22; IV. 6) but not all are equally vague. The man concerned in this miracle is a Briton: Oswald's miraculous healing power is not confined to his former Northumbrian subjects.

p. 244, ll. 31–2. III. 11. **quid uirtutis . . . ostensum.** Bede is careful in his use of *uirtus* in such a context as this. It does not mean 'virtue' in our sense. 'Healing power' perhaps comes nearest to it, as sometimes in the Gospels and subsequently in the literature of the Church.

p. 244, l. 32–p. 246, l. 1. III. 11. **cum ossa eius inuenta.** It is unknown where Oswald's bones lay between his death in 642 and their translation to Bardney *c.*679. I do not see why Plummer thinks 'probably at Maserfelth'. For Bede it was sufficient that they were 'discovered' by the Mercian King Æthelred and his queen Osthryth, niece of Oswald, and translated by them to Bardney. The saintly reputation of Oswald may have been fairly widely recognized by this date but it is his kindred who take the critical step in establishing his tomb, and thus his cult, in the church of a monastery. On the significance, for the cult, of enshrinement and entombment, see A. C. Thomas, *Bede, Archaeology, and the Cult of Relics* (Jarrow Lecture, 1973), 6–8. The length of this chapter is by itself evidence of the great importance of the event in Bede's eyes. A royal martyr-saint is a national acquisition. The unexplained assassination of

Osthryth by the Mercians, who tended to dislike queens from Northumbria, is discussed by Finberg, *The Early Charters of the West Midlands*, pp. 176-7.

p. 246, l. 12. III. 11. **ueteranis ... odiis.** Lindsey was repeatedly and alternately dominated by Northumbrians and Mercians, for neither of whom can the inhabitants have had much love. Bede appears to be saying that the community of Bardney, being men of Lindsey, felt hatred towards a Northumbrian king, however holy. But if, as Wormald suggests (personal communication), Bardney was already a Mercian house, then it may have been Mercian resentment that excluded Oswald. Bardney could have been Mercian since its foundation, though we can only claim it as effectively so since Osthryth's intervention and the subsequent retirement there of her husband Æthelred. Stenton, *Preparatory*, p. 181, thinks that it may have been a colony of Medeshamstede (in Middle Anglian territory under Mercian control). Its early history is well summarized by Krüger, *Königsgrabkirchen*, pp. 316-23. Bede and his informant do all they can to emphasize the miraculous circumstances that led the community to change its mind about Oswald's bones.

p. 246, ll. 23-5. III. 11. **regia uiri ... adposuerunt.** The royalty of the saint is demonstrated by the placing of his banner above his tomb. A Northumbrian, he continued to be venerated by Mercian kings (e.g. Offa, as noted by Plummer, ii. 155). To Bede, his sanctity cut across provincial boundaries. He belongs to an uncommon class of royal saint: those killed by pagan invaders. For other classes see D. W. Rollason, 'The Cults of Murdered Royal Saints in Anglo-Saxon England', *ASE* 11 (1983), 1-22.

p. 246, ll. 30-5. III. 11. **Denique tempore ... habebat.** These details are a necessary introduction to the miracle that follows, not an attempt to squeeze in some more local history.

p. 248, ll. 18-19. III. 11. **dicebat presbyter exorcismos.** Plummer's excellent note on exorcism fails to draw attention to Bede's point: exorcism, a proper remedy of the Church, failed where a miracle performed by Oswald (through water used to wash his bones) succeeded. Gregory of Tours records another case where exorcism failed (*Hist.* VII. 44), though the correct procedure for dealings with evil spirits had been followed by a bishop. I discuss the passage above, pp. xxx–xxxi. Æthelhild's community was clearly a double monastery of a type commoner in Francia than in England. A good recent account is J. Godfrey, 'The Place of the Double Monastery in the Anglo-Saxon Minster System', *Famulus Christi*, pp. 344–50.

p. 248, l. 27. III. 11. **Conticuere omnes . . . tenebant.** Hunter Blair comments: 'this line is part of the grammarians' stock-in-trade, a Virgilian cliché which will have been familiar to every schoolboy' ('From Bede to Alcuin', *Famulus Christi*, p. 244). This may be true, at least of Bede's schoolboys, but it is no proof that Bede himself did not know what followed in *Aeneid* II: Aeneas' vivid account to Dido of the sack of Troy. Hunter Blair's paper is an important contribution to the problem of how much Virgil Bede was actually acquainted with. There can be no doubt that the insertion of the Virgilian line at this point heightens the dramatic suspense that Bede himself feels: will the miracle work? The *exitus* would be proof of very much.*

p. 250, l. 22–p. 252, l. 4. III. 12. **Denique ferunt . . . condidit.** Bede continues with the miracle of the cure of the oblate at Oswald's tomb in Bardney and appears to rely on the source that provided the previous chapter; and the following passage, an oral tradition concerning Oswald's habit of prayer, is connected in a general way with a miracle that depended on Oswald's continuing prayers in heaven. But the translation of his head to Lindisfarne and his hands and arms to Bamburgh might have fitted in earlier in the narrative and seems unconnected with the rest of the chapter. The placing of the hands and arms at Bamburgh sounds like a secular event; certainly their exposure, with the head ('in stipitibus suspendi', p. 252, l. 1), by Penda was common Germanic practice as evidence of vengeance taken. The hand and arm of Grendel were hung up in Heorot by Beowulf for men to wonder at. The Roman tradition was that saint's bodies should remain entire in their resting-places. The case of Oswald was exceptional: 'Bede's emphasis should perhaps be seen as a deliberate effort to explain the fragmentation of a body, which did in fact lead to a confusing multiplicity of relic-claims' (Rollason, *ASE* 7 (1978), 81). However, Bede did not object to limbs of other saints being placed in Alban's tomb (I. 18).

p. 252, ll. 7–8. III. 13. **Denique ... Acca solet referre.** This is the only miracle of Oswald's that Bede says he derives from Acca (but cf. IV. 14). It may have been the direct record of conversation between Bede and Acca but on the other hand it might have been based on a written narrative that was itself the result of conversation. The length of the account suggests the latter.

p. 252, ll. 8–10. III. 13. **cum Romam uadens ... moraretur.** Bede sees nothing incongruous in the companionship of Acca and Wilfrid on their continental journey in 703 and visit to Willibrord, presumably at Utrecht or Echternach. He does not see one as worldly and the other as unworldly. Willibrord will have taken relics of Oswald to Frisia. On the continental cult of Oswald (German rather than French) see P. Clemoes, *The Cult of St Oswald on the Continent* (Jarrow Lecture, 1983), 4 ff. The king's day, 5 August, is noted in the original hand in Willibrord's calendar.

p. 252, ll. 19–21. III. 13. **scolasticus ... gerens.** Bede or Acca appears to associate the scholar's vice with his scholarship, and indeed it seems unlikely that a dedicated scholar would be living fast and loose. Bede may have had in mind Pseudo-Cyprian's *De XII Abusivis Saeculi* (composed before 700) or one of its sources. This begins with the words: 'Primus abusionis gradus est, si sine bonis operibus sapiens et praedicator fuerit.'

p. 254, ll. 25–30. III. 14. **Translato ... Oidilualdo.** The heart of this chapter is the life of Oswine and its necessary introduction is to explain how he came to be reigning over Deira while his second cousin, Oswiu, reigned in Bernicia. Bede does not pause to explain why Oswiu should have been challenged by Alhfrith and Ethelwald or why Oswiu and Oswine were enemies. He recounts the facts as briefly as he can. On the length of Oswiu's reign see Harrison, 'The Reign of King Ecgfrith of Northumbria', *Yorks. Archaeol. Journ.* 43 (1971), 83. McClure, *Ideal and Reality*, p. 86, comments on the level of importance in Bede's mind, 'upon which modern historians naturally pounce', of linking material such as the political troubles following Oswald's death; was he influenced by the way in which the compilers of the first Book of Samuel added sentences to give structure to their account? In particular, was the account of Saul's jealousy of David, and 'his ploys when his rival sought to refuge among the Philistines', in Bede's mind when he came to the clashes between Oswiu and Oswine (p. 90)?

p. 254, l. 32-p. 256, l. 5. III. 14. **pater Paulinus ... aequandum.** This insertion may derive from a source other than that of the main material of the chapter. Paulinus' nineteen years as a bishop may have been much commented upon, but Kirby, 'Bede and Northumbrian Chronology', *EHR* 78 (1963), 516, persuades me that Bede's calculation is correct. The great bishop is buried in his church at Rochester which Æthelberht had built 'a fundamentis' (i.e. it was not a refurbished pagan shrine) and is succeeded by Ithamar, equally learned although he was a local product.

p. 256, ll. 26-8. III. 14. **Quod factum ... Ingetlingum.** The ultimate source of Bede's information on Oswine's murder may well be the monastery of Gilling or possibly Whitby, though more immediately it could be Bede's own abbot, Ceolfrith, who had been a novice at Gilling. If this is so, then most of the chapter may derive from Ceolfrith, another driving-force behind the composition of *HE*. On the foundation of Gilling, in which Oswiu himself may have played a part, Rollason speculates (*ASE* 11 (1983), 21) that this could be a case where a royal murderer, in presenting himself as a benefactor of his victim's cult, was seeking to diminish the effectiveness of the cult as a focus for the forces of social tension and political opposition. One would not expect Bede to say this—indeed, he rather implies that it was God himself who needed propitiating—but there can be no doubt about the rapidity with which the cult took root. Oswine appears, apparently as a saint, in Willibrord's calendar. Kirby, *BJRL* 48 (1965-6), 351, emphasizes the distinctions between Bede's Bernician information about Oswiu and his Deiran information about Oswine.*

p. 256, l. 32–p. 258, l. 4. III. 14. **Erat autem ... exemplo.** This exuberant summary of Oswine's virtues sounds, and partly is, conventional, though Bede's treatment does not follow a normal hagiographical pattern. But the summary is important to Bede as a model for his own contemporaries: this is how a Christian king should be. The crux for Bede was that Oswine was a *rex humilis*. R. Folz, *Les Saints Rois*, pp. 222–3, insists that the recorded personality of a saintly king is reconstructed humility; and it is this that gives the seal of authenticity to the portrait. *Humilitas* was not among the virtues attributed to Christian emperors of the fourth century, though Ambrose praised Gratian for the 'lofty humility' he showed in writing to him in his own hand. By the sixth century, a Frankish king can be urged to practise humility in what amounts to an early example of a Mirror of Princes. I have considered the matter in *The Long-Haired Kings*, pp. 191 ff. See also Roger Collins, *Ideal and Reality*, p. 22. However, Patrick Wormald, reflecting on Bede in relation to *Beowulf*, writes: 'It now seems very likely that King Oswald of the Bernicians (633–42) was actually much more like King Hygelac of the Geatas than any reader of Bede's famous chapters would immediately appreciate, and both kings certainly met the same sort of death' ('Bede, "Beowulf" and the Conversion of the Anglo-Saxon Aristocracy', in *Bede and Anglo-Saxon England* (Brit. Arch. Reports, 46; 1978), 35). The same may be true of Oswine, at least as far as 'manu omnibus ... largus' (p. 256, ll. 33–4) can take us.

p. 258, ll. 35–6. III. 14. **Vnde animaduerto ... rectorem.** Kirby, *BJRL* 48 (1965–6), p. 351, comments: 'It is to be noted that in the stories about Aidan and the kings, Oswald and Oswine, the intention is less to illustrate the saintliness of Aidan than to extol that of the kings. Aidan was intended to be a figure of only secondary importance.' None the less, their saintliness, and particularly the lesson of humility, was the result of Aidan's mission.

p. 260, l. 5. III. 15. **internus arbiter.** The Moore and Leningrad MSS agree on the reading 'internus'. It is not biblical. Bede also uses it in *De Tabernaculo* (ed. D. Hurst, p. 98): 'et in conspectu interni arbitri oportet esse gloriosa'. He was clearly influenced by

Gregory's 'internus iudex' (e.g. *Curia Past*, 2. 3, and several times in the *Moralia*), of which 'internus arbiter' is a variant. Full reference in Dom Michael Frickel, *Deus Totus Ubique Simul* (1956), 113 n. 73, for knowledge of which I am indebted to Ann Freeman.

p. 260, ll. 6–7. III. 15. **Presbyter quidam nomine Utta.** Bede now relates the first of three miracles attributed to Aidan, and it is clearly biblical in inspiration. Mayr-Harting, *Coming of Christianity*, p. 48, comments: 'If one looks at the groups of miracles which Bede told about a particular saint, one sometimes sees a very interesting thing; some of the stories will come from the monastery where the saint was specially revered, but one will perhaps come from a personal friend of Bede who had nothing to do with that monastery. Thus there are three miracles about Aidan. Two of them probably came from Whitby ... but the third ... was told to Bede by a monk of his own monastery'. I agree with Plummer that this Cynemund (l. 31) is likely to be Cynemund of Lindisfarne. Tugène, 'L'Hist. "eccl." ', p. 150, makes this point on Bede's account of miracles: 'ce qui compte pour lui, c'est la valeur du miracle en tant que "signe", et non son côté merveilleux.' It is the interior significance of a miracle that counts, and thus it may not be chance that the chapter begins with 'internus arbiter'.

p. 260, ll. 9–10. III. 15. **ob adducendam ... Eanfledam.** Presumably Oswiu's second queen, the first having been a princess of Rheged according to the Anglo-Saxon genealogies in the *Historia Brittonum*. See K. Jackson on the evidence (*Celt and Saxon*, p. 41).*

p. 260, l. 27. III. 15. **per prophetiae spiritum.** On the medieval understanding of prophecy, see R. W. Southern, 'Aspects of the European Tradition of Historical Writing: 3. History as Prophecy', *TRHS* 5th ser. 22 (1972), 159–80.

p. 262, l. 4. III. 16. **peruenit ... regiam.** This miracle, known to many, is evidence for Bede's readers of a different aspect of the miraculous help a saint can afford: he can save an *urbs regia*. God can protect a town as well as individuals, using the saint as his instrument. We should know nothing of Penda's expedition against Bamburgh if Bede had not introduced it incidentally into his narrative to provide the occasion for Aidan's miracle. 'Vide, Domine, quanta mala facit Penda' (ll. 18-19) sounds like the crystal round which the story has come to be shaped, as is not uncommon in accounts of miracles.

p. 264, l. 38. III. 17. **quasi uerax historicus.** Bede closes his account of Aidan with a miracle associated with his death and summarizes what he thinks of the saint's character and work. He, more even than Cuthbert, is Bede's holy bishop. The summary has been much commented upon; see for example C. W. Jones, *Saints' Lives*, pp. 84-5. Bede is saying two things and wishes them to be taken in conjunction: first, that Aidan had all the episcopal virtues so notably absent in the *segnitia* of present times and, secondly, that Aidan was quite wrong (if understandably) about the date of Easter. In other words, the 'uerax historicus' will benefit his readers by frankly ('simpliciter') rebuking error and praising virtue. Was Bede influenced here, as so often, by Gregory the Great? 'Gregory is always willing to acknowledge the "bonum" wherever it may be found. Despite the many hard things he has to say about heretics in general . . .' (Meyvaert, 'Diversity within Unity', p. 149 n. 1).

p. 264, ll. 1-2. III. 17. **ut adclinis destinae.** Mayr-Harting, *Coming of Christianity*, p. 30, comments: 'Aidan's pillar succeeded Thor's.' Though not meant literally, this makes the important point that even in Aidan's day, and after, Christianity subsumed what it could of pagan practices still dear to ordinary people. It had to.

p. 264, ll. 8-9. III. 17. **translata ... ad dexteram altaris.** 'The Vitae [sc. of Cuthbert] always use *ecclesia Lindisfarnensium* al. *Lindisfarnensis*—never *ecclesia sancti Aidani*, even though his relics had been translated to the right side of the altar in the later 650s' (Bullough, 'Missions to the English', p. 94 n. 44). This is evidence of the eclipse of the cult of Aidan by that of Cuthbert.

p. 266, ll. 20-3. III. 17. **Vnde et hanc ... ad uicesimam.** Bede makes every excuse for Aidan's Easter observance at the wrong time. The Irish did not fall under the same condemnation as the British. They were no heretics, even though the accusation is allowed to stand unchallenged in a papal letter (II. 19). 'The important thing is that the justice of God was exemplified in their *correctio* for it was *per gentem Anglorum*. The spiritual debt was discharged' (Charles-Edwards, 'Bede, the Irish and the Britons', p. 44). See Harrison, *Framework*, p. 31 n. 1, on Quarto-decimanians, and 'Easter Cycles and the Equinox in the British Isles', *ASE* 7 (1978), 1-8; also C. W. Jones, *Saint's Lives*, p. 6: 'Bede, who has often been accused of excessive rancor on the subject [sc. of the Easter controversy], turns out to be the mildest controversionalist of them all.'

p. 266, ll. 27-8. III. 18. **His temporibus ... eius praefuit.** Bede turns to a saintly East Anglian king, Sigeberht, who retires to his own monastery and is brought out by his warriors to inspire them in their fight against Penda. He falls in battle. Bede records no miracle associated with him; it was enough that he had chosen the monastic life despite his obvious success as king; and of this Bede strongly approves. It is unknown where Sigeberht was buried; and where no recognized tomb survived there was unlikely to be a cult. This account clearly illustrates Bede's indifference to the secular obligations of kingship. Stenton calls the East Anglian kings of the seventh century 'an unlucky house'. 'It is remarkable that under these kings, whose reigns were generally short and sometimes disastrous, Christianity should have become rooted in East Anglia so firmly that it was unaffected by the fortunes of local rulers' (*Preparatory*, p. 399). I doubt if Bede would have called them 'an unlucky house', or meant them to be seen so.

p. 266, l. 32. III. 18. **instituit scholam ... erudirentur.** This almost amounts to a standard form in continental texts relating to education at a cathedral school. Sigeberht is inspired by schools he has seen in Gaul to attempt something of the same kind in East Anglia but it is Bishop Felix who provides teachers from Kent. The school must therefore be called Kentish rather than Frankish, despite Sigeberht's Frankish affinities and the likelihood that there may have been very little difference between them. But it should warn us not to belittle Canterbury before Theodore's arrival, as does Brooks, *Early History*, p. 94, though not Chaplais, 'Who introduced Charters', pp. 531-2. The correspondence to which Plummer refers between the Frankish king, Sigibert III, and Bishop Desiderius of Cahors is genuine (*MGH Epp*. 3. 194-5) and is relevant to the relations of the East Anglian kings with their clergy in as much as the East Anglian Sigeberht was familiar with precisely this Frankish context. See Pierre Riché, *Education et culture dans l'occident barbare* VIe-VIIIe *siècles* (1962), 362-3; and, on Sigeberht's Frankish associations, Lohaus, *Die Merowinger und England*, pp. 31-3, 130. Bede goes on to distinguish between the 'pedagogos' and 'magistros' of Sigeberht's school, meaning perhaps those in charge of the children and those who taught the older boys, as P. F. Jones first suggested ('The Gregorian Mission and English Education', *Speculum*, 3 (1928), 347).

p. 268, ll. 13-14. III. 18. **duce . . . et eximio.** Bede does not conceal the reason why his former warriors compelled Sigeberht to join them against Penda: he had himself been a distinguished warrior and leader before entering his monastery. It was not his piety that had moved them. For Bede, however, he gains added merit by appearing in battle with 'nonnisi uirgam tantum' (l. 16) though this in context may have been a symbol of authority (as also the crozier in III. 22, p. 284). Compare Gregory of Tours, *Hist.* VII. 32.

p. 268, ll. 24-5. III. 19. **superuenit . . . Furseus.** Bede turns to Felix's contemporary, the Irishman, Fursa, of whom he has a Life (Gallo-Irish) that he can resume, omitting some gruesome details and rearranging to permit the emphases he wants, but sticking to the facts. 'Bede's chapter on St Fursa resembles so much the earliest *Vita S. Fursei* . . . that the latter is either a close reproduction of Bede's *libellus* or, more probably, identical with it' (L. Bieler, 'Ireland's Contribution to the Culture of Northumbria', *Famulus Christi*, pp. 222-3). Bede's knowledge of the *Vita* may have come from Abbot Esi, as C. W. Jones suggests (*Saint's Lives*, p. 49). Whatever the field of Fursa's activity in East Anglia, or its success, it is for his visionary experience that Bede thinks him worthy of extended treatment. I see no reason for associating Fursa with Felix, as does Françoise Henry, 'Irish Enamels of the Dark Ages and their Relation to the Cloisonné Techniques', in *Dark-Age Britain* (1956), 81. Claude Carozzi, *Spoleto*, 29 (1983), 449 ff., emphasizes the very different treatment of the after-world in Bede's accounts of Fursa and of Dryhthelm (v. 12). Once again, Bede feels bound by what he sees as facts in his sources. To him, as to Fursa, the vivid impression must have remained that it was a hard matter to get into heaven; only penitence could clear the way. The same difficulty struck King Oswiu at the synod of Whitby. Charles-Edwards, 'The Social Background to Irish *peregrinatio*', *Celtica*, 11 (1976), 57-8, shows from Fursa's *Vita* how the saint progressed in the Irish manner from asceticism to the lower, and finally to the superior, grade of *peregrinatio*, which could involve missionary work. Bede stresses this work in a way that his source does not, but does not suggest that the activities of Fursa, or of Aidan, were exclusively Irish. He sees them rather as 'models of orthodox holiness, practitioners of virtues inculcated by the Fathers, above all Gregory the Great' (A. Thacker, 'Bede's Ideal of Reform', *Ideal and Reality*, p. 146).

p. 270, ll. 10-11. III. 19. **in castro quodam ... uocatur.** The name of the site is Bede's addition. He does not often record the foundation of monasteries, unless connected with Iona. There may have been hundreds such in his lifetime. (See Campbell, 'First Century', p. 15.) The identification of Cnobheresburg with Burgh Castle (excavation still incomplete) is questioned by Campbell (in *Names, Words and Graves*, p. 36 n. 6). Bullough argues ('Missions to the English', p. 88 n. 25) that the extensive remains there of Christian burial and occupation may point to the early siting of the East Anglian see-church rather than Fursa's monastery. At least it is certain that Fursa's site was a royal gift, and thereafter an object of royal bounty; and this interests Bede.

p. 270, ll. 34-5. III. 19. **legat ipsum ... accipiet.** Bede envisages no 'popular' audience for *HE*; there will be readers to whom the text of the *libellus* will be available in a (presumably) monastic library.

p. 274, l. 22. III. 19. **Superest adhuc frater.** An excellent example of Bede's reporting of a verbally transmitted recollection: (1) Fursa himself; (2) 'ueracem ac religiosum hominem'; (3) 'frater . . . senior' at Jarrow; (4) Bede.

p. 274, l. 30. III. 19. **ut ad superiora redeamus.** The chapter, as Plummer observed (ii. 169–70), seems untidily arranged, possibly because Bede had already drafted his account of Fursa in East Anglia before the *Vita S. Fursei* reached his hands. The vision is introduced by give-away words, 'in quibus . . . duximus' (p. 272, ll. 1–2), that betray that Bede is 'conscious of inserting something intrusive into his narrative' (Markus, *Bede and the Tradition of Ecclesiastical Historiography* (Jarrow Lecture, 1975), 8).

p. 274, l. 34. III. 19. **in prouinciam Anglorum.** As Wormald notes ('Bede, the *Bretwaldas* and the Origins of the *Gens Anglorum*', *Ideal and Reality*, p. 121 n. 94), Bede substitutes 'Angles' for the 'Saxons' of the continental *Vita*, since 'Saxons' would have been inaccurate.

p. 276, l. 6. III. 19. **Dein turbatam . . . uidens.** On the invasions that prompted Fursa's move to the continent, see D. Whitelock, 'The Pre-Viking Age Church in East Anglia', *ASE* 1 (1972), 5 ff. The plural, as she notes, is of interest. She summarizes what more can be gleaned from the account of Fóillán, Fursa's half-brother, written at Nivelles not later than 655–6. 'The interest of the Nivelles account for ecclesiastical history is that it suggests that the monastery of *Cnobheresburg* came to an end by c. 651, or at least that it was then deserted by its Celtic inmates. There is no further evidence of Celtic influence in the East Anglian church' (p. 6). For a fuller account of the Nivelles material, P. Grosjean, *Anal. Boll.* 78 (1960), 365–9.

p. 276, ll. 9–10. III. 19. **monasterium construxit . . . nominato.** A reliable account of the founding of Lagny and Péronne is F. Prinz, *Frühes Mönchtum*, pp. 128 ff. The basic work on the Irish contribution to the spiritual and intellectual revival of northern France remains Ludwig Traube, *Perrona Scottorum* (reprinted in *Vorlesungen und Abhandlungen* (1920), iii. 95–119). Bernhard

Bischoff's 'Il monachesimo irlandese nei suoi rapporti col continente' (*Spoleto* 4 (1957), 121–38) is a valuable general survey, and Ludwig Bieler, *Ireland, Harbinger of the Middle Ages* (1963), contains useful summaries. The claim that the *paruchia Fursei* supported by some Frankish magnates 'played some part in Frankish politics' (K. Hughes, *The Church in Early Irish Society* (1966), 82) is certainly as far as one should go. Irish missionaries on the continent, as in England, were dependent on royal patronage, despite their acerbic rebuking of royal vice. Krusch's introduction to his edition of the *Vita S. Fursei*, together with the saint's (later) *Virtutes* and the Nivelles *Additamentum de Fuilano* (the two last not known to Bede), reveals the limited impact of the Irish migration on Frankish 'politics' (*MGH SRM* 4. 423–9). Uncertain of Merovingian support, the Irish turned to the early Carolingians (on the political aspect, see R. Sprandel, *Der merowingische Adel* (1957), 51 ff.; and on their cults, L. Gougaud, *Les Saints irlandais hors d'Irlande* (1936), 108–13). A more immediately significant point is that the Irish *peregrini* were as welcome in Frankish circles as they had been in East Anglia, and for this they had ultimately to thank the great pioneer, St Columbanus, and their own adoption of the mixed Columbanic–Benedictine Rule.*

p. 276, l. 25. III. 20. **Interea, defuncto Felice.** The link with the preceding chapter is the death of Felix, whom Bede plainly thinks more important, if less interesting, than Fursa. Episcopal lists are clearly being used for the following summary of episcopal succession. Harrison, *Framework*, p. 96, notes that Bede knew the length of reign of two East Anglian bishops but did not have enough information to supply dates *Anno Domini* and was not prepared to guess. 'The *Historia* is littered with expressions like *interea, mox, plus minus, eo tempore, circiter*, which may fairly be said to outnumber the positive dates' (ibid., n. 21). It is Archbishop Honorius who consecrates Felix's successor, Thomas, but neither here nor elsewhere in the chapter could I go so far as Brooks, *Early History*, p. 66, in claiming that Canterbury's authority was 'virtually limited to the kingdoms of Kent and East Anglia'. 'Virtually' is an extendible concept.

p. 276, l. 27. III. 20. **de prouincia Gyruiorum.** On the Gyrwe, an example of a minor English grouping that persisted, see H. Loyn, *Anglo-Saxon England and the Norman Conquest* (1962), 24.

p. 278, ll. 4-5. III. 20 **Ordinatus est ... duos dies.** Harrison, *Framework*, p. 93, accepts Grosjean's argument for dating Deusdedit's consecration as 12 March 655, which, as must have been known, was the feast of Gregory the Great. It is unclear whether the slip, 26 March, was due to Bede or to his Canterbury informant. Stenton, *Anglo-Saxon England*, p. 129, prefers reading 'menses vii' to 'menses iiii', thus placing the synod of Whitby in 663 instead of 664; but this is not generally accepted. Deusdedit was the first English archbishop of Canterbury: Thomas, Berhtgisl, Deusdedit, and Damian were all Englishmen. What is more interesting is the spread of English provinces from which they came. There is no valid reason for thinking that Honorius was an Englishman.

p. 278, ll. 8-10. III. 21. **Middilengli ... perceperunt.** A possible source for this report on the conversion of the Middle Angles, so notably short on exact dating, would be Utta ('presbyter inlustris', l. 29), brother of Adda. It reads like information received by word of mouth. (Jones, *Saints' Lives*, p. 48, surveys the few records we have for early Mercia and concludes that 'any dated record purporting to originate in Mercia in the seventh century is suspect'.) Of the kings Bede here discusses, he says, and perhaps knows, nothing that is irrelevant to conversion. For example, there is no mention of Merewalh, ruler of the Magonsæte, allegedly Penda's third son and father of St Mildburg of Much Wenlock. (See Finberg, *Lucerna*, pp. 70 ff., and *Early Charters of the West Midlands*, pp. 217 ff.) Nor does Bede develop reasons for the surprising attitude to Christianity of Penda towards the end of his life: it seems to go rather further towards acceptance than the attitude of Redwald (a personal insurance-policy). Whereas Bede is clear about the essential unity of Deirans and Bernicians, he is equally clear that Mercians and Middle Angles are distinct. See however Wendy Davies, 'Middle Anglia and the Middle Angles', *Midland History*, 2 (1973-4), 18-20, who argues that Middle Anglia was neither more nor less than southern Mercia and was never a separate kingdom but a dependent province. The Middle Angles were not 'a close-knit group but a conglomeration of different Anglian groups in the Midlands. In so far as they have a political identity it is artificially imposed and it does not appear to last beyond Peada's administration.' However, as she also notes, Middle Anglia supports, and continues to support, a bishopric.

p. 278, ll. 15-19. III. 21. **audita praedicatione ... Alchfrido.** Peada is converted partly by Irish preaching, partly by the arguments of Alhfrith, a Roman sympathizer. This suggests that the two 'parties' enjoyed a measure of common ground, which is also implied by the consecration of the Englishman Trumhere as bishop by the Irish, at the end of the chapter; an incident that seems to surprise Bede. As to Alhfrith's arguments, an alliance between Deirans and Middle Angles might have other than religious consequences: but these do not concern Bede or presumably his source or sources of information. All that mattered was that Peada had sought alliance by marriage in Northumbria and ended a convert.

p. 278, ll. 24-5. III. 21. **acceptis quattuor presbyteris.** Of one of the three Englishmen, Betti, we may have the shrine-lid from Wirksworth in Derbyshire. See A. C. Thomas, *Early Christian Archaeology*, p. 158.*

p. 280, l. 1. III. 21. **Ad Caprae Caput.** B. Dickins, 'Place-Names Formed from Animal-Head Names', appendix 1 to J. E. B. Gover, A. Mawer, and F. M. Stenton, *The Place-Names of Surrey* (EPNS 11; Cambridge, 1934), 403-6, argues that the name contains a reminiscence of pagan goat-sacrifice. Bede will also have been aware of the implications of this practice from a passage in Gregory's *Dialogues* (III. 28) concerning Lombard goat-sacrifice.*

p. 280, l. 3. III. 21. **libenter auditi sunt.** The missionaries met with no opposition to their preaching from Middle Angles or Mercians of any rank. However, conversion did not go very deep with some, as Penda disdainfully observed.

p. 280, ll. 15–16. III. 21. **Paucitas enim sacerdotum.** Clear evidence that in Bede's view the Mercians and Middle Angles were distinct *nationes* and, further, that a *natio* was entitled to a bishop.

p. 280, ll. 26–7. III. 22. **Orientales Saxones fidem ... receperunt.** Hingeing his narrative on the missionary zeal of Oswiu—whose 'instantia' is 'pressure'—Bede is able to give a fuller account of the re-conversion of the East Saxons than of the conversion of the East Angles. He does not mean by 'eo tempore', as Plummer says, that missionary activity was 'strictly contemporary' in Essex and Middle Anglia; he means that he does not know. His information for this chapter and the next appears to come from the monks of Lastingham (in the fortunes of which Cedd played an important part), and they seem to have been short on any chronological information. (See C. W. Jones, *Saints' Lives*, pp. 49, 196, though I do not know what Jones means by adding that 'the history they [the Lastingham monks] compiled may well have been taken from contemporary letters'.) If Cedd and his colleagues kept any chronological records they would have presumably have been in Irish. There is no justification for thinking that Oswiu put pressure on Essex because he was a Bretwalda; indeed, he was put to some trouble to persuade Sigeberht II to convert; but it is certainly evidence of his power that he was able to move Cedd from the Middle Angles to the East Saxons.*

p. 280, l. 31–p. 282, l. 11. III. 22. **solebat eum hortari ... praemia essent percepturi.** This is a basic statement by Bede on the nature of God and of idols, with which one naturally compares the advice given by Bishop Daniel of Winchester to St Boniface (Letter 23, ed. Tangl, pp. 38–41), and, equally relevant, Gregory of Tours, *Hist.* II. 10, rich in Old Testament parallels. Bede turns spontaneously to the language of the prophets and the Psalms; the Old Testament provides the natural parallel when it comes to stigmatizing idolatry. Tugène, 'L'Hist. "eccl."', pp. 152–3, adds that Bede's wish to present ancestral history as a kind of collection of *exempla* for his contemporaries is associated with the conviction that the reward of piety or of sin was the real

motive force of history; and this was an essential message of the
Old Testament.

p. 284, l. 3. III. 22. **disciplinam uitae regularis.** Bede is speaking
of two sites in particular where churches were established and
clergy appointed. They appear to have been minsters, centres
from which clergy operated in the surrounding countryside.
Such clergy would naturally live under discipline, that is to say
under a local rule appropriate to secular clergy, as happened in
Francia. Bede does not mean that they lived under a recognized
monastic rule. For the royal gift of *Ythancæstir* see Campbell, *The
Anglo-Saxons*, p. 50, and A. C. Thomas, *Early Christian Archaeology*, p. 34. H. M. and J. Taylor, *Anglo-Saxon Architecture*, i. 91-3
accept the present remains of *Ythancæstir* at Bradwell-on-Sea as
those of Cedd's church. They do not point out that the Kentish
style of the building—and what else could it have been?—is a
further warning not to distinguish too sharply between the
Celtic and Roman approaches to conversion in England.

p. 284, ll. 7-9. III. 22. **contigit ipsum regem ... interfici.** The
murder of Sigeberht II by his kinsmen is suggestive of pagan
conservatism: it was no business of a king to pardon his enemies
merely because he was a Christian. Vengeance should be taken.
However, he had himself sinned by entering the house of one of
them, unlawfully married in Cedd's eyes, when he had been
forbidden to do so. Bede does not specify what he means by
'inlicitum coniugium' (l. 17): presumably it was a marriage within
the Church's prohibited degrees, though perfectly proper in
Germanic pagan practice. I have looked at the general issues
involved in *The Frankish Church*, XVI (ii). One might suspect that
Bede did not see eye to eye with Cedd on the degree of the
king's guilt. On the often menacing demeanour of Irish missionaries see Campbell, 'First Century', p. 23.

p. 284, l. 35. III. 22. **in uico regio ... Rendlaesham.** R. L. S.
Bruce-Mitford judiciously summarized what was then known of
Rendlesham and its possible connection with Sutton Hoo in
'Saxon Rendlesham', *Proc. Suffolk Inst. of Archaeol. and Nat. Hist.* 24
(1948), iii. 228-51. Baptism in the *uicus regius* does not neces-
sarily indicate a church or a baptistry. There had been no church

on the banks of the Swale and the Glen. Rendlesham had been pagan, residence of a pagan king, until the occasion of his baptism.

p. 286, ll. 6–7. III. 23. **postulauit ... monasterium accipere.** Ethelwald envisages burial in a monastic church founded by himself and for that purpose. He does not plan to lie with his kindred. The security of a burial-place is not infrequently the motive for the foundation of churches. The long description of the process of foundation that follows, 'in montibus arduis ac remotis' (l. 17), is very much a literary topos. Compare for example the founding of Condat by St Romanus (*Vie des pères du Jura*, ed. F. Martine (*SC* 142; 1968), pp. 242 ff.). In fact the old road from York and Malton to Whitby passed Lastingham some 10 km to the east. The pollution from which the site had to be cleared by fasting was not that of pagan shrines but of evil spirits that inhabited any deserted place. Bede believes in these as firmly as did Cedd and his brothers, and his thoughts move to Isaiah's habitations where once dragons lay. The comparison assists his monastic readers to place the process within a biblical category they understood (Tugène, 'L'Hist. "eccl."', p. 147 n.). See Krüger, *Königsgrabkirchen*, pp. 300–4, and H. M. and J. Taylor, *Anglo-Saxon Architecture*, i. 372–3 (for what evidence remains of Anglo-Saxon occupation).

p. 288, ll. 13–14. III. 23. **Dedit autem ... Ceadda.** Hereditary succession to monasteries occurred from time to time in seventh-century Northumbria as elsewhere (in Ireland and on the continent). A proprietary right remained with the founder.

p. 290, ll. 4–5. III. 24. **rex perfidus ... praeberet.** Plummer draws attention to 'Nennius' ' account, where Oswiu's bribe is extorted by Penda. 'Nennius' may not have been wrong; or there may have been two offers of treasure, one accepted and the other rejected (according to Campbell, 'Bede', p. 170). Bede, less warm about Oswiu personally than about others of his house, excuses the king, 'necessitate cogente' (p. 288, l. 37), for offering a bribe in the first place: it was not a kingly thing to do (see Cross, 'The Ethic of War', p. 269). There are other features of Bede's account that suggest inaccuracies somewhere down the line of the reporting of this major engagement. But in any case it was not the engagement itself that focused Bede's attention but Oswiu's offer to God and the Church, 'si uictor existeret' (p. 290, ll. 9–10).*

p. 290, ll. 8–9. III. 24. 'Si paganus . . . Deo nostro'. Judith McClure, *Ideal and Reality*, pp. 88 ff., draws attention to the parallels between Bede's account of the occasion and what he would have read in his Old Testament: 'The battle of the Winwaed itself was described in terms all to be found in the Vulgate text of Samuel and Kings.' I think it is true that he had learned from the Old Testament how 'to ask the pertinent questions about significant military encounters in the history of his own people'; in other words, to reduce to certain formulae the reports (possibly conflicting) of such encounters as reached him.

p. 290, l. 26. III. 24. **auctor ipse belli.** Since Plummer's time this passage has raised problems. How could Æthelhere, a comparatively unimportant figure, be the cause of the war without further explanation? There seems to be no doubt about what Bede wrote, and one might suppose that in his anxiety to get to the religious outcome of Oswiu's victory he chose not to pause over explanations. P. Hunter Blair considers the account of Penda's death in 'The Bernicians and their Northern Frontier', in *Studies in Early British History*, pp. 163 ff. However, J. O. Prestwich, 'King Æthelhere and the Battle of the Winwaed', *EHR* 83 (1968), 89–95, offers another explanation: if a full-stop is allowed after 'regnauit' (and there is some justification for this) then the 'auctor' could be not Æthelhere but Penda, who may have been slain in the battle (Bede is obscure here) and could most reasonably be considered its 'auctor'. Even so, and attractive as the argument is, Bede's sentence strikes me as clumsy rather than dramatic. Has something dropped out between 'regnauit' and 'auctor', perhaps in the report that reached him? One might have expected to see another sentence like 'Auctor . . . interemptus' or, for that matter, another ending like 'in quibus . . . regnavit'. That would be more in Bede's style. However, he may simply be copying his source. Prestwich does not prove his point (*pace* Campbell, *The Anglo-Saxons*, p. 249) but one would like him to be right.

p. 292, ll. 2-5. III. 24. **donatis . . . suppeteret.** Oswiu's gifts in land, which for Bede come significantly after the gift of his daughter, are scarcely proof, as E. John argued (*Land Tenure in Early England* (1960), 74) that the lands were freed from military service. See N. Brooks, 'The Development of Military Obligations in Eighth- and Ninth-Century England', *England before the Conquest*, p. 74 n. 2. In particular, John's interpretation of Bede's 'facultas' (ibid., pp. 13-14 and *Orbis Britanniae*, pp. 265-71) must be questioned. I think 'means' an adequate translation without reference to any technical sense derived from Roman Law. *Possessiunculi* does not imply disparagement for it probably means 'component settlements, in distinction from *villae* or *vici* meaning estate centres, generally royal' (Campbell, '*Bede's* Reges *and* Principes' (Jarrow Lecture, 1979), 11); but Bede may be taking the word from his source without having much interest in the distinction.

p. 292, ll. 11-12. III. 24. **Streanaeshalch.** Mayr-Harting, *Coming of Christianity*, pp. 149-52, clearly summarizes what is known of the early history of Whitby. See also Krüger, *Königsgrabkirchen*, pp. 305-15.*

p. 292, ll. 16-17. III. 24. **pater matris eius Eduini.** Colgrave, *Celt and Saxon*, p. 135, comments on 'Bede's failure to use the story of the translation of Edwin's relics to Whitby. Bede obviously knows nothing about it. Yet it seems extraordinary that news of the event should not have reached Bede, even if the Whitby *Life* never came into his hands'; for a quarter of the Life is devoted to Edwin and his relics. It may be extraordinary but Bede's information from Whitby was patchy and in any case, as Bullough argues ('Hagiography as Patriotism', pp. 340 ff.), 'English hagiography before the Danish invasions is not evenly distributed in time or space.' A cult could be very localized. One can agree with R. Folz, *Les Saints Rois*, pp. 45-6, that there may never have been a true cult.

p. 292, ll. 22-3. III. 24. **desecto capite perfido.** Penda was not 'destroyed' by Oswiu: his head was cut off and doubtless displayed as a sign of vengeance taken. As Prestwich notes of this brief reference ('King Æthelhere and the Battle of the

Winwæd', p. 90), it seems to imply that Penda's death was already known to the reader. Bede is equally short but clear about Penda's death in his chronological summary s.a. 655: 'Penda periit, et Merci sunt facti Christiani' (v. 24, p. 564). But what is 'prominent' about the entry seems to me to be the conversion of the Mercians.

p. 292, ll. 24-5. III. 24. **Primus autem ... Diuma.** Bede now comes to a summary of Mercian bishops. Diuma ruled over Mercia, Lindsey, and the Middle Angles. Hunter Blair, *Studies in Early British History*, p. 146 and n. 4, discusses Bede's use of the same word to describe the inhabitants of Lindsey and of Lindisfarne: 'it is open to question whether this is adequate ground for postulating that the inhabitants of Lindisfarne came from Lindsey'. If not adequate, it is suggestive.*

p. 292, ll. 27-8. III. 24. **secundus Cellach ... rediit.** It may not follow that Ceollach's withdrawal was connected with Wulfhere's revolt. It was a very Irish thing to do. Moreover, Trumhere, his successor, came from Gilling which had been founded by Oswiu as propitiation for the murder of Trumhere's own relative, Oswine. In making his episcopal appointments Oswiu was exercising the power of a conqueror, Bretwalda or not.

p. 292, ll. 35-7. III. 24. **orationes assiduae pro utriusque regis ... salute.** Compare the alleged foundation of Minster-in-Thanet by Eormenberga on land given as a wergeld for her two murdered brothers. (See Finberg, *Early Charters of the West Midlands*, p. 218.) Bede several times uses *assiduus* in connection with prayer and it may have the sense of 'continuous' somewhat like the *laus perennis* of certain continental monasteries, for which special arrangements had to be made, involving large bodies of monks who relieved each other on duty, day and night.*

p. 294, ll. 2-3. III. 24. **gentem Pictorum ... subiecit.** 'Irish sources say nothing of an invasion of Pictland by Oswiu, and Bede gives only the most general of accounts, possibly because, at a time of peaceful relations with the Picts by *c.* 730, he was not anxious to emphasize previous Northumbrian aggression' (Kirby, *Famulus Christi*, p. 289). Or possibly because that was all he knew and wanted to know? Wainwright, *Problems of the Picts*, p. 7, considered that Oswiu's power in Pictland involved annexation as distinct from overlordship because of Bede's later description (IV. 3) of Wilfrid's episcopal authority.

p. 294, ll. 6–7. III. 24. **familiarum quinque milium ... VII milium.** Bede means hides, a word not used in *HE*. What these were has been discussed since Maitland's time. Whatever they may have signified in later times, to Bede they were simply units of tenure, each theoretically capable of supporting a family and therefore varying according to the yield of land. They may later have become units of revenue or *feorm*.

p. 294, l. 11. III. 24. **rebellarunt ... duces.** Bede clearly approves of the Mercian rebellion against Oswiu. He accepts the blood-right of Penda's kin to rule and welcomes the loyalty of the Mercians to that kin. However, the more significant consequence for Bede is that they could now freely serve Christ, 'uero regi' under Wulfhere his vicar. One can give little credence to the claim made in a much later *passio* that Wulfhere killed two of his own sons because they had been converted to Christianity (see Rollason, *ASE* II (1983), 11). C. W. Jones, *Saints' Lives*, p. 188, sees evidence in the whole passage from the death of Penda to the Mercian rebellion against Oswiu of 'repetition and disorder'. They suggest to him that 'Bede was concentrating upon two separate sources, the first a record from Lindsey which showed the *successio sacerdotalis* ... the second a Mercian record giving an episcopal succession from the appointment of Trumhere, derived from Lastingham. Bede made little effort to correlate his two sources'. He earlier suggests that 'Lastingham probably created a history in imitation of Whitby and Wearmouth'; hence presumably the hints of a saga-atmosphere. But there is no evidence of this.

p. 294, ll. 33–4. III. 25. **contra uniuersalis ecclesiae morem.** Bede starts this famous and lengthy account of the synod of Whitby with what for him was the vital issue: the universality of the

Church of Rome, itself heir to the apostolic tradition of conversion of the gentile world.

p. 294, ll. 34-5. III. 25. **acerrimus . . . defensor nomine Ronan.** It seems likely that this Irishman belonged to a Columbanian context in Gaul, as equally others in England who, Bede says, came 'de Gallis' (Campbell, 'First Century', p. 21). I do not see why, because Rónán is 'acerrimus' in this respect, it is he and not Fínán who was 'homo ferocis animi' (p. 296, ll. 2-3). Bede is not specific about the 'regula ecclesiasticae ueritatis' championed by Rónán and practised by James the Deacon ('uerum et catholicum pascha', p. 296, ll. 5-6). 'That Bede himself understood the "catholic observance" to be the one that involved use of the Dionysiac Paschal tables can hardly be doubted' (D. Ó Cróinín, 'The Irish Provenance of Bede's Computus', p. 232). Ó Cróinín goes on to emphasize Bede's unacknowledged but preponderant debt to southern Ireland, as against the continent, for his computistical knowledge, thus partly following C. W. Jones. However, Harrison (*Framework*, pp. 61-75, and 'The Synod of Whitby and the Beginning of the Christian Era', pp. 108-14) seems to me to make a better case, following R. L. Poole, for the view that 'the Easter Tables of Dionysius—and by implication, the notion of the Christian Era—were formally adopted at Whitby through the influence of Wilfrid . . . and perhaps of Benedict Biscop'. Wilfrid will have studied these matters at Rome and in Gaul.*

p. 296, ll. 10-11. III. 25. **ut bis in anno uno pascha celebraretur.** If P. Grosjean is right (*Anal. Boll.* 78 (1960), 234-55) it is not true that this would have happened, 'which seems to confirm that in this matter emotion and polemic were more important than literal truth' (Bullough, 'Missions to the English and Picts', p. 91). It remains possible that Bede was misled by his sources, but there can be no question that the business of Whitby was intensely personal to the kings concerned, as later to Bede himself on other grounds.

p. 296, ll. 23-5. III. 25. **grauior de obseruatione . . . nata est.** Bede is saying that with the arrival of Colmán controversy sharpened in Northumbria over the date of Easter and other matters affecting ecclesiastical discipline; but his own report of the debate at Whitby is confined to the Easter question, though he admits that other matters were raised there. In fact, Bede's report of Whitby does not profess to be full: it concentrates on the issue that was most significant to him, as probably also to the participants. I do not understand Mrs Chadwick's claim that Bede's report is 'certainly an elaborate form of ecclesiastical saga' (*Celt and Saxon*, p. 177) since I do not know what an 'ecclesiastical saga' is. There is more to be said for the view of C. W. Jones, *Saints' Lives*, p. 181, that Bede models his report on the *Acta Synodi Caesareae*, or rather, on a comparable document drawn after the synod by the Roman party: 'That literary creation Eddius then summarized for his account ... I hazard the guess that Bede copied the document verbatim'. If so, the document can have had no official status or he would have shown that it had, as in other contexts where *acta* are involved. Mayr-Harting, *Coming of Christianity*, p. 112, wonders whether Bede did not also see Whitby in an Irish context, using for example Cummian's letter to Ségéne of Iona (*PL* 87, cols. 969–78) where the Roman arguments advanced at Whitby also occur; and this is emphasized by Duncan, *The Writing of History*, pp. 37 ff. But why should not Wilfrid himself have deployed these arguments, having acquainted himself with the *computus paschae* during his visit to Rome in 654? (See Harrison, 'Synod of Whitby', p. 113.) I have not seen Gabriele Isenberg, *Die Würdigung Wilfrieds von York in der Historia Ecclesiastica Gentis Anglorum Bedas und der Vita Wilfridi des Eddius* (1978), who is said to argue that Aldhelm's letter to Gerontius of Cornwall (ed. Ehwald, *MGH AA* 15, 480–6) may have influenced the writing of Bede's account of Whitby.*

p. 296, ll. 27–8. III. 25. **Peruenit et ad ipsas principum aures.** The two kings, then, though already holding different opinions on Easter reckoning, were not the originators of the Whitby meeting. Bede seems to imply that the sharpening of the issue was due to their advisers, and in particular to Wilfrid. I am not convinced that Bede depends for his information on Eddius' Life of Wilfrid: they may have drawn upon a common source.

p. 298, l. 11. III. 25. **in praefato suo monasterio.** A detailed account of the building and consecration of the monastic church at Ripon is provided by Eddius, ch. 17. All that survives of the church is Wilfrid's crypt, on which see H. M. and J. Taylor, ii. 516-18. It is some indication of the force of Wilfrid's personality, as also of his convictions, that for his sake his patron Alhfrith was prepared in effect to evict from Ripon the Irish-trained monks whom he himself had placed there.

p. 298, ll. 14-16. III. 25. **dispositum est ... synodus fieri.** This was no synod of the whole English Church but of Northumbrian clergy and such others as happened to be present. Canterbury in particular was not represented. In the strict sense it was not a synod but a meeting. However, synod is what Bede calls it. That it should have taken place under kings would not have surprised the Frankish Church. It is no evidence that Oswiu was, or was acting in the capacity of, a Bretwalda. The best summary of its proceedings is Mayr-Harting, *Coming of Christianity*, pp. 103-13. Contrast the allusion in ASC s.a. 664, which is purely insular, whereas Bede sees the doctrinal dispute within a wider framework, as an issue between orthodoxy and schism, which ends, rightly but tragically, in the victory of orthodoxy. 'It is almost certain that Bede ... invested the synod with a larger and more entirely religious significance than it in reality possessed' (Cowdrey, 'Bede and the "English People"', p. 511). But this may already have been the work of a contemporary Roman account. Roman or not, the meeting and Bede's account of it betray no break in communication between England and Ireland.*

p. 298, l. 25. III. 25. **unam uiuendi regulam tenere.** Bede would have agreed with Oswiu, and so too would Gregory the Great. However, 'if Bede and his contemporaries could have consulted Gregory on the question of the tonsure and on the issue of conformity with Roman practice on a wider scale they would probably have received an answer which would have caused them some surprise' (Meyvaert, *Bede and Gregory the Great*, p. 17).

p. 300. ll. 4-5. III. 25. **'Loquatur, obsecro, uice mea discipulus'.** Agilbert, formerly West Saxon bishop but now about to become bishop of Paris, is present by chance as it seems. As bishop, he should have answered for the Romanists but pleads his imperfect English as an excuse for putting Wilfrid forward to argue their case. There can be little doubt that Wilfrid was the mainspring of the meeting, whether or not Agilbert could speak English. Wilfrid speaks not only for Agilbert but for Rome. On the other hand, Oswiu could speak Irish.

p. 300, ll. 30–1. III. 25. **Hinc est enim quod Paulus Timotheum circumcidit.** 'As Bede narrates it in the *Historia*, the debate at the Synod of Whitby contained a crucial interpretation of Acts 16: 3 ... The text, rightly construed, was the answer to a central argument of the Irish party. It is therefore striking that in the *Retractatio* ... Bede reassessed Acts 16: 3 along the very lines followed in the Whitby narrative ... Bede was still investigating sacred history in the interests of calendrical orthodoxy' (Ray, *Famulus Christi*, p. 126).*

p. 304, ll. 15–17. III. 25. **cum plurimi fuerint ... praebuerunt.** Colmán appeals to the good life lived by Columba and his successors as an additional reason why they were likely to be right about Easter. This placing of good living above doctrine and discipline is characteristic of the Irish, as Joseph Kelly points out (*Medievalia*, 4 (1978), 116).

p. 306, ll. 10–13. III. 25. **si audita decreta ... peccatis.** Conformity is a matter of belief. 'The seventh-century *Romani* were treating the Celtic peculiarities of liturgical practice as the church had once treated the Quartodecimans' (Hughes, *Church in Early Irish Society*, p. 106). No doubt Wilfrid treated his opponents harshly but he was not contemptuous of the great men of the Irish tradition and Bede did not think that he was. I see no reason for Colgrave's conclusion that 'Wilfrid's speech is Bede's own version of what Wilfrid said'.*

p. 306, ll. 21–2. III. 25. **'haec illi Petro dicta sunt a Domino?'** The presiding king, Oswiu, reaches his decision for the Roman party on the one factual point that all accept. He is not prepared to be turned away from the gates of heaven by St Peter, and he means this literally. With St Peter's primacy goes Petrine approbation of the Roman Easter. Eddius (ch. 10) adds that Oswiu spoke *subridens*, clearly not because he was bored by the lengthy speeches but because he was relieved to have reached firm ground for a decision—a decision that went against his personal preference for the Irish. However, Bede omits *subridens*. Those present agreed: the decision was binding on all, to the extent that any who could not accept it had to leave Northumbria.

p. 308, ll. 4-7. III. 26. **Colman ... Scottiam regressus est.** Bede neatly summarizes the immediate consequences of Whitby, with a further warm tribute to the Irish mission. 'That Colmán should have withdrawn in dudgeon from Northumbria after the "Synod" of Whitby in 664, almost certainly reflected his distaste for the settlement of an ecclesiastical dispute by an earthly ruler' (Byrne, *Irish Kings and High-Kings*, p. 34). Distaste he may have felt but his withdrawal was due to the settlement itself, not to the nature of the synod. Duncan (*The Writing of History*, p. 5) suggests that Colmán's return to Iona may have prompted Cummian, the abbot, to write his *Liber de Virtutibus Sancti Columbae* to answer the challenges of Whitby; of this only a brief extract survives in Adomnán's Life of Columba (ed. A. O. and M. O. Anderson, pp. 474-6).

p. 308, ll. 10-11. III. 26. **Facta est ... DCLXquarto.** Bede's dating of Whitby to 664 has been challenged by Stenton (*Anglo-Saxon England*, p. 129), who prefers 663; but the case for 664 is a sound one. See Kirby, *EHR* 78 (1963), 519, and M. Miller, *ASE* 8 (1979), 54, on Bede's method here of assembling and presenting a network of dates. The Irish had held the episcopate in Anglian (not 'English') territory for thirty years.*

p. 308, ll. 16-17. III. 26. **Tuda ... ordinatus episcopus.** Tuda clearly was, and was intended by Oswiu to be, bishop of Lindisfarne. I cannot accept the view of E. John, 'The Social and Political Problems of the Early English Church' (*Agricultural History Review*, 18 (1970), suppl., pp. 42 ff.) that Oswiu really meant Tuda to be bishop of York.

p. 308, ll. 29-31. III. 26. **Multum namque ... diligebat.** Bede's emphasis on Oswiu's affection for Colmán is further evidence for the seriousness of the reason (St Peter's primacy) that compelled the king to decide against Colmán's party at Whitby. A better translation of 'prudentia' than 'prudence' would be 'discernment' or 'wisdom'.

p. 310, l. 1. III. 26. **Quantae autem parsimoniae** ... No doubt Bede's description of the life-style of the Irish missionaries glows, as Plummer observes; but it does so because he wishes to emphasize to his contemporaries how the religious life should be lived. Plummer also points out that even in St Cuthbert's time monks were not always popular in Northumbria.

p. 310, l. 5. III. 26. **Nil pecuniarum absque pecoribus habebant.** This is no necessary sign of poverty. Apropos Jarrow's Codex Amiatinus R. L. S. Bruce-Mitford writes: 'The three pandects, or great copies of the Holy Scriptures, would thus together represent the utilization of the skins of some 1,550 calves, implying the existence of great herds of cattle. Only rich and well-run communities could afford to produce books of this calibre' (*The Art of the Codex Amiatinus* (Jarrow Lecture, 1967), reprinted in *Journ. Brit. Archaeol. Assoc.* 3rd ser. 32 (1969), 2). Lindisfarne also produced books. As for the church, no fabric of pre-Conquest date remains, and the many carved stones from the burial-ground almost all belong to the ninth or tenth centuries (Cramp, *Corpus of Anglo-Saxon Stone Sculpture*, i/1. 194–208).

p. 310, ll. 29–30. III. 26. **ut nemo territoria ... coactus acciperet.** The qualification is illuminating but may have no connection with the situation described by Bede in his letter to Egbert, which he says has persisted 'per annos circiter triginta, hoc est, ex quo Aldfrid rex humanis rebus ablatus est' (ed. Plummer, i. 416): that is, since 705, which is a generation later than what he describes in this chapter. For a persuasive interpretation of the letter's bearing on Anglo-Saxon bookland and charters see Wormald (Jarrow Lecture, 1984), 19 ff.

p. 310, ll. 33–4. III. 27. **facta erat eclipsis.** First recorded for England in Bede's *Chron. Maj.* as occurring on 3 May 664, and substantially repeated here with the addition of the *Annus*

Domini. The true day is 1 May. Harrison, *Framework*, p. 94, explains how the error may have arisen.

p. 312, l. 1. III. 27. **subita pestilentiae lues.** Plummer's long note raises problems that still await solution. For example, it is often assumed that Cuthbert sickened of bubonic plague in 664 but recovered. Plummer draws attention to the fact that before his removal to Lindisfarne in that year he was prior (provost?) of Melrose 'per aliquot annos' (*Two Lives of St Cuthbert*, ed. B. Colgrave (1940), 184-5). The nature of his illness is clear: 'tumor in femore', coupled with the statement (ibid., p. 180) that very many were carried off (i.e. in 664), which is usually taken to mean bubonic plague. Bubonic plague can be endemic but apart from human reservoirs the disease can also be carried by rodents, in which case it is properly called enzootic. It is therefore possible that Cuthbert's infection could have taken place while he was at Melrose (661-4), from an enzootic source. Perhaps a few others were affected but the outbreak (over the whole of England?) will have been on a far smaller scale than that of 664. I owe the substance of this information to Mr Kenneth Harrison. The best short account of plague is a review by C. Morris, *Historical Journal*, 14 (1971), 205-15. The death from plague of Tuda, and its spread to Ireland, brings Bede quite naturally to the exodus of Anglo-Saxons to Ireland.

p. 312, l. 10. III. 27. **relicta insula patria.** If Iona was the main channel by which Irish–Latin culture reached Northumbria in the seventh century, it is none the less clear from Bede's account that the direct link between England and Ireland was significant. 'One of the Northumbrians who studied in Ireland is clearly the Edilberict son of Berictfrid who wrote in an Irish-trained hand and from an Irish exemplar or Irish sources the *Commentarium in Psalmos* in Vatican MS. Pal. Lat. 68' (Bullough, 'Columba, Adomnan and the Achievement of Iona', *SHR* 43 (1964), 121 n. 4). See also K. Hughes, 'The Distribution of Irish Scriptoria and Centres of Learning from 730 to 1111' (*Studies in the Early British Church*, pp. 243-72). On the significance of the pilgrim's vow and Bede's understanding of *patria* in this respect, see Charles-Edwards, 'The Social Background to Irish *Peregrinatio*', p. 45.*

p. 312, l. 18. III. 27. **Edilhun et Ecgberct.** It is clear that for them as Roman sympathizers, as for Bede, there was nothing unnatural about their going to Ireland for study and the ascetic life: and they were received honourably by the Irish clergy. Egbert, a man of real importance in Bede's eyes, probably 'held the position of power which the laws assign to the *deorad Dé* [exile of God]' (Charles-Edwards, 'Social Background to Irish *Peregrinatio*', p. 54). 'Like the bishop or the chief poet, the *deorad Dé* has a legal status equal to that of the normal Irish king' (ibid., p. 53). Bede has his information about Egbert's recovery from the plague from an old priest who had heard of it from Egbert himself. It is likely, then, that the substance of the whole chapter came from the same source.

p. 312, l. 23. III. 27. **Rathmelsigi.** Mellifont has been suggested as a possible identification, as Plummer notes. Mrs Chadwick (*Celt and Saxon*, pp. 203–4) thinks that Egbert may have spent some time with the English community at Mayo, which would explain the reputation of the monastery.*

p. 314, ll. 28–9. III. 28. **ad regem Galliarum.** Chlotar III, son of Clovis II and Balthildis, inherited his parents' interest in monastic reform in Francia. No less than five of his 'original' diplomas in favour of St Denis survive. (Facsimiles in Lauer and Samaran, *Les Diplômes originaux des mérovingiens* (1908), plates 9–13.) Alhfrith would naturally intend that Wilfrid should go for consecration to Agilbert of Paris, with Chlotar's permission. That the consecration should take place at the royal villa of Compiègne, by courtesy of Chlotar and presumably also of Balthildis, does, as Janet Nelson points out ('Queens as Jezebels', in *Medieval Women: Essays presented to Rosalind Hill*, p. 66 n. 184), cast doubt on Eddius' story (*Vita S. Wilfridi*, ch. 6) that Wilfrid had experienced Balthildis' malevolence during his earlier residence at Lyons. Lohaus, *Die Merowinger und England*, p. 60, suggests that while Wilfrid was with Agilbert in Paris he may have acquired plans of a Parisian church (possibly St Denis) for use when he returned to England. On possible reforming influences on him during his stay see Wormald, *Famulus Christi*, p. 145.*

p. 316, l. 1. III. 28. **imitatus industriam filii.** Bede seems to mean that Oswiu was not to be caught out by Alhfrith's quick decision to send Wilfrid to Agilbert for consecration; in other words, Oswiu's action was meant to forestall Alhfrith's and was thus an act of hostility. I see no reason why Chad might have been intended to assist Wilfrid. Bede's information presumably comes from Lastingham and thus his account of Chad is entirely sympathetic. Note that Oswiu's intention was that Chad should be consecrated at Canterbury, the vacancy at which alone accounted for Chad's subsequent consecration in Wessex by Wine and two Celtic bishops (whose collaboration suggests improved Anglo-British relations in the south-west).*

p. 316, l. 21. III. 28. **oppida ... castella.** 'This marked clustering of words for places which [Bede] does not generally use except when following a written source strongly suggests that in the passage where they occur he is in fact following written sources now lost, very possibly letters' (Campbell, in *Names, Words and Graves*, p. 39). I doubt 'letters' but otherwise agree.

p. 316, ll. 26-8. III. 28. **perplura catholicae ... contulit.** Having given Chad his due, Bede ends rather abruptly with Wilfrid's introduction of 'catholic' principles on his return to England and the total surrender of 'Scotti omnes'. This, more than Whitby, marks the true end of Celtic dominance in the northern Church; and both were effectively the work of Wilfrid.

p. 318, ll. 1-3. III. 29. **reges Anglorum ... habito inter se consilio.** The interpretation of this difficult chapter turns on what sources we think Bede was using. He appears to be saying that the two kings collaborated in sending a candidate to Rome for consecration to Canterbury, and this has been taken to mean that Oswiu was acting as Bretwalda, Egbert as the king directly interested in the appointment. As Plummer saw, Bede's earlier account in *Historia Abbatum*, chapter 3, simply states that Egbert sent Wighard to Rome for consecration, where he and all his companions died of the plague. Some fifteen years later Bede has changed his mind. He no longer relies on his earlier report but on Pope Vitalian's letter to Oswiu, of which he had a copy, presumably from a Northumbrian source. As Campbell first suggested ('Bede', p. 187), Bede now seems to have made a deduction based on a conflation of Vitalian's letter with his account of Egbert's sending a candidate (doubtless Wighard) to Rome. He could have deduced 'first, that Oswy's gift-bearer ... was none other than Wighard himself; and second, that the Northumbrian king had exercised this wide-ranging authority and had involved himself in Wighard's promotion and dispatch to Rome' (Brooks, *Early History*, p. 69). The pope writes as if he had been asked to find an archbishop, not merely to consecrate one. It looks therefore as if his letter was simply a reply to Oswiu's independent initiative, but he clearly infers from Oswiu's letter that Oswiu had some sort of overriding prestige in England (which we need not interpret as that of a Bretwalda). In other words, the two kings acted independently. However, as Brooks observes, Oswiu had good reason to consult with Egbert, who might easily have wanted the election of the dreaded Wilfrid. What is really hard to credit is that either king or both kings could have acted on the authority of 'sanctae ecclesiae gentis Anglorum' (l. 6), though Bede may well be right in seeing ecclesiastical interests common to Northumbria and Kent. As usual, Bede has made sense of what was before him though he may unintentionally mislead in doing so.

p. 318, l. 27. III. 29. **sicut scriptum est in Esaia.** On Vitalian's repeated citation of Isaiah with its implication of the historical development of God's plan, actualized by St Paul's mission to the Gentiles and Gregory's to the English, see Tugène, 'L'Hist. "eccl."', p. 161.

p. 320, ll. 13–14. III. 29. **Et post nonnulla ... uero pascha loquitur.** Bede may have felt that he had already said enough about Easter. On the other hand, Vitalian's views may in some respect have displeased him. The omitted passage attributed to Vitalian is cited by C. W. Jones (ed.), *Bedae Opera de Temporibus*, p. 104 (a better text than that in Plummer's note); it is in favour of uniformity following the Dionysiac *ratio*. On whether or not there was a papal shift in regard to the *ratio*, see Harrison, *Framework*, pp. 59–63 (with whom I agree) and the contrary opinion of Duncan, *The Writing of History*, p. 38.

p. 320, ll. 27-9. III. 29. **reliquias ... Gregorii atque Pancrati.**
Nothing is known of these relics. Gregory's relics, or some
portion of them, might naturally reach Canterbury; but St
Pancras is a problem, though the Canterbury church dedication
to him is most likely to date from Augustine's time or soon after.
Was he then considered to be the patron saint of children?
There seems to be no evidence for this in *Acta Sanctorum* (*Acta
Martyrii S. Pancratii*, *AA SS Maii* iii. 21). According to legend he
was martyred at the age of thirteen or fourteen. His name occurs
virtually throughout F. Wormald's *English Kalendars to 1100*
whereas that of Nicholas of Myra (our present children's saint) is
not found before the eleventh century. There are no known
dedications to Pancras in Northumbria. However, it is curious
that Ceolfrith was elected abbot of Wearmouth-Jarrow on
12 May 688 (*Vita Ceolfridi*, in Plummer, i. 394; Plummer, i. 393,
and ii. 364, by a slip gives 13 May), which was a Tuesday and the
feast of St Pancras. One would have expected such a ceremony
to have taken place on a Sunday or a major festival? I am grateful
to Mr Harrison for information.

p. 322, l. 21. III. 30. **misit ad corrigendum errorem.** Bede is not
at all concerned about the nature of the authority by which
Wulfhere intervened in East Saxon affairs. It was enough that he
had the power to send his bishop to deal with a relapse into
paganism: and this quite clearly without any invitation from the
king and people who had relapsed (though possibly from the
other king, Sebbi). One would like to know why Jaruman was
successful in destroying temples and reopening churches: was it
that the plague had suddenly loosened its hold? There is an
interesting treatment of the question in Vollrath-Reichelt,
Königsgedanke, pp. 108-9 (and compare Diesner, 'Fragen', p. 26).
Note Bede's sole source for a significant relapse: a priest who
accompanied Jaruman; and it is the priest's credentials ('religi-
osus et bonus uir', l. 25) that are vouched for, not Jaruman's; a
priest, moreover, who in the intervening years between 664-5
and his meeting with Bede had made his way from Mercia or
Essex to Northumbria. Jaruman's mission had been a risky
undertaking, requiring 'multa sollertia' (l. 23), without any
military backing. At least he started with the goodwill of that
part of the East Saxons that had not relapsed.

Book IV

p. 328, l. 17. IV. 1. **habito de his consilio.** The pope seeks advice not generally but from the English survivors of the plague that had carried off Wighard and most of their companions.

p. 328, ll. 20–1. IV. 1. **sacris litteris . . . inbutus.** Neither nationality nor age plays any part in the qualifications for a new archbishop in Britain; what matters is scriptural learning, experience of ecclesiastical and monastic discipline, and unimpeachable character. Theodore, however, is so old that Bede makes a virtue of it. Obviously he cannot have been expected to last long. The pope no doubt expected to consecrate Hadrian in his place before many years had passed.

p. 330, l. 3. IV. 1. **Theodorus, natus Tarso Ciliciae.** Professor Henry Chadwick has pointed out to me that at the Lateran council of 649 there were many Greek monks present, including some from a monastery of the Cilicians *ad Aquas Salvias* (Tre Fontane) by St Paul's on the road to Ostia. They had been there some time. It seems highly probable that Theodore had lived in Rome a long time as a Greek monk in a Cilician monastery, and so was familiar with Latin and Western usages as well as being zealously anti-Monothelite; in which case Hadrian's choice of him was not so very surprising.

p. 330, ll. 15–16. IV. 1. **tonsuram more orientalium sancti apostoli Pauli.** Bede appears to be the first writer to equate the Eastern tonsure with that of St Paul. See Bullough, 'Missions to the English and Picts', p. 92 n. 36, and P. de Puniet, *The Roman Pontifical* (1932), 109–14, on the different forms of tonsure.*

p. 330, ll. 16–18. IV. 1. **Qui ordinatus ... dominica.** Grosjean, *Anal. Boll.* 78 (1960), 238, argues that Bede has confused the date of Theodore's consecration with that of Deusdedit.

p. 330, ll. 20–1. IV. 1. **Iohanni archiepiscopo ciuitatis.** Strictly, John was not archbishop but metropolitan of Arles. Bede or his informants interpret the Gallo-Frankish hierarchy in terms of

the English. There were no Gallo-Frankish archbishops in 668.
See E. Lesne, *La Hiérarchie épiscopale* (1905), p. 26 n. 3, and p. 28
n. 2. The English archbishopric was something exceptional, but
see Wolfgang Fritze, 'Zur Enstehungsgeschichte des Bistums
Utrecht', *Rheinische Vierteljahrsblätter*, 35 (1971), 122 ff., on the
use of the title by the Roman Church before St Boniface's time.

p. 330, l. 22. IV. 1. **Ebrinus maior domus.** Further to Ebroin, see
my *Long-Haired Kings*, pp. 236, 246. He plays a negative but
significant role in Frankish hagiography. The best modern
assessment of his influence is that of J. Fischer, *Der Hausmeier
Ebroin* (1954) and he appears *passim* in Prinz, *Frühes
Mönchtum.**

p. 330, ll. 26-7. IV. 1. **primum ad Emme ... postea ad Faronem.**
Speaking of Benedict Biscop, who accompanied Theodore and
Hadrian, Wormald, *Famulus Christi*, p. 146, rightly notes that
'Burgundofaro was as closely tied to the Luxeuil connection as
was Agilbert, while Emmo was at least a patron of the joint rule.'

p. 332, ll. 3-4. IV. 1. **ad portum ... Quaentauic.** Campbell, *Names,
Words*, p. 40 observes that this is the only occasion when Bede
calls a place *portus* when he is not using the words of another; if
indeed he is not.

p. 332, ll. 6-8. IV. 1. **suspicabatur ... aduersus regnum.** On
Frankish touchiness about foreign travellers and their possible
links elsewhere, see my *Early Medieval History*, p. 63.

p. 332, l. 19. IV. 2. **peragrata insula tota.** Brooks, *Early History*,
p. 72, is certainly right to claim that Theodore and his two
immediate successors exercised greater authority than Canterbury was ever to possess again. But, though evidence is lacking,
there can be no doubt to my mind that this was the result of
papal instructions. An obvious reason for the general acceptance
of Theodore's authority is that for most of his reign he was
working through diocesans of his own appointment. There is no
good reason to suppose that his general acceptance was the
result of any Bretwalda-like authority exercised by Oswiu. See
Vollrath-Reichelt, *Königsgedanke*, p. 107.

p. 332, l. 26. IV. 2. **congregata discipulorum caterua**. It is to Bede that we owe most of our knowledge, and certainly our appreciation of the significance of, the effective re-establishment of the English Church by Theodore and Canterbury. It has, as he shows, a disciplinary and an organizational side, but equally important is its intellectual aspect. Of the teaching, writing, and pupils of the school of Canterbury more is known than when Plummer wrote. However, Jones, *Famulus Christi*, p. 263, reminds us that Bede's list of subjects (which, though incomplete, plainly influenced the school of Jarrow) 'is a list of content, not a course of study; we have to study the remains of textbooks and manuals from the period to find that'. He goes on to point to the direct line from Theodore's instruction to Charlemagne's educational programme. Theodore's pupils—and we know the names of several—were instructed in metre, astronomy, computus, and, above all, the Scriptures with their patristic literature. Aldhelm, Canterbury's most distinguished pupil, adds in a letter that he also studied Roman Law, musical chant, and poetry—this last suggesting the school's interest in secular as well as Christian literature. Aldhelm's stylistic skills may have owed more to his Canterbury training, with its continental links, than to Malmesbury and the Irish. But we know nothing of Theodore's books or library. There is some evidence that medicine was not neglected, rather less that the use of written English was practised. Greek was certainly taught. Theodore's scriptural teaching seems to have relied more on the Greek fathers than on the Latin and stood somewhat apart from the main western allegorical tradition in being more obviously factual and literal. This was to have little effect on Bede's own exegesis. Indeed, the impetus of the Canterbury school faltered at the death of its founder. Uncertainty surrounds the evolution of so important a Canterbury text as Theodore's Penitential. But this is not to say that his immediate successors, Berhtwald, Tatwine, and Nothhelm, were unlearned or unable to conduct a school. See the admirable summary of Brooks, *Early History*, pp. 94 ff., and Mayr-Harting, *Coming of Christianity*, pp. 240 ff.; and on Greek teaching at Canterbury, T. J. Brown, *Spoleto*, 22 (1975), 255 ff., and the fundamental study of B. Bischoff, 'Das griechische Element in der abendländischen Bildung des Mittelalters', *Mittelalterliche Studien* (1967), ii. 246–75. That the great Julian of Toledo corresponded with Hadrian of Canterbury was suggested by Bischoff (*Spoleto*, 22 (1975), 59–86) but Julian's correspondent could have been a Spanish Abbot Hadrian of whom, like most Spanish abbots of the time, no trace remains.*

p. 334, l. 12. IV. 2. **cantandi magister Nordanhymbrorum.** This may be evidence that the head of the post-Gregorian *schola cantorum* in Rome was by now known as the *magister cantandi* as well as prior. It is by no means clear that the singing-master Ædddi, surnamed Stephen, should be identified with the author of the *Vita S. Wilfridi*, who is not called Eddius Stephanus before the seventeenth century. See D. P. Kirby, 'Bede, Eddius Stephanus and the "Life of Wilfrid"', *EHR* 98 (1983), 102. However, it is a Stephanus who is here summoned by Wilfrid from Kent and it is a Stephanus who writes Wilfrid's *Vita*.

p. 334, ll. 14–15. IV. 2. **qui primus ... tradere didicit.** Bede may be referring to western practices generally, as opposed to Celtic, as Colgrave suggests; or more likely, to Wilfrid's influence upon monastic life (the view of Hamilton Thompson, *BLTW*, p. 82 n. 5). Either way, it is no 'extraordinary statement', as Plummer thought it.*

p. 334, ll. 16–17. IV. 2. **ordinabat locis oportunis episcopos.** Rome was alert to the propriety of placing bishops only in 'locis oportunis'. See the warning of Pope Zacharias to Boniface on this matter in 743: *Die Briefe des heiligen Bonifatius und Lullus*, ed. Tangl, No. 51.

p. 334, ll. 18–19. IV. 2. **Ceadda ... non fuisse rite consecratum.** 'St Chad received episcopal consecration from a Saxon bishop of Winchester and two British bishops. There is no need to suppose that his two co-consecrators came from Wales or Cornwall' (Finberg, *Lucerna*, p. 6). Note that when Theodore reconsecrated Chad he did not restore him to York but allowed him to spend some years in retirement at Lastingham.

p. 336, ll. 5–7. IV. 2. **Putta ... peritum.** Meyvaert, *Bede and Gregory the Great*, pp. 7–8, comments that 'it is clear from the context ... that what Bede had in mind was the chant as "Roman" rather than as specifically "Gregorian". It was because Gregory's missionaries came from Rome that they were skilled in the chant.'

p. 336, l. 8. IV. 3. **Eo tempore ... rex Uulfheri praefuit.** C. W. Jones, *Saints' Lives*, p. 188–9, notes the vagueness of the time reference. 'Bede here adjusts to his outline as best he can the Life of St Chad, supplied by the monks of Lastingham.' Trumberht 'may have substantiated the story and provided additional information, but the story of Owin was almost certainly copied with little change from a local hagiography exalting the founder of the monastery'. I agree with Kirby, *BJRL* 48 (1965–6), 369, that 'Chad's conspicuous position in the *HE* results simply from the fact that Bede was in touch with Lastingham.' His knowledge of Mercian affairs, always patchy and seemingly not confirmed by any direct information from any Mercian monastery or bishopric, rests on information from 'a haphazard selection of individuals all with probably only a limited knowledge of Mercian affairs'. This did not matter. Bede had as much background material as he required for a lengthy account of the last days and burial of Chad; and this account is not fill-in material in lieu of anything better, but exactly what he wanted: the substance of ecclesiastical history. What matters is not Mercia. It is an accident that that is where a saintly bishop happened to meet his exemplary end.

p. 336, l. 10. IV. 3. **non eis nouum uoluit ordinare episcopum.** It is Theodore, not Wulfhere, who asks Oswiu to send Chad to be bishop of the Mercians. Why Theodore found no suitable replacement for Jaruman apart from Chad may depend on what Bede understood by 'eo tempore' (l. 8) but the likelihood is that Theodore had had too little time to satisfy himself that there were other candidates trained in his own way of thinking.

p. 336, ll. 28–9. IV. 3. **in loco qui uocatur Licidfelth.** This difficult place-name may go back no further than Chad's time. 'Lichfield clearly came into being as a new English settlement in a *feld*, or stretch of open country, which derived its name from the adjacent Roman works of Letocetum' (Stenton, *Preparatory*,

p. 259). It is not known that Wulfhere had a *uilla regalis* there; but Tamworth lies only some ten miles to the south-east.

p. 344, ll. 15-16. IV. 3. **ipse peregrinus ... permansit.** Bede does not say, as Colgrave translates, that Egbert remained in Ireland till his death. He died on Iona. See Duncan, *The Writing of History*, p. 41.

p. 346, ll. 2-5. IV. 3. **locus idem sepulchri ... adsumere.** A more correct translation, supplied by A. C. Thomas (*Early Christian Archaeology*, p. 147) is: 'Moreover the place of his burial' (that is, of the reburial of Chad's bones) 'is covered with a wooden coffin made in the shape of a little house, having a hole in one side through which those who go thither out of devotion may insert their hands and take some of the dust.' So Chad's second grave was open and only covered by a wooden structure; and the material is wood not stone. Thomas recalls the Kerry slab-shrines (of stone) but also Germanic shrines for the dead. Bede is, as usual, precise in describing what was visible in his own day, even if not to him personally.

p. 346, ll. 15-16. IV. 4. **Interea Colmanus ... relinquens Brittaniam.** Nora Chadwick, *Celt and Saxon*, p. 187, may well be right in arguing that 'Bede's narrative of Colmán is not confined to the chapter relating specifically to Mayo, but is related piecemeal in several places, and Bede is perhaps drawing upon a continuous saga or *Vita*, a *navigatio* of Colmán, the thread of which he is following and weaving into his account.' Clearly his source is Irish in origin and is written, not oral. The chapter fits not too comfortably into the narrative but is excused by 'interea', as also by its brevity. For corrections to Mrs Chadwick's account of Mayo, see K. Hughes, *England before the Conquest*, pp. 51 ff., who questions whether Mayo was ever Egbert's base and notes that, whether or not Mayo became an exponent of Roman practice under Colmán (surely unlikely?), the interesting point is that by the 730s it supported a bishop who seems to have regarded himself as subject to, or in close communion with, the metropolitan of York. Bede's words suggest to me that the conversion of Mayo to Roman usages was subsequent to

Colmán's rule. His concern is less with Colmán than with his need to account for a flourishing English community in Ireland.

p. 348, ll. 3-4. IV. 4. **ut pro ipso ... preces offerrent.** That land for a monastery should be given on condition that prayers should be offered for the founder (indeed, for his family in perpetuity) was common throughout the western Church and could be illustrated many times over from Frankish evidence alone. Also, as Bede knew, there were instances of family-interference in the subsequent history of such foundations.

p. 348, l. 14. IV. 5. **Anno dominicae incarnationis DCLXXmo.** This and other datings in the chapter have given rise to much discussion, notably by R. L. Poole, W. Levison, and D. P. Kirby. Plummer in effect acknowledges himself defeated. One way of clearing up the difficulties is suggested by Harrison, 'The Reign of King Ecgfrith', pp. 79 ff., who reminds us that Bede was not writing a political history and often has to make his reckonings of reigns from one assured date or episode. Harrison concludes that Ecgfrith did not succeed Oswiu immediately but in September of the same year; but S. Wood, *EHR* 98 (1983), 284, shows that this need not follow and explains how Bede arrived at the dates he records: 673 was indeed the year of the synod of Hertford.

p. 348, ll. 20-1. IV. 5. **Uilfridumque ... donatione rogaret.** Wilfrid refused the bribe according to Bede, but this casts no light on his reason for not agreeing to accompany Oswiu to Rome. We do not know why he refused, any more than we know why he was not present at the synod of Hertford, though the fact that he sent proctors shows that he acknowledged his right and duty to be present. 'Proprios legatarios' (p. 350, l. 3) are more than mere observers, and Theodore appears to have been content.

p. 348, ll. 28-9. IV. 5. **Cuius synodicae ... textus est.** Bede is our sole source for this, the earliest synodical record of the English Church, and it is presumably taken from a Canterbury copy. Chaplais points out ('The Origin and Authenticity of the Royal Anglo-Saxon Diploma', p. 50) that 'the Hertford document falls into the same diplomatic category as the *acta* of papal synods, on which it may have been modelled', though it contains a *rogatio* clause concerning the notary Titillus not then used in papal documents but 'regularly found in Italian private deeds of the sixth and seventh centuries'. Theodore knew how to draw up a document in the true Italian fashion. On the other hand, 'the Anglo-Saxon charters which were drawn up in Kent during Theodore's pontificate ... show no apparent trace of notarial influence'. This may be an argument against Theodore as the introducer of written grants into England, as has often been maintained. If Chaplais is right, these go back to Augustine.*

p. 350, ll. 4–5. IV. 5. **castelli Cantuariorum quod dicitur Hrofaescaestir.** Theodore is precise: Rochester is not a 'town' but a *castellum*, as sometimes in charters. 'The area associated with Rochester appears to have been known as *regio Caestruuara*; *Burgwara* appears in connection with the area associated with Canterbury ... Perhaps in early Kent Canterbury was known simply as the *burg* and Rochester as the *ceastre*' (Campbell, in *Names, Words*, p. 40).

p. 350, ll. 18–19. IV. 5. **ex eodem libro x capitula.** Theodore draws the synod's attention to specific disciplinary matters affecting bishops, clergy, and monks without impinging (apart from one instance) on secular relations and notably relations with kings. (Similarly with the synod of Hatfield.) Theodore's synods were quite unlike Oswiu's council at Whitby in terms of royal control, or Wihtred's at Bapchild.*

p. 352, l. 5. IV. 5. **in loco qui appellatur Clofaeshooh.** The place remains unidentified. There is nothing to be said for Brixworth nor any firm evidence to support the ascription to Cliffe at Hoo. See the interesting note by Vollrath-Reichelt, *Königsgedanke*, p. 136, who points out Cliffe's significant position between the Medway and the Thames on the frontiers of Kent, Mercia, and Essex. See also Stenton, *Preparatory*, pp. 189–90, for suggestive charter material, though he does not risk an identification of Clofeshoh.

p. 352, ll. 8-10,. IV. 5. **Nonum capitulum ... ad praesens siluimus.** I see no reason why this discussion should have been anticipated by Wilfrid and avoided by him. The division of dioceses will depend on what has yet to happen, 'crescente numero fidelium'. Nor do I feel that grounds exist for speculating on which bishops at Hertford opposed Theodore's plans for diocesan reorganization (*pace* Mayr-Harting, *Coming of Christianity*, p. 131). No decision was taken. There was simply a discussion.

p. 352, l. 11. IV. 5. **Decimum capitulum pro coniugiis.** Theodore deals with the degree of consanguinity within which Christian marriage is permissible and (more problematical) with divorce and remarriage. These considerations would sharply affect a lay society still living within the traditional Germanic ethos. By 'legitimum coniugium' is understood marriage recognized by the church. It is equally clear from this provision that laity had been remarrying in the belief or hope that they had not contravened the Church's teaching.

p. 352, ll. 28-9. IV. 5. **Facta est ... DCCLxxtertio.** Note the discrepancy between this date and the date in Theodore's own *acta* of the synod, where 'indictione prima' is added. Against Levison's opinion that Bede made a slip by forgetting that 'the indictions did not change, with the years of Incarnation, on Christmas Day, but almost four months earlier' (*England and the Continent*, p. 267), Harrison believes that we can exonerate Bede 'by supposing him faced with an entry in a Dionysiac table: (in the margin) "concilium in loco Herutford die xx°iiii° Sept." and (in the adjacent columns of the table) "AD DCLXXIII, Ind. I". People accustomed to using these tables would find no problem here ... As it turned out, the acts of the council were dated by the date of the month and the indiction only, and Bede filled in the Year of Grace quite correctly. If he had written 672 he would have broken his own rule.' (*ASE* 2 (1973), 56-7.)

p. 352, ll. 29-30. IV. 5. **quo anno rex Cantuariorum ... obierat.** Bede finishes the chapter with a brief summary of the succession of Hlothhere in Kent and the division of the East Anglian diocese. (He records no more than East Anglian bishops till 731 and probably had no occasion to do so.) These matters fit in here because of the date-linking between the synod of Hertford and King Egbert's death and also because Bisi had been present at the synod. D. Whitelock, *ASE* 1 (1972), 8, rightly notes that 'some writers when assessing the influence of the church of Canterbury established by Augustine tend to ignore its permanent influence in East Anglia'.

p. 354, ll. 1-2. IV. 5. duo sunt pro illo ... consecrati episcopi. The division of the East Anglian diocese was the result of an accident: the illness of Bisi. Nothing remains of Ælcci's church at Dunwich (for the South Folk) but at Baduwine's North Elmham (for the North Folk) the foundations of his church may remain. See H. M. and J. Taylor, *Anglo-Saxon Architecture*, i. 228-31, for North Elmham and also Biddle, *England before the Conquest*, p. 407. Bede had seen a Dunwich MS of the Life of St Paul which included, he says, pictures of almost all St Paul's sufferings or labours (*Aliquot Quaestionum Liber, PL* 93, col. 456). See Levison, *England and the Continent*, p. 133. Theodore's bishops were monks, their houses and sees remaining closely associated, as they were also to be in Boniface's German foundations. The sites of the sees were not important to Bede. What identified a bishop was the people over whom he ruled.

p. 354, ll. 5-6. IV. 6. Theodorus ... deposuit eum. There is no justification for thinking that Winfrith's disobedience arose from his objection to a proposed division of the Mercian diocese. We do not know why he crossed the Channel, as Eddius reports. What moves Bede is not his deposition or the reason for it but the holiness of his life. Still more is he moved by the holiness of Eorconwald: by his 'uita et conuersatio'. This was how bishops should be. Holiness is a test that survives Theodore's un-exampled use of his authority (on which Bede makes no direct comment).

p. 354, l. 9. IV. 6. Medeshamstedi in regione Gyruiorum. 'The date of the foundation is quite uncertain, but it must have taken place long before Saxulf, its founder, became bishop of the Mercians, and Saxulf's consecration cannot be later than 675'

(Stenton, *Preparatory*, p. 179 n. 4). See also Whitelock, *ASE* 1 (1972), 13, on Peterborough and its early colonies.

p. 354, ll. 23-4. IV. 6. **duo praeclara monasteria.** Bede does not go out of his way to mention the names of monasteries, of which there were certainly many more than he records. When he does so, it is for a particular reason, often connected with the sanctity of a founder or inmate. Such is the case here. Chertsey and Barking were certainly important houses, but that in itself is not why they appear in *HE*. The early charters of Barking are discussed by C. Hart, *The Early Charters of Eastern England*, pp. 117-45. Stenton notes (*Preparatory*, p. 80) that Bede's 'Inberecingum' (p. 356, l. 1) is 'important as a link between the folk-names and place-names restricted to some particular spot. The established cases in which a folk-name ending in -*ingas* has passed into and survived as a place-name are rare. Barking is one'. The meaning of the place-name 'Cerotaesei' (p. 354, l. 27) would not have been obvious to a northerner; therefore Bede explains it. See A. Mawer, *The Chief Elements Used in English Place-Names* (EPNS 1/ii, under *eg*, p. 24). Bede does not say what kind of rules Eorconwald imposed on his two houses. It may be that none of this account of foundations would have appeared in *HE* if it had not been that Eorconwald's sister was Æthelburh, to whom Bede had already determined to devote much space. Kirby, *BJRL* 48 (1965-6), 360, is no doubt right that the report on Æthelburh he received from Barking, whether directly or indirectly, also contained information about Eorconwald. However, it was not just any information from other East Saxon monasteries that he lacked, but information of the right kind.*

p. 356, l. 8. IV. 7. **descripta habentur a multis.** It is no doubt correct that this and the following three chapters are based on the *libellus* of Barking. However, it should also be noted that copies were to be had elsewhere. I agree with Plummer that the style suggests Bede himself. We must suppose him to have 'worked up his materials in his own way'. The chapter casts some light on the degree of collaboration between men and women in a double monastery. The miracles that follow are, as Bede explains, evidence of Æthelburh's holy living and care for those subjected to her rule as abbess. That is why they are included, and at some length. That special provision had to be made for a new cemetery was presumably because the plague was expected to carry off large numbers at the same time.

p. 358, ll. 24–5. IV. 8. **domum hanc tanta luce inpletam.** G. Bonner (Jarrow Lecture, 1966, pp. 9–10) draws attention to comparable passages in Bede's biblical commentaries: e.g. Rev. 2: 28 and 20: 5–6, on Christ as the morning star of the resurrection.

p. 360, ll. 1–2. IV. 9. **Cum autem et ipsa mater ... rapienda de mundo.** D. Whitelock, *Famulus Christi*, p. 30, writes that 'it seems to me likely that it was Nothhelm who brought to Bede the *Life* of St Æthelburg of Barking, which Bede used, and who supplied him with information about Eorcenwald, bishop of London, who was buried in Nothhelm's own church, St Paul's'. The account may have influenced the illustrations of the bodily assumption of the Virgin in the twelfth-century York Psalter, for which there existed no known fixed or standard visual form: 'a body and not a soul had to be shown to be conveyed by angels to heaven' (Henderson (Jarrow Lecture, 1980), 22). What Bede sees in these miracles of holy dying is the reward of holy living and good works; and they are here associated with women, at least one of whom was of high birth.

p. 364, l. 5. IV. 10. **Sane nullatenus praetereundum arbitror miraculum sanitatis.** Bede decides to include this miracle of restored sight for the sake of his own comment upon it: the lady's blindness was itself a gift, so that her cure before the relics of saints should illustrate the grace of healing.

p. 364, l. 25. IV. 11. **uir multum Deo deuotus ... Sebbi.** Sebbi now appears not because something needed to be said of the East Saxons but because the Barking *libellus* recounted two miracles associated with his death as a monk. Bede seems to share the common view that Sebbi ought to have been a bishop rather than a king. However, he reigned for thirty years and his queen was reluctant to see him renounce his rule and become separated from her. E. John, *Orbis Britanniae*, p. 34, takes the word 'ordinari' in a technical sense: 'What can this mean but that kings, like bishops, were ordained?' Bede frequently uses the verb *ordinare* for the making of bishops—indeed, of priests and deacons—but never of kings. I doubt if he had a technical meaning in mind in this passage.

p. 366, ll. 6-8. IV. 11. **Attulit ... pauperibus erogandam, nil omnimodis sibi reseruans.** Bede seems to be echoing a provision of the Rule of St Benedict (ch. 58): 'Res ... aut eroget prius pauperibus aut ... conferat monasterio, nihil sibi reservans ex omnibus', as Mayr-Harting (Jarrow Lecture, 1976, p. 8) points out. The provision otherwise phrased is however common to other rules.

p. 366, ll. 11-13. IV. 11. **timere coepit ... membrorum.** Sebbi is still king enough to wish to die with dignity. Bede approves. Bishop Waldhere of London is glad enough to be present at the end and to bury him in his cathedral. The interesting point about Waldhere's letter to his archbishop (mentioned by Colgrave) is its explicit evidence of a diocesan's subjection to his metropolitan. See Brooks, *Early History*, p. 80. Bede's employment of *urbs* here for London is curious: it reflects his sense of its importance (see Campbell, *Names, Words*, p. 37). On royal burials in St Paul's see Krüger, *Königsgrabkirchen*, p. 328.

p. 366, l. 30. IV. 11. **Cuius corpori ... sarcofagum lapideum.** It was clearly a mark of distinction to be buried in a stone sarcophagus, probably a re-used Roman sarcophagus. If the one prepared for Sebbi had not been miraculously lengthened, another would have been looked for—not made afresh. See R. Cramp, in *Saint Wilfrid at Hexham*, pp. 127, 139.

p. 368, l. 9. IV. 12. **Quartus ... antistes Leutherius fuit.** It is difficult to spot the heart of this chapter, which looks like a rag-bag based on materials derived from several sources that must include Winchester and Canterbury. It is not impossible that the Northumbrian material with which it closes was obtained from Canterbury rather than from local contacts. In fact the chapter is a deft survey of episcopal succession over comparatively few years in which Archbishop Theodore was the moving force. The amount of secular history included by Bede is precisely what is needed to explain episcopal flux, and no more.

p. 368, l. 11. IV. 12. **Cumque mortuus est Coinualch.** It is likely that the ASC is right in reporting that Cenwalh was succeeded by his queen, Seaxburh, who reigned for a year (Stenton, *Preparatory*, p. 314). 'Thus when Bede was writing, in 731, we can envisage a source of information beyond his ken, which is not unusual, though he may have heard of a disputed succession' (Harrison, *Framework*, pp. 135-6). Bede himself—and Bishop Daniel if he was Bede's informant—seems entirely unclear about the decade of West Saxon history covered by the 'subreguli'. He did not need to be clear. All that mattered to him was that the 'subreguli' did not prevent Haeddi from succeeding Leuthere as bishop. (See Dumville, *ASE* 8 (1979), 19, commenting on Kirby's views.) I do not understand what Plummer means by calling the rule of the 'subreguli' a 'temporary reversion to a form of government anterior to the institution of royalty'.

p. 368, ll. 14-15. IV. 12. **episcopatu functus Haeddi pro eo.** Finberg, *Early Charters of the West Midlands*, p. 173, suggests that Bede means that Haeddi was consecrated as an assistant bishop while Leuthere was still alive. Though possible, this is not how I should translate the Latin.*

p. 368, ll. 16-17. IV. 12. **Caedualla suscepit imperium.** Bede is not concerned with Cædwalla's claim to rule or with possible rival dynastic confrontations (on which see Kirby, *EHR* 80 (1965), 21, 24), but with his resignation after two years and his retreat to Rome; all this within the episcopate of Haeddi. Wheeler, *EHR* 36 (1921), 164 n. 3, suggested that this information might have come from a Roman Life of Cædwalla rather than from Bishop Daniel; but this seems unnecessary.

p. 368, ll. 21-2. IV. 12. **Aedilred ... adducto maligno exercitu.** The army was not 'cruel' (Colgrave) but 'wicked', as the Old English translator of Bede makes clear ('wærge'); and the source is surely Canterbury, outraged by a fierce attack for which no explanation can be advanced aside from the alternating attempts of Mercia and Wessex to control Kent (see Stenton, *Preparatory*, p. 51). However, Æthelred's otherwise pious reputation and the special attention he paid to the destruction of churches and monasteries suggests particular anger with the Church of

Canterbury. Why should Putta have sought refuge with Æthelred's own bishop, Seaxwulf? If Bede's information was right, Putta of Rochester cannot have been the Putta who was first bishop of Hereford. One can hardly make a new bishop's see out of 'possessione ecclesiae cuiusdam et agelli non grandis' (l. 28). But the see of Rochester was not finished: though very poor, it could support Theodore's replacement of Putta and his 'substituted' successor. 'Bede does not use such terms to describe the actions of other archbishops, so we may accept his words at face value to mean that Theodore himself took the initiative in choosing the bishops whom he consecrated and if necessary in removing them' (Brooks, *Early History*, p. 73). In the end, Bede's episcopal succession is assured.*

p. 370, l. 2. IV. 12. **apparuit mense Augusto stella.** Harrison, discussing the date of Ecgfrith's succession, agrees with Levison that the true year of the comet was 676, not 678; but the mistake will probably have occurred in Bede's source ('Reign of King Ecgfrith', p. 79). For Bede, a comet in mid-August was indeed a portent: it is followed by the downfall of Bishop Wilfrid (Harrison, *ASE* 2 (1973), 56; see also M. Miller, *ASE* 8 (1979), 53).

p. 370, ll. 7–8. IV. 12. **duo in locum eius substituti episcopi.** Bede seems to be in some uncertainty about what happened when Wilfrid was deposed by Ecgfrith; but he may simply be reducing a complicated situation to the few words that say all that need to be said. Furthermore, 'in Hagustaldensi siue in Lindisfarnensi' need not express doubt. What may have happened, if Michael Roper is right (in *St Wilfrid at Hexham*, p. 74), is that 'Wilfrid was from the outset intended to retain part of his original diocese and only his own refusal to compromise frustrated this intention. If this was so, then the administration of two sees by Eata could be explained by supposing that one of them was that offered to Wilfrid in 680 and probably in 678 also.' Hexham was clearly Wilfrid's northern base, where he had supporters whom Ecgfrith may have been unwilling to ignore.

p. 370, l. 14. IV. 12. **superato in bello et fugato Uulfhere.** Eddius is more explicit on Wulfhere's defeat, supplying 'a useful warning against building overmuch on the silence of Bede, whose only reference to this war is a bare statement of Wulfhere's defeat introduced casually into an account of the appointment of the first bishop of Lindsey' (Stenton, *Preparatory*, p. 50). However, Bede's statement is not casual but a necessary parenthesis to explain why Eadhæd was appointed to Lindsey with Ecgfrith's approval. 'No one would learn from the *Historia Ecclesiastica* that Lindsey was ruled by kings of no less noble ancestry than Ecgfrith and Æthelred themselves' (Stenton, *Preparatory*, p. 127). As Mr Harrison has pointed out to me, while there were several bishops of Lindsey between 678 and 767, Bede mentions no king. Did Ecgfrith's victory make him a Bretwalda? He does not appear in Bede's list. See Vollrath-Reichelt, *Königsgedanke*, p. 95, commenting on John, *Orbis Britanniae*, p. 13.

p. 370, l. 25. IV. 12. **Trumuini ad prouinciam Pictorum.** 'That Trumwine's ecclesiastical jurisdiction extended beyond the Forth is proved by the events of 685. It is quite clear that during the second half of the seventh century Oswiu and Ecgfrith, not content with the vague overlordship exercised by their predecessors, had pushed northwards to annex Pictish territory beyond the Forth' (Wainwright, *Problem of the Picts*, p. 7). Hunter Blair (*Studies in Early British History*, p. 169) adds that 'The Picts had of course long been Christian, but at this date they still observed Celtic forms and no doubt their conversion to orthodox ways was among the purposes for which this see was established.' Abercorn on the Forth, Trumwine's see, lay in English territory, but this need not cast doubt on Bede's statement that his responsibility extended (north) 'ad prouinciam Pictorum'. Considering the complicated episcopal movements that are the subject of this chapter, Bede shows great skill in inserting just that amount of secular activity that provides the essential framework.

p. 370, ll. 29-30. IV. 13. **Pulsus autem ... Brittaniam rediit.** Bede proceeds with an account of Wilfrid's South Saxon mission. Not as warm as that of Eddius (on whose account he is not relying), it probably reflects the approach of his sources. These could have included a written report from Bishop Daniel, perhaps based on information from Wilfrid's monastery of Selsey, and more information from Hexham and Bishop Acca. Kirby, *EHR* 98 (1983), 111, emphasizes the different approach to Wilfrid of Hexham on the one hand and Ripon (Eddius' source) on the other; and he is right to detect a keener interest in the miraculous in Bede's account than in that of Eddius, who was more concerned with political vicissitudes. Levison clearly thought that Bede added material from Eddius to III. 25, 28, and IV. 2, 3, 12, 13, but does not suggest at what stage (*BLTW*, p. 138). See the perceptive study of Mayr-Harting, 'St Wilfrid in Sussex' (*Studies in Sussex Church History*, ed. M. J. Kitch (1981), 1–17), which has the additional merit of drawing attention to Wilfrid's knowledge of missionary enterprise on the continent and its possible effect on his Sussex mission.

p. 372, ll. 7–10. IV. 13. **Aedilualch ... filii susceptus est.** Eddius held that Wilfrid converted the king; Bede, that he had already been baptized at the instance of Wulfhere of Mercia. Since Æthelwalh's queen, a Christian, came from the Hwicce, who were subordinate to Mercia, it sounds as if Bede's information was accurate. It is difficult to believe, as some do, that the differences between Eddius and Bede were due to Bede's ability to 'doctor' his material. It is less a question of which writer displays greater veracity than of which writer uses the more reliable sources; and on this we can only remain unsure.

p. 372, ll. 10–11. IV. 13. **duas illi prouincias donauit.** Since these territories were West Saxon, and were soon to be reclaimed, there could be no better evidence that Wulfhere's control of Sussex was the result of conquest, and was resented. It appears from IV. 16 that the native dynasty of the Isle of Wight survived. The apparent failure of Wulfhere to convert the South Saxons until Wilfrid's arrival is further evidence of resentment against the Mercian coup. The fact that there was a South Saxon bishop of Rochester (Damian) before Wilfrid's arrival in Sussex is no evidence that the bishop had come from a people already converted.

p. 372, ll. 27–9. IV. 13. **Uilfrid non solum ... temporalis interitus eripuit.** Bede reaches the miraculous with two events: first, the ending of a terrible drought as soon as Wilfrid's mission began, and secondly his teaching them how to fish, 'diuina se iuuante gratia' (p. 374, l. 12). They may derive from different strata of tradition and are here woven together by Bede or his source. As to the fish, Kirby, *EHR* 98 (1983), 111, draws attention to Eddius' account, not mentioned by Bede, of a large haul of fish on Wilfrid's first coming to Frisia, which disposed the Frisians to listen to him. Eddius and Bede were presumably drawing on different accounts of the same miracle. At all events, such happy coincidences certainly assisted the mission; and Bede empha- sizes this here, as on other occasions elsewhere.

p. 374, ll. 20-1. IV. 13. **suos homines, qui exules uagabantur.** Clearly Wilfrid's followers were exiles in a political sense. Bede does not mean that, like Wilfrid, they were all *peregrini* devoted to a mission of evangelization. Wilfrid was always a man who could attract and hold a following. Among them were the *fratres* who became the core of his monastery at Selsey.

p. 374, l. 32. IV. 13. **omnes quae ... facultates.** Colgrave and Mynors prefer the reading *quae* to Plummer's *qui*; and despite E. John's objection (*Orbis Britanniae*, p. 266) I think they are right, and the sense of the sentence is as they translate it. While it seems unnecessary to give 'facultates' the technical sense that John champions (ibid., pp. 275-71), his excursus is a valuable exercise in pondering the exact meaning of Bede's words.

p. 376, l. 1. IV. 13. **seruos et ancillas.** Mayr-Harting, 'St Wilfrid in Sussex', p. 13, makes the point that the manumission and baptism of slaves was often a first step towards the priesthood. This will not of course have applied to all the 250 freed by Wilfrid; but from them he could have formed the nucleus of a local clergy. Such was the practice of missionaries abroad.

pp. 376-80. IV. 14. 'The type of text which Plummer calls C appears to preserve one recension slightly earlier than the last, differing from it chiefly in not including chapter xiv of the fourth book: traces of other insertions into an earlier version or versions appear in the text as we have it' (Campbell. 'Bede, p. 167). This, as Campbell observes, will probably be due to the fact that Bede did not have all his material available when he made his first draft. Since the miracle in this chapter is derived from Acca, as a late insertion, the case is rather strengthened for holding that the previous material on Wilfrid in Sussex did not come from Acca. I have difficulty in accepting Jones' judgement (*Saints' Lives*, p. 49) that 'Bede's information about Sussex was limited to that supplied by Acca' and that when he had completed his first draft and shown it to Acca, the latter then recalled further information, and also sent him a copy of Eddius (ibid., pp. 49–50). Acca had in fact told him the story of the South Saxon boy 'saepius', not just once as a sudden recollection.

p. 376, ll. 22–3. IV. 14. **puerulus quidam de natione Saxonum.** Wilfrid had clearly reinforced his own followers at Selsey with some recently converted South Saxons, including boys on whom the future of the mission might well depend. This was common practice among the continental missionaries. This boy's experience contains an important lesson: a natural disaster's effects may be stemmed, after suitable monastic fasting, by the intervention of a saintly intercessor whose messengers will be saints of much higher standing—in this case, St Peter and St Paul. Such indeed is the final message of the chapter: 'Ex qua nimirum uisione multi . . . sunt mirabiliter accensi' (p. 380, ll. 12–15).

p. 378, l. 4. IV. 14. **possessiunculis.** Not necessarily pejorative. As in III. 24, Bede here uses the diminutive in a context where there can be no such intention. *Possessio* could mean a settlement or several such; there was an ambiguity in the word and its diminutive which may also be reflected in charter-formulae, as in *CS* No. 229 (Sawyer, No. 115). See Campbell, *Names, Words*, p. 47. Bede probably understands single settlements.*

p. 378, l. 15. IV. 14. **Quaerant in suis códicibus.** Selsey was already provided with texts of record. 'We do not know how far Bede himself used obituaries' (Levison, *BLTW*, p. 143 n. 2), but Selsey clearly did. However, Harrison writes (*Framework*, p. 89) that 'By the combination of regnal years with obits and other events Bede had an important source at his disposal, quite apart from what Paschal annals could contribute.' Continental instances of the recording of deaths, with or without dates, are by no means confined to Willibrord's calendar. Important examples are the *Libri Memoriales* of Reichenau and Remiremont.

p. 378, l. 19. IV. 14. **in memoriam praefati regis Osualdi.** Wilfrid and his pupil Acca clearly shared an interest in miracles associated with Oswald. The king was remembered at Hexham and in Wilfrid's two missionary areas of Frisia and Sussex. (See Kirby, *St Wilfrid at Hexham*, p. 26, and Mayr-Harting, 'St Wilfrid in Sussex', p. 17.) It is clear that Wilfrid, not Bede in *HE*, was the propagator of the cult. A missionary would see in such a king a natural protector of, and Christian model for, peoples in the early stages of conversion. To what extent Oswald had 'ruled' the South Saxons is unknown. One bears in mind that the king's cult was primarily Northumbrian, that Acca, Wilfrid, and Bede were Northumbrians, and that Selsey was effectively a Northumbrian monastery. Oswald's 'rule' has thus to be seen as through Northumbrian eyes. But it may have been real enough. Bishop Daniel, quite independently, could have known something about it.

p. 380, l. 18. IV. 15. **Interea superueniens ... Caedualla.** This short chapter (really a continuation of chapter 14: see Colgrave and Mynors, p. 326 n. *a*) gives a picture of Cædwalla that differs from that of Eddius (ch. 42). If, as Jones asserts (*Saints' Lives*, pp. 48-9), Bede owes his material on Cædwalla to Acca alone, one may well ask why Acca also entrusted to Bede a copy of Eddius. However Bede obtained his information, he and Eddius had widely different interests. Eddius is concerned with Wilfrid, while Bede wishes to explain why it came about that after Wilfrid's withdrawal the South Saxons were without a bishop of their own for so long a time. The brief summary of Cædwalla and Ine explains why. As always, Bede has his eye fixed on episcopal succession. I am not clear why Jones holds that 'a study of Wessex material indicates that Bede overstated his debt to Bishop Daniel of Winchester'; nor, as so often, can we know what material came from Canterbury, from where some information at least about the West Saxons was available. It is certainly true, as Jones points out, that the Anglo-Saxon Chronicle is a better guide to West Saxon history than is *HE*.

Bede would not have supposed that his reference to Cædwalla was any sort of an account of West and South Saxon history.

p. 382, l. 2. IV. 16. **insulam Uectam . . . idolatriae dedita.** The Isle of Wight, according to Bede's informants, was the last part of Britain to be converted, and therefore its inclusion at this point was important to him. Even so, a chapter would hardly have been justified had it not been for the story of the baptism and execution of the two princes. He is not concerned with the reasons for Cædwalla's treatment of the territory nor with Wilfrid's involvement in them. The only section of the chapter that has no bearing on conversion is the geographical detail in the final paragraph.

p. 382, l. 3. IV. 16. **omnes indigenas exterminare.** Bede is clear that the slaughter went far beyond the native royal *genus*: a subsequent settlement of West Saxons was also intended. The Merovingians behaved in much the same way east of the Rhine, estabishing Frankish communities as territory fell to them. Cædwalla's policy of extermination of rival lines is discussed by Dumville, *ASE* 8 (1979), 19.

p. 382, l. 6. IV. 16. **quartam partem . . . Domino daret.** It may well be, as Finberg argues (*Early Charters of Wessex*, p. 216) that it was 'under Wilfrid's influence that the kings of Wessex began to issue charters when making grants of land'. However, none survives for the Isle of Wight and Bede does not use charter-evidence.*

p. 382, ll. 12–13. IV. 16. **erat filius sororis eius.** It does not seem that Bede, any more than Benedict Biscop, objected to the succession of kindred to ecclesiastical office, provided that they had the necessary qualifications. He raises no eyebrow at Wilfrid's bestowal of 300 hides upon his nephew who, though a *clericus*, needed a priest for teaching and baptism.

p. 382, l. 19. IV. 16. **in proximam Iutorum prouinciam.** See Myres, *PBA* 56 (1970), 149–50, on the survival of the Jutes to Bede's time. The place 'Ad Lapidem' to which the two young princes were taken is less likely to be Stoneham than Stone

Farm (see Ekwall, *Concise Oxford Dictionary of English Place-Names*, under *Stone, Bk.*)

p. 382, ll. 23-4, IV. 16. **monasterium ... Hreutford.** An otherwise unrecorded monastery. There will have been others such in early Wessex. Kirby, *BJRL*, 48 (1965-6), 364, considers that Bede's information about the Isle of Wight came from Bishop Daniel, which seems likely enough. The detail suggests that it reached Bede in writing. Bede sees no unwarranted severity in the execution of the young princes once Abbot Cyneberht had baptized them. On the other hand, he does object to the absence of a bishop till Daniel's time, which absence was attributable to alien rule.

p. 384, ll. 17-18. IV. 17. **hunc synodalibus litteris ... curauit.** No doubt using what Canterbury provided, unless a copy were already at Jarrow, Bede gives part of the council of Hatfield's confession of faith. Its decrees were 'formed after the model of a Roman council, but with the names of the Emperors superseded by the names of the kings to whose realms the attending bishops belonged' (Levison, *BLTW*, p. 148). This implied a troublesome reckoning for Bede, as Levison observes, and did not correspond to the unity of the English Church. But it was plainly Canterbury, not Bede, that was responsible. The date of the council remains a matter for argument: whether 679 or 680. Kirby, *EHR* 78 (1963), 517, opts for 680, basing his case on the year of accession of Hlothhere of Kent; but Harrison, *Framework*, pp. 41, 83, shows why 679 is to be preferred, and S. Wood, *EHR* 98 (1983), 287, follows him with some provisos. The form of heresy debated was in fact Monothelitism, of which Bede makes very little mention, and none at all of Maximus the Confessor, the great Greek theologian under whose influence Pope Martin I had summoned the Lateran synod of 649. See Bonner, *ASE* 2 (1973), 88: Bede was a stranger to 'the sophisticated world of Greek patristic theology'. It was perhaps less the theology of the issue than the demonstration of Theodore's authority, and of his reliance on Rome, that persuaded Bede to include extracts from Hatfield at this point. The doctrine that he would have taught at Jarrow must have been Latin, and specifically Augustinian, to judge from what is known of the books available to him.

p. 388, l. 2. IV. 18. **uir uenerabilis Iohannes.** The council of Hatfield reminds Bede of the presence there of the Archchanter John, about whom it seems that Monkwearmouth-Jarrow had information because of his connection with Benedict Biscop. It also reminds him that John's brief from Pope Agatho went a good deal further than the teaching of Roman chant.

p. 388, ll. 5–6. IV. 18. **Benedicto, cuius supra meminimus.** A slip that may best be explained by D. Whitelock's query (*Famulus Christi*, p. 22): 'is it possible that in the early stages of composing this work Bede included some account of the abbots of his monastery, but removed this part after writing his *Historia Abbatum*?'*

p. 388, l. 13. IV. 18. **epistulam priuilegii.** Biscop's charter is lost but Wormald (*Famulus Christi*, pp. 146 ff.) shows how its main outlines may be recovered by comparison with what we have or know of contemporary privileges, e.g. those obtained by Abbot Hadrian for Canterbury and Bishop Wilfrid for Ripon. They may all belong to a new class of monastic privilege, quite possibly owing much to Irish–Frankish example. If continental examples be accepted, 'they set up a shocking contrast with the impression of Biscop's horizons that is given by Bede. In Bede's view, it is Rome and almost only Rome that counts in the making of Biscop; the Gallic episodes are asides and afterthoughts' (ibid., p. 149). In brief, what Biscop's privilege secured would be: freedom of abbatial elections, protection of property and revenues from outside interference, and the reservation of jurisdiction to the pope except in limited disciplinary and sacramental matters proper to the diocesan. These apart, the diocesan only entered a monastery by invitation.

p. 388, l. 18. IV. 18. **cursum canendi annuum.** C. W. Jones (*Famulus Christi*, p. 266) observes that strictly speaking there could have been no texts, since musical notation was not invented for a century or more. However, John did commit something to writing. On the nature of the *cantus* taught, see

Margot H. King, *Saints, Scholars*, i. 149. What is more impressive is Bede's evidence that instruction by John was widely sought by monastic communities.

p. 390, ll. 3-4. IV. 18. **secum ueniens adtulit . . . transscribendam commodauit.** Bede could thus have studied the decrees of Pope Martin's council in his own monastery, though it does not follow that the copy of the Hatfield decrees that John took for the pope was also made at Jarrow.

p. 390, l. 16. IV. 18. **propter amorem sancti Martini.** Like Biscop, John has his connection with St Martin at Tours and, as abbot of a monastery under the same patronage, feels strong affection for the saint. He had even been provided by Tours with 'adiutores' on his way to Britain, which can only mean monastic advisers. This is the kind of link that best explains a copy of Gregory of Tours' *History* at Jarrow, then or slightly later. Bede is respectful to St Martin's memory though one would not guess from his pages the immense influence of the saint's career on western Christianity: it was not part of the story of Rome. Evidence of the honouring of St Martin in Wessex comes from Ine's laws (688-98), ch. 4: 'Church dues shall be rendered at Martinmas'. Lohaus, *Die Merowinger und England*, p. 46, attributes this West Saxon link with Frankish practice to Bishop Agilbert.

p. 390, l. 25. IV. 19. **Accepit . . . Aedilthrydam.** Ecgfrith's first wife, Æthelthryth, is Bede's ideal of the virgin queen; an ideal, if widely practised, that could not have been congenial to kings in search of heirs. Wilfrid's part in keeping her virgin and facilitating her taking the veil clearly cost him the goodwill of his king. Her entry into Coldingham may have coincided with her donation of land at Hexham to Wilfrid but exact dating is impossible. (See Roper, in *St Wilfrid at Hexham*, pp. 169-71.) The story also illustrates how little say a royal princess had in the bestowal of her hand. For comparable situations on the continent see R. Folz, 'Tradition hagiographique et culte de Sainte Bathilde, reine des Francs', *Acad. des Inscriptions et Belles-Lettres* (1975), 369-84. Bede presumably used an Ely Life of St Æthelthryth but added information based on a conversation with Wilfrid, 'beatae memoriae' (ll. 33-4). The account of the abbess at Ely centres on her uncorrupt body, years after death, as proof of her virginal life.

p. 390, ll. 28–9. IV. 19. **princeps ... uocabulo Tondberct.** As Campbell points out (Jarrow Lecture, 1979, p. 5), this is 'the only marriage Bede records of the offspring of one *rex* to someone who was not the offspring of another'. On the limits of the territory of the South Gyrwe see Whitelock, *ASE* 1 (1972), 7.

p. 392, ll. 3–7. IV. 19. **Nec diffidendum ... pollicetur.** Anxious to bolster the authenticity of Æthelthryth's virginity, Bede remarks that what has happened in the past may easily be repeated today with the help of the same Lord. 'Aucun discours théorique ne pouvait, mieux que ces quelques mots, exprimer l'assurance sereine d'une perpétuelle présence de Dieu à l'histoire humaine' (Tugène, 'L'Hist. "eccl." ', p. 156).

p. 392, ll. 13–14. IV. 19. **in loco quem Coludi urbem nominant.** Thomas, *Early Christian Archaeology*, p. 35, discusses the fortress-site of Æbbe's monastery.*

p. 392, ll. 24–5. IV. 19. **raro praeter ... manducauerit.** 'The fact that his [sc. Wilfrid's] pupil, St Æthelthryth, failed to fast on festivals is a further hint of Gallic influence' (Wormald, *Famulus Christi*, p. 144, who also notes the close links between her family and Faremoutiers, p. 158).

p. 396, ll. 27–8. IV. 20. **Videtur oportunum ... inserere.** It is not vanity that moves Bede to insert his poem on Æthelthryth but a desire to link her through verse, in a traditional way, with the succession of virgins that had always marked the history of the Church. She thus becomes a new link between the Early Church and Bede's Church: 'Nostra quoque egregia iam tempora uirgo beauit' (p. 398, l. 23). Bede is very proud of Æthelthryth. He is not urging all royal ladies to take the veil, at least while they are marriageable, but he is insisting that this is the highest calling for the elect minority and a credit to any Christian people.

p. 396, ll. 30–1. IV. 20. **imitari morem sacrae scripturae.** The poem is in deliberate imitation of biblical practice: songs should

be inserted into history. Bede's piece is not an outpouring of the heart but a mannered composition (see Kendall, in *Saints, Scholars*, i. 177-8). It lacks the ecstatic warmth of Venantius Fortunatus' great poem on virginity and the calling of the nun to be Christ's bride (see my 'Bede and Plummer', above, p. xxix), a poem known to Bede. Bede's lines tell us nothing factual about Æthelthryth that had not already been recounted in the previous chapter and in this sense fall within the well-tried device of *opus geminatum*, a verse version (not always by the same writer) of a prose account. On *opus geminatum* see P. Godman, 'The Anglo-Latin *Opus Geminatum*, from Aldhelm to Alcuin', *Medium Aevum*, 50 (1981), 215-29, summarized in his *Alcuin, The Bishops, Kings and Saints of York* (OMT, 1982), lxxviii–lxxxviii.*

p. 400, l. 11. IV. 21. **conserto graui proelio.** It is not clear why hostilities broke out in 679, culminating in the battle of the Trent. It may have been connected with control of the province of Lindsey (see Stenton, *Preparatory*, p. 51) but Bede does not say so; nor does he appear to favour either side. What concerns him is the prospect of feud, following the death in battle of Ælfwine, and the intervention of Archbishop Theodore. Colgrave's translation does not make it clear that the likelihood of continued fighting resulted from Ælfwine's death. For some observations on feud see my 'Bloodfeud of the Franks', *The Long-Haired Kings*, pp. 121-47.

p. 400, ll. 17-19. IV. 21. **Theodorus ... extinguit incendium.** Bede does not report whether Theodore was invited to act as arbitrator (which would have been normal in a case of feud) or whether he took the initiative. Either way, it is a remarkable tribute to the reach of his prestige and the respect in which both Mercia and Northumbria held him. While it is true, as Colgrave observes, that the Church encouraged the settlement of feud, the interests of the feuding parties equally welcomed a chance to settle by arbitration. The following chapter also contains a threat of feud at a lowlier level, but that is not why Bede tells the story.

p. 400, ll. 24-5. IV. 22. **In praefato autem proelio ... memorabile quiddam factum.** Though this circumstantial story (no doubt recast by Bede) also concerns the battle of the Trent, its source appears to be different: 'quidam eorum' (p. 404, l. 29), who had it from Imma himself, may have been monks of 'Tunnacaestir' (p. 402, l. 14, unidentified). It is rightly inserted at this point. For some implications of the story see my 'Bede and Plummer', pp. xxv–xxvi.

p. 402, ll. 5–8. IV. 22. **rusticum ... uenisse testatus est.** Imma's attempt to pass as a peasant includes the statement that he was married, presumably so that his captor should not forcibly marry him to a female slave. Had Imma been a West Saxon, he might not have found it easy to claim that a peasant came to battle merely as a bearer of provisions; but he was a Northumbrian, a member of 'a society in which warrior-peasants were thin on the ground' (L. Alcock, *Angles, Saxons and Jutes*, p. 177, who seems to imply that Bede should have known that Imma's pose would have cut no ice with a Mercian *gesith*). On the position of the *gesith* (*comes*), see Loyn, *EHR* 70 (1955), 536.

p. 402, ll. 19–20. IV. 22. **Quarum celebratione ... continuo solueretur.** It is the thegn, not Bede, who had heard tales of 'litteras solutorias', and clearly believes in them, though a Christian. What interests Bede is the loosening of Imma's bonds when his brother is celebrating mass. There was a Petrine background to stories of the loosening of bonds (Acts 12: 7). See also Gregory of Tours, *Hist.* x. 6. Bede's account is closely paralleled in Gregory the Great's *Dialogues*, IV. 59 (ed. de Vogüé and Antin, iii. 196), where a captive's chains are loosened whenever his wife 'pro eo offerebat sacrificium'. Bede was familiar with the *Dialogues*.*

p. 404, ll. 1–2. IV. 22. **dignus es morte ... interemti.** As Plummer saw, the implication is that the feud must be carried by any member of a hostile force that kills one's brother and kindred.

p. 404, l. 4. IV. 22. **uendidit eum Lundoniam Freso.** On Frisians and the slave trade see Mayr-Harting, 'St Wilfrid in Sussex', p. 12. Imma was now worth selling because he was known to be a thegn. He was equally worth ransoming, but not by a Mercian to Northumbrians with whom he felt himself to be at feud.

p. 404, ll. 23-6. IV. 22. **Multique ... qui de saeculo migrauerant.**
Bede has a wider interest in the story than the possibility that
others like Imma might be delivered from captivity: it is for the
bodies and souls of those already dead that the offering of the
mass may secure everlasting redemption. This is why Bede
inserts the story in 'historiae nostrae ecclesiasticae' (l. 31).

p. 404, l. 33-p. 406, l. 3. IV. 23. **religiosissima Christi famula
Hild ... transiuit.** Bede's long account of Hild, presumably
based on a report from Whitby, enables him to explain why such
a life was important and at the same time to catch up with some
bishops. Its slant is not consciously pro-Celtic. Though it was
Aidan who recalled her to Northumbria and instructed her, she
had earlier been taught and baptized by Paulinus and had
intended to pursue her vocation in Francia, at Chelles. It is a
further warning not to distinguish too sharply between the
labours of Celtic and Roman missionaries, or indeed missionaries in Francia.

p. 406, l. 16. IV. 23. **in monasterio Cale peregrinam.** For Chelles
see note on III. 8 (p. 236, l. 25). Hild planned to be rather more
than a 'stranger' (Colgrave). Technically, her aim was to be an
exile (*peregrina*) in a foreign land, devoted to the duties of such.
At Chelles she wished to join her sister Hereswith, also a
peregrina. Stenton, *Preparatory*, p. 87, comments on the name
Hereswith: Hereric and Breguswith give their daughter a
compound name, derived from their own names. Bede is clear
about the royal connections of the two ladies; their high
connections were important for the furtherance of religious
foundations.*

p. 406, ll. 26-7. IV. 23. **in monasterio, quod uocatur Heruteu.** On
the doubtful remains of Hartlepool monastery see Cramp,
Famulus Christi, p. 9.

p. 408, ll. 6-7. IV. 23. **monasterium in loco, qui uocatur
Streanaeshalch.** H. M. and J. Taylor, *Anglo-Saxon Architecture*, ii.
654-5, describe the foundations of a substantial part of the
domestic buildings of Hild's Whitby; the church presumably lay
under the present-day ruins of the medieval abbey. What has

been excavated justifies Campbell's view ('The Church in Anglo-Saxon Towns', p. 121) that 'A monastery such as Whitby, with its numerous buildings, its crafts and its maritime contacts must have been considerably more like a town than were most places.'

p. 408, ll. 10–11. IV. 23. **maxime pacis et caritatis custodiam docuit.** As Bede well knew, peace and charity were not easily to be enforced in any monastery—male, female or, as here, mixed. Great ladies and those more humbly born could not be brought together in a closed community without giving opportunities for trouble. An example of what might happen is vividly described by Gregory of Tours (*Hist.* IX. 39–43): an account of the rioting in the monastery founded by Queen Radegundis at Poitiers and of the great difficulty experienced by kings and bishops in bringing it to a conclusion. The need for peace within and outside the community is reinforced later in the chapter (p. 412, ll. 9–10) when the dying Hild exhorts her community to preserve 'pace euangelica'. The Gospels had already been recalled by reference to the egalitarianism practised by the Early Church, as Plummer rightly observes.

p. 408, ll. 18–20. IV. 23. **facillime uiderentur . . . repperiri.** Bede refers to men under Hild's rule (whatever technically that may have been) and not to nuns. This is made clear by the following sentence: they included five future bishops, and of the career of one of them, Oftfor, bishop of the Hwicce (Worcester), Bede now gives an account which is likelier to be based on Mercian information than on what Whitby provided. On the foundation of the see of Worcester see Finberg, *The Early Charters of the West Midlands*, p. 172. Bede's 'multo tempore' (p. 410, l. 2), adequate for his purposes, gives no help to historians whose business it is to determine Hwiccian regnal years on the difficult evidence supplied by charters.

p. 408, ll. 33–4. IV. 23. **Romam adire . . . aestimabatur.** Bede can only mean that what was proper 'eo tempore' is no longer so in his own day, and he wishes it were. Compare what he writes about the 'segnitia nostri temporis' in III. 5. But the journey to Rome was not lightly to be undertaken. See Levison, *England and the Continent*, p. 39.

p. 410, ll. 18-19. IV. 23. **etiam plurimis longius ... occasionem salutis.** Industry and virtue are not only effective within the community. Their report spreads salvation far afield. This had been foretold of Hild at the time of her birth. It is a common feature of prophecy to be recognized only after its fulfilment; and Breguswith's dream was a prophecy.

p. 414, l. 6. IV. 23. **Pulchraque rerum concordia.** This limpid phrase sounds more like Bede than his source. The visions of the death of Hild, 'matrem illarum omnium' (p. 412, l. 30), are not in fact visions of her death but of her soul's ascent to heaven. They are the final proof of the exemplary life vouchsafed to the faithful.

p. 414, ll. 24-5. IV. 24. **frater quidam ... specialiter insignis.** No passage in *HE* has received more attention than this beautiful story obviously derived from Whitby and recast by Bede. It might have excited less attention if an Old Northumbrian version of the lines of poetry cited in Latin by Bede had not survived, in addition to a late West Saxon version. However, what actually happened and what Bede makes of it are distinct issues. As to the first, we are in the realm of conjecture; but as to the second, an attempt at understanding is possible.

p. 414, ll. 29-30. IV. 24. **multorum saepe ... accensi.** Bede's first point: Cædmon's songs were an inspiration to many to think of heavenly things. The gift of song was not for the edification of a restricted company. There is no problem about their being in English: Bede says that it was Cædmon's own language. Too much is made of his name, which is British in origin (Jackson, *Language and History*, p. 244); but all that this suggests is 'inter-marriage and intimate fusion between the two races, which, in any case, must presumably have taken place on a considerable scale; and therefore some degree of bilingualism'.

p. 414, ll. 32-3. IV. 24. **Namque ipse ... artem didicit.** Bede cites St Paul's epistle to the Galatians: Paul was 'an apostle not of men, neither by man, but by Jesus Christ and God the Father' (Gal. 1: 1). Bede's thoughts are on St Paul in relation to Cædmon, and remain so. (How often Bede is reminded of St

Paul is remarked by Tugène, 'L'Hist. "eccl." ', pp. 158-9.)
Cædmon owes his art not to man but to God direct. Moreoever,
he could recite no secular poetry, as did other lay workers in the
community. This is a significant matter since it means that he
had no background of versification before the miracle of his
dream.

p. 416, ll. 12-14. IV. 24. **ipse coepit cantare ... iste est sensus.**
The Old Northumbrian version (nine lines) is edited by A. H.
Smith, *Three Northumbrian Poems*, revised edn. (1968), pp. 38-40.
Smith observes that the earliest use of *dryhten* (lord) as a
Christian term in any Germanic language is by Cædmon. On its
secular sense see D. H. Green, *The Carolingian Lord*, pp. 276ff.
There are other words in the poem that belong to secular
heroic-poetic tradition. Another edition is that of E. Van
K. Dobbie, *The Anglo-Saxon Minor Poems* (1942), 105, who also
discusses the manuscript transmission of the poem. C. L. Wrenn,
'The Poetry of Cædmon', *PBA* 32 (1946), asks wherein the
miracle of the poem lay and proposes that it was that 'one
obviously quite untrained in the aristocratic heroic tradition of
the Anglo-Saxon poetic manner—its highly technical diction,
style and metre—suddenly showed that ... he had acquired the
mastery over this long and specialized discipline' (p. 286).
Perhaps even more miraculous was that Cædmon should have
been the first to apply the discipline to Christian edification.
Crépin, *Famulus Christi*, p. 179, sees no particular miracle in the
issue of technique: 'the rhythm of poetry was not different from
that of ordinary prose ... The miracle in Cædmon's story is that
he succeeded in adapting ancient traditional themes and
formulas to new revolutionary ideas.' Cædmon had never heard
Christian poetry though he had often listened to secular recita-
tions and absorbed their formulaic patterns. His achievement
was thus sanctity working upon memórization. Cædmon's
poetic diction still raises problems; but Bede, himself a poet,
chose rather to see the miracle in divine inspiration conveyed in
the traditional vehicle of a dream. It was God who spoke to and
through Cædmon.*

p. 416, ll. 20-2. IV. 24. **neque enim possunt carmina ...
transferri.** Bede speaks as a poet. I agree with Crépin, *Famulus*

Christi, p. 183, that Colgrave's translation of 'decoris ac digni-
tatis' misses the point: '*decor* ... refers to sound and *dignitas* to
sense'. Therefore Bede means that you cannot translate literally
'without damage to sound and sense'.

p. 418, ll. 9-11. IV. 24. **At ipse cuncta ... conuertebat.** Of this
very extensive programme of further versification nothing
certainly survives, though there can be no doubt of Cædmon's
effect on the course of Old English poetry up to King Alfred's
time. Nor can his high repute be attributed solely to Bede. But
his general method of composition is made plain by Bede:
passages of the Bible in the vernacular were read to him; he
memorized them; then he meditated upon them, innocently
chewing the cud; and finally they fell into metrical form in his
mind. Still the miracle remained and equally the purpose of the
miracle, which was to spread knowledge and love of the biblical
message. This was how Cædmon himself saw it; and this,
together with his strict observance of the rule of his house,
explained 'pulchro uitam suam fine' (ll. 24-5), of which he had
foreknowledge.

p. 418, ll. 12-13. IV. 24. **Canebat autem de creatione mundi.**
Virginia Day, *ASE* 3 (1974), 54 ff., notes that Bede's description
of the corpus of Cædmon's poetry 'is no less than a description
of the catechetical *narratio* as well', and, noting the break
marked by 'item' (l. 17) at the end of the catechetical *narratio*
proper, she draws attention to Augustine's view (*De Cat. Rud.* 8.
2) that the subject of future judgement should be raised *narra-
tione finita*. And so it is.

p. 420. l. 6. IV. 24. **'Quid opus est eucharistia?'.** It may well be
that in this account of Cædmon's death, as elsewhere in *HE*,
Bede is turning into *oratio recta* what he found in *oratio obliqua*.
There is a stylistic similarity between such accounts that points
to Bede's unfailing literary sense of how to secure dramatic
effect.

p. 420, ll. 28-9. IV. 25. **monasterium uirginum ... cognominant.**
A double monastery is inhabited by Irish and Angles and is
probably, as Kirby says (*BJRL* 48 (1965-6), 355), 'the Bernician

counterpart of the Deiran monastery of Whitby'. It was clearly important in royal eyes but Bede had little information because it was burnt down in the 680s. His present story, as he remarks in conclusion, came from the priest Eadgisl, once of Coldingham and then of Jarrow. I do not doubt that he could have provided Bede with much more information had it been required.

p. 420, ll. 30–2. IV. 25. **Quod tamen a malitia ... aduertere.** The fire was God's judgement on the 'malitia' of the community and especially, one infers, of aristocratic ladies. There are continental instances of the same trouble. Bede bolsters his narrative with citations from both Testaments that illustrate the continuous presence of God in the affairs of man. God will take vengeance for shortcomings today, as in Hebrew times, and particularly on religious houses dedicated to his service. See Tugène, 'L'Hist. "eccl."', p. 156.

p. 422, IV. 25. The story of the ascetic Adomnán (not the abbot of Iona) indicates that those who are truly obedient to God will be vouchsafed warnings that could save others. This is one function of prophecy.

p. 424, ll. 33–4. IV. 25. **domunculae ... factae erant.** As at Whitby, these separate dwellings show that Coldingham was organized on a Celtic and not a Roman model. See Addleshaw, Jarrow Lecture, 1963, p. 9.*

p. 424, ll. 37–8. IV. 25. **texendis subtilioribus indumentis.** Reliable studies of what remains of Anglo-Saxon embroidery and related techniques are those of Elizabeth Plenderleith, Grace Crowfoot, and others in *The Relics of Saint Cuthbert*, ed. C. F. Battiscombe (1956), 375–469. Also relevant is the apparel of Aunegundis, queen of the Frankish king Chlotar I, buried at St Denis (Paris) c. 570. Peter Lasko has attempted a reconstruction of her appearance at burial in *The Dark Ages*, ed. D. Talbot Rice (1965), following p. 198. Splendid apparel for nuns should have nothing to do with bridal finery on earth, as Bede observes, but, as he probably had in mind from a reading of Venantius Fortunatus' *De Virginitate*, with their ultimate appearance as brides of Christ in heaven.*

p. 426, ll. 21–3. IV. 25. **temporalibus damnis ... tollat.** The lesson Bede draws from the ruin of Coldingham is that God's vengeance can still today cost Christian communities temporal loss and even eternal perdition. This is the other facet to the temporal gain that results from conversion and obedience to his will.

p. 426, ll. 26–7. IV. 26. **uastauit misere gentem ... amicissimam.** Bede does not concern himself with the reasons for the once-admired Ecgfrith's raid on the Irish; unprovoked as Bede sees it, and against the advice of holy men, it explains Ecgfrith's death next year at Nechtanesmere and the consequent decline of the Northumbrian kingdom. But Ecgfrith does not die directly because of his unprovoked aggression. He dies because his victims had called down God's vengeance upon him. A Christian king's duties outweigh sentiments of national loyalty. Contrast Gregory of Tours' appreciation of Clovis' attack on the kingdom of Sigebert (*Hist.* II. 40). Bede recalls St Paul to the Corinthians (1 Cor. 6: 10): those who curse will not inherit the kingdom of God but their cursing may be effective all the same. Duncan, *The Writing of History*, pp. 14 ff., sees Bede's source in a narrative based on Irish annals, perhaps Pictish-mediated. I do not see why the narrative should not have been Northumbrian. On the political significance of Nechtansmere see Kirby, *Famulus Christi*, p. 291. Good reasons for Ecgfrith's Irish expedition are given by A. P. Smyth, *Warlords and Holy Men*, p. 26. See also Bullough, 'Missions to the English and Picts', p. 92, and, for chronology, Harrison, 'The Reign of King Ecgfrith of Northumbria'.*

p. 428, ll. 22–3. IV. 26. **uir Domini Trumuini ... recessit cum suis.** One consequence of the collapse of Northumbrian 'spes ... et uirtus' (l. 16) was the retreat to Whitby of Bishop Trumwine; not a large matter in the general débâcle perhaps, but the one on which Bede focuses. As on other occasions, Trumwine's life of austerity was a benefit to many. The reference to his burial there must come from Whitby itself.

p. 430, l. 4. IV. 26. **uir in scripturis doctissimus.** No doubt Aldfrith owed his education to the Irish, though Bede does not make the point. His learning was the exception, not the rule, among kings. Another such was Sigeberht of the East Angles, educated in Frankish Gaul. What impresses Bede is that the learned Christian king does something to restore the fortunes of Northumbria. Irish sources record that Aldfrith's maternal grandfather was the high-king Colmán (Byrne, *Irish Kings and High-Kings*, p. 260).

p. 430, ll. 8–18. IV. 26. **Quo uidelicet anno ... liberaret.** This is one of the few passages in *HE* that have no immediate bearing on ecclesiastical history. Bede has the annalistic record or king-list before him and decides to include this entry. On chronological issues raised by Bede's dating for Hlothhere as against charter-evidence, see Harrison, *Framework*, pp. 83–4, 142–5; and for the 'reges dubii uel externi' (l. 15), Hart, *Early Charters of Eastern England*, pp. 120–1.

p. 430, ll. 20–1. IV. 27. **fecerat ordinari ... Cudberctum.** Bede concludes his fourth book with a series of chapters on St Cuthbert, about whom he was well informed, having indeed already written a Life of him. Both Bede and the author of the anonymous Life, on which he drew, owe something to the Life of St Martin by Sulpicius Severus. See my remarks above, pp. xxxii–xxxiii. Unlike Aidan, Cuthbert was a saint with a future, as Bede saw: a romanized product of the Celtic discipline, he was 'the great unifier: a national or sectarian label for his inner spiritual life is irrelevant and inappropriate' (Bullough, 'Missions to the English and Picts', p. 94). I doubt, however, if Bede felt the force of this unifying of Celtic and Roman traditions as keenly as we do; he was more impressed by the life itself than by its components. Whether or not he saw Cuthbert as a northern St Martin, what he grasped about the Englishman was his combination of Martinian gifts.

p. 430, l. 25. IV. 27. **studio religiosae uitae.** Colgrave translates as 'life under a Rule' and is probably right. But we cannot tell what rule. Presumably it was that of Iona, or a variant. It will not have been that of St Benedict but rather the Rule of Eata and Boisil.

p. 432, ll. 13–14. IV. 27. **ad erratica idolatriae medicamina concurrebant.** Cuthbert's rustics were formally Christians; what they reverted to in time of stress was not the formalized practices of such as Redwald but hedge-paganism which never could be wholly eradicated.

p. 432, ll. 21–2. IV. 27. **cuncti ad eius imperium.** An instance of the loose sense in which Bede employs a word full of implications to the modern scholar. Here it obviously has no political meaning: people gathered together at the preacher's 'command'. *Imperium* ushers in *praedicatio*.

p. 434, ll. 10–11. IV. 27. **episcopus cum clero et abbas ... monachis.** Thacker, *Ideal and Reality*, p. 144, thinks that 'Bede was anxious to set Lindisfarne in a Gregorian context'. Certainly he goes on to cite the example of Augustine at Canterbury. Yet I doubt if Bede is 'gliding over the fact that the bishop ... was subject to the abbot within the monastery', a very un-Roman arrangement. All that he is stressing is the common life proper to all Christians living in community since the days of the Early Church.

p. 434, ll. 24–5. IV. 28. **silentia secreta peruenit.** Bede's picture of Cuthbert increasingly takes on the flavour of Gregory's *Dialogues* while not departing from the spirit of St Martin. The life of contemplation is the highest endeavour and dearest wish of the holy man, though he may be called from it to other duties.

p. 434, ll. 32–3. IV. 28. **spiritum malignorum ... minus accommodus.** One of several passages that reveal Bede's full acceptance of the world of evil spirits. Compare Cuthbert's reaction with that of St Guthlac in Felix's Life of him (ed. Colgrave), constantly surrounded by evil spirits in his fenland retreat.

p. 436, ll. 34–5. IV. 28. **ad synodum pertrahunt.** The picture of the holy man dragged protesting to public office is sufficiently conventional, but it is plainly Bede's opinion that such beginnings will make the best bishop. The inference is that the bishop's office was thought well worth having by ambitious men, and these not the best. It is not so much unanimity that overcomes Cuthbert's reluctance as Boisil's 'mente prophetica' (p. 438, ll. 2–3). Once elected, Cuthbert's conception of his office follows the apostolic pattern: we are back in the New Testament.

p. 438, ll. 9–13. IV. 28. **Hagustaldensis ... primo fuerat ordinatus.** See IV. 12 (p. 370).

p. 438, l. 30. IV. 29. **Duobus ... in episcopatu peractis.** This does not mean that Cuthbert then ceased to be bishop of Lindisfarne but only that he ceased his visitations on the mainland, having been warned by divine inspiration ('diuino ... oraculo') of his approaching end.

p. 440, l. 10. IV. 29. **ad ciuitatem Lugubalium.** 'Bede rather pedantically calls this *Lugubalia* in his History, using the British Latin form from some written source', though in his prose Life he follows the Anonymous in calling Carlisle *Luel*, a spoken form (Thomas, *Early Christian Archaeology*, p. 18).

p. 440, ll. 16–18. IV. 29. **Certus sum ... tabernaculi mei.** Cuthbert evokes approaching death by recalling the words of St Peter. Once again, Bede sees a correspondence between events of his own time and those of the New Testament (Tugène, 'L'Hist. "eccl."', p. 158). The whole chapter is an essay in prophecy with correspondences. It should be compared with the longer account in the prose Life, from which it differs in some respects.

p. 442, ll. 9–10. IV. 29. **episcopatum ... antistes Uilfrid.** Bede omits a passage from his prose Life which claims (without mentioning Wilfrid) that the year of Wilfrid's control was a time of consternation at Lindisfarne. Peace returned with Eadberht. The passage is in fact a quotation from Herefrith. 'It is likely enough that Wilfrid would use his year of authority to impose his own ideas of monastic observance on reluctant monks, and Bede might be out of sympathy with his methods, if not with his aims' (Whitelock, *Famulus Christi*, p. 33). However this may be, Bede seems to have revised his views when he came to write *HE*, where he is uniformly respectful to Wilfrid's memory.

p. 442, l. 21. IV. 30. **transactis sepulturae eius annis XI.** So the monks of Lindisfarne took eleven years before they decided to treat Cuthbert as a saint by reburying him in a raised reliquary-shrine that could be venerated by all. This marks the start of the cult. On his shrine at Durham, his final resting-place, see Battiscombe, *Relics of Saint Cuthbert*. Fragments of the reliquary-coffin still exist. Thomas, *Early Christian Archaeology*, pp. 146-7, thinks that the idea of such a coffin will have come from Francia, not from Ireland. Clapham, *English Romanesque Architecture*, i. 43, compares Cuthbert's coffin with a well-known stone slab in the Hypogeum at Poitiers: 'there can be little doubt of their common origin'. Wormald considers (*The Anglo-Saxons*, ed. Campbell, p. 93) that the Lindisfarne Gospels were 'probably made for the translation of Cuthbert's relics in 698'.*

p. 446, ll. 16-17. IV. 31. **prosternens se ad corpus uiri Dei.** Bede completes his sketch of Cuthbert with two new miracles that emphasize what he had already written in the Life: the holy life of a bishop is immediately efficacious but its effects are even more notable after death. They prove the quality of life. Indeed, Bede might have given less attention to Cuthbert if miracles had not witnessed his sanctity. It is further clear from Bede that the cult of Cuthbert, centred on Lindisfarne, was a thriving concern in a matter of a few years.

p. 446, ll. 33-4. IV. 32. **in monasterio ... constructum.** Stenton, *Preparatory*, p. 215, notes that Bede records nothing of the history of the later *Westmoringa land* beyond this one miracle in the monastery at Dacre, and adds that the names of its abbots show it to have been an English, not a Celtic foundation. The foundations of the monastery lie chiefly under the present church and are at present under excavation. It is true, as Colgrave remarks, that the opening sentence contains verbal echoes of Gregory's *Dialogues* IV. 57 (ed. de Vogüé and Antin, iii. 188). The *Dialogues* were constantly in Bede's mind, and for much more than verbal reminiscence.

BOOK V

p. 450, v. It is noteworthy that Book V alone does not include the words 'the ecclesiastical history of the English people' in its heading; indeed, it lacks a heading of any sort. This could be because the book's thrust is to bring the Picts and the Irish within the Catholic fold. The theme of English conversion was already complete. It may well be that this final book was planned to end in 716, together with some concluding matter. In the opinion of Duncan, *The Writing of History*, p. 42, Bede 'had precious little material on the Picts and Scots before 716 to put in book V, and created a narrative of sorts with miracles, pilgrimages to Rome, episcopal successions (all evidence of catholicity), the Frisian mission, and an obituary of Wilfrid'. Certainly this last book looks less well structured than the others but there is still a shape to it. The miracles, pilgrimages, episcopal successions and above all the Frisian mission are major themes. They add up to more than 'a narrative of sorts'.

p. 454, ll. 1–3. v. 1. **Successit ... uir uenerabilis Oidiluald.** Bede begins his last book with a Farne miracle, thus linking Ethelwald with Cuthbert, his predecessor as hermit. It is a miracle of stilling the waters that has its roots in the New Testament. It illustrates two points: first, the 'meritum uel uita' of the hermit, and secondly the efficacy of intercession by prayer with Christ. Bede seems to have had access, through Abbot Guthfrith, to a cycle of stories about Ethelwald, of which the present miracle is an element. Such at least is the view of Kirby, *BJRL* 48 (1965–6), 355, who adds that Bede, already affected by the spiritual decline of his own generation, had little he wished to say about it. Is it distaste or absence of information that explains his silence about such centres as Whitby or Lindisfarne after c. 680–90? Or is it that their contribution to English ecclesiastical history was already complete in his eyes? In other words, had they no more information of the right sort? Ethelwald's miracle may not be a chance piece of flotsam but a vital clue to an understanding of his purpose.

p. 454, ll. 28–9. v. 1. **tumida aequora placauit.** Clearly an echo of Virgil's 'tumida aequora placat' (*Aeneid* 1. 142). Hunter Blair, *Famulus Christi*, p. 245, points out that the phrase could have been met with in the grammarians with whom Bede was familiar. Of the seven alleged quotations from Virgil in *HE*, 'one is doubtfully an echo at best, two are used by Augustine, and three are found in the works of the grammarians'. Furthermore, 'the 78 Virgilian quotations in the [sc. Bede's] school treatises were all derived directly or indirectly from the grammarians and not from Virgil's own works' (ibid., p. 247). This seems to dispose of the claim that Bede knew Virgil's writing direct; but an element of doubt lingers.*

p. 456, ll. 12–13. v. 2. **Iohannes … praesulatum suscepit.** Uncertain, or perhaps uninterested, in exact dates, Bede turns to the careeer of John of Beverley, bishop of Hexham and then York, with whom he was intimate: it was enough that he became bishop 'at the beginning of Aldfrith's reign'. But again, what matters most about John are his miracles, as recalled by Abbot Berhthun.

p. 456, ll. 21–2. v. 2. **clymiterium sancti Michahelis.** This oratory, if that is what it is, and whether at St John's Lee, Acomb, or at Warden, was clearly a remote spot suitable for contemplation. Hence the dedication to St Michael, who is often to be found presiding over hermits' fastnesses where his protection against evil spirits was especially welcome. The cult spread from Gaul to Celtic Britain in the seventh century, and thus to Northumbria. For a comment on *clymiterium* see J. H. Mozley, *Latomus*, 19 (1960), 578. On the fastnesses dedicated to the archangel see Robin Flower, *The Western Isle* (1944), 34.*

p. 458, ll. 10–11. v. 2. **dicito** *gae.* Crépin, *Famulus Christi*, pp. 184 ff., contrasts Bede's attitude to language with that of Guthlac in Felix's Life of the saint. When Bishop John sets out to teach English to the dumb (but not deaf) boy he follows Quintilian's practice: 'a boy must learn both the peculiarities and the common characteristics of letters and must know how they are related to each other' (*Institutio Oratoria* 1. 4. 12). From individual letters one proceeds to syllables and words and finally longer sentences. Bede advocates the same method in *De Orthographia* and *De Arte Metrica*. He is clear that God's truth and glory may be sought in any language. The only possible hint in *HE* of depreciation of native speech occurs in v. 7, in Cædwalla's Italian epitaph. However, and despite the care with which the cure of the dumb youth is described, it remains for Bede a miracle; the sign of the cross on the tongue precedes the cure, which thus comes under the heading 'plura uirtutum miracula'; and the miraculous is emphasized by reference to the healing of the lame man by SS Peter and John in Acts 3: 2–8. Why did he not cite Mark 7: 32–7?

p. 460, l. 8. v. 3. **et cum esset in studio.** Plummer notes that he recollects no other instance of the use of *studium* for medical treatment. However, the verb *studere* certainly has this sense, as in Gregory of Tours, *Hist.* VI. 32: 'iussitque rex ut studeretur a medicis'.

p. 460, ll. 18–20. v. 3. **Memini enim . . . in cremento est.** Bishop John considers the case hopeless because Archbishop Theodore's teaching on bleeding has not been followed; but he is persuaded to pray over Cwenburh and bless her, thus bringing about her cure. This girl is more explicit than the dumb boy in the preceding miracle in giving thanks to God for her cure. Plummer rightly considers that the tract *De Minutione Sanguinis* is unlikely to be Bede's work. It depends not on the phases of the moon but on a mathematical allotment of lunar days. Bede has something to say of certain lunar superstitions in *De Temporum Ratione*, 28 ('De effectiua lunae potentia'), though without reference to bleeding. See C. W. Jones, *Bedae Pseudepigrapha* (1939), 89.

p. 460, ll. 22–3. v. 3. **abbatissam eam pro se facere disposuerat.** Bede expresses no disquiet at this proposal. There was no objection to Cwenburh succeeding her mother as abbess.

p. 462, ll. 9–10. v. 4. **Villa erat comitis . . . Puch.** Here and in the succeeding chapter Berhthun transmits to Bede two miraculous cures by Bishop John which involve 'gesiths' whom he had visited in order to dedicate private churches. See Loyn's note

(*EHR* 70 (1955), 536) where he remarks that 'both these miraculous cures come to be associated with the granting of estates to the church at Beverley'. Escomb is sometimes cited as an example of the kind of church Puch and Addi would have built, but nothing is known of its early history. Other examples might be the Visigoth churches (some royal) built in northern Spain in the seventh century. Thinking of the churches of Puch and Addi, Addleshaw writes (Jarrow Lecture, 1963, p. 11) that 'already in Bede's day churches like a modern village church were being built to supplement the work of the early minsters'; but there is no suggestion of this in Bede's narrative: they were private churches.

p. 462, l. 32. v. 4. **imitata socrum beati Petri.** In what sense did Puch's wife 'imitate' St Peter's mother-in-law in Matt. 8: 14-15? It can hardly mean conscious or voluntary imitation; 'without being attributed to God's will, the imitation goes beyond the person's intention, as if history were imitating history virtually without the participant's knowledge'. What we are meant to appreciate is the permanence of God's ways manifested in the similarity of two situations. So Tugène, 'L'Hist. "eccl." ', p. 157. What is not in question is that the instantaneous cure of Puch's wife after drinking holy water used for a church dedication is a miracle which Bede thinks not unlike the miracle of the cure of Cwenburh.

p. 464, ll. 5-6. v. 5. **loculus iam tunc ... praeparatus.** Commenting on the coffin, Bullough (*Ideal and Reality*, p. 185 n. 20) writes that this 'confirms other evidence that coffin burial is not in itself evidence of superior social standing'. Bede shows no particular interest in the burial of the dead. The miracle recalls in some respects that of the centurion's servant in Matt. 8: 5-13 and Luke 7: 2-10. In both, the faith of the servant's master is critical.

p. 464, ll. 27-8. v. 6. **famulus Christi Herebald ... miraculum.** Plummer's view (ii. 277) was that 'in the story as told by Bede there is nothing distinctly miraculous'; and he shows how the miracle was made more explicit by Folcard. But Bede is clear that it was a miracle as related to him by Herebald. It was not the physician but the bishop himself who brought about the recovery by prayers and benediction; and the recovery was spiritual as well as physical. See Benedicta Ward, *Famulus Christi*, p. 75.

p. 468, l. 11. v. 6. **an me esse baptizatum.** It thus appears that Bishop John's views on re-baptism differed from Bede's own, as Plummer observes. But the inefficacy of Herebald's first baptism lay not only in the priest's inadequacy but also in his direct disobedience to his bishop in performing a rite that had been specifically forbidden him. The inadequacy of the first baptism is revealed to the bishop by a further act of disobedience: that of Herebald himself. His recovery enables this to be put right.

p. 468, ll. 28–9. v. 6. **et sic caelestia regna conscendens.** Bede's series of miracles associated with Bishop John ends with the bishop's death. They were made possible, as Herebald sees, by his way of life, 'worthy of a bishop in every particular so far as it is lawful for a man to judge' (p. 464, ll. 31–2). And such indeed is the burden of the entire series: a holy bishop can perform miracles, even today. Clearly they were of the first importance to Bede and were very far from being chance scraps with which to gloss over his ignorance of more important events. They witness, as nothing else does, to his passionate acceptance of Gregory the Great's teaching: God continues to act through the course of history in miracles performed by his chosen instruments.

p. 468, l. 35. v. 7. **Anno autem regni Aldfridi tertio.** The manner in which Bede associates Cædwalla's pilgrimage with Aldfrith's reign may suggest that the source was Northumbrian. On the other hand, this and the following chapter could equally well be based on Canterbury material, which would best explain the epitaphs of Cædwalla and Theodore.

p. 470, ll. 5–6. v. 7. **mox baptizatus, carne solutus . . . transiret.** As Stenton saw, it sounds as if the king, a young man, knew he was ill before he decided to resign and seek baptism at Rome. It is not known why his baptism had been delayed so long but it need not imply that he had ever been a practising pagan. It does seem to be implied by the epitaph ('Barbaricam rabiem . . .

conuertit ouans', ll. 29–30) but the author may simply have been following convention. See also Paul the Deacon's account, *Hist. Langobard.* VI. 15 ('ad Christum conversus'), *MGH SRG in usum Schol.*, p. 217. What he certainly had been was a great suppressor of rivals (Dumville, *ASE* 8 (1979), 19). Bede is plainly satisfied that Cædwalla did the right thing. More than that, his exceptional treatment by the pope was itself an honour to the English Church. Bede is more concerned with this than with the rights and wrongs of resignation after a mere two years of ruling 'strenuissime'. The best treatment of English pilgrimages to Rome is that of Levison, *England and the Continent*, pp. 36–44.

p. 470, ll. 16–17. v. 7. **epitaphium in eius monumento scriptum.** For another version of the epitaph see J. Hammer, *Speculum*, 6 (1931), 607–8. On the career of Benedict Crispus, supposed author of the epitaph, see F. J. E. Raby, *A History of Secular Latin Poetry in the Middle Ages* (1934), i. 159. I do not understand why 'Bede must have obtained a copy from some traveller to Rome' (Colgrave). It is likelier that the epitaph was already incorporated in written material at Bede's disposal.

p. 472, ll. 17–18. v. 7. **ad tempus peregrinari in terris.** Bede naturally links Ine's pilgrimage with that of his predecessor. But the cases are different. Ine had reigned for a long time and plainly felt that he had done enough. He left his kingdom to 'iuuenioribus' in whom Bede shows no interest. He certainly did not seek baptism at Rome, nor does Bede say that he wished to remain at Rome and die there. That he did in fact do so gains some support from the lack of any record of his death in English sources. As far as Bede is concerned, Ine falls within the category of English pilgrims to Rome who simply sought to increase their chances of a warm welcome in heaven.

p. 474, ll. 2–4. v. 8. **tantum profectus . . . ceperunt.** Bede speaks of spiritual progress. What has he in mind? He is usually taken to mean the benefits accruing from the new diocesan organization of the Church and educational challenge of the school of Canterbury. The latter gains support from the fourth line of Theodore's epitaph. It may be so. If we knew more, we might say that proliferation of monasteries in Theodore's reign was an equally healthy sign of spiritual progress. But perhaps the clearest sign to Bede of such progress might have been the miracles and pilgrimages of the time. He nowhere mentions Theodore's concern with penitential matters (see Hughes, *England before the Conquest*, pp. 61 ff.)

p. 474, l. 17. v. 8. **Successit autem ... Berctuald.** Equally notable are the time-lag between Theodore's death and Berhtwald's election and the consecration of Berhtwald in Gaul rather than by English bishops. It may be, as Brooks argues (*Early History*, pp. 76–8), that the succession was disputed. Wilfrid may have been a candidate favoured by kings and clergy in Mercia, Northumbria, and East Anglia, but not in Wessex and Kent. Such at least could be the reason for the two letters from Pope Sergius I (less suspicious than Plummer thought) with which Berhtwald returned from Rome. They imply that he would meet with opposition without strong papal support. The course of events remains unclear (see Levison, *England and the Continent*, p. 242 n. 1) and what we are left with is Bede's version, which is presumably that of Canterbury: Berhtwald earns respect as a learned man and Wilfrid is not mentioned. The charter of King Hlothhere of Kent making a grant in 679 to Berhtwald, then abbot of Reculver, is the earliest extant original Anglo-Saxon charter (*CS* No. 45, Sawyer, No. 8). It is illustrated in *The Anglo-Saxons*, ed. Campbell, p. 98, and discussed by Chaplais, 'Origin and Authenticity', pp. 51, 53.*

p. 474, ll. 29–30. v. 8. **Latina Greca ... instructum.** It is clearly his learning that causes Bede, and perhaps Canterbury, to distinguish Tobias among the 'many bishops' consecrated by Berhtwald. Bede is not claiming that English was a learned language in the sense in which Greek and Latin were; but it was a language properly to be used for Christian instruction, and the mastery of it for these purposes was not possessed by all bishops. See Wormald, 'The Uses of Literacy', p. 103.

pp. 474–86. v. 9–11. Bede now devotes three chapters to the English contribution to the conversion of the Frisians and Saxons. He sees it as what in truth it was: a contribution to place beside that of the Franks, without whom nothing could have

been attempted. More important, he sees the English missionaries not simply as seizing opportunities for indulging personal
piety but as representatives of a missionary Church whose duty
it was to convert other *Germani*. In other words, the missions
were a natural, even a national, extension and culmination of the
Christian rebirth of the *gens Anglorum*. See Tugène, 'L'Hist.
"eccl."', p. 143.

p. 476, ll. 8-9. v. 9. **Sunt autem Fresones ... Boructuari.** This
famous list raises questions and hackles. Is Bede giving a general
description of Germanic peoples or does he mean exactly what
he says? We cannot assert that none of these peoples invaded
and settled in Britain. Myres takes the list seriously (*PBA* 56
(1970) 151): 'Bede was fully conscious that the invaders included
elements from many peoples other than the Angles, Saxons and
Jutes of *Hist. Eccles.* i, 15. It probably belongs to an early stage in
the composition of his work, certainly earlier than the passage in
i, 15, which I have suggested to be an insertion at a comparatively late point in his revision of the text.' My own feeling is that
Bede is simply quoting his source: it is Egbert, not Bede, who
knows about these people. 'Bede's inclusion of the Huns and the
Rugini among the peoples ... suggests the possibility that an
early source lies behind what he says, for these names belong to
a fifth rather than an eighth century context' (Campbell, *Studia
Hibernica*, 15 (1975), 179). Whatever the truth, the burden of the
argument must be that a great variety of Germans contributed
to the settlement of Britain and that this constituted their claim
to be converted from Britain.

p. 476, ll. 13-14. v. 9. **Romam uenire ... cogitauit.** It is clear to
Bede that it was no part of Egbert's plan to visit Iona. If he were
unable to reach his Germans he intended to go to Rome, and
this links him with the *Romipetentes* of the preceding chapters. It
was the vision of Boisil's pupil that turned his thoughts to the
crooked furrow (on which see Plummer's note). In other words,
it was divine intervention. The vision is confirmed by the loss of
his ship, which turns his thoughts to Jonah. A miracle can take
the form of a catastrophe. However, the application is to Egbert
himself, not to others who could undertake the continental
mission.

p. 480, l. 1. v. 9. **reuersus ... locum peregrinationis.** Wihtberht's
place of exile is Ireland, not Frisia; and it is to exile that he
retreats after the failure of his preaching to the Frisians. I am not
sure that I follow the note in *Famulus Christi*, p. 168 n. 92.*

p. 480, ll. 8–9. v. 10. **temtauit adhuc ... uiros sanctos et
industrios.** Bede is clear that the Frisian mission continued to
rest on Egbert's initiative after Wihtbert's failure. Willibrord, too,
is sent by Egbert. The likeliest source for Bede's information on
Willibrord is Bishop Acca, who visited him in Frisia during the
winter of 703–4. Bede's, and presumably Acca's, version of the
establishment of the Frisian mission does not in all respects
agree with continental accounts, or with that of Alcuin, Willibrord's biographer. The chronological difficulties are best
explained by Wolfgang Fritze, 'Zur Enstehungsgeschichte des
Bistums Utrecht: Franken und Friesen 690–734', *Rheinische
Vierteljahrsblätter*, 35 (1971), 107–51.

p. 480, l. 13. v. 10. **citeriorem Fresiam.** What is meant is south-
western Frisia up to the Lek, reconquered by Pippin II in 690,
with its headquarters at Antwerp. Bede's account makes it
appear that Willibrord always meant to co-operate with
Frankish military power though in fact he may have hoped to
work more independently among Germanic peoples not under
Frankish control.

p. 480, ll. 14–15. v. 10. **ipse quoque imperiali auctoritate
iuuans.** I doubt if Bede meant more than that Pippin was
exercising authority beyond Francia. See however E. E. Stengel,
DA 3 (1939) and 16 (1960), reprinted in his *Abhandlungen und
Untersuchungen* (1965).

p. 480, ll. 19–21. v. 10. **duo quidam presbyteri ... ad
prouinciam Antiquorum Saxonum.** This accords with the list of
nationes given in v. 9 (p. 476), as equally with the mission of
Swithberht to the Bructeri. Clearly the Hewalds, and Egbert
who sent them, counted on no Frankish support. It does not
appear that martyrdom was their goal though it was certainly
their fate.

p. 480, ll. 29-30. v. 10. **ad satrapam qui super eum erat.** Bede only uses *satrapa* in this chapter and presumably had it from his informant. A title of adjustable import is borrowed from the Old Testament. 'Viceroy' (Colgrave) is an unhappy translation. The Old English translation *ealdorman* is nearer the mark. 'Chieftain'? See Loyn, *Anglo-Saxon England*, pp. 25-6. Bede describes what he seems to think is still the constitutional practice of the Old Saxons simply because they had no king, which to an Anglo-Saxon would call for explanation.

p. 482, ll. 20-1. v. 10. **Passi sunt . . . quinto nonarum Octobrium die.** In Willibrord's Calendar the two Hewalds were commemorated on 3 October. 'Possibly the eve of their festival, or the day itself if emended, was thought to be suitable for a consecration' (Harrison, *Framework*, p. 112). They are still venerated at Cologne, where Pippin caused their bodies to be brought. He may have hoped to link the new Anglo-Saxon missions with the ancient Church of Cologne, according to H. Löwe, 'Entstehungszeit und Quellenwert der Vita Lebuini', *DA* 21 (1965), 365n. To Bede the martyrdom of the Hewalds was an additional credit to the English Church.

p. 484, ll. 6-7. v. 11. **Uilbrord datam sibi . . . uenire Romam.** The best survey of Willibrord's mission remains that of Levison, 'St Willibrord and His Place in History', reprinted in *RuFF*, pp. 314 ff., which also contains three further papers on the saint. See also Levison, *England and the Continent*, pp. 53 ff. There are some useful contributions in *Willibrordus*, ed. N. Goetzinger. That Willibrord should have made for Rome as soon as possible is what Bede would have expected of an English missionary. The papacy was the proper initiator of foreign missions and especially so for the English. Pippin II does not send him to Rome: he merely permits him to preach in territory under his control.

p. 484, ll. 18-20. v. 11. **fratres, qui erant in Fresia . . . Suidberctum.** It is not clear whether Swithberht was sent for consecration with Willibrord's permission. Wilfrid's early involvement in the Frisian mission made him an appropriate consecrator, as the 'fratres' appreciated. It may be that it was always intended to send him to the Bructeri.

p. 486, ll. 4–5. v. 11. **Pippinum petiit ... dedit ei locum mansionis.** Early Carolingian estates, including those of Plectrudis, lay largely in and near the northern area of the Middle Rhine; and it was here that Willibrord received liberal endowments. Kaiserswerth is not far north of Cologne. For Willibrord's endowments see my *Frankish Church*, pp. 145 ff., and *Early Medieval History*, pp. 142 ff.

p. 486, l. 13. v. 11. **postulans ut ... archiepiscopus ordinaretur.** There are no grounds for questioning Bede's statement that what Pippin wanted from the pope was an archbishop, i.e. a metropolitan who could consecrate other bishops. The English Church was not alone in understanding the office of archbishop. The author of the *Vita Sergii* describes how the pope consecrated named persons as archbishops: Damian to Ravenna, Berhtwald to Britain, and Clemens (i.e. Willibrord) to the Frisians. Archbishop, metropolitan, and recipient of a *pallium* were now drawing together in a recognized pattern. The precision of Bede's statement suggests that his informant might have been Canterbury rather than Bishop Acca. See Fritze, 'Zur Entstehungsgeschichte', pp. 120–4. As to the date of Willibrord's consecration, Bede was certainly at fault by a year, though we do not know why. See Harrison, *ASE* 2 (1973), 69–70. There was an appropriateness in giving Willibrord the name of the martyr Clement since Sergius was much interested in propagating the martyr traditions and relics of Rome. A pilgrim-missionary was likely enough to meet with martyrdom.

p. 486, ll. 19–21. v. 11. **Donauit autem ei Pippin ... Traiectum uocatur.** It was Pippin, not Sergius (who simply consecrated and nominated him to the Frisians), who placed Willibrord in Utrecht. Though it was intended from the start as a Church province directly dependent on Rome, its beginnings must have been more modest and even more doubtful than those of the German Church under St Boniface. Bede knows nothing of the prior claims of the Church of Cologne to exercise authority in these parts, nor does he know whether Pippin fully understood the implications of the establishment of a new Church province. Willibrord's establishment in Utrecht appears to belong to the winter of 703-4, not to his immediate return from Rome. What is clear to Bede is that the universal mission of Rome to convert the heathen had taken a step forward.

p. 486, l. 24. v. 11. **monasteria nonnulla construxit.** Among these, as Plummer notes, was Echternach, a foundation particularly indebted to Carolingian generosity. Lying too far south for missionary work in Frisia, it has often been seen as Willibrord's place of retreat. It is possible that it could have been intended as a rear base for operations over the Rhine among the Hessians. The grants to Echternach are now best studied in C. Wampach, *Geschichte der Grundherrschaft Echternach* (2 vols.; 1929-30).

p. 488, l. 1. v. 12. **miraculum memorabile et antiquorum simile.** This lengthy and precise account of Dryhthelm is included not because of the occurrence but because of its interior significance. The miracle itself, of one returning from the dead to relate his experiences, is of a conventional kind—'antiquorum simile'— which indeed lends support to its authenticity in Bede's eyes; but the spiritual warning to Dryhthelm's hearers is what counts. Salvation lies in present recognition of the reality of paradise and heaven, purgatory and hell. Dryhthelm returns to the world to help others, not himself, though he does in fact do that also. Compare the account of Fursa's vision (III. 19), which differs in important respects as being more conventional. Dryhthelm's vision shows something new that corresponds to Augustine's teaching on categories of good and evil (*Enchiridion*, XXIX. 110): the four categories of purgatory, hell, paradise, and heaven find their earthly reflections in the self-knowledge men have of their own merits. See Claude Carozzi, *Spoleto*, 29 (1983), 448-54.

p. 496, ll. 18-19. v. 12. **per cuius relationem ... perstrinximus.** Bede's account is excerpted from the *relatio* of Hæmgisl, which appears to have reached him either from Ireland or from Æthelwald of Lindisfarne. It may be that the new features of the vision were already in the *relatio*. The importance of the vision is enhanced by the keen interest in it shown by the learned King

Aldfrith. However, Aldfrith's knowledge of it was derived *viva voce* and not from the *relatio*.

p. 496, ll. 25-6. v. 12. **abbas et presbyter Ediluald praeerat.** Further to Æthelwald, D. N. Dumville, 'Liturgical Drama and Panegyric Responsory from the Eighth Century? A Re-examination of the Origin and Contents of the Ninth-Century Section of the Book of Cerne', *JTS* NS 23 (1972), 374-406.

p. 498, ll. 14-16. v. 13. **quidam in prouincia ... ipsi, profuit.** Unlike Dryhthelm, the layman in this grim story benefits nobody by his vision, except as a general warning. He appears to have been a thegn in King Cenred's entourage, and a literate thegn. The reason he gives for refusing to confess and do penance for his sins despite his king's advice is interesting: to confess when one is ill could look like cowardice to one's companions. This has the ring of a good pagan morality that survives conversion. It makes a point that Bede makes nowhere else. As against such spurious bravery one should weigh the evidence of one's whole life recorded by God and the Devil—in books, black and white. The 'codicem horrendae uisionis' reminds Plummer of the Apocalypse of Paul (doubtless unknown to Bede) and he cites Tischendorf's text. The most relevant passage is ch. 17 (tr. by M. R. James, *The Apocryphal New Testament* (1924), 534): 'And the angel of the sinful soul came, having a writing in his hands, and said "These, Lord, that are in mine hands, are all the sins of this soul from its youth up unto this day".' As James notes, the Apocalypse of Zephaniah has a comparable passage.

p. 502, l. 1. v. 13. **sicut beatus papa ... scribit.** Bede recalls Gregory's *Dialogues*, IV. 40, a selection of stories showing how visions of the punishment awaiting sinners hereafter are sometimes meant to benefit the sinners themselves, sometimes *ad aedificationem audientium* (ed. de Vogüé and Antin, iii. 138-46). One can suppose that Bede, familiar with Gregory's categories in such matters, would be on the lookout for contemporary stories making the same points.

p. 502, l. 18. v. 13. **Hanc historiam ... Pecthelmo didici.** It is not known when Bede met Pehthelm, once a monk at Malmesbury and later bishop of Whithorn. Harrison, *Framework*, p. 134 n. 12, commenting on Bede's ignorance of the hypothetical West Saxon annals (subsequently drawn upon by the Anglo-Saxon Chronicle) which he feels might have been compiled at Malmesbury, seems surprised that, if this were so, Pehthelm conveyed nothing of it to Bede: 'their talk may only have been of visionary matters'. I do not doubt that it was so. One imagines that Bede's first question to a new West Saxon acquaintance would not have been 'Can you explain the succession-problems of Wessex?' but 'Do you know any good miracle-stories?'

p. 502, l. 21. v. 14. **Noui autem ipse fratrem.** Bede concludes his series of powerful didactic chapters with an account of the vision of hell vouchsafed to a monk-craftsman known personally to him. The lesson is that it may be too late to repent: confession and penance must precede death if there is to be any chance for the sinner to escape hell. The darkness seen by the wretched monk is contrasted with the brightness seen by St Stephen at his execution. See Henderson (Jarrow Lecture, 1980, p. 12).

p. 504, ll. 26-7. v. 14. **Quod utinam ... litterarum fiat.** The didactic purpose of *HE* could not be more clearly expressed. The immediate effect of the monk's death had been widespread; many had done penance as a consequence. But the lesson has still to be learnt: the need for confession and penance is as urgent as ever it was. This is the darker side of the picture of which Bede's pride in the English religious achievement is the lighter. See Cowdrey, 'Bede and the "English People" ', p. 518.

p. 504, l. 31-p. 506, l. 2. v. 15. **Adamnan ... uenisset ad Aldfridum.** Bede knows of Adomnán (whom he could have met at Jarrow in his youth) as a new champion of the Roman Easter, 'uel in aliis quibusque decretis' (p. 506, ll. 5-6), and as the transmitter of Arculf's experiences in the East. He begins with the Roman Easter and it is clear that, whatever his source, annalistic or narrative, his account is inaccurate in detail. This may be due to his wish to abbreviate a complicated career. A good summary of the facts is Smyth, *Warlords and Holy Men*, pp. 128 ff., though his judgement on Bede is unnecessarily harsh, but reference should also be made to Hughes, *England before the Conquest*, pp. 53–4; Duncan, *The Writing of History*, pp. 12 ff.; and Byrne, *Irish Kings and High-Kings, passim*. Bede has certainly simplified the situation in Ireland; he seems not to know that Adomnán visited Aldfrith (possibly his former pupil) not once but twice; Adomnán lived longer than he implies; and Adomnán's greatest achievement was his Life of St Columba. What is left, however, is an acceptable outline of what struck Bede as significant: Adomnán was converted to the Roman Easter in Northumbria, taught successfully in Ireland, and finally failed to persuade his own monstery of Iona to abandon its old ways. Bede, but not Adomnán, prepares the way for Egbert. I do not agree with Hughes that Bede is 'condescending' to Adomnán.

p. 506, l. 27. v. 15. **Scripsit idem uir de locis sanctis.** The subject was clearly of great interest to Bede. Here, and in the following two chapters of excerpts, he gives it extended treatment, for the book has been and will continue to be of help to many. What matters most to Bede is Jerusalem: readers are brought, as so often in *HE*, face to face with the historical roots of the universal Church. His sense of relevance precludes his quoting Adomnán's attractive accounts of Arculf darting about among his sites, measuring and computing, taking a dip in the Jordan, seeing if he can walk though Alexandria in one day, watching the Nile crocodiles, and comparing the salt of the Dead Sea with Sicilian rock-salt. Bieler, *Famulus Christi*, pp. 219–20, reveals the pains Bede took to check the literary references which Adomnán added to what Arculf told him. Denis Meehan's introduction to his edition of *De Locis Sanctis* (1958) is valuable. Bullough, 'Columba, Adomnan and the Achievement of Iona', p. 121, emphasizes the value of Adomnán's text as evidence of the Latin culture of Iona.

p. 506, ll. 32–3. v. 15. **patriamque nauigio ... dilatus est.** Arcuulfus is an odd name behind which may lie such a form as Arnulfus (Meehan) or even Eorconwulfus; but it may equally lie hidden under a latinized form like Lupus. In any case he cannot be identified. The name sounds Germanic, but this is no good reason for supposing 'that the bishop's ship was bound for the 'north of France' (Colgrave) or that he held a northern Frankish see.

p. 508, l. 13. v. 16. **Scripsit ergo ... in hunc modum.** I would translate 'he wrote about the Lord's birthplace after this fashion'. In other words, he does not claim to be quoting Adomnán's words exclusively. He is in fact quoting from his own survey of the subject (which he does not mention in the list of his writings). Levison, *England and the Continent*, pp. 42 ff., is valuable on western interest in the geography and topography of eastern lands; an interest that Bede obviously shared.

p. 512, ll. 17–18. v. 17. **ad sensum quidem uerborum illius.** Bede ends his excerpts by making it still clearer that he has not been quoting literally from Adomnán, and then refers readers to Adomnán's own book and his abridgment of it.

p. 512, ll. 23–4. v. 18. **Anno dominicae ... necdum impleto.** The chronology is difficult but it does not depend wholly on Bede. Harrison, *Framework*, pp. 85, 89–91, argues that Aldfrith died on 14 December 705, and was succeeded by the intruder Eadwulf (not mentioned by Bede) for two months, Osred beginning to reign about the middle of February 706. Kirby, *EHR* 98 (1983), 113, prefers to place Aldfrith's death in 704.

p. 512, ll. 26–7. v. 18. **Huius regni principio ... migrauit ad uitam.** Bede employs a Northumbrian regnal date to introduce a chapter devoted to West and South Saxon bishops. The bulk of his information presumably came from Bishop Daniel. Bede's interests in Haeddi is confined to the sanctity of his life as proved by subsequent miracles; and perhaps this is all the information he had asked for. Another side of Haeddi is revealed in 'the first letter known to have been written by one Englishman to another' (Stenton, *ASE*, p. 142). It is written by Wealdhere, bishop of London, to the archbishop asking for guidance on a proposed settlement between East and West Saxons, at which Haeddi was to represent the West Saxons. 'The terms of the settlement were left to the discretion of Bishops Wealdhere and Haedde, an indication of the important part played by bishops in Anglo-Saxon government and diplomacy'

(Chaplais, 'The Letter from Bishop Wealdhere', in his *Essays in Medieval Diplomacy and Administration* (1981), No. 14, p. 4). The letter is translated by Whitelock, *EHD*, i. 729–30.

p. 514, ll. 7–8. v. 18. **Quo defuncto ... diuisus est.** It does not follow that Haeddi had opposed the division of his diocese.

p. 514, ll. 21–2. v. 18. **nam et sermone ... eruditione mirandus.** It is still often accepted that Aldhelm's learning and style derived from Ireland by way of Malmesbury, whereas those of Bede came from the continent. M. Winterbottom, 'Aldhelm's Prose Style and its Origins', *ASE* 6 (1977), 39–76, has shown that Aldhelm's real debt was not to the Irish but to Theodore and Hadrian, his Canterbury masters. So far from his style being quirkily Irish, it 'is a monument to the enduring attractions of classical methods of expansion' (p. 64). Parallels to it can be found on the continent: 'the continentals remained perfectly capable of constructing complex sentences at least until 650 and in some parts of Europe beyond that date' (p. 56). See also Michael W. Herren (ed.), *The Hisperica Famina* (1974), 36. Bede attributes no miracles to Aldhelm and is chiefly moved by his efforts to convert Britons in Wessex to the correct date for celebrating Easter.*

p. 514, l. 23. v. 18. **pontificatum pro eo suscepit Fortheri.** On the division of the West Saxon diocese and Bishop Forthhere see Finberg, *Early Charters of Wessex*, p. 217.

p. 514, l. 25. v. 18. **Quibus episcopatum administrantibus.** Considering the few traces of rearrangement or remains of earlier efforts in *HE*, Levison, *BLTW*, pp. 144–5, notes that in this chapter 'a real continuity is established only by removing the sentences on his [sc. Aldhelm's] writings, which seem to have been added by Bede subsequently', i.e. the sentences from 'Denique Aldhelm, cum adhuc esset presbyter' to 'erat eruditione mirandus'. Plummer shares this view. I am not sure that this is necessary. On the origin of Sherborne see Finberg, *Lucerna*, pp. 98 ff.

p. 516, l. 4. v. 19. **Anno autem imperii Osredi quarto.** This might be called a chapter of *Romipetentes*. Cenred, Offa, and Wilfrid are linked by more than a date. It is the Roman aspect of Wilfrid's life, not his wanderings among English kings and the reasons for them, that Bede wishes to emphasize. This can be overlooked in our surprise to find Bede so warmly approving the departure of an excellent king and the heir of another king as Roman pilgrims. The career of Wilfrid therefore fits in comfortably at this point. There are difficulties about seeing it as an insertion after the completion of the first draft of *HE*, though it may still be true. Bede may have met Eddius' Life of Wilfrid at a late stage. However, as Plummer realized, the account is much more than an excerpt from that Life. Bede not only omits material in Eddius but adds to it, e.g. from what Acca and Ceolfrith, his own abbot, could tell him. Something more would surely have had to be said about Wilfrid if Bede had never read Eddius.

p. 516, ll. 12-14. v. 19. **Offa, iuuenis ... exoptatissimus.** It appears that Offa may actually have reigned in Essex. See Finberg, *Early Charters of the West Midlands*, pp. 181-3. But it is odd that Bede did not know this.*

p. 516, ll. 22-3. v. 19. **diem clausit ... Inundalum.** Bede is even clearer than Eddius, his likely source, that Wilfrid died in a district, not a place, called Oundle. 'Thus Oundle is a clear example of an area name which later became a place-name. It is likely that all the names of English places which Bede gives in such a form as *In Getlingum, Ingyruum* were of the same kind, related to his *In Brige*' (Campbell, *Names, Words*, p. 48). It is plausible that Wilfrid died at Peterborough (*Saint Wilfrid at Hexham*, p. 98).*

p. 516, ll. 26-7. v. 19. **De cuius statu uitae ... memoremus.** Bullough, 'Hagiography as Patriotism', p. 347, compares Bede's treatment of Wilfrid with Alcuin's and concludes that Alcuin was more influenced by Bede than by Eddius—if he read Eddius. However, I find it hard to accept that 'Bede had not written anything about him [sc. Wilfrid] that allowed him to be admired'. Bede does seem to admire Wilfrid though not to like him. In any case Wilfrid was a major figure who could never be ignored, whether for his relations with Rome or for his role in the establishment of York. But I agree with Brooks, *Early History*, p. 72, that 'there is no evidence that the issue of York's metropolitan status lay at the centre of Wilfrid's quarrels with Archbishop Theodore and with his successor, Berhtwald'. Campbell, 'Bede', pp. 178, 189, contrasts Bede's Wilfrid with Eddius' and argues that R. L. Poole's conclusion that Bede was more often factually right than Eddius needs qualification. Bede's picture is certainly nuanced but whether this was due to discretion or to his intention to portray only those parts of Wilfrid's career that were relevant to his general purposes is open to question. Discretion may indeed be operative in such a matter as Wilfrid's relations with Canterbury but on the other hand it is hard to see why his Merovingian career and contacts should figure at all prominently in Bede's account, which does not aim to be a full biography.

p. 518, ll. 9–10. v. 19. **uerum eis ... sunt uirtutibus.** If this is not praise of Wilfrid I do not know what would be.

p. 518, l. 15. v. 19. **proposuitque animo venire Romam.** A wish to see what ecclesiastical and monastic practices were observed at Rome may have been Wilfrid's initial intention, though something more is already implied by his reason for refusing to stay at Lyon with the bishop. So far as is known, he was the first Englishman to go to Rome on pilgrimage. He later expressed the desire to stay indefinitely there. Only at the pope's orders did he return home, without abandoning his intention. See Stancliffe, *Ideal and Reality*, p. 170.

p. 518, l. 34. v. 19. **Uilfrid a Dalfino ... retentus est.** The bishop's name was in fact Aunemundus. Dalfinus was the family-name. Continental sources provide no name for the bishop's brother. The matter has been exhaustively investigated by A. Coville, *Recherches sur l'histoire de Lyon* (1928), 381–5. Bede seems to have had no other source than Eddius.

p. 520, l. 17. v. 19. **computum paschae rationabilem.** 'Wilfrid learnt the correct *computation* of Easter, a matter far removed

from the tame acceptance of reckonings made by somebody else
... Thus it will have been the Dionysiac system, down to detail,
that Wilfrid learnt from Boniface, the correct computation in
Bede's eyes' (Harrison, *Framework*, p. 63). This was to have far-
reaching effects on English computation when Wilfrid returned
home.

p. 520, ll. 25-6. v. 19. **Baldhild ... iussit interfici.** On the queen's
initiative in the downfall of the bishop of Lyon and his family, in
which Wilfrid was involved, see Janet Nelson, 'Queens as
Jezebels', in *Medieval Women*, ed. D. Baker, pp. 63-7.

p. 520, ll. 28-9. v. 19. **sed hunc ubi peregrinum.** Eddius uses the
word *transmarinus*, which Bede changes to *peregrinus*. This puts
Wilfrid in a different category.

p. 520, ll. 33-5. v. 19. **mox donauit terram ... Inhrypum.** The
best treatment of Wilfrid's northern possessions is Michael
Roper, 'Wilfrid's Landholdings in Northumbria', *Saint Wilfrid at
Hexham*, pp. 61-79. Bede's account of the reason for the Irish
abandonment of Ripon is not in Eddius. Wilfrid's Roman
orthodoxy is again emphasized.

p. 522, l. 24. v. 19. **flante Fauonio pulsus est Fresiam.** Eddius'
account of the crossing is not essentially different. Bede does not
imply that Wilfrid was unwilling to go to Frisia because the west
wind drove him there. Kirby, *EHR* 98 (1983) 109, suggests that
'our extant version of Stephen's [sc. Eddius'] *Life* was revised
after Bede used it'; and further (p. 112): 'Bede's non-use of large
parts of the *Vita Wilfridi*, dealing with various adventures and
misadventures of the bishop, may be the consequence not of a
dislike of the material or of Wilfrid or a distrust of the material
but of the absence of many episodes now present in the *Life*
from the earlier edition which Bede used.' This might reduce
Eddius' 'earlier edition' to a skeleton? I think that the easiest
solution is that Bede excerpted what was relevant to him.

p. 522, ll. 30-1. v. 19. **sic Romam ueniendi iter repetiit.** Bede
omits Eddius' vivid account of Aldgisl's rejection of the Frankish
bribe to assassinate Wilfrid and of Wilfrid's subsequent visits to

Dagobert II and the Lombard Perctarit. Bede's concern is to get
Wilfrid to Rome.

p. 522, ll. 34-7. v. 19. **papa Agatho ... et Uilfridum.** Bede's
shortened account of Wilfrid's first appearance before the pope
in council is markedly different from that of Eddius, in part
because he was unwilling to record Wilfrid's differences with
Archbishop Theodore as well as his subsequent treatment by
King Ecgfrith and his allies. Any account of the quarrelsome
council at Austerfield, as recorded by Eddius, could well have
proved embarrassing to Bede. The events surrounding it are
examined by Brooks, *Early History*, p. 79. Bede moves straight to
the conversion of the South Saxons and thus to Wilfrid's second
visit to Rome.

p. 526, ll. 25-6. v. 19. **ubi esset Acca presbyter.** Despite Bede's
intimacy with Acca, his account of Wilfrid's vision at Meaux
differs in no significant respect from that of Eddius, with the
exception of 'quam te audire ac silentio tegere uolo', as noted by
Plummer.

p. 528, ll. 10-11. v. 19. **Coinredum ... regem fecerat.** On kings,
as here, choosing their successors, see Dumville, *ASE* 8 (1979),
18-19.

p. 528, ll. 22-3. v. 19. **hoc de illo ... scriptum.** Eddius does not
record the epitaph. It insists on achievements with which Bede
could have no quarrel: Wilfrid's generosity to Ripon, his
teaching of the true Easter and other Roman rites—probably
'Wilfrid is being credited with the promotion in England of the
Dionysiac cycle', Harrison, *Framework*, p. 75—his establishment
at Ripon of 'regula patrum', and his long reign. Jaager, *Bedas
metrische Vita sancti Cuthberti* (1935), 50-1, notes that little in the
epitaph suggests the normal form of such verse and thinks it
very likely on stylistic grounds that Bede himself composed it.
For Ripon? All dates associated with Wilfrid's last years are
treated by Bede 'in an oblique fashion' (Harrison, *Framework*,
p. 91). See also Levison, *England and the Continent*, pp. 278-9.

p. 530, l. 4. v. 20. **Anno post obitum praefati patris proximo.** The death of Hadrian and the accession of Acca are linked chronologically by Bede to Wilfrid's death in such a way as to suggest that it always had been his intention to place a chapter on Wilfrid immediately before. It also gives him an opportunity to pay tribute to Acca to whom, with Albinus, *HE* owed most. But whereas he had only known Albinus indirectly, through Nothhelm, Acca had long been a close friend. It is clear that Acca had emphasized to Bede his close association with Wilfrid and his debt to him.

p. 530, ll. 15–16. v. 20. **Suscepit uero ... Acca presbyter eius.** It is remarkable how closely Acca's achievements at Hexham seem to parallel those of Wilfrid: he was a church builder and embellisher, a relic collector, a church musician, and a visitor to Rome where he had learnt what could not be learnt in England. The nature of Acca's debt to Bosa is not specified. In 731 Acca was deposed from his see and exiled. 'These events must have been traumatic both for Bede ... and for the Wilfridian communities, particularly Hexham' (Kirby, *EHR* 98 (1983), 107).

p. 530, ll. 24–5. v. 20. **amplissimam ... bibliothecam.** For Acca as a library builder in a setting of contemporary book collectors see Levison, *England and the Continent*, pp. 132 ff. Acca specialized in *passiones*. His library was quite unlike that of Charlemagne less than a century later.

p. 532, ll. 6–8. v. 20. **cum quo etiam ... utilia didicit.** Meyvaert, *Bede and Gregory the Great*, p. 24 n. 39, speculates that Bede's original plan was to end Book V with this chapter. If this were so (and Meyvaert gives reasons why it might be) one imagines that the conclusion of the chapter would originally have been less abruptly structured.

p. 532, ll. 17–18. v. 21. **misit legatarios ... Ceolfridum.** Duncan, *The Writing of History*, pp. 20 ff., emphasizes the possible significance of this Pictish embassy to Abbot Ceolfrith as the route by which Bede acquired not only verbal but written information about the Irish Church and Iona. Hughes (Jarrow Lecture, 1970, p. 2) also thinks that 'the most likely people to give him [sc. Bede] his account of Columba's settlement at Iona on land given by a Pictish king were the messengers sent by King Nechton to Ceolfrith'. Duncan further argues that the man who persuaded King Nechtan to reform Pictish practice and to seek help from Abbot Ceolfrith was Egbert, the converter of Iona to Roman usage. This conjecture makes good sense. Smyth, *Warlords and Holy Men*, p. 75, makes the reasonable point that 'Nechtan's plea for help to Jarrow, and his expulsion of Columban monks ... in 717 may not have been the actions of a strong ruler about to implement radical cultural reforms, but those of an insecure king about to be swamped by those very influences he sought to curtail.' It is certainly clear that Nechtan was on the defensive: he wanted more information to confute those who celebrated Easter at the wrong time.*

p. 534, l. 2. v. 21. **misit illi et litteras.** Bede does not state that this is the precise reply sent by Ceolfrith to Nechtan but only that it was composed 'in hunc modum'. It remains an open question whether Bede himself wrote it; there were others who might have done it ('tanta hodie calculatorum exuberat copia', p. 546, ll. 7–8). However, he was a master of the subject, may well have contributed to it, and may further have worked over and abbreviated the official reply for incorporation in this chapter. The stress on Roman and specifically Petrine obedience, in conjunction with apt biblical quotations, is at least as characteristic of Bede as citations from his own computistical writings which would have been available to all at Jarrow. It is not clear whether the letter itself would have been basic to the first draft of *HE* or was a later addition. I am inclined to think it basic. We do not have Nechtan's letter to which this is the reply.

p. 534, l. 20. v. 21. **Tres sunt ... inditae litteris.** See Harrison, *ASE* 7 (1978), 1–8, on Easter cycles and the equinox.

p. 542, ll. 5–6. v. 21. **Quae disputatio ... uel debeat.** Bede would have agreed that this letter (or his revision of it), long as it is, does not cover the entire issue. It only deals, as briefly as may be, with the particular points on which Nechtan asked for further guidance. Nechtan is not provided with cycles of times for the future because he only ('tantum') asked for reasons for Easter dating (p. 546), not for tables which he already had.*

p. 544, l. 34. v. 21. **Sed per industriam Eusebii.** What was the source of Ceolfrith's (or Bede's) information that Eusebius had reduced the computation of the 19-year cycle to a plainer system? L. W. Barnard, *Famulus Christi*, p. 108, gives reasons why it is likely that their information 'was based on knowledge of a work on the Easter cycle mediated through Jerome which Eusebius had composed'.

p. 548, ll. 1–4. v. 21. **inter omnes tamen ... Dominus ait.** The letter deals at some length with the question of tonsure. It is careful not to elevate the matter to the same level of importance as Easter dating but nevertheless it is best to follow St Peter. Outward conformity is an indication of inward obedience.*

p. 550, l. 8. v. 21. **dixi illi inter alia conloquens.** This passage of *oratio recta* is typical of Bede but can only refer to a conversation between Ceolfrith and Adomnán, not between Bede and Adomnán. He would not have attributed to Ceolfrith a conversation that he never had.

p. 552, ll. 14–15. v. 21. **quae dixerat, regia auctoritate perfecit.** This surprising exercise of royal authority outside the English kingdoms (on 'Pictorum prouincias' see Kirby, *Famulus Christi*, p. 292) is Bede's gloss on the effects of the letter. The scriptorial activity involved in replacing the old 84-year cycle with the new 19-year cycle is commented on by Bullough, 'Missions to the English and Picts', p. 93.

p. 552, ll. 19–21. v. 21. **et quasi nouo ... gaudebat.** The chapter ends with Bede's insistence on what really mattered to *HE* about Nechtan's appeal: another victory for St Peter, and this time through the good offices of the monastery of SS Peter and Paul.

p. 552, ll. 28–31. v. 22. **pater ac sacerdos ... deuotissimus.** In this short rhetorical chapter Bede brings together much that he had been saying throughout *HE*. The last stronghold of Irish particularism yields to the teaching of a remarkable Englishman; the Irish, to whom English Christianity owed so much, are at one in Christian observance with the English, whereas the British are left out in the cold. I agree with Charles-Edwards, 'Bede, the Irish and the Britons', pp. 42 ff., that Bede's picture of the British is conditioned less by ethnic or political antipathy (if he felt such) than by horror at their failure to preach the Gospel to their neighbours. So, at the end, they remain isolated and out of communion with the universal Church.

p. 552, ll. 32–3. v. 22. **inmutauit piis ... parentum eorum.** It is not clear why Egbert succeeded in Iona where others had failed, nor whether his lengthy mission involved one or more visits. Bede's conclusion is that it was an act of divine dispensation, as by the same dispensation Egbert died on the very Easter Day in 729 that saw the first celebration according to Roman dating. Bede is writing not more than two years later and the triumph is fresh in his mind. In this sense it marks a culmination of *HE* (see Cowdrey, 'Bede and the "English People"', p. 513) but it was not necessarily a foreseen culmination when he first planned the outlines of *HE*. It is hard to believe that Egbert's success was the cause of the writing of *HE*.

pp. 556–60. v. 23. This seems to be the final narrative chapter of Bede's revision of *HE* and is a survey of the episcopal scene against a royal background.

p. 556, ll. 6–7. v. 23. **Tobias ... doctissimus.** The effective start of the chapter is the death of Tobias of Rochester, about whom a little more can now be reported than in v. 8. That little has to do with his learning, which he owed to the two great Canterbury teachers. At the end, Bede still turns to Canterbury.

p. 556, ll. 16–17. v. 23. **cometae duae circa solem.** Presumably one and the same comet before and after perihelion (see R. R. Newton, *Medieval Chronicles and the Rotation of the Earth* (1972), 671: I owe this reference to Mr Harrison). Bede reports this carefully as a presage of calamity, soon to be fulfilled by the Arabs in Gaul and by troubles unspecified in Northumbria.

p. 556, ll. 24-5. v. 23. **grauissima Sarracenorum lues ...
uastabat.** Note Gregory of Tours, *Hist.* v. 34: 'sed haec prodigia
gravissima lues est subsecuta', a chapter used by Bede in his
Expositio Actuum Apostolorum et Retractatio, ed. Laistner (1939),
p. 146. I see no reason why Bede should be thinking of Charles
Martel's defeat of the Arabs near Tours in 732. He might be
drawing on the account of the victory of Odo, duke of Aquitaine,
over the Arabs in 721, as recorded in the notice of Pope
Gregory II in the *Liber Pontificalis*. On Bede's view of the Arabs
generally see my Jarrow Lecture, 1962 (reprinted in *Early
Medieval History*, pp. 60-75) and G. Bonner, *ASE* 2 (1973), 73.

p. 558, ll. 2-5. v. 23. **cuius regni ... necdum sciri ualeat.** Though
I agree with Campbell, 'Bede', p. 172, that one can say of Bede,
as contrasted with Gregory of Tours, that 'the more he knew the
less he wrote', and further that he had to show some discretion
at this point, the fact remains that what would be relevant to an
ecclesiastical history was not yet apparent to him. In Tugène's
phrase, 'L'Hist. "eccl." ', p. 150, it was difficult for Bede—I should
say impossible—to discern the significance of events 'encore
immergés dans l'actualité'; that is, their ecclesiastical significance. Bede's dating of the Northumbrian reigns is discussed by
Harrison, 'The Reign of King Ecgfrith', p. 83.

p. 558, l. 10. v. 23. **in monasterio quod uocatur Briudun.** On
Breedon in Leicestershire and its role in Mercia see Stenton,
Preparatory, pp. 183 ff. Bede does not mean Bredon in Hwiccian
Worcestershire. That Breedon, a comparatively recent founda-
tion from Peterborough, should have produced an archbishop of
Canterbury is some measure of the standing of a monastery
about which Bede has nothing more to say. I take it that Bede's
list of contemporary bishops came from Canterbury.

p. 558, ll. 27-9. v. 23. **hae omnes prouinciae ... subiectae sunt.**
Of Æthelbald's effective power there can be no question. He is
himself a witness to it in his charters. See Stenton, *Preparatory*,
pp. 361 ff. But this does not explain the nature of Bede's
reference to him. His name is inserted in a strictly episcopal
context. Was it that Canterbury, now under an archbishop from
Mercia, recognized an advantage in the effective control of

southern England by one king and one archbishop, and so
represented it to Bede? Æthelbald's reign is well summarized in
The Anglo-Saxons, ed. Campbell, pp. 94 ff.

p. 560, ll. 18–19. v. 23. **Quae res ... aetas uidebit.** Generally
taken as a veiled reference to what Bede was to say more openly
about bogus monasteries in his letter to Bishop Egbert of York.
Another possibility is that he has in mind not what coming
generations of Northumbrians will see but the remainder of the
Sixth Age, clear only in the sight of God. 'I cannot help asking
myself whether Bede did not mean it to remind us that the
historian must not anticipate that which shall be made clear only
in the judgement at the end. It would have been very like him to
end his account of the ecclesiastical history of the English
people on this note' (Markus (Jarrow Lecture, 1975), 15). Bede
not only must not but cannot go further. He has reached the
barrier of silence and stops before it: let Britain rejoice in the
rule of God, the true king.

p. 560, ll. 26–7. v. 24. **Verum ea ... placuit.** This *recapitulatio* was
apparently not added after completion but drawn up as a
working summary before writing. It contains matter that Bede
did not use in the text. As a model he may have used Italian
annals or paschal tables containing marginal extracts from such
annals (Levison, *BLTW*, pp. 136–7; C. W. Jones, *Saints' Lives*,
p. 32, agrees in part; Harrison, *Framework*, p. 102, adds that 'it is
not clear why an unwieldy Easter table should be resorted to,
when a single sheet of parchment would suffice'). R. L. Poole,
Studies in Chronology and History (1934), 58, summarizes the
contents of the *recapitulatio* thus: notices of natural phenomena,
accessions, abdications, and deaths of kings, conversion, synods,
appointments and deaths of bishops. A chronicle fragment of
early British history, now at Bern, is based on the *recapitulatio*
and is seen by Dumville, *EHR* 88 (1973), 312–14, as 'another
item of evidence ... for Charles Plummer's estimate of the
importance of Bede's summary chronicle in the development of
annalistic writing in Britain'. Janet Bately discusses the use of the
recapitulatio in the Anglo-Saxon Chronicle (*Saints, Scholars*, i.
244). The dates provided in the *recapitulatio* will have come from
Bede's sources. When composing his narrative he sometimes

saw reason to change them slightly. Harrison, *Framework*, ch. 5, and S. Wood, *EHR* 98 (1983), *passim*, explain his methods. I have not noticed all the changes here. Bede's narrative often departs widely from the chronological order of the *recapitulatio*, as Plummer noted.

p. 560, l. 28. v. 24. **Anno igitur ante incarnationem.** To Bede 'we owe the reckoning Before Christ ... which follows when 28 cycles of 19 years each are subtracted from the first year of the Dionysiac cycle. A year 0 is intolerable in everyday thinking' (Harrison, *Framework*, p. 37). M. Miller, 'Bede's Roman Dates', *Classica et Mediaevalia*, 31 (1970), considers why Bede's Roman dates in *Chron. Maj.*, the *recapitulatio*, and *HE* do not always agree among themselves and shows (e.g. for Claudius) how they can be straight recalculations from Orosius in the *recapitulatio* without reference to Jerome whom he used for *Chron. Maj.*

p. 562, ll. 14–16. v. 24. **Anno CCCCXLVIIII Marcianus ... adierunt.** See Harrison, *Framework*, pp. 123 ff.

p. 562, ll. 21–2. v. 24. **Anno DXLVII Ida ... permansit.** Not mentioned in *HE* because irrelevant. Ida's twelve years were calculated backwards from a king-list, not taken from an annal, according to Kirby, *EHR* 78 (1963), 515. Hunter Blair, 'The Moore Memoranda on Northumbrian History', p. 247, takes the same view, and describes how Bede may have reached his year 547: 'The method would be to add together the regnal years of all the Bernician kings and to subtract the total so reached from the year of the Christian era in which the calculation was made' (*Studies in Early British History*, p. 145); but the accuracy of the method would be affected by the correctness of the regnal years and by the assumption that all the kings in question ruled in regular succession. S. Wood, *EHR* 98 (1983), 281–2, notes that 'Bede does not say that 547 was Ida's first year; he says that in 547 Ida "began to reign" ... if Ida's first year worked out for Bede as 548, then the *presumption* would be that he "began to reign" in 547'.

p. 564, l. 12. v. 24. **Anno DCLV Penda periit.** 'This fitting end to the man responsible for the deaths of Edwin and Oswald will

have remained long enough in memory for it to be recorded
retrospectively in a Dionysiac annal, with the regnal year of
Oswiu as a further check' (Harrison, 'Synod of Whitby', p. 113).
More interesting is what follows: the Mercians became
Christians. This reads like a note to remind Bede that an
important step in a long process of conversion should be
considered at this point.

p. 564, ll. 22-3. v. 24. **Anno** DCLXXV **Uulfheri rex ... imperium.**
'This phrase may or may not be a stylistic variation, instead of
Aedilredus regnare coepit. In any case we should not neglect the
possibility that Æthelred had ruled with his brother, as joint-
king or sub-king, for a while before the latter's death' (Harrison,
Framework, p. 80). 'Imperium' can signify no more than 'rule' or
'power' in context.

p. 564, l. 24. v. 24. **Anno** DCLXXVI **Aedilred uastauit Cantiam.** 'A
study of Bede's Kentish dates demonstrates how errors could
arise in the transmission of historical information in the early
eighth century, and throws light on the written records the
Kentish scribes sent to Bede ... The Kentish scribes did mislead
Bede on a number of chronological points' (Kirby, *EHR* 78
(1963) 521).

p. 564, l. 29. v. 24. **Anno** DCLXXX **synodus ... Haethfeltha.** The
date is correct if Bede is following his own rule derived from
Dionysius. If he had written 679, which in fact was the year of
the synod, he would have broken his rule (Harrison, *Framework*,
p. 83). S. Wood, *EHR* 98 (1983), 287, marshals the arguments.

p. 564, ll. 38-9. v. 24. **Anno** DCXCVII **Osthryd ... interemta.** Not
recorded in the narrative. Finberg, *Lucerná*, p. 77, considers a
possible political motive which, if accepted, would explain why
Bede found the assassination irrelevant to his text.

p. 564, ll. 40-1. v. 24. **Anno** DCXCVIII **Berctred ... interfectus.**
Presumably the Berht of p. 426, l. 25 (IV. 26), is identical but
derived from a different source. See Hunter Blair, *Studies in Early
British History*, pp. 170-1.

p. 566, ll. 1–2. v. 24. **Anno** DCCIIII **Aedilred . . . regnum dedit.** See Dumville, *ASE* 8 (1979), 18, and Harrison, *Framework*, p. 80.

p. 566, l. 3. v. 24. **Anno** DCCV **Aldfrid ... defunctus est.** See Harrison, *Framework*, pp. 89–90.

p. 566, ll. 7–9. v. 24. **Anno** DCCXVI **... uir Domini Ecgberct ... tonsuram.** Duncan, *The Writing of History*, p. 41, taking 'uir Domini' in conjunction with 'Sanctus', s.a. 729, places more weight than I would on this 'unique distinction of epithets'.

p. 566, ll. 13–15. v. 24. **Anno** DCCXXXI **Berctuald ... annum imperii.** On Tatwine see Brooks, *Early History*, pp. 98–9, and on Æthelbald, *The Anglo-Saxons*, ed. Campbell, p. 99. This annal s.a. 731 is the last entry in Bede's *recapitulatio* but is not in itself evidence that he stopped composition in the same year. This was as far as his written material went.

p. 566, l. 16. v. 24. **Haec de historia.** Compare the conclusion of Gregory of Tours' *History* where, after a survey of his predecessors as bishops, he gives an account of his own episcopate and a brief résumé of his writings. Bede, a monk, has less to say of his careeer but is more elaborate in his account of his writings. 'Gregory thus may have influenced the design of his not unworthy Anglo-Saxon successor in historiography' (Levison, *BLTW*, p. 132). Levison also notes that 'Bede's list closely compares with the *Indiculus* of Augustine's writings appended to his Life by Possidius'. I should not go so far as C. W. Jones, *Famulus Christi*, p. 285, in claiming that Bede's autobiographical matter was 'written in pious imitation of Gregory of Tours'. Bede's opening phrase should be translated: 'I have put together this account of the ecclesiastical history of the British and especially of the English peoples'. His list of writings is complete, with the exception of his letter to Egbert, provided that we allow that the *Retractatio* is mentioned and that *De Locis Sanctis* is adequately covered by v. 17. There is no mention of a penitential and no good reason for thinking that he composed one.*

p. 566, ll. 24–5. v. 24. **omnem meditandis scripturis operam dedi.** This meditation or study has been the mainspring of

Bede's life and is the key to all his writings. 'Authentically committed to the programme of Christian studies best described in Augustine's *De Doctrina Christiana*, Bede wanted it known that among his works there was nothing superfluous. Every title, including the *Historia* no less than such treatises as *De Arte Metrica*, fell precisely within the tight biblical economy of his learned purposes' (Roger Ray, *Famulus Christi*, p. 125).

p. 568, l. 2. v. 24. **In primam partem Samuhelis.** 'Like Gregory, Bede recognized that the Vulgate's first Book of Kings was more properly the first Book of Samuel, because it was the prophet who by his words and deeds shed light on the meaning of events … Bede even changed the title of the book to *In primam partem Samuhelis*' (McClure, *Ideal and Reality*, p. 98 and n. 122).

p. 568, l. 8. v. 24. **In Cantica Canticorum libros** VII. 'In relation to which he performs, four centuries before St Bernard, some of the most astonishing feats of exegesis in all theological literature' (C. Jenkins, *BLTW*, p. 153).

p. 568, l. 24. v. 24. **In Actus Apostolorum libros** II. I accept the assessment of Laistner, *Bedae Venerabilis Expositio Actuum Apostolorum et Retractatio* (1939), pp. xiii ff., that Bede here means both his commentary and his *Retractatio*.

p. 568, l. 34. v. 24. **Item de historiis sanctorum.** The *Vita Felicis* is a prose version of Paulinus of Nola's *Natalicia*. It is examined and warmly praised by Thomas Mackay, *Famulus Christi*, pp. 77–92. Bede recognized in his reference to his *Vita Anastasii* 'that if one were dealing with a translation and did not have the text in the original language, the situation could become almost hopeless' (Meyvaert, *Famulus Christi*, p. 49, where, by a slip, Anastasius becomes Athanasius). Apropos Bede's 'ad sensum correxi', Meyvaert asks (*England before the Conquest*, p. 32 n. 4), 'Is there perhaps a clue in this last phrase: as long as Bede thought he could get meaning out of a text it was better to leave it intact?'. For his Lives of St Cuthbert, Bede first composed a long version in verse which he later reduced to prose. In Levison's opinion, *BLTW*, p. 126, these Lives 'were composed principally with regard to the form', but this hardly does justice to Bede's personal feelings about St Cuthbert. Bede's contribution to *opus geminatum* is well treated by Godman, 'The Anglo-Latin *Opus Geminatum*, from Aldhelm to Alcuin', *Medium Aevum*, 50 (1981), 222 ff.*

p. 570, l. 7. v. 24. **Historiam ecclesiasticam nostrae insulae ac gentis in libris v.** Again, 'ecclesiastical history', not 'history of the Church'.

p. 570, l. 8. v. 24. **Martyrologium de nataliciis ... diebus.** The importance of Bede's martyrology, 'fundamental for the development of this literature' (Levison, *BLTW*, p. 124), lies not only in his remarkably wide reading, which included some fifty hagiographical texts, but in what he did with his material. What he created was the historical narrative martyrology. A jumble of names and dates, as in the past, was not enough; summaries and assessments of saints' careers were required. Bede's sources have been investigated by Dom H. Quentin, *Les Martyrologes historiques du moyen âge* (1908), 17–119.

p. 570, l. 13. v. 24. **Librum epigrammatum.** C. W. Jones, *Famulus Christi*, p. 266, suggests that this lost work could have been composed 'to lighten the rigour for youngsters' of the study of the Psalter, and further notes (p. 280) that Bede 'grouped all his didactic writings together' in this list and includes his *Liber Epigrammatum* in it. Levison, *BLTW*, p. 128 n. 2, agrees with Plummer that the nine distichs of a lost poem on Eadberht, alluded to in Bede's metrical Life of St Cuthbert (ch. 39) may be a fragment of the *Lib. Epig.**

p. 570, l. 17. v. 24. **Item librum de metrica arte.** Despite its title, 'the aim of this textbook is practical instruction in pronunciation. Bede concentrates most of his effort on quantity and accentuation' (Margot King, 'Grammatica Mystica', *Saints, Scholars*, i. 149, and she explains why this should be so). Mayr-Harting, *Coming of Christianity*, p. 215, has a useful comparison of Bede and Aldhelm as writers on grammar.

p. 570, ll. 20–3. v. 24. **Teque deprecor ... faciem tuam.** Mayr-Harting, *Coming of Christianity*, p. 190, notes that this concluding prayer provides one of the occasions when Bede addresses neither God the Father nor any saint but Christ (to be precise, Jesus). 'Teque' suggests that what we have might have been the conclusion of a longer prayer. The metrical *oratio* appended to the end of Bede's *De Die Iudicii* is the work of Eugenius of Toledo, not of Bede (see Laistner and King, *A Hand-List of Bede Manuscripts* (1943), 126). Gildas too concludes his *De Excidio* with a prayer, but of a very different nature. Eusebius, Orosius, and Gregory of Tours conclude their narratives with no prayer. Bede's prayer, like the rest of v. 24, is clearly not an integral part of his narrative but its appearance in its present position in the Moore and Leningrad MSS is reasonable evidence that that is where Bede meant it to be.*

ADDENDA

Note: The addenda mainly refer to points made in the Commentary, but some are further observations on Colgrave's translation or notes.

PRAEFATIO

p. 2, l. 1. Gloriosissimo ... Ceoluulfo. On Ceolwulf's interest in the *Historica Ecclesiastica* see D. P. Kirby, 'King Ceolwulf of Northumbria and the *Historia Ecclesiastica*', *Studia Celtica*, 14–15 (1979–80), 168–73. Since Acca was expelled from his see in 731, when a coup temporarily drove Ceolwulf from his throne (p. 572, l. 2), it may be supposed that he was a close supporter of the king (see Kirby in *Saint Wilfrid at Hexham*, p. 24). Hexham is thus just as likely a place for Ceolwulf to have had the *HE* copied as was Lindisfarne. But there are several other possibilities.

p. 2, l. 5. et nunc ad transcribendum. Bede's own definition of *transcribere* (*De Orthographia*, ed. C. W. Jones (*CCSL* 123 A), p. 19) suggests that it was a technical term for the moment at which the author relinquished his rights by releasing his work for general copying: 'transcribere: cum ius nostrum in alium transit'.

p. 6, ll. 19–21. uera lex historiae ... studuimus. See also R. Ray, 'Bede's *vera lex historiae*', *Speculum*, 55 (1980), 1–21, who argues that the phrase is to be translated 'a true law of history' not 'the true law of history', still less 'the principles of true history' as Colgrave renders it.

Book I

p. 14, l. 26, I. 1. **fontes calidos.** On the *Historia Brittonum*, see also D. N. Dumville, 'The Historical Value of the *Historia Brittonum*', *Arthurian Literature*, 6 (1986), 1–26.

p. 16, l. 21. I. 1. **iuxta numerum librorum.** On the significance of these numerical divisions compare C. W. Jones's preface to his edition of Bede's *Libri quattuor in Principium Genesis* (*CCSL* 118 A), p. x.

p. 16, ll. 22–6. I. 1. **quinque gentium linguis … facta communis.** On the Picts Bede's information appears to have been incomplete. K. Jackson, 'The Pictish Language', in *The Problem of the Picts*, ed. F. T. Wainwright, p. 152, concludes: 'There were at least two languages current in northern Scotland before the coming of the Irish Gaels in the fifth century. One of them was a Gallo-Brittonic dialect not identical with the British spoken south of the Antonine Wall, though related to it. The other was not Celtic at all, nor apparently even Indo-European, but was presumably the speech of some very early set of inhabitants of Scotland.'

p. 16, l. 30. I. 1. **Pictorum de Scythia.** For analyses of the various forms of this origin-legend see G. Mac Eoin, 'On the Irish Legend of the Origin of the Picts', *Studia Hibernica*, 4 (1964), 138–54, and M. Miller, 'Matriliny by Treaty: The Pictish Foundation Legend', in *Ireland in Early Mediaeval Europe*, ed. D. Whitelock *et al.*, pp. 133–61.

p. 26, l. 10. I. 5. **apud Eboracum.** See also M. Biddle, 'Towns', in *The Archaeology of Anglo-Saxon England*, ed. D. Wilson, pp. 117–18.

p. 28, l. 10. I. 7. **Siquidem in ea passus est sanctus Albanus.** For a recent statement on the excavations of St Albans see M. Biddle, 'Archaeology, Architecture, and the Cult of Saints', pp. 13–16. On British survival in the Chiltern area see K. Rutherford Davis, *Britons and Saxons: The Chiltern Region 400–700* (1982).

p. 34, l. 28. i. 8. **Arrianae uaesaniae.** There is evidence for Arianism in Britain in the letter of Vinisius to Nigra preserved on a lead tablet at Bath: see Thomas, *Christianity in Roman Britain to A.D. 500*, pp. 126-7. Bede is here echoing Gildas, *De Excidio*, ch. 12. The phrase 'insulae noui semper aliquid audire gaudenti' echoes, as Colgrave noted, Acts 17: 21, but it was suggested by Gildas's 'patriae noui semper aliquid audire uolenti'. That it hints 'at the existence of various heresies in Britain' (Plummer) is therefore shown by Gildas's text with its mention of 'cuiuslibet haereseos' and by the summary (ch. 2), where 'de diuersis haeresibus' corresponds to the second part of ch. 12.

p. 36, l. 19. i. 9. **Maximus ... strenuus et probus.** On later British traditions about Maximus, entangled with stories about other Roman figures, see J. F. Matthews, 'Macsen, Maximus, and Constantine', *Welsh History Review*, 11 (1982-3), 431-8. These traditions are like Bede, but unlike Gildas, in that they present a favourable picture of Maximus.

p. 38, l. 3. i. 10. **Pelagius Bretto.** For arguments against the view that Gildas' geographical perspective is confined to northern Britain see N. Wright, 'Gildas's Geographical Perspective: Some Problems', in *Gildas: New Approaches*, ch. v, and P. Sims-Williams, 'Gildas and the Anglo-Saxons', *Cambridge Medieval Celtic Studies*, 6 (1983), 5-15. (A purely northern perspective will not, therefore, explain why he does not mention Pelagianism.) On the other hand, there are the arguments summarized by Dumville, *Gildas: New Approaches*, pp. 78-80, for thinking that he was largely writing about one area of Roman Britain, perhaps the north-west. One should distinguish between what he intended to be the geographical scope of his account (and here Wright seems to have persuasive arguments) and the area on which Gildas had reliable information, which may be much more limited and is certainly very difficult to locate. Gildas's view of Pelagianism is not clear though Ian Wood points to some possible clues, 'The End of Roman Britain', *Gildas: New Approaches*, p. 8 n. 62. New evidence for later British interest in Pelagius is discussed by D. N. Dumville, 'Late-Seventh- or Eighth-Century Evidence for the British Transmission of Pelagius', *Cambridge Medieval Celtic Studies*, 10 (1985), 39-52.

R. A. Markus in his review-article on E. A. Thompson, *Saint Germanus of Auxerre and the End of Roman Britain*, in *Nottingham Medieval Studies*, 29 (1985), 118–22, argues that the main tradition of British Christianity was labelled Pelagian only by foreign churchmen, and that this is the explanation why British sources such as Gildas may not have felt the need to expatiate on Pelagianism as a phenomenon native to their province. See further R. A. Markus, 'Pelagianism: Britain and the Continent', *JEH* 37 (1986), 191–204.

p. 40, l. 20. I. 12. **Scottorum a circio, Pictorum ab aquilone.** The re-interpretation of Gildas's text involved in this paragraph is discussed by N. Wright, 'Gildas's Geographical Perspective: Some Problems', pp. 92–6, who shows that in his *Chron. Maj.* Bede still followed Gildas in regarding the Picts and the Irish as attacking Britain from outside the island. Now they are seen as *transmarinae gentes* simply because they came from across the firths of Forth and Clyde. The re-interpretation therefore occurred between 725 and 731.

p. 40, l. 26. I. 12. **urbem Giudi.** Kenneth Jackson defends the identification with Stirling in '*Varia*: I. Bede's *Urbs Giudi*: Stirling or Cramond?', *Cambridge Medieval Celtic Studies*, 2 (1981), 1–7, against the counter-arguments of I. Rutherford, '*Giudi* Revisited', *Bulletin of the Board of Celtic Studies*, 26 (1974–6), 440–4.

p. 44, ll. 3–4. I. 12. **ubi et Seuerus ... fecerat.** N. Wright, 'Did Gildas read Orosius?', *Cambridge Medieval Celtic Studies*, 9 (1985), 31–42, gives reasons for believing that Gildas may have known Orosius.

p. 46, l. 1. I. 13. **anno imperii octauo Palladius.** The most important treatment of the relationship between Patrick and Palladius is D. A. Binchy, 'Patrick and his Biographers: Ancient and Modern', *Studia Hibernica*, 2 (1962), 7–173.

p. 46, l. 4. I. 131. **Aetius uir inlustris.** On the identification (made by Bede) of Gildas' Agitius with Aetius, see D. N. Dumville, 'The Chronology of *De Excidio Britanniae*, Book I', pp. 67–8, who concludes that 'what makes the identification with Aëtius seem reasonably secure is the appellation *ter consul*. The spelling of Agitius is not a serious problem if we may allow for the influence of Vulgar Latin: to avoid hiatus a *j* sound (as English *y* in *yet*) was sometimes introduced, so that Aetius might be pronounced *Ajetius*. This *j* could be spelt with a *g*: see V. Väänänen, *Introduction au latin vulgaire* (Paris, 1967), paras. 75 and 95. The first -*i*- in Agitius (rather than Agetius) may be explained either by the Vulgar Latin confusion of short *i* and long *e* or by the influence of British final -*i*-affection which occurred *c.* 500 (K. H. Jackson, *Languages and History*, p. 603).

Morris's theory about the 'perpetual consulship' referred to by a Pelagian writer is refuted by A. Cameron, 'Celestial Consulates: A Note on the Pelagian Letter *Humanae Referunt*', *JTS* NS 19 (1968), 213-15. The honour in question was celestial, not earthly.

p. 46, l. 22. I. 14. **Interea Brettones.** But this 'interea' appears to correspond to the 'interea' of Gildas, *De Excidio*, ch. 20. 2, not the 'interea' at the beginning of ch. 22. The 'mox' of *Chron. Maj.* (para. 484) has no direct counterpart in Gildas, though it may have been suggested by the 'approprinquabat siquidem tempus' of 22. 3. There is thus no evidence that 'interea' has the same sense in this instance as 'mox' *pace* Miller, 'Bede's Use of Gildas', p. 248.

p. 48, ll. 25-6. I. 14. **cum suo rege Uurtigerno.** The deductions made from the forms of the name need qualification. The Old English *Wyrtgeorn* is indeed derived from *Vurtigernus* but so also are Welsh *Gwrtheyrn*, Old Breton *Gurdiern*. Here the variant is certainly early, and Bede's source could be Celtic. The form found in *Chron. Maj.*, *Vertigernus*, does not necessarily imply an earlier source than that lying behind *Vurtigernus*. Fluctuation in the vocalism of the Celtic prepositions **wer/*wor* and **wo* is as old as the Roman period (for example, Gallo-Latin *vassus* for an earlier **wossos*) and is still found in Middle Welsh. There is no evidence to show that such fluctuations did not occur in the seventh and eighth centuries. All Bede's forms, however, reflect a written tradition, not eighth-century oral informants, either British or English, for they preserve the *i* in -*tigernus* which had been syncopated in Old English by AD 700 and the *t* which had developed to *th* in Welsh *c.* 600. It does not follow that Bede's sources were themselves earlier than *c.* 600, but they must have derived the form of the name from earlier texts.

p. 48, l. 30–p. 50, l. 1. i. 15. **Anno ... Tunc.** For Bede this is the 'aduentus ... Anglorum in Britanniam' (I. 23), the coming of members of at least three distinct Germanic peoples, Jutes, Angles, and Saxons, but all under the leadership of Hengest, ancestor of the kings of Kent (II. 5), and of his brother Horsa. Bede placed the accession of Marcian a year too soon (so also in v. 24). His chronology thus appears to be as follows (with an assimilation of regnal years to AD years in the manner proposed by Levison, *England and the Continent in the Eighth Century*, pp. 271–5):

446: appeal of the Britons to Aetius; the failure of this appeal leads to the invitation issued by Vortigern to the 'Angles or Saxons'.

449: accession of Marcian, who reigns for seven years (the regnal years of Marcian are given in roman numerals).

450: I

454: V: killing of Aetius 'cum quo Hesperium cecidit regnum neque hactenus ualuit releuari' (*Chron. Maj.* from Marcellinus).

455: VI: Valentinian III killed 'anno imperii Marciani sexto cum quo simul Hesperium concidit regnum' (I. 21).

456: VII: death of Marcian.

Although the date of the accession of Marcian was put a year too soon, the implied AD date for the death of Valentinian is correct. The entry on the 'aduentus' in v. 24 (p. 562, ll. 14–16) is more explicit in one respect. After stating that in 449 'Marcian acquired the imperial office, as co-ruler with Valentinian, and reigned for seven years' (one should correct Colgrave's translation thus), he adds 'quorum tempore Angli a Brettonibus accersiti Britanniam adierunt'. The use of the plural 'quorum' implies that the *aduentus Anglorum in Britanniam* occurred before the death of Valentinian in 455, in other words, in the period 449 to 455.

There remain two problems. First, Bede's notice of the death of Valentinian (p. 66, ll. 23-6; I. 21) is a conflation of Marcellinus' entries for the deaths of Aetius (in 454) and Valentinian (in 455). As a result Bede now states that the Roman Empire fell with Valentinian, whereas Marcellinus had ascribed its fall, much more plausibly, to the death of Aetius, and so indeed had Bede in *Chron. Maj.* The synchronism between the death of Valentinian in 455 and the date of the *aduentus Anglorum in Britanniam* (between 449 and 455) may be one reason for this otherwise extraordinary reapplication of Marcellinus' comment on the killing of Aetius to the murder of Valentinian. The change appears to be deliberate since, whereas in *Chron. Maj.* Bede follows Marcellinus more or less word for word, in *HE* he emphasizes his point by means of the change of *cecidit* to *concidit* and the addition of *simul*. He thus stresses the synchronism between the death of Valentinian in the sixth year of Marcian's reign and the fall of the *Hesperium regnum*. Further reasons for the change may be (1) that, in Marcellinus, the sack of Rome by the Vandals in 455 follows, and is occasioned by, the killing of Valentinian, and (2) the link between the death of Germanus and that of Valentinian. On the occasion of the first visit of Germanus to Britain the alliance of the Saxons and Picts was defeated by the Britons under his leadership. After his second visit to Britain, Germanus went to Ravenna and was received 'summa reuerentia' by Valentinian and his mother Placidia (p. 66, ll. 20-2; I. 21); 'nec multo post' Valentinian was killed in 455. In other words, for Bede, the *aduentus Anglorum in Britanniam*, their rebellion against the Britons and alliance with the Picts, and both the visits of Germanus all occurred within the period 449-55.

Secondly, all Bede's other dates for the *aduentus Anglorum in Britanniam* make it a little earlier than 449-55. In I. 23, the sending of Augustine by Gregory the Great in 596 is said to have occurred 'aduentus uero Anglorum in Britanniam anno circiter CL', implying an approximate date of 446 (not 445 as Colgrave asserts). In II. 14, the year 627 is 'ab aduentu ... Anglorum in Britanniam annus circiter CLXXXmus' implying an approximate date of 447. In V. 23, similarly, 731 is roughly the 285th year since the *aduentus*, implying an approximate date of 446. In this third case it is clear that Bede cannot be giving an approximate reference to a date between 449 and 455 since otherwise he would have said that it was roughly the 280th year since the *aduentus* (implying *c.*451). Bede's date for *Mons Badonicus* is phrased in the same terms as he uses for the rough datings from 446/7, 'quadragesimo circiter et quarto anno aduentus eorum in Britanniam', and this suggests that the date he intended was *c.*490, though it could have been *c.*493 to 499. The reason is very probably that Bede is counting from the third consulship of Aetius for he assumes that it was after the failure of the appeal of the Britons to Aetius that Vortigern issued the invitation to the English. That was the beginning of the process which culminated in the arrival of Hengest and Horsa between 449 and 455. There is thus no reason to think that Bede ever departed from the limits 449-55 for the arrival of the English (both 446 and 449-455/6 are already implied by *Chron. Maj.*). Thompson, *Saint Germanus of Auxerre and the End of Roman Britain*, pp. 91-2, has a different theory. According to him, the date 446/7 does not refer to the appeal to Aetius, but rather to the same conquest of British territory as that reported by the Gallic 'Chronicler of AD 452'. This, according to Thompson, took place in the southeast of the island, whereas the events associated with the *superbus tyrannus* occurred in the north. Whatever the general merits of Thompson's reconstruction of events in fifth-century Britain, this cannot represent Bede's view. For him the invitation of the *superbus tyrannus* brought the ancestor of the Kentish kings to Britain. Indeed, the story as he tells it, with Hengest and Horsa assuming the *ducatus* of a mixed force of Angles, Saxons, and Jutes, may be intended to claim for the founder of the Kentish royal line the same kind of *imperium* as that mentioned in II. 5. Thompson argues that there is no reason to associate the date 446/7 with the invitation to Aetius mentioned in the *De Excidio*, for the latter was 'in quite a different part of the book' from Gildas' account of the invitation of the *superbus tyrannus*. The argument loses its force, however, when it is noted that the two events are brought together in *Chron. Maj.* (paras. 483-4). Finally, Thompson's argument requires us to accept that Bede had two distinct *aduentus Anglorum in Britanniam* in mind, though he describes them in the same terms, though he never sees fit to explain the relationship between them, and though both would already have existed side by side in the chronological summary in v. 24 (*sub annis* 449 and 597), which was probably drawn up before he began writing (see note on p. 560, ll. 26–7).

p. 50, l. 15. l. 15. **Saxonibus, Anglis, Iutis.** See also J. N. L. Myres, *The English Settlements* (Oxford, 1986), chs. 3 and 5.

p. 50, ll. 26–7. l. 15. **Duces fuisse perhibentur ... Hengist et Horsa.** On the Hengest of *Beowulf* and the *Fight at Finnesburg*, see the detailed discussion by J. R. R. Tolkien, *Finn and Hengest: The Fragment and the Episode* (1982), 63–76 (and cf. the reconstruction, pp. 159–62). For Tolkien, Hengest is an historical character and his coming to Britain was subsequent to the events in Frisia alluded to in an excursus in *Beowulf* and partially recounted in the fragmentary *Fight at Finnesburg* or *Freswael*. For a much more sceptical view see P. Sims-Williams, 'The Settlement of England in Bede and the *Chronicle*', pp. 21–5. As he shows, it is likely that Bede's Canterbury source has conflated two distinct traditions. First, there is the origin of the dynasty of the Oiscingas from the Oisc who is probably to be identified with the Ansehis (for Anschis) of the Ravenna Cosmographer (it is less likely that Ansehis stands for Hengest); the Cosmographer saw Anschis as the leader of a migration. Secondly, there is the tradition which made the heroic figure Hengest into the leader of an alliance of peoples.

p. 52, l. 25. l. 15. **alii transmarinas regiones.** On Britons in Ireland at the time of Patrick, see E. A. Thompson, 'St. Patrick and Coroticus', *JTS* NS 31 (1980), 12–27.

p. 52, l. 29. l. 16. **domum reuersus est.** See also Dumville, 'The Chronology of *De Excidio Britanniae*, Book I', p. 75, for whom the *domus* is the territory granted by the terms of the agreement made with the *superbus tyrannus*, Bede's Vortigern.

p. 54, l. 1. l. 16. **duce Ambrosio Aureliano.** On Bede's date for *Mons Badonicus*, probably intended to be *c.*490, though possibly *c.*493–9, see the addendum to p. 48, l. 30–p. 50, l. 1; 1.15.

p. 54, l. 6. l. 16. **Badonici montis.** A new interpretation of Gildas's sentence is given by I. N. Wood, 'The End of Roman

Britain', pp. 22–3, but the syntactical objections are insurmountable: see the review of *Gildas: New Approaches* by T. M. Charles-Edwards in *Cambridge Medieval Celtic Studies*, 12 (1986), 118–19. If the traditional translation is unacceptable, it is necessary to emend; for one suggestion see M. Miller, 'Relative and Absolute Publication Dates of Gildas's *De Excidio* in Medieval Scholarship', *Bulletin of the Board of Celtic Studies*, 26 (1974–6), 169–74.

p. 54, l. 19. 1. 17. **Germanus Autisidorensis.** See now E. A. Thompson, *Saint Germanus of Auxerre and the End of Roman Britain* (1984). According to Thompson, pp. 55–70, the death of Germanus is to be dated to 437; I. N. Wood, 'End of Roman Britain', pp. 14–16, favours either 437 or 442. In any event Bede put the date too late (not long before 455). On Victricius see R. P. C. Hanson, *St Patrick: His Origins and Career* (1968), 143–5, and A. C. Thomas, *Christianity in Roman Britain*, pp. 50–1. For arguments against the association of Patrick with Auxerre, or anywhere else in Gaul, see D. A. Binchy, 'Patrick and his Biographers: Ancient and Modern', pp. 76–90.

p. 64, ll. 23–4. 1. 1. **Elafius ... primus.** See E. A. Thompson, *Saint Germanus of Auxerre and the End of Roman Britain*, p. 12.

p. 66, ll. 18–26. 1. 21. **Itaque conpositis ... concidit regnum.** It should be noted that whereas Marcellinus (s.a. 454) has the Western Empire fall with the death of Aetius, Bede, in the *HE*, places it in the next year, with the death of Valentinian III (see the addendum to p. 48, l. 30–p. 50, l. 1. 1. 15).

p. 68, ll. 6–7. 1. 22. **historicus eorum Gildas.** Duncan's accusation presupposes the correctness of Colgrave's translation of 'inter alia inenarrabilium scelerum facta' by 'to other unspeakable crimes'. The translation suggests that the 'alia ... facta' are in addition to those previously recounted by Bede, whereupon the reference to Gildas does not amount to an acknowledgement of indebtedness for material that Bede has used but is only a statement of where further horrid details may be found. If, however, one translates 'to *the* other unspeakable crimes', the natural implication is different. Since Bede has listed several such crimes (1. 14) and has recalled them in the previous sentence, he may well have expected the reader to take this passage as an acknowledgement of his source. Moreover one cannot take 'inenarrabilium' too literally: Cadwallon is 'infandus' (p. 214, l. 9), but Bede speaks of him in three chapters. Gildas is admittedly not mentioned in the Preface, but Bede did not there give by name any of his sources for the period before the arrival of Augustine (they are all included under the phrase 'ex priorum maxime scriptis', p. 4, l. 12).

p. 68, ll. 7–12. I. 22. **ut numquam ... destinauit.** The argument of T. Charles-Edwards, 'Bede, the Irish and the Britons', was that by *digniores praecones* Bede meant not only the missionaries sent from Rome, but also the Irish from Iona and elsewhere.

p. 70, ll. 1–18. I. 23. **Gregorius ... indictione** XIIII. Contrary to what Colgrave says in his note, this letter was part of the Register, as Norberg showed (*In Registrum Gregorii Magni Studia Critica* (1939) ii. 35). It is included in his recent edition of the Register as *Ep.* VI. 53 (*CCSL* 140; p. 426).

p. 72, ll. 12–13. I. 25. **rex Aedilberct ... potentissimus.** On possible Frankish hegemony over southern England and the context of the marriage of Bertha to Æthelberht, see I. N. Wood, *The Merovingian North Sea*, pp. 12–17.

p. 76, ll. 3–4. I. 26. **coeperunt ... imitari.** On Gregory's and Augustine's knowledge of the Rule of St Benedict one should distinguish between Gregory and Augustine and between knowledge and influence. That Gregory knew the Rule is very probable: see de Vogüé in the introduction to the edition of the Rule by himself and J. Neufville (*SC* 181), pp. 150–7. The extent of this influence of the Rule on his monastic life is much more difficult to estimate. That Augustine knew the Rule is quite uncertain—there is simply no evidence—but he may well have been influenced by it via Gregory even if he never read the text himself.

p. 82, ll. 5–6. I. 27. **et haec quasi ... depone.** A better translation of the original than that given by Colgrave in n. 1 would be: 'and when you have collected them as it were into one dish, place them on the table of the English by way of menu'.

Book II

p. 132, ll. 3–4. II. 1. **in tumba ipsius epitaphium.** On the sylloge of Cambridge see P. Sims-Williams, 'William of Malmesbury and *La Silloge Epigrafica di Cambridge*', *Archivum Historiae Pontificiae*, 21 (1983), 9–33.

p. 138, l. 2. II. 2. **Dinoot abbas.** The evidence of this name is crucial, for if the source is an English document of the early seventh century, as claimed by Kenneth Jackson, it can hardly come from anywhere other than Canterbury. Unfortunately, when discussing the name *Brocmail* which occurs later in the same chapter (p. 140, ll. 22, 31), Jackson comes to a different conclusion: 'the form could have been derived ultimately from a Latin written document of British origin' (*Language and History*, p. 568), and not therefore a Canterbury text. Yet the two names are unlikely to come from different sources. What is certain is that the name *Dinoot* was not transmitted orally through English intermediaries during the seventh century, for otherwise it would have a short *o* (*oo* is simply a way of spelling the long vowel): on this Primitive Old English shortening of unaccented long vowels see A. Campbell, *Old English Grammar*, §§ 355 and 394. It thus comes either from an English written source of the early seventh century or from a British source, which might be of any date from 603 to 731. The arguments in favour of an English origin are the more cogent. In the case of *Dinoot*, the appearance of *i* in place of *u* in the first syllable is telling evidence: a British source should have had *Dunoot* or *Dunot*, where *u* stands for a fronted and rounded vowel similar to French *u* or Old English *y* though not pronounced so far forward in the mouth. (We may represent it by *y*.) The explanation favoured by Jackson (*Language and History*, pp. 295, 309) is that in the early seventh century Old English had not yet developed the sound *y* (by i-mutation of *u*), though it had certainly done so by the end of Bede's lifetime. An Anglo-Saxon or an Italian missionary (for whom the sound *y* would also be foreign) substituted *i* for the strange *y*. This substitution is well-attested in place-names. The alternative is to suppose an abnormal British use of *i* for *y*; this may be attested in the name CIMESETLI in an inscription dated to the fifth or early sixth century, but this example lacks corroboration and may well be a mere error for CVMESETLI (see *Language and History*, p. 312). In the case of *Brocmail*, the difficulty lies in the use of -*c*- rather than -*ch*-; an earlier British -*cc*- had developed to -*ch*- in the course of the sixth century. An English document of the early seventh century might thus have been expected to use -*ch*- rather than -*c*-, whereas a British text would be far more likely to maintain the earlier spelling out of conservatism; hence Jackson's attribution of the form to a British source. His argument is, however, dependent on the earliest sources for Old English, such as the names in Bede's *HE*. Yet their orthography betrays the influence of the Irish way of spelling and pronouncing Latin, and so cannot antedate the mission of Aidan (for examples see K. Brunner, *Altenglische Grammatik*, 3rd edn. (1965), p. 12). Among the conventions probably taken over from the Irish is the use of *ch* to represent the final sound heard in German *Buch*; but this borrowing would be too late to appear in a Canterbury document of the early seventh century. It is true that the same use of *ch* is to be found in Frankish names and in the Malberg glosses to *Lex Salica*, so that it is quite likely that this spelling convention also spread from Francia to England. To explain the form *Brocmail* as stemming from an early Canterbury document we must suppose that the missionaries had not yet adopted the Frankish use of *ch*. Gregory's spellings of Germanic names (e.g. *Reg.* XIII. 11-13) suggest that this use of *ch* was foreign to him, and therefore presumably also to his missionaries when they left Rome. There is thus little difficulty in assuming a Canterbury written form of the early seventh century which had *c* rather than *ch* in *Brocmail*. The form *Brocmail* is therefore entirely consistent with the theory of a Canterbury provenance for the whole story of Augustine's dealings with the British Church, whereas to suppose a British source one must invoke orthographic conservatism. The evidence of the two names points in the same direction, to Canterbury.

p. 140, l. 3. ii. 2. **si pacem ... bellum.** The arguments of Kenneth Jackson (for which see the addendum to p. 138 l. 2; ii. 2) are inconsistent with the theory of oral tradition if it is assumed that any considerable part of that transmission was English.

p. 146, ll. 20–2. ii. 4. **Columbanum abbatem ... didicimus.** It is very possible that Columbanus never set foot in Britain. For arguments against the identification of Jonas's *Britannici sinus* (to which Columbanus came on his way to Gaul) with the coast of Britain, as opposed to Brittany, see E. James, 'Ireland and Western Gaul', in *Ireland in Early Mediaeval Europe*, ed. D. Whitelock *et al.*, pp. 376–7.

p. 148, ll. 22–7. ii. 5. **Nam primus ... obtenuit.** The form Caelin could be either Kentish or Northumbrian; the form Ceaulin is specifically West Saxon, as Bede implies: see Campbell, *Old English Grammar*, pp. 69–70.

p. 148, ll. 26–7. ii. 5. **quartus Reduald ... obtenuit.** While Brooks's interpretation certainly makes good historical sense, it should be remembered that it relies on Vollrath-Reichelt's argument (*Königsgedanke und Königtum bei den Angelsachsen*, p. 83) that in 'qui etiam uiuente Aedilbercto eidem suae genti ducatum praebebat' one should not take *suae genti* together with *eidem* as indirect object of *praebebat*. She interprets *suae genti ducatum* as constituting a distinct phrase meaning 'the *ducatus* over his people'. Yet she has no convincing parallel to justify this interpretation of the syntax. Both of the examples she offers are sentences where the sphere of authority is given in the dative because it is construed with the verb *ordinare*; thus Augustine was ordained archbishop 'for the English people', 'archiepiscopus genti Anglorum ordinatus est' (p. 78, ll. 9–10); Pippin sent Willibrord to Rome 'to be ordained archbishop for the aforementioned Frisian people', 'ut eidem Fresonum genti archiepiscopus ordinaretur' (p. 486, l. 13). Moreover in both cases the verb is in the passive. If turned into sentences with active verbs (cf. the active *praebebat*) *genti* becomes the indirect object; for example 'papa Sergius ordinauit uenerabilem uirum Vilbrordum ... Fresonum genti episcopum' (*Chron. Maj.* para. 566). Yet this syntactical pattern is precisely the basis of Colgrave's translation.

One may also note that in the first sentence about Willibrord's ordination *eidem* goes with *genti*, whereas Vollrath-Reichelt's interpretation of the clause about Redwald separates *eidem* from *suae genti*. Her evidence supports, not her translation, but the one she attacks. Yet all the recent reinterpretations of this clause rest on this fragile foundation.

But neither is Colgrave's translation ('who was gaining the leadership for his own race') acceptable. It is not just that the meaning assigned to the verb *praebebat* is unparalleled; the sense given to the whole clause is contrary to the only way in which the phrase *eis ducatum praebere* is used in Christian Latin. *Ducatum praebere* (or its variant *ducatum praestare*) is well-attested in sources familiar to Bede. Thus Gregory the Great, *Moralia in Iob* XXVII. 11 (ed. M. Adriaen (*CCSL* 143 B), p. 1345): 'Moyses ... cum priusquam plebi israeliticae ducatum praeberet ...'; 2 Macc. 10: 29: 'uiri quinque ... ducatum Iudaeis praes-tantes' (cf. Quodvultdeus (Ps. Prosper), *De Promissionibus* 2. 40. 1: 'Maccabaei ducatum Hebraeo populo praebuerunt'); Matt. 15: 14: 'caecus autem si caeco ducatum praestet' (Itala: 'caecus caeco ducatum praebens'). Whether the *ducatus* is that of the guide or the military leader, the syntax remains the same: the *dux* provides leadership (guidance) for those who are led or guided (in the dative). To accept Colgrave's translation one has to allow that Bede used the phrase *ducatum praebere* in a way which would have flouted the usage, not merely of the Vulgate, but of Gregory the Great. The only possible way to take Bede's clause is to suppose that Redwald himself provided leadership for his own people. Bede is not saying that his people had the leadership over other peoples given to them by Redwald, as Colgrave would have it, but simply that Redwald led his own people in war. Since Redwald was king of the East Angles, and kings were meant to lead in war, this may seem a grossly redundant thing for Bede to have said. The implication must be, however, that the holder of the *imperium* over the southern English would have been expected to exercise military leader-ship, *ducatus*, over the East Angles and the other southern English peoples. Æthelberht, however, lost the *ducatus* over the East Angles to Redwald before his death in 616. Redwald, for his part, may not have gained the *imperium* over the southern English during the lifetime of Æthelberht, but he did secure a measure of military independence and thus had the *ducatus* over his own people. There is nothing here to suggest 'a friendly relationship between the two kings'. On the other hand, Vollrath-Reichelt's view that a military *ducatus* was a constituent element of the *imperium* over the southern English is confirmed even though her translation is faulty. The clause may thus be translated 'the fourth was Redwald, king of the East Angles, who, while Æthelberht was still alive, acted as the military leader of his own people'.

p. 152, ll. 3–4. II. 5. **tres suos filios ... reliquit.** For a possible identification of these East Saxon kings from the extant genealogy see B. Yorke, 'The Kingdom of the East Saxons', *ASE* 14 (1985), 17–18.

p. 160, ll. 9–10. II. 8. **Susceptis ... Adulualdi regis.** Adulwald can hardly be merely a ruler in western Kent for Boniface writes in his letter of his confidence that the *uera conuersio* of Adulwald will secure 'non solum suppositarum ei gentium plenissimam salutem immo quoque uicinarum'. The pope still believes in the power of the king of Kent. Confusion between -*b*- and -*v*- is normal in Late Latin of this period except in the British Isles. Furthermore it is difficult to separate the Adulwald of this letter with his *suppositae gentes* from the Audubald of Boniface's letter to Edwin (*HE* II. 10), for Audubald also, according to the pope, has his *gentes subpositae*. Yet Audubald is certainly Eadbald, for Aud- is the continental Germanic counterpart to Old English Ead-. It remains true, however, that Adul- corresponds to Old English Æthel- (Aedil-), as in Gregory the Great's letter to Theodelinda, queen of the Lombards, on the Catholic baptism of her son Adulouuald (*Reg.* XIV. 12), and that Kent was more than once divided between two rulers (see D. W. Rollason, *The Mildrith Legend: A Study in Early Medieval Hagiography in England* (1982), 38).

p. 162, l. 1. II. 9. **Quo tempore ... Nordanhymbrorum.** On the chronological problems concerning the reign of Edwin see also S. Wood, *EHR* 98 (1983), 290–1.

p. 162, l. 8. II. 9. **Quin et Meuanias insulas.** Although for Bede the Isle of Man is British, for Orosius it is Irish ('aeque a Scottorum gentibus habitatur', i. 2. 82). Irish evidence suggests that in the half-century before Edwin's conquest it had been mainly under British control but was subject to Irish invasion, which led to conquest for short periods: see T. F. O'Rahilly, *Early Irish History and Mythology* (1946), 503-4.

p. 164, l. 3. II. 9. **quasi comes.** Lilla is not a *comes*, but a *minister* (thegn) and a *miles*. Bede makes a distinction between the *comes* (in the sense of a *gesith*), a nobleman after he has received a grant of land from the king, and a *minister* (thegn), normally a noble before he has received such a grant. The *comes* is generally resident on his own estate; the *minister* is part of the king's household or that of another member of the royal family. For a brief summary see T. M. Charles-Edwards, 'The Distinction between Land and Moveable Wealth in Anglo-Saxon England', in *Medieval Settlement*, ed. P. H. Sawyer (1976), 181-3.

p. 188, ll. 24-7. II. 15. **Tantum autem ... suscipere.** Though Ceolwulf may have been the source of the story, there is no particular reason to suppose that he was. The marriage of Hereswith to Æthelric of East Anglia did not make it family history for him: Hereswith was a survivor of the Deiran royal kindred, whereas Ceolwulf was a Bernician. The Deiran monastery of Whitby is the more plausible source.

p. 190, ll. 13-19. II. 15. **Verum Eorpuald ... curauit.** The hypothesis that the Wuffingas came from Sweden should not be allowed to harden into assured fact: J. L. N. O'Loughlin, who supported the idea of the link with Sweden ('Sutton Hoo—the Evidence of the Documents', *Medieval Archaeology*, 8 (1964), 1–19), never claimed that the evidence was conclusive.

p. 190, ll. 20-3. II. 15. **Felix episcopus ... nationi Anglorum.** Ewig, 'Bemerkungen zu zwei merowingischen Bischofsprivilegien und einem Papstprivileg des 7. Jahrhunderts für merowingische Klöster', in *Mönchtum, Episkopat und Adel*, ed. A. Borst (1974), 246-8, discusses Felix, and suggests (p. 248) that he came from Luxeuil.

p. 190, l. 29. II. 15. **in ciuitate Dommoc.** On the site of Dommoc
see also S. E. Rigold, 'Further Evidence about the Site of
"Dommoc"', *Journ. Brit. Arch. Assoc.* 3rd ser. 37 (1974), 97–102.

p. 198, l. 22. II. 19. **Misit idem papa ... genti Scottorum.** Ewig
points out ('Bemerkungen zu zwei merowingischen Bischofsprivilegien', pp. 245–6) that the two popes to concern
themselves with Irish paschal practices, Honorius and John IV,
were also in touch with the Columbanic monasteries in
Neustria.

For new evidence on the development of opinion in Ireland
after the letter of Honorius, and also on the letter of the pope-
elect John and his fellow-writers, see D. Ó Cróinín, 'A Seventh-
Century Irish Computus from the Circle of Cummianus', *Proc.
Royal Irish Acad.* 82 C (1982), 405–30, and the discussion by
K. Harrison, 'A Letter from Rome to the Irish Clergy, AD 640',
Peritia, 3 (1984), 222–9. Ó Cróinín has identified in the Munich
computus, of Irish provenance and dating from *c.* 718, a passage
from the letter of John, which Bede omitted from his text.
'Iohannes consiliarius ait: "xiiii. dies lunae ad umbras pertinet."'
'John, the councillor, said: "The fourteenth day of the lunar
month belongs to the shadows."' The point of this statement is
to associate the Irish with the Quartodecimans and with the
Jewish custom of celebrating the Passover on the fourteenth day
of their first lunar month. The reference is to Hebrews 8: 5 on
the priests of the Old Covenant 'qui exemplari, et umbrae
deserviunt caelestium' and 10: 1, 'Umbram enim habens lex
bonorum futurorum, non ipsam imaginem rerum'. The Irish
Romani used these texts to belabour their opponents (*Collectio
Canonum Hibernensis*, xx. 6; lii. 6, ed. Wasserschleben, pp. 61,
212). But, as Ó Cróinín, '"New Heresy for Old"', argues, the
problem in fact arose out of the paschal table of Victorius of
Aquitaine. Because Victorius placed the *saltus lunae* at a different
point in the 19-year cycle from that prescribed by Dionysiac
tables, their days of the month were out of step by one day for
several years out of the cycle. As a result, what was for the table
of Victorius the fifteenth day of the lunar month was often, for
the Dionysiac tables, the fourteenth. When the fifteenth day was
a Sunday, Victorius gave alternative dates for Easter: he placed
the 'Greek' date on the fifteenth and the 'Latin' date on the

twenty-second. If, however, this occurred in the part of the 19-year cycle when the two tables were one day out, the effect was to make the 'Greek' date, supposedly on the fifteenth day of the lunar month, occur on what was, for all followers of Dionysius, the fourteenth day. Thus in 641 the Victorian table put the 'Greek' date of Easter on what, to the followers of Dionysius and the Alexandrians, was the fourteenth day of the lunar month. Hence the mistaken notion on the part of Rome that those who addressed the query were attempting to revive the Celtic paschal limits which allowed Easter to occur on the fourteenth day. It was, therefore, this trap in the table of Victorius which appears to have caught the synod of northern Irish churchmen. According to Ó Cróinín, they are thereby shown to have gone over to the Victorian paschal table and to have abandoned the Celtic 84-year cycle. Moreover the papacy is shown to have gone over to the Alexandrian Easter championed by Dionysius. The discovery of the new passage makes it possible, according to Harrison, 'A Letter from Rome to the Irish Clergy, AD 640', p. 228, 'to clear Bede of fraud'. He knew that John's argument was misdirected; in III. 4 he explicitly rejects the claim that the Irish were ever Quartodecimans, even when they followed the 'Celtic' Easter. It was thus only reasonable to go no further than he does in the phrase 'et XIIII luna cum Hebreis celebrare nitentes'. He does not conceal the nature of the charge, but also he does not wish to emphasise it by including the whole letter. There is, however, one difficulty in Ó Cróinín's theory: among the recipients of John's letter was Ségéne, probably the abbot of Iona; yet Iona was to remain faithful to the 84-year cycle for another seventy-six years.

The connection between Easter and Pelagianism is explained in the letter of Ceolfrith to Nechtan v. 21, p. 544, ll. 14–30. It there relates to anyone who allows Easter to be celebrated before the vernal equinox. In the Victorian paschal table the first lunar month might begin as early as 5 March and thus the day of the paschal full moon could occur before the equinox. It is, however, clear from the letter of the pope-elect John that the same charge was made against the followers of the 84-year cycle in that they were prepared to celebrate Easter before the fifteenth day of the lunar month (for Bede, the day of the full moon).

p. 204, l. 7. II. 20. **Adlatum est ... Eburacum.** A fragment of a
Welsh poem, *Gofara Braint*, claims that Edwin's head was taken
to Aberffraw (in Anglesey). The date of the poem is unknown.
See R. G. Gruffydd, 'Canu Cadwallon ap Cadfan', in *Astudiaethau
ar yr Hengerdd/Studies in Old Welsh Poetry* (1978), 41–3, with an
English summary, pp. 3–4.

Book III

p. 212, ll. 5–6. III. 1. **nam in has duas ... diuisa erat.** But Charles-
Edwards may be wrong in suggesting that Bede created the term
Northumbria. Stenton, *ASE*, p. 32, points out that it is attested
in the text, given by Bede in IV. 5, of the proceedings of the
council of Hertford in 673, where Wilfrid is 'Nordanhymbrorum
gentis episcopus'. It is further argued by Hunter Blair, 'The
Northumbrians and their Southern Frontier', *Archaeologia
Aeliana*, 4th ser. 26 (1948), 98–126, that such terms as *Transhumbrenses*, though earlier attested than *Nordanhymbri*, were merely
Latinized versions of the vernacular *Norðanhymbre*. On the other
side, Myres argued ('The Teutonic Settlement of Northern
England', *History*, NS 20 (1935), 250–62) that the term *Nordanhymbri* was Bede's creation and that the earlier term was
Humbrenses. For him, *Humbrenses* covered both those to the
north and those immediately to the south of the Humber. There
are thus two questions: first, how old is the term *Nordanhymbri*,
and, secondly, were the English north of the Humber considered
to be a single *gens* before the destruction of the Deiran dynasty
(finally accomplished in 651 with the killing of Oswine)? To
answer the first question we need to know whether the phrase
Nordanhymbrorum gens was an authentic part of the original text
of the proceedings of the council of Hertford or was due to Bede.
It is also worth noting that the proceedings purport to attest not
only the term *Nordanhymbri* but the notion of the Northumbrians as a single *gens*. Moreover, the unity of the Northumbrian
gens may have been an important part of Wilfrid's arguments
against any proposed division of his diocese. On the issue as to
whether Bede is likely to have updated the wording of the
document, the evidence is conflicting. On the one hand, the text

of the *responsa* of Gregory to Augustine suggests that Bede did not improve the wording of documents which he quoted, even to the point of tolerating nonsense. On the other hand, Bede did sometimes make such changes to his sources (see the notes on p. 198, l. 21, and p. 274, l. 34). What one can say is that the evidence of the Life of Wilfrid and the Whitby Life of Gregory shows that *Nordanhymbri* was not the standard term in Latin before Bede; terms for the Northumbrians fluctuate (*Aquilenses*, *Humbrenses*, *Transhumbrenses*, *Ultrahumbrenses*) whereas the terms *Deiri* and *Bernicii* are fixed. On Stenton's and Hunter Blair's view these other terms for the Northumbrians are merely various Latin renderings of the vernacular *Norðanhymbre*. But *Nordanhymbri* is not the only term to be based directly on English vernacular: the same is true of *Nordi* (*Historia Brittonum*, ch. 63), which may underlie the Latin *Aquilenses*. On the second question, Hunter Blair's argument for the antiquity of the notion of the Northumbrians as a single *gens* is tied up with his whole conception of the fundamental importance of the Humber as a boundary from the early days of the settlement. For him, the *Mierce* (*Mercii*) are the people of the frontier, *mearc*, because they lived to the south of the Humber and its *contigui termini* (II. 5). The *mearc* was the frontier with the Northumbrians, not with the Welsh. Yet this theory is open to grave objection. Before Edwin's conquest of Elmet, a British kingdom in the West Riding of Yorkshire, the Mercians did not have a significant common frontier with the Northumbrians. The centre of Mercia lay in the upper, not the lower, Trent valley, and thus well away from Northumbria. The list of estates given to Ripon—a list read out by Wilfrid at the dedication of the church some time in the 670s—suggests that the English had been slow to make permanent conquests of British territory to the west of the Pennines (*Vita S. Wilfridi*, ch. 17). It is more likely, not only that the *mearc* of the *Mierce* was with the Britons, but that *Nordanhymbri* began as a purely geographical term for the English north of the Humber. Only some time after 651, and as a result of Bernician efforts to assimilate Deira, did the notion of a single Northumbrian *gens* take root. The process of unification may not have owed much to Wilfrid's defence of the unity of the Northumbrian diocese, for the *Vita S. Wilfridi* is a more ambiguous supporter of the unity of the *gens* than is Bede in *HE* (for example, *Vita S. Wilfridi*, ch. 15, where Ecgfrith is 'rex Deyrorum et Berniciorum'). Wilfrid's ambition was to be recognized as a metropolitan (*Vita S. Wilfridi*, ch. 16), not just as the bishop of a single *gens*, however large. Moreover, the process of unification was slow. The Whitby Life of Gregory perceived Æthelfrith's rule over Deira as tyranny (ch. 16) even though he was the direct ancestor of the current ruler (Aldfrith or his son Osred). Even Bede himself in *Chron. Maj.* could regard the Deirans and Bernicians as separate *gentes* (para. 531), though in the later *HE* there are only two traces of this conception (p. 50, ll. 24–5, I. 15; p. 216, l. 19, III. 2). The evidence suggests therefore, that the unification of Deira and Bernicia under the Bernician dynasty preceded the emergence of a concept of the *gens Nordanhymbrorum*, whereas for Bede the unity of the *gens* came first and the division into Deira and Bernicia came second.

Myres' theory, however, is also unacceptable, though it is still maintained in his *The English Settlements* (1986), ch. 7. Admittedly Hunter Blair's counter-argument ('The Northumbrians and their Southern Frontier', p. 103), that Ecgfrith is described as *rex Humbronensium* in the proceedings of the synod of Hatfield, two years after he had lost the battle of the Trent and with it all his territories south of the Humber, is inaccurate: both the synod of Hatfield and the battle of the Trent took place in 679 and there is no evidence to determine which occurred first. A better example is the Whitby Life of Gregory, written early in the eighth century, which talks of 'gens nostra quae dicitur Humbrensium' (ch. 12) and of the Mercian King Æthelred as the ruler of the *Sudrangli* (ch. 18). For the Whitby monk, therefore, the Humber appears to be the boundary between the *Humbrenses* and the *Sudrangli*.

p. 212, ll. 9–10. III. 1. **cum magna nobilium iuuentute.** The 'not totally unintelligible' Welsh poem has now been edited and translated, but only into Modern Welsh, in R. G. Gruffydd, 'Canu Cadwallon ap Cadfan', pp. 27–34.

p. 218, ll. 27–9. III. 3. **Porro gentes Scottorum ... didicerunt.** Harrison's claim that some of the southern Irish were followers of Victorius as late as the 650s has been overtaken by more recent work, especially that of Ó Cróinín, 'A Seventh-Century

Irish Computus', and '"New Heresy for Old"'. It is necessary to distinguish between use of Victorius's paschal table and adherence to the Victorian paschal limits by which Easter could not be celebrated before the sixteenth day of the lunar month. Churches were reluctant to abandon old tables entirely; collections of computistical texts may thus contain both Victorian and Dionysiac material, and even discussion of the 84-year cycle. The Lindisfarne Life of St Cuthbert quotes from the preface to Victorius's paschal table, but it is not thereby convicted of abandoning the Roman and Alexandrian Easter. Cummian, *c.*632, argues for Victorius's paschal limits, though he certainly believes that he is following the Roman Easter. According to Harrison, *Framework*, pp. 60-1, it is not possible to show that Rome itself had abandoned Victorius until the letter of John in 640 (II. 19). The computus from the circle of Cummian, identified by Ó Cróinín, is probably to be dated to *c.*650; it argues for *luna xv-xxi*, namely the Dionysiac limits. It thus seems likely that while Irish *Romani* after 640 may have used Victorius, they did so only in conjunction with Dionysius and with the latter's paschal limits.

p. 220, ll. 28-9. III. 4. **Siquidem anno ... quinto.** But Harrison is wrong to say that it is v. 24 (p. 562, ll. 23-4) which implies that Columba's preaching to the Picts preceded his foundation of Iona. What shows that this was Bede's belief is rather p. 220, ll. 26-7 (and similarly the 'unde' of p. 222, l. 16).

p. 222, ll. 24-8. III. 4. **Ex quo ... principatum teneret.** But Duncan is wrong to say that *princeps* is consistently used of the abbot: the Irish *princeps* may be an abbot (e.g. *Collectio Canonum Hibernensis*, ed. Wasserschleben, XVIII. 6*a*) or a *praepositus* (*propositus*) (ibid., XXXVII. 24*c*), a bishop (ibid., XXXVII. 20*d*), a superior of *clerici* (ibid., XXXVII. 15). It may even be used of a secular ruler (ibid., XXV. 5). When used in an ecclesiastical context it is applied to any head of a church, whether monastic or secular, whether the head in question has authority over other churches than his own or, on the contrary, is subject to the head of another church. Bede is not here using *principatus* in some technical sense derived from an Irish source.

p. 222, l. 29–p. 224, l. 3. III. 4. **Habere autem . . . et monachus.**
This *ordo inusitatus* is not said by Bede to be widespread in the
Irish Church, still less to be prevalent throughout the 'Celtic
Church'. The idea of the Irish monastic *paruchia* put forward in
Hughes, *The Church in Early Irish Society*, chs. 6–8, has been
questioned by Sharpe, 'Some Problems concerning the Organisation of the Church in Early Medieval Ireland', *Peritia*, 3
(1984), 230–70. He distinguishes three functions: the sacramental role of the bishop, authority in all matters of pastoral
concern, and control of temporal possessions. He argues that the
bishop did not lose pastoral authority to the abbot. The growth
of monastic federations depended on control of temporal
possessions only.

p. 224, ll. 14–15. III. 4. **reuerentissimo . . . Ecgbercto.** For the
identification of the site of Rathmelsigi, the monastery at which
Egbert was staying in 664 (Clonmelsh, Co. Carlow), see below,
addendum to p. 312, l. 23 (III. 27).

p. 230, ll. 3–5. III. 6. **sed et regna . . . consecutus est.** It may have
been during Oswald's reign that the Bernicians conquered
Lothian, as suggested by Jackson, 'Edinburgh and the Anglian
Occupation of Lothian', in *The Anglo-Saxons*, ed. P. Clemoes,
pp. 35–47, on the basis of an admittedly inconclusive entry in the
Annals of Ulster (s.a. 637/8, *obsesio Etin* 'the siege of Edinburgh').
The entry probably derives from Iona, as shown by J. Bannerman, 'Notes on the Scottish Entries in Early Irish Annals', *Studies
in the History of Dalriada* (1974), 15–16. Nor is it clear that Penda
was successful in resisting pressure from Oswald: the 'uaria
sorte' of II. 20 (p. 202, l. 15) suggests military reversals as well as
victories. Moreover Adomnán's *totius Britanniae imperator* cannot
be entirely dismissed: Binchy's point is that Adomnán, a member
of the Uí Néill dynasty, claimed that the leading king of the Uí
Néill was *totius Scotiae regnator* even though he certainly did not
rule over the whole of Ireland. Adomnán's parallel claim on
behalf of Oswald may, therefore, be just as remote from fulfilment. In both cases Iona had an interest in the claim. The
evidence of Adomnán does not show the real extent of Oswald's
power, but it does show that the ambition was recognized, and

welcomed, by Iona. (Compare F. J. Byrne, *The Rise of the Uí Néill and the High-Kingship of Tara* (1969), 6-7.)

p. 232, ll. 13-20. III. 7. **contigit tunc ... sedem episcopalem.** Angenendt, *Kaiserherrschaft und Königstaufe*, pp. 181-7, argues in favour of a link between the role of godfather and that of Bretwalda (for Oswald and Cynegisl see pp. 183-4). His parallels include, however, instances where it is not said that the kings became godfather and godson (Æthelberht and Sæberht, II. 3; Oswiu or Alhfrith and Peada, III. 21; Oswiu and Sigeberht, III. 22), and an instance where there is no question of the godfather having held an *imperium* over the southern English (Æthelwald and Swithhelm, III. 22). His best parallel is the relationship between Wulfhere and Æthelwealh of Sussex (IV. 13).

p. 232, ll. 18-19. III. 7. **Donauerunt ... ambo reges.** The suggestion that Oswald made use of some land which came to him with his West Saxon wife in order to participate in the grant of Dorchester to Birinus was originally made by Dr Vollrath-Reichelt, *Königsgedanke und Königtum*, p. 110. There are, however, serious objections to her explanation if it assumes that dynastic marriages between members of English royal kindreds were accompanied by considerable dowries and that these might take the form of land in the wife's natal kingdom placed at the disposal of a husband who was the ruler of another kingdom. Even in southern Europe, where dowry was standard, this was not true: the dowries of Brunhild and of Galswintha did not consist of land in Visigothic Spain (Gregory of Tours, *Hist.* IV. 27-8). Ine chapter 31 attests bridewealth but not dowry (so also Theodore's Penitential, II. 12. 34); there is no evidence that dowry was the custom either in Wessex or Northumbria in the seventh century. In *Ideal and Reality*, p. 112, Wormald suggests that Oswald 'may have attested Cynegils's grant simply because he was there'.

p. 234, l. 25. III. 7. **emit pretio ab eo.** The charter of Leuthere to Malmesbury is a forgery, though some elements, including the witness-list, may be early: see Lapidge and Herren, *Aldhelm: The Prose Works* (1979), 173-5, and Wormald (Jarrow Lecture, p. 29

n. 14). There is no other evidence for Leuthere's role in the foundation of Malmesbury.

p. 236, l. 25. III. 8. **Cuius filia Earcongotae.** One of the Frankish monasteries mentioned in this chapter, Chelles, was not founded, or possibly refounded, by Balthildis until 660, and even then the foundation may not Have been complete (see Ewig, *Spätantikes und fränkisches Gallien*, ii. 578). For the same reason it is unlikely that in 647 Hild could have intended to enter Chelles and that her sister Hereswith should already have been a nun there, as implied by Bede in IV. 23 [21]: see Ewig, 'Bemerkungen zu zwei merowingischen Bischofsprivilegien', p. 247. Though the early A recension of the *Vita Balthildis*, ch. 18, says of Chrodechildis, the wife of Clovis I, 'aecclesias in honore sancti Petri Parisius et sancti Georgii in coenobiolo virginum in Kala prima construxit' (*MGH SRM* 2. 506), it is unlikely that an English princess would have been attracted to a decayed *coenobiolum*. Balthildis' first abbess of Chelles came from Jouarre which had been founded by Bishop Agilbert's uncle Ado *c.* 635: if English nuns from Jouarre accompanied her to Chelles *c.* 660 this could have led Bede or his source to suppose that Chelles itself was sufficiently flourishing to attract English princesses in the 640s.

p. 248, l. 27. III. 11. **Conticuere omnes ... tenebant.** On Bede's knowledge of Virgil see now N. Wright, 'Bede and Vergil', *Romanobarbarica*, 6 (1981–2), 361–79.

p. 256, ll. 26–8. III. 14. **Quod factum ... Ingetlingum.** On the foundation of Gilling see also D. W. Rollason, *The Mildrith Legend*, pp. 50–1.

p. 260, ll. 9–10. III. 15. **ob adducendam ... Eanfledam.** On Oswiu's union with a princess of the Cenél nÉogain branch of the Uí Néill (probably before his return to Northumbria in 634/5) see H. Moisl, 'The Bernician Royal Dynasty and the Irish in the Seventh Century', *Peritia*, 2 (1983), 122–3. It is worth remembering that Aldfrith, the child of this union, would not have been regarded as illegitimate by the Irish (in Irish law polygyny was permissible) unless Oswiu had denied paternity.

Since Aldfrith eventually succeeded to the throne of Northumbria in 685 we may assume that Oswiu had acknowledged him as his son.

p. 276, ll. 9-10. III. 19. **monasterium construxit ... nominato.** Ian Wood, 'The *Vita Columbani* and Merovingian Hagiography', *Peritia*, 1 (1982), 69-70, points to differences between the monastic traditions of Columbanus and Fursa.

p. 278, ll. 24-5. III. 21. **acceptis quattuor presbyteris.** The shrine-lid from Wirkworth is probably to be dated to the first half of the ninth century. See R. Cramp in *Mercian Studies*, ed. A. Dornier, pp. 218-25.

p. 280, l. 1. III. 21. **Ad Caprae Caput.** Margaret Gelling, 'Place-Names and Anglo-Saxon Paganism', *University of Birmingham Historical Journal*, 8 (1961-2), 16-18, argues against the theory of animal sacrifices, while admitting that there is, as yet, no other satisfactory explanation.

p. 280, ll. 26-7. III. 22. **Orientales Saxones fidem ... receperunt.** On the chronology of these events see T. M. Charles-Edwards, 'The Foundation of Lastingham', *Ryedale Historian*, 7 (1974), 13-21, according to whom the mission to the East Saxons must have begun in 653, the same year as the start of the mission to the Middle Angles. It is most unlikely that Cedd and his colleagues would have kept any chronological records in Irish. Cedd was English, though he appears to have learnt Irish (p. 298, ll. 21-3; III. 25). Moreover, until the late eighth century Irish is hardly used in the *Annals of Ulster*: see D. N. Dumville, 'Latin and Irish in the *Annals of Ulster*, A.D. 431-1050', in *Ireland in Early Mediaeval Europe*, ed. D. Whitelock *et al.* (1982), 320-41.

p. 288, l. 6. III. 23. **statutis propositis.** Colgrave's translation 'whose rules he had established' ignores Plummer's note and the supporting evidence assembled in his introduction (Plummer, i, pp. xxviii-xxix n. 5). Clear examples of *propositus* with the meaning 'head of a subordinate monastic house' are p. 432, ll. 1 and 6, and p. 434, l. 7 (IV. 27). It should be noted that the Leningrad MS reads *praepositis* (*praepropositis* with *pro* deleted) at this point (fo. 66*b* of the fascimile), although Colgrave and Mynors give no variant. Although this can hardly have been what Bede wrote, it helps to confirm Plummer's argument. The phrase therefore means 'having appointed priors'.

p. 290, ll. 4–5. III. 24. **rex perfidus . . . praeberet.** On the account in the *Historia Brittonum* see Jackson in *Celt and Saxon*, pp. 35–9. His contention that 'Nennius' incorporated an earlier 'Northern History' more or less wholesale into his text has been disputed by D. N. Dumville, 'On the North British Section of the *Historia Brittonum*', *Welsh History Review*, 8 (1976–7), 345–54. The text as it stands is no earlier than 829–30, but the question of its sources for its account of relations between Britons and English in North Britain remains open.

p. 292, ll. 11–12. III. 24. **Streanaeshalch.** See now P. Hunter Blair, 'Whitby as a Centre of Learning in the Seventh Century', in *Learning and Literature in Anglo-Saxon England: Studies presented to Peter Clemoes*, ed. M. Lapidge and H. Gneuss (Cambridge, 1985), 3–32.

p. 292, ll. 24–5. III. 24. **Primus autem . . . Diuma.** In spite of Hunter Blair's doubts it is likely that the name *Lindisfari*, Old English *Lindesfaran* in *Lindisfarna eg*, Lindisfarne, is identical with *Lindisfari*, the people of Lindsey. Hunter Blair cites the etymology given by Simeon of Durham according to whom the name derives from a stream called *Lindis* which came out opposite the island. Hunter Blair suggests that the British word **lindon* was applied to the water between Lindisfarne and the mainland. If this were so the *Lindisfari* of Lindisfarne would not be connected with the *Lindisfari* of Lindsey but would merely be the people who crossed the water to and from the island. He fails to give evidence in support of this supposition that a British word **lindon* meaning 'lake' or 'pool' (so not only Welsh *llyn*, Breton *lenn*, but also Old Irish *lind*) might be applied to a part of the sea. The only known parallels are in a small number of Cornish names: see O. J. Padel, *Cornish Place-Name Elements* (EPNS 56–7 (1985), s.v. *lyn*). Ekwall's theory (*The Concise Oxford Dictionary of English Place-Names*, 4th edn., under Lindisfarne) by which the people of Lindisfarne were so named because of their association with Lindsey is accepted both by Förster, *Der Fluss-name Themse*, p. 167, and by Jackson, *Language and History*, p. 543; it is as certain as anything in place-name studies can be. The compound *Lindisfari* is to be compared with the continental Germanic type of name exemplified by *Burgundofara* and the *fara* place-names of Lombard Italy: the *Lindisfari* of Lindsey were the people who migrated, *faran*, to the territory of the *Lindenses* centred on *Lindum*, modern Lincoln. For *faran* 'migrate' compare Ine's laws, chapters 63-4 (ed. Liebermann, i. 118). For the continental parallels see G. P. Bognetti, *L'età longobarda* (Milan, 1967), iii. 3-46.

p. 292, ll. 35-7. III. 24. **orationes assiduae pro utriusque regis . . . salute.** See also Rollason, *The Mildrith Legend*, pp. 54-7.

p. 294, ll. 34-5. III. 25. **acerrimus . . . defensor nomine Ronan.** The views of Harrison and Ó Cróinín are not inconsistent. It may be true both that Bede's debt to Irish computistic texts was great and that the influence of Wilfrid at Whitby was decisive. There was some English presence at Rath Melsigi already in 664 in an area where the influence of Dionysiac tables goes back to the 640s, after the letter of the pope-elect John (*HE* II. 19). Harrison argues that Dionysiac tables were unknown in Kent when Wilfrid stayed there on his way to Rome, which he probably reached in 654. If true, this would show how relatively advanced some Irish circles were. Yet Harrison himself makes the important distinction between possession of paschal tables and expertise in their use; what Wilfrid got from the archdeacon Boniface in Rome was expertise, not just tables. Even if teaching such as that given to Wilfrid by the archdeacon Boniface were not to be had in Kent before 654, it does not follow for a moment, as Harrison's own distinction makes clear, that Dionysiac tables were not to be found in Canterbury by that date.

p. 296, ll. 23-5. III. 25. **grauior de obseruatione . . . nata est.** On the issue of the tonsure see now E. James, 'Bede and the Tonsure Question', *Peritia*, 3 (1984), 85-98. Aldhelm's letter to Gerontius is translated in Lapidge and Herren, *Aldhelm: The Prose Works*, pp. 155-60.

p. 298, ll. 14–16. III. 25. **dispositum est ... synodus fieri.**
Continuing communications between England and Ireland after
the synod of Whitby are discussed by K. Hughes, 'Evidence for
Contacts between the Churches of the Irish and the English
from the Synod of Whitby to the Viking Age', in *England before
the Conquest*, pp. 49–67. There is no reason why there should
have been a break in communications: the *Scotti* of this chapter
are the party owing allegiance to Iona and thus to the 84-year
cycle; yet the followers of the old paschal table were already in a
minority in Ireland itself. The significance of Whitby was that it
ended the authority of Iona over the Northumbrian church and
its offshoots.

p. 300, ll. 30–1. III. 25. **Hinc est enim quod Paulus Timotheum
circumcidit.** It is an implication of Ray's point that this element,
at least, in the argument cannot have been in any written source
used by Bede for his account of the synod. If it was a recent idea
of Bede's own, present in the *Retractatio* but not in the original
commentary on Acts, it was hardly an argument deployed at
Whitby. Ray further argues ('The Triumph of Greco-Roman
Rhetorical Assumptions in Pre-Carolingian Historiography', in
The Inheritance of Historiography 350–900, ed. C. Holdsworth and
T. P. Wiseman, pp. 79–81) that the speeches in Bede's Whitby
narrative exhibit the characteristics of rhetorical *inuentio*: he
arrived at their contents 'by asking what arguments would have
carried the day, by imagining things which could have happened
on the occasion as he knew it' (p. 81).

p. 306, ll. 10–13. III. 25. **si audita decreta ... peccatis.** Hughes's
point is that Wilfrid argued in the same spirit as the Irish
Romani. The remoteness of Iona and its followers and their
numerical insignificance set against the unanimity of the rest of
the Church are already central points in Cummian's letter to
Ségéne and Beccán *c.* 632.

p. 308, ll. 10–11. III. 26. **Facta est ... DCLXquarto.** Colgrave's
translation of 'Anglorum' as 'English' rather than 'Anglian' can
be defended: Fínán seems to have had authority over Cedd's
mission to the East Saxons (*HE* III. 22).

p. 312, l. 10. III. 27. **relicta insula patria.** As this phrase shows, 'ibidem' in l. 8 means 'in Ireland', not 'in England' as it is translated by Colgrave.

p. 312, l. 23. III. 27. **Rathmelsigi.** This has been identified with Clonmelsh (Cluain Melsige), Co. Carlow: see Ó Cróinín, 'Rath Melsigi, Willibrord, and the Earliest Echternach Manuscripts', *Peritia*, 3 (1984), 23, and T. Fanning, 'Some Field Monuments in the Townlands of Clonmelsh and Garryhundon, Co. Carlow', *Peritia*, 3 (1984), 43-9.

p. 314, ll. 28-9. III. 28. **ad regem Galliarum.** Isenberg, *Die Würdigung Wilfrieds von York*, p. 44, notes that, whereas Bede here has Alhfrith alone send Wilfrid to Gaul for consecration, Stephanus ('Eddius'), chs. 12-14, stresses that both Oswiu and Alhfrith participated in the decision to send Wilfrid. In v. 19, Bede's phrase 'cum consilio atque consensu patris sui' (p. 522, ll. 10-11) expresses a view of the transaction closer to that of Stephanus. In Isenberg's view, this is one instance of a more general point: Bede's debt to Stephanus is clear in v. 19, but not in the rest of the *HE*.

p. 316, l. 1. III. 28. **imitatus industriam filii.** Isenberg, *Die Würdigung*, pp. 43-4, discusses the relationship between this passage (favourable to Oswiu), Stephanus's account in chapter 14 of the *Vita S. Wilfridi* (hostile to Oswiu) and the brief summary in v. 19 (neutral).

Book IV

p. 330, ll. 15-16. IV. 1. **tonsuram more orientalium sancti apostoli Pauli.** See also E. James, 'Bede and the Tonsure Question', *Peritia*, 3 (1984), 85-98.

p. 330, l. 22. IV. 1. **Ebrinus maior domus.** See also P. Fouracre, 'The Merovingians, the Mayors of the Palace and the Notion of a Low-Born Ebroin', *Bulletin of the Institute of Historical Research*, 57 (1984), 1-14.

p. 332, l. 26. IV. 2. **congregata discipulorum caterua.** See M. Lapidge, 'The School of Theodore and Hadrian', *ASE* 15 (1986), 45–72, and the bibliography given by Lapidge on p. 45 n. 1.

p. 334, ll. 14–15. IV. 2. **qui primus . . . tradere didicit.** Plummer's note (ii. 206), citing the names of five English bishops before Wilfrid who were certainly not followers of the Celtic Easter, shows that Colgrave's explanation can hardly stand, unless one is willing to accept that Bede is guilty of gross exaggeration.

p. 348, ll. 28–9. IV. 5. **Cuius synodicae . . . textus est.** See now Wormald (Jarrow Lecture, pp. 11–19), according to whom English charters have more than one source.

p. 350, ll. 18–19. IV. 5. **ex eodem libro x capitula.** Wihtred's Bapchild synod is attested only in *CS* No. 91 (Sawyer, No. 22), which has been shown to be a forgery by Brooks, *Early History*, pp. 191–7. On the other hand, the close collaboration between king and archbishop during the reign of Wihtred is noted by Brooks (pp. 78–9) and is exemplified by the synod which issued *CS* No. 99 (Sawyer, No. 20) as well as by Wihtred's laws.

p. 354, ll. 23–4. IV. 6. **duo praeclara monasteria.** *Cerotaesei* contains the normal Anglian *ei*, *eg*, 'island', 'land partly surrounded by water'. The first element is British, but there is no other reason to think that the meaning of the name 'would not have been obvious to a northerner'. Cf. A. H. Smith, *English Place-Name Elements*, i (EPNS 25), p. 147.

p. 368, ll. 14–15. IV. 12. **episcopatu functus Haeddi pro eo.** Finberg's main point is rather that *CS* No. 43 (Sawyer, No. 51) indicates that Haeddi was consecrated in the lifetime of Leuthere.

p. 368, ll. 21–2. IV. 12. **Aedilred . . . adducto maligno exercitu.** For a possible reason for Æthelred's attack on Kent see Rollason, *The Mildrith Legend*, p. 39.

p. 378, l. 4. IV. 14. **possessiunculis.** Diminutives in -*ul*- are sometimes used in charters for small parcels of land, but on other occasions the land in question is of considerable extent. *CS* No. 229 (Sawyer, No. 115) refers to a fairly small area, 'exiguam ruris portiunculam .iiiior. videlicet manentium', and *CS* No. 148 (Sawyer, No. 23) to an even smaller area (the *terrula* is a quarter of a sulung); but in *CS* No. 154 (Sawyer, No. 89) the *particula* is rated at ten hides.

p. 382, l. 6. IV. 16. **quartam partem ... Domino daret.** Finberg's suggestion must be a mere oversight for he himself dates *CS* No. 107 between AD 670 and 676 (*Early Charters of Wessex*, p. 155, No. 551). For reference to comments on this charter see Sawyer, No. 1164.

p. 388, ll. 5-6. IV. 18. **Benedicto, cuius supra meminimus.** Judith McClure, 'Bede and the Life of Ceolfrid', *Peritia*, 3 (1984), 83-4, argues that the *Historia Abbatum* was composed *c.* 730, that it is complementary to the *Ecclesiastical History*, and that this is the reason why information on Wearmouth-Jarrow is so thin in the larger work. The difficulty in accepting the explanation put forward by Whitelock is that this phrase is omitted from the earlier *c*-text (cf. Mynors' arguments on the relationship between the two branches of the tradition in the Textual Introduction, p. xli). A further argument for the chronological priority of the *c*-text is the omission from the *m*-text of a passage in the last *responsum* of Gregory to Augustine (*uel infirmitate... superfluitate*, p. 98, ll. 29-30). The cause of the error was the repetition of the words 'superfluitate uel infirmitate' in Gregory's text. This passage is omitted by the Leningrad MS (L) as well as by the other MSS recorded in Plummer's *apparatus*, though this is not noted by Colgrave and Mynors.

p. 392, ll. 13-14. IV. 19. **in loco quem Coludi urbem nominant.** The site is being excavated. See L. and E. A. Alcock, *Excavations on St Abb's Head, Berwickshire, 1980: An Interim Report* (University of Glasgow, Department of Archaeology; 1981).

p. 396, ll. 30-1. IV. 20. **imitari morem sacrae scripturae.** Venantius Fortunatus' *De Virginitate* was the only one of his poems known to Bede: see the appendix by Michael Lapidge to R. W. Hunt, 'Manuscript Evidence for Knowledge of the Poems of Venantius Fortunatus in Late Anglo-Saxon England', *ASE* 8 (1979), 291.

p. 402, ll. 19–20. IV. 22. **Quarum celebratione ... continuo solueretur.** On the *litterae solutoriae* see R. I. Page, 'Anglo-Saxon Runes and Magic', *Journ. Brit. Arch. Assoc.* 3rd ser. 27 (1964), 21–3, who argues that the English evidence for magical runes is inconclusive.

p. 406, l. 16. IV. 23. **in monasterio Cale peregrinam.** Chelles, however, had not yet been refounded in 647: see the addendum to p. 236, l. 25; III. 8.

p. 416, ll. 12–14. IV. 24. **ipse coepit cantare ... iste est sensus.** Colgrave's note is in error in implying that the Early Northumbrian version is to be found in N (the Namur MS): it is to be found in the Leningrad (L) and Moore (M) MSS of the eighth century and two later MSS. A detailed discussion of the MSS is provided in E. Van K. Dobbie, *The Manuscripts of Caedmon's Hymn and Bede's Death Song* (1937).

p. 424, ll. 33–4. IV. 25. **domunculae ... factae erant.** The Whitby excavation by Sir Charles Peers was not well enough conducted to prove that Whitby was a collection of *domunculae*: see R. Cramp (pp. 223–9) and Rahtz (pp. 459–62), both in *The Archaeology of Anglo-Saxon England*, ed. D. M. Wilson (1976).

p. 424, ll. 37–8. IV. 25. **texendis subtilioribus indumentis.** See M. Budny, 'The Anglo-Saxon Embroideries at Maaseik', *Mededelingen van de Koninklijke Academie voor Wetenschappen, Letteren en Schone Kunsten van België*, 45 (1984), ii. 57–133.

p. 426, ll. 26–7. IV. 26. **uastauit misere gentem ... amicissimam.** For suggestions as to the reasons for Ecgfrith's attack see also H. Moisl, 'The Bernician Royal Dynasty and the Irish in the Seventh Century', *Peritia*, 2 (1983), 120–4.

p. 442, l. 21. IV. 30. **transactis sepulturae eius annis** XI. The association of the Lindisfarne Gospels with the translation of the relics of St Cuthbert in 698 was suggested by T. J. Brown and R. L. S. Bruce-Mitford in T. D. Kendrick *et al.*, *Evangeliorum Quattuor Codex Lindisfarnensis*, ii. 11–16. Ó Cróinín, 'Pride and Prejudice', *Peritia*, 1 (1982), 357–8, argues for a date closer to 721, in other words towards the end of Eadfrith's episcopate.

BOOK V

p. 454, ll. 28–9. v. 1. **tumida aequora placauit.** N. Wright, 'Bede and Vergil', *Romanobarbarica*, 6 (1981–2), 361–79, gives evidence for Bede's direct knowledge of Virgil.

p. 456, ll. 21–2. v. 2. **clymiterium sancti Michahelis.** On dedications to St Michael see also *Millénaire monastique du Mont Saint-Michel*, iii. *Culte de Saint Michel et pèlerinages au mont*, ed. M. Baudot (Paris, 1971).

p. 474, l. 17. v. 8. **Successit autem ... Berctuald.** On Hlothere's charter (*CS* No. 45, Sawyer, No. 8) see Chaplais, 'Some Early Anglo-Saxon Charters on Single Sheets: Originals or Copies?', *Journ. Soc. Archivists*, 3 (1965–9), 317–27.

p. 480, l. 1. v. 9. **reuersus ... locum peregrinationis.** Wihtbert may appear, spelt as Ichtbricht, in the witness-list in *Cáin Adomnáin* (The Law of Adomnán) promulgated at a synod at Birr in AD 697: see Ó Cróinín, 'Rath Melsigi, Willibrord and the Earliest Echternach Manuscripts', pp. 25–6.

p. 514, ll. 21–2. v. 18. **nam et sermone ... eruditione mirandus.** On Aldhelm, see M. Lapidge and M. Herren, *Aldhelm: The Prose Works* (1979) and M. Lapidge and J. Rosier, *Aldhelm: The Poetic Works* (1985).

p. 516, ll. 12–14. v. 19. **Offa, iuuenis ... exoptatissimus.** For a new discussion of Offa's status see B. Yorke, 'The Kingdom of the East Saxons', *ASE* 14 (1985), 17–18.

p. 516, ll. 22-3. v. 19. **diem clausit ... Inundalum.** But there was a community at Oundle, at least by the ninth century: D. W. Rollason, 'List of Saints' Resting-Places', p. 89. Moreover, Peterborough appears to have been in the district of the Northern Gyrwe, quite distinct from the *prouincia* of Oundle which was further to the west: P. A. Stafford, *The East Midlands in the Early Middle Ages* (1985), 30-2.

p. 532, ll. 17-18. v. 21. **misit legatarios ... Ceolfridum.** On the different forms of the Pictish name Naiton (Bede's form at the beginning of v. 21), Naitanus (the Latin form given in the address of Ceolfrith's letter, ibid.), and Nechtan, see K. H. Jackson, 'The Pictish Language', p. 145. Nechton is the older form of the name which then developed to Neiton. Bede's Naiton is an approximation to this later form. Meanwhile Irish sources used their form of the name, namely Nechtan (very close to the earlier Pictish form Nechton), and this is normally preferred by historians.

p. 542, ll. 5-6. v. 21. **Quae disputatio ... uel debeat.** On the link made in the letter between paschal observance and doctrinal orthodoxy see Ó Cróinín, '"New Heresy for Old"', pp. 515-16; cf. the addendum to the commentary on p. 198, l. 22 (II. 19).

p. 548, ll. 1-4. v. 21. **inter omnes tamen ... Dominus ait.** See now E. James, 'Bede and the Tonsure Question', pp. 85-6; and cf. notes on p. 298, l. 25 (III. 25); p. 330, ll. 15-16 (IV. 1).

p. 566, l. 16. v. 24. **Haec de historia.** If Lehmann is right ('Wert und Echtheit einer Beda abgesprochenen Schrift', pp. 10-20), Bede produced 'Eight Questions on Kings' as well as the more familiar 'Thirty Questions'. On the penitential ascribed to Bede see A. J. Frantzen, 'The Tradition of Penitentials in Anglo-Saxon England', *ASE* 11 (1983), 32-5, who also rejects the attribution.

p. 568, l. 34. v. 24. **Item de historiis sanctorum.** The text of the *Vita Anastasii* which Bede improved has recently been discovered: see C. Vircillo Franklin and P. Meyvaert, 'Has Bede's Version of the "Passio S. Anastasii" come down to us in "BHL" 408?', *Anal. Boll.* 100 (1982), 373-400.

p. 570, l. 13. v. 24. **Librum epigrammatum.** For some fragments of this work see M. Lapidge, 'Some Remnants of Bede's Lost *Liber Epigrammatum*', *EHR* 90 (1975), 798–820.

p. 570, ll. 20–3. v. 24. **Teque deprecor . . . faciem tuam.** On the prayer appended to *De Die Iudicii* see also Hunter Blair in *Celt and Saxon*, pp. 85–6.

BIBLIOGRAPHY

A. PRIMARY SOURCES

Acta Synodi Caesareae. Ed. A. Wilmart, OSB, *Analecta Reginensia: Extraits des manuscrits de la Reine Christine conservés au Vatican* (Studi e Testi, 59; Rome, 1933), 19–27.

Adomnán, *De Locis Sanctis*, ed. D. Meehan (*Scriptores Latini Hiberniae*, 3; Dublin, 1958).

—— *Vita S. Columbae*. Ed. W. Reeves, *Adamnani Vita S. Columbae* (Irish Archaeological and Celtic Society; Dublin, 1857). Ed. A. O. and M. O. Anderson, *Adomnan's Life of St Columba* (London and Edinburgh, 1961).

Agnellus, *Liber Pontificalis Ecclesiae Ravennatis*, ed. O. Holder-Egger, *MGH SS Rerum Langobardicarum et Italicarum Saec. VI–IX* (1878), 265–391.

Alcuin, *Versus de Patribus Regibus et Sanctis Euboricensis Ecclesiae*. Ed. P. Godman, *Alcuin, The Bishops, Kings, and Saints of York* (OMT; 1982).

Aldhelm, *Opera Omnia*, ed. R. Ehwald (*MGH AA* 15; 1919). Tr. by M. Lapidge and M. Herren, *Aldhelm: The Prose Works* (Ipswich, 1979). M. Lapidge and J. Rosier, *Aldhelm: The Poetic Works* (Cambridge, 1985).

The Annals of Ulster (to A.D. 1131), ed. S. Mac Airt and G. Mac Niocaill. Part 1 (Dublin, 1983).

Anonymous of Whitby, *Vita S. Gregorii Magni*. Ed. B. Coigrave, *The Earliest Life of Gregory the Great* (Kansas, 1968; repr., Cambridge, 1985).

The Apocalypse of St Paul, tr. M. R. James, *The Apocryphal New Testament* (Oxford, 1924), 525–55.

Augustine, *Enchiridion*, ed. E. Evans (*CCSL* 46; 1969), 21–114.

—— *De Catechizandis Rudibus*, ed. I. B. Bauer (*CCSL* 46; 1969), 117–78.

Bede, *Aliquot Quaestionum Liber. PL* 93, cols. 455–78.

—— *Chronica Maiora*. Ed. Th. Mommsen, *Chronica Minora Saec. IV. V. VI. VII.*, iii (*MGH AA* 13; 1898), 223–354. Ed. Th. Mommsen and C. W. Jones (*CCSL* 123; 1977), 461–544.

—— *De Arte Metrica*. Ed. H. Keil (*Grammatici Latini*, 7; Leipzig, 1880), pp. 227–60. Ed. C. B. Kendall and M. H. King (*CCSL* 123; 1975), 59–171.

— *De Orthographia*. Ed. H. Keil (*Grammatici Latini*, 7), 261-94. Ed. C. W. Jones (*CCSL* 123 A), 1-57.

— *De Tabernaculo*, ed. D. Hurst (*CCSL* 119 A; 1969), 1-139.

— *De Templo*, ed. D. Hurst (*CCSL* 119 A; 1969), 142-234.

— *De Temporum Ratione*. Ed. C. W. Jones, *Bedae Opera de Temporibus* (Cambridge, Mass., 1943), 174-291. Also ed. C. W. Jones (*CCSL* 123 B; 1977).

— *Epistola ad Ecgbertum*, ed. C. Plummer, *Venerabilis Baedae Opera Historica* (2 vols.; Oxford, 1896), i. 405-23.

— *Explanatio Apocalypsis. PL* 93, cols. 129-206.

— *Historia Abbatum*, ed. Plummer, i. 364-87.

— *Historia Ecclesiastica*. Ed. C. Plummer, *Venerabilis Baedae Opera Historica*. Ed. B. Colgrave and R. A. B. Mynors, *Bede's Ecclesiastical History of the English People* (OMT; 1969).

— *In Cantica Canticorum Allegorica Expositio*, ed. D. Hurst (*CCSL* 119 B; 1983), 166-375.

— *In Ezram et Neemiam Prophetas Allegorica Expositio*, ed. D. Hurst, *CCSL* 119 (1969), 235-392.

— *In Lucae Evangelium Expositio*, ed. D. Hurst (*CCSL* 120; 1960), 1-425.

— *In Primam Partem Samuhelis Libri IIII*, ed. D. Hurst (*CCSL* 119; 1962), 1-287.

— *In Regum Librum*, ed. D. Hurst (*CCSL*, 119; 1962), 289-322.

— *Libellus Retractationis in Actus Apostolorum*. Ed. M. L. W. Laistner, *Bedae Venerabilis Expositio Actuum Apostolorum et Retractatio* (Cambridge, Mass., 1939), 91-146. Also ed. Laistner (*CCSL* 121; 1983), 101-63.

— *Libri Quattuor in Principium Genesis*, ed. C. W. Jones (*CCSL* 118 A; 1967).

— *Super Acta Apostolorum Expositio*, ed. M. L. W. Laistner, *Bedae Venerabilis Expositio Actuum Apostolorum et Retractatio*, pp. 1-90.

— *Vita Felicis*, ed. J. A. Giles, *Venerabilis Bedae Opera quae supersunt Omnia* (London: 1843-4), iv. 173-201.

— *Vita S. Cuthberti Metrica*. Ed. W. Jaager, *Bedas metrische Vita sancti Cuthberti* (Palaestra, 198; Leipzig, 1935).

— *Vita S. Cuthberti Prosaica*. Ed. B. Colgrave, *Two Lives of Saint Cuthbert: A Life by an Anonymous Monk of Lindisfarne and Bede's Prose Life* (Cambridge, 1940).

Benedict, *Regula*. Ed. A. de Vogüé and J. Neufville (6 vols., *SCS* 181-6; 1971-2).

Boniface, *Letters*. Ed. M. Tangl, *S. Bonifatii et Lullii Epistolae* (*MGH Epp. Selectae*, i; 1916). English tr. by E. Emerton, *The Letters of Boniface* (Columbia Records of Civilization; New York, 1940).

Caedmon's Hymn. Ed. A. H. Smith, *Three Northumbrian Poems* (London, 1933). Ed. E. Van K. Dobbie, *The Anglo-Saxon Minor Poems* (The Anglo-Saxon Poetic Records, 7; New York, 1942), 106–7. Ed. D. Whitelock, *Sweet's Anglo-Saxon Reader in Prose and Verse* (Oxford, 1967), 181–2.

Cartularium Saxonicum. Ed. W. de Gray Birch (3 vols. and index; London, 1885–99).

Collectio Canonum Hibernensis. Ed. H. Wasserschleben, *Die irische Kanonensammlung*, 2nd edn. (Leipzig, 1885).

Columbanus, *Opera*, ed. G. S. M. Walker (*Scriptores Latini Hiberniae*, 2; Dublin, 1957).

Constantius, *Vita Germani*. Ed. W. Levison (*MGH SRM* 7; 1919), 247–83. Ed. R. Borius, *Constance de Lyon: Vie de Saint Germain d'Auxerre* (*SC* 112; 1965).

Councils and Ecclesiastical Documents relating to Great Britain and Ireland, ed. A. W. Haddan and W. Stubbs (3 vols.; Oxford, 1869–71).

Cummian, *Epistula de Controversia Paschali. PL* 87, cols. 969–78.

Donation of Constantine, ed. H. Fuhrmann (*MGH Fontes Iuris Germanici Antiqui in usum Schol.* 10; 1968).

Eddius Stephanus, *Vita S. Wilfridi*. Ed. B. Colgrave, *The Life of Bishop Wilfrid by Eddius Stephanus* (Cambridge, 1927). Ed. H. Moonen, *Eddius Stephanus: Het Leven van Sint Wilfrid* ('s-Hertogenbosch, 1946).

Edictus Rothari. Ed. F. Beyerle, *Leges Langobardorum, 643–866* (Germanenrechte, NF, Westgermanisches Recht; 2nd edn., Witzenhausen, 1962).

Einhard, *Vita Karoli Magni*. Ed. O. Holder-Egger (*MGH SRG in usum schol.*; 1911). Ed. L. Halphen, *Eginhard, Vie de Charlemagne*, in *Les Classiques de l'histoire de France au moyen âge*, 2nd edn. (1938).

English Kalendars before AD 1100, ed. F. Wormald (Henry Bradshaw Soc. 72; 1934).

Eusebius, *Ecclesiastical History*. Ed. E. Schwartz, *Eusebius Werke* (3 vols.; Leipzig, 1903–9), ii.

Felix, *Vita S. Guthlaci*. Ed. B. Colgrave, *Felix's Life of St Guthlac* (Cambridge, 1956).

Fredegar, *Chronicarum quae dicuntur Fredegarii Scholastici Libri IV cum Continuationibus*. Ed. B. Krusch (*MGH SRM* 2; 1888), 1–193. Book IV and continuations ed. and tr. J. M. Wallace-Hadrill, *The Fourth Book of the Chronicle of Fredegar with its Continuations* (Nelson Medieval Classics; London, 1960).

Gesta Dagoberti, ed. B. Krusch (*MGH SRM* 2; 1888), 396–424.

Gildas, *De Excidio Britanniae*. Ed. Th. Mommsen, *Chronica Minora Saec. IV. V. VI. VII.*, ii (*MGH AA* 13; 1898). Ed. and tr. H. Williams, *Gildae*

De Excidio Britanniae (Cymmrodorion Record Ser. 3-4; London, 1899-1901). Ed. and tr. M. Winterbottom, *Gildas: The Ruin of Britain and Other Works* (Chichester, 1978).

Gregory the Great, *Cura Pastoralis. PL* 767, cols. 13-128.

— *Dialogues*, ed. A. de Vogüé and P. Antin (3 vols., *SC* 254, 260, 265; Paris, 1978-80).

— *Moralia in Iob*, ed. M. Adriaen (*CCSL* 43, 43 A, and 43 B, 1979-85).

— *Registrum Epistolarum*. Ed. P. Ewald and L. M. Hartmann (*MGH Epp*, 1-2; 1891-9). Ed. D. Norberg (*CCSL* 140 and 140 A; 1982).

Gregory Nazianzen, *Oratio in Laudem Caesarii Fratris. PG* 35, cols. 755-88.

Gregory of Tours, *Liber in Gloria Confessorum*, ed. B. Krusch (*MGH SRM* 1/ii; 1885), 744-820.

— *Libri Historiarum X*, ed. B. Krusch and W. Levison (*MGH SRM* 1/i; 1951).

Hisperica Famina. Ed. M. W. Herren, *The Hisperica Famina: 1. The A-Text* (Toronto, 1974).

Historia Augusta: see *Scriptores Historiae Augustae*.

Isidore, *De Natura Rerum*. Ed. J. Fontaine, *Isidore de Séville, Traité de la nature* (Bordeaux, 1960).

— *Etymologiarum sive Originum Libri XX*, ed. W. M. Lindsay (2 vols., OCT; 1911).

— *Historia Gothorum*. Ed. Th. Mommsen, *Chronica Minora Saec. IV. V. VI. VIII.*, ii (*MGH AA* 11; 1894), 267-303.

— *Sententiarum Libri Tres. PL* 83, cols. 537-738.

Jerome, *Adversus Helvidium de Mariae Virginitate Perpetua. PL* 23, cols. 183-206.

Jonas, *Vita S. Columbani*, ed. B. Krusch (*MGH SRG in usum schol.*; 1905).

Laws of Ine, ed. F. Liebermann, in *Die Gesetze der Angelsachsen* (Halle, 1903-16), i. 88-123.

Liber Pontificalis, ed. L. Duchesne and C. Vogel (3 vols.; Paris, 1886-1956).

Marcellinus Comes, *Chronicon*. Ed. Th. Mommsen, *Chronica Minora Saec. IV. V. VI. VII.*, ii (*MGH AA* 9), 39-108.

Martin of Braga, *Formula Vitae Honestae*. Ed. C. W. Barlow, *Martini Episcopi Bracarensis Opera Omnia* (New Haven, 1950), 236-50.

'Nennius', *Historia Brittonum*. Ed. Th. Mommsen, *Chronica Minora Saec. IV. V. VI. VII.*, iii (*MGH AA* 13; 1898), 111-222. Ed. F. Lot, *Nennius et l'Historia Brittonum: Étude critique suivie d'une édition des diverses versions de ce texte* (2 vols., Bibl. École des hautes études, sci. hist. et philol. 263; Paris, 1934). Ed. D. Dumville, *The Historia Brittonum*, iii. *The 'Vatican' Recension* (Cambridge, 1985: the 1st vol. to appear of a complete edn.).

248 BIBLIOGRAPHY

Orosius, *Libri Historiarum Adversum Paganos*, ed. C. Zangemeister (*CSEL* 5; 1882), 1–600; also Teubner edn. (Leipzig, 1885).
Passio SS. Albani, Amphibali et soc. Ed. W. Meyer, *Nachrichten Göttingen*, 7/i (1904), 35–62.
Paul the Deacon, *Historia Langobardorum.* Ed. L. Bethmann and G. Waitz, *MGH SS Rerum Lang. et Ital. Saec. VI–IX*, pp. 12–192. Ed. G. Waitz, *MGH SRG in usum schol.* (1878).
Paulinus Diaconus, *Vita S. Ambrosii.* Ed. J. G. Krabinger (Tübingen, 1857). Ed. A. A. R. Bastiaensen (*Vite dei Santi*, 2; 1975), 52–125.
Paulinus of Nola, *Natalicia*, ed. G. van Hartel, *S. Ponti Meropii Paulini Nolani Carmina* (*CSEL* 30; 1984), carm. 12–16, 18–23, 26–8.
Prosper of Aquitaine, *Epitoma Chronicon.* Ed. Th. Mommsen, *Chronica Minora Saec. IV. V. VI. VII.*, i (*MGH AA* 9; 1891), 342–485.
Pseudo-Cyprian, *De Duodecim Abusivis Saeculi*, ed. S. Hellmann (Texte und Untersuchungen, 34/i; Leipzig, 1909), 32–60.
Quintilian, *Institutionis Oratoriae Libri Duodecim*, ed. M. Winterbottom (2 vols., OCT; 1970).
Quodvultdeus (Pseudo-Prosper), *Liber Promissionum et Praedictorum Dei*, ed. R. Braun (*CCSL* 60; 1976), 1–189.
Rufinus, *Historia Ecclesiastica. PL* 21, cols. 465–540. Ed.Th. Mommsen, in *Eusebius Werke*, ii, ed. E. Schwartz and Th. Mommsen (3 vols.; Leipzig, 1903–9).
Scriptores Historiae Augustae, ed. E. Hohl (2 vols., Leipzig, 1955–65).
Sulpicius Severus, *Vita Martini*, ed. J. Fontaine (*SC* 133–5; 1967–9).
Venantius Fortunatus. Ed. F. Leo, *Venantii Fortunati Opera Poetica* (*MGH AA* 4), i. 136–46.
Vita S. Balthildis Reginae, ed. B. Krusch (*MGH SRM* 2), 482–508.
Vita Bertilae, ed. W. Levison (*MGH SRM* 6), 95–109.
Vita Ceolfridi, ed. C. Plummer, *Baedae Opera Historica*, i. 388–404.
Vita S. Cuthberti Auctore Anonymo. Ed. B. Colgrave, *Two Lives of Saint Cuthbert*, pp. 60–139.
Vita S. Fursei. Ed. L. d'Achery and J. Mabillon (*AA SS Ben.* 2; 1669), 299–315. Ed. (without the visions) B. Krusch (*MGH SRM* 4; 1902), 423–51.
Vita S. Genovefae, AA SS Jan. i. 138–47.
Vita Lebuini Antiqua, ed. A. Hofmeister (*MGH SS* 30), ii. 789–95.
Vita S. Lupi, ed. B. Krusch (*MGH SRM* 7; 1920), 284–382.
Vita Patrum Iurensium. Ed. F. Martine, *Vie des pères du Jura* (*SC* 142; Paris, 1968).

B. Secondary Works

Addleshaw, G. W. O., *The Pastoral Organization of the Modern Dioceses of Durham and Newcastle in the Time of Bede* (Jarrow Lecture, 1963).

Addyman, P. V., 'The Anglo-Saxon House: A New Review', *ASE* 1 (1972), 273–307.

Alcock, L., 'Quantity or Quality: The Anglian Graves of Bernicia', in *Angles, Saxons and Jutes*, ed. V. I. Evison (Oxford, 1981), 168–86.

—— and E. A. Alcock, *Excavations on St Abb's Head, Berwickshire, 1980: An Interim Report* (Univ. of Glasgow, Department of Archaeology; 1981).

Allen, P. S., F. M. Stenton, and R. I. Best, 'Charles Plummer', *PBA* 15 (1929), 463–76.

Angenendt, A., 'Rex et Sacerdos: Zur Genese der Königssalbung', in *Tradition als historische Kraft: Interdisziplinäre Forschungen zur Geschichte des früheren Mittelalters*, ed. N. Kamp and J. Wollasch (Berlin and New York, 1982), 100–18.

—— *Kaiserherrschaft und Königstaufe: Kaiser, Könige und Päpste als geistliche Patrone in der abendländischen Missionsgeschichte* (Schriftenreihe des Instituts für Frühmittelalterforschung der Universität Münster; Berlin and New York, 1984).

Antin, P., '"Aureum illud nomisma . . . de Cantia . . .", Bede, H. E., III. 8', *Journées internationales d'études mérovingiennes: Actes des journées de Poitiers, 1er–3 mai* (Paris, 1953), 8–12.

Armitage Robinson, J., 'The Early Community at Christ Church, Canterbury', *JTS* 27 (1926), 231–3.

Aylmer, G. E., and R. Cant (eds.), *A History of York Minster* (Oxford, 1977).

Bannerman, J., 'Notes on the Scottish Entries in the Early Irish Annals', in his *Studies in the History of Dalriada* (Edinburgh, 1974), 9–26.

Barley, M. W., and R. P. C. Hanson (eds.), *Christianity in Britain, 300–700* (Leicester, 1968).

Barnard, L. W., 'Bede and Eusebius as Church Historians', *Famulus Christi*, ed. G. Bonner, pp. 106–24.

Bately, J., 'Bede and the Anglo-Saxon Chronicle', in *Saints, Scholars*, ed. M. H. King and W. M. Stevens, i. 233–54.

Battiscombe, C. F. (ed.), *The Relics of St. Cuthbert* (Oxford, 1956).

Biddle, M., 'Archaeology and the Beginnings of English Society', *England before the Conquest*, ed. P. Clemoes and K. Hughes, pp. 391–408.

—— 'Archaeology, Architecture, and the Cult of Saints in Anglo-Saxon

England', in *The Anglo-Saxon Church*, ed. L. A. S. Butler and R. K. Morris, pp. 1-31.

Bieler, L., *Ireland, Harbinger of the Middle Ages* (London, 1963).

—— 'St Patrick and the British Church', *Christianity in Britain 300-700*, ed. M. W. Barley and R. P. C. Hanson, pp. 123-30.

—— 'Ireland's Contribution to the Culture of Northumbria', in *Famulus Christi*, ed. G. Bonner, pp. 210-28.

Binchy, D. A., 'Patrick and his Biographers: Ancient and Modern', *Studia Hibernica*, 2 (1962), 7-173.

—— *Celtic and Anglo-Saxon Kingship* (Oxford, 1970).

Bischoff, B., 'Il monachesimo irlandese nei suoi rapporti col continente', *Spoleto*, 4 (1957), 121-38. Repr. in his *Mittelalterliche Studien*, i. 195-205.

—— *Mittelalterliche Studien* (3 vols.; Stuttgart, 1966-81).

—— 'Paläographie und Frühmittelalterliche Klassikerüberlieferung', *Spoleto*, 22 (1975), i. 59-86. Repr. in his *Mittelalterliche Studien*, iii. 55-72.

Bodmer, J. P., *Der Krieger der Merowingerzeit und seine Welt* (Zürich, 1957).

Bognetti, G. P., 'L'influsso delle istituzioni militare romane sulle istituzioni longobarde del secolo VI e la natura della "fara"', in his *L'età longobarda* (Milan, 1967), iii. 3-46.

Bonner, G., *Saint Bede in the Tradition of Western Apocalyptic Commentary* (Jarrow Lecture, 1966).

—— 'Bede and Medieval Civilization', *ASE* 2 (1973), 71-90.

—— (ed.), *Famulus Christi: Essays in Commemoration of the Thirteenth Centenary of the Birth of the Venerable Bede* (London, 1976).

Brechter, Dom S., *Die Quellen zur Angelsachsenmission Gregors des Grossen: Ein historiographische Studie* (Beiträge zur Geschichte des alten Mönchtums und des Benediktinerordens, 22; Münster in Westfalen, 1941).

—— 'Zur Bekehrungsgeschichte der Angelsachsen', *Spoleto*, 14 (1967), 191-215.

Brooks, N., *The Early History of the Church of Canterbury* (Leicester, 1984).

Brown, P. R. L., 'Pelagius and his Supporters: Aims and Environment', *JTS* NS 19 (1968), 93-114; repr. in his *Religion and Society in the Age of Saint Augustine* (London, 1972), 183-207.

Brown, T. J., 'An Historical Introduction to the Use of Classical Authors in the British Isles from the Fifth to the Eleventh Century', *Spoleto*, 22 (1975), 237-93.

Bruce-Mitford, R. L. S., 'Saxon Rendlesham', *Proc. Suffolk Inst. of Archaeol. and Nat. Hist.* 24 (1948), iii. 228-51. Repr. in his *Aspects of*

Anglo-Saxon Archaeology: Sutton Hoo and Other Discoveries (London, 1974), 73–113.

— *The Art of the Codex Amiatinus* (Jarrow Lecture, 1967), repr. in *Journ. British Archaeol. Assoc.* 3rd ser. 32 (1969), 1–25.

— *The Sutton Hoo Ship-Burial* i (London, 1975), ii (1978), iii, parts 1 and 2 (1983).

— *The Sutton Hoo Ship-Burial: A Handbook*, 3rd edn. (London, 1979).

Brunner, K., *Altenglische Grammatik*, 3rd edn. (Tübingen, 1965).

Budny, M., 'The Anglo-Saxon Embroideries at Maaseik: Their Historical and Art-Historical Context', *Medelingen van de Koninklijke Academie voor Wetenschappen, Letteren en Schone Kunsten van België, Klasse der Schone Kunsten*, 45 (1984), ii. 57–133.

Bullough, D. A., 'Columba, Adomnan and the Achievement of Iona', *SHR* 43 (1964), 111–30; 44 (1965), 17–33.

— 'Roman Books and Carolingian *Renovatio*', in *Renaissance and Renewal in Christian History*, ed. D. Baker, *Studies in Church History*, 14 (1977), 23–50.

— 'Hagiography as Patriotism: Alcuin's "York Poem" and the Early Northumbrian "Vitae Sanctorum"', in *Hagiographie, cultures et sociétés, ive–xiie siècles* (Études Augustiniennes; Paris, 1980), 339–59.

— 'The Missions to the English and Picts and their Heritage (to c.800)', in *Die Iren und Europa im früheren Mittelalter*, ed. H. Löwe (2 vols., Veroffentlichungen des Europa zentrums Tübingen, Kultur-wissenschaftliche Reihe, Stuttgart, 1982), i. 80–98.

— 'Burial, Community and Belief in the Early Medieval West', in *Ideal and Reality*, ed. P. Wormald *et al.*, pp. 177–201.

— 'Alcuin and the Kingdom of Heaven', in *Carolingian Essays*, ed. U.-R. Blumenthal (Andrew W. Mellon Studies in Early Christian Studies; Washington DC, 1983), 1–69.

Butler, L. A. S., and R. K. Morris (eds.), *The Anglo-Saxon Church: Papers on History, Architecture, and Archaeology in Honour of Dr H. M. Taylor* (The Council for British Archaeology, Research Report, 60; 1986).

Byrne, F. J., *The Rise of the Uí Néill and the High-Kingship of Tara* (O'Donnell Lecture, Dublin, 1969).

— *Irish Kings and High-Kings* (London, 1973).

Cameron, A., 'Celestial Consulates: A Note on the Pelagian Letter *Humanae Referunt*', *JTS* NS 19 (1968), 213–15.

Campbell, A., *Old English Grammar* (Oxford, 1959).

Campbell, J., 'Bede', in *Latin Historians*, ed. T. A. Dorey (London, 1966), 159–90. Repr. in his *Essays in Anglo-Saxon History* (London, 1986), 1–27.

— 'The First Century of Christianity in England', *Ampleforth Journal*,

76 (1971), 12-29. Repr. in his *Essays in Anglo-Saxon History*, pp. 47-67.

—— 'Observations on the Conversion of England: A Brief Commemorative Review Article', *Ampleforth Journal*, 78 (1973), ii. 12-26. Repr. in his *Essays in Anglo-Saxon History*, pp. 69-84.

—— Review of J. Morris, *The Age of Arthur*, in *Studia Hibernica*, 15 (1975), 177-85. Repr. in his *Essays in Anglo-Saxon History*, pp. 121-30.

—— *Bede's Reges and Principes* (Jarrow Lecture, 1979). Repr. in his *Essays in Anglo-Saxon History*, pp. 85-98.

—— 'Bede's Words for Places', in *Names, Words and Graves*, ed. P. H. Sawyer (Leeds, 1979), 34-53. Repr. in his *Essays in Anglo-Saxon History*, pp. 99-120.

—— 'The Church in Anglo-Saxon Towns', in *The Church in Town and Countryside*, ed. D. Baker, *Studies in Church History*, 16 (1979), 119-36. Repr. in his *Essays in Anglo-Saxon History*, pp. 139-154.

—— (ed.), *The Anglo-Saxons* (Oxford, 1982).

Carozzi, C., 'La Géographie de l'au-delà et la signification pendant le haut moyen âge', *Spoleto*, 29 (1983), 423-81.

Chadwick, N. K. (ed.), *Studies in Early British History* (Cambridge, 1954).

—— 'Intellectual Contacts between Britain and Gaul in the Fifth Century', in *Studies in Early British History*, pp. 189-253.

—— (ed.), *Studies in the Early British Church* (Cambridge, 1958).

—— (ed.), *Celt and Saxon: Studies in the Early British Border* (Cambridge, 1963).

—— 'The Battle of Chester: A Study of Sources', in *Celt and Saxon*, pp. 167-85.

Chadwick, O., *John Cassian*, 2nd edn. (Cambridge, 1968).

Chambers, R. W., 'Bede', *PBA* 32 (1936), 3-30.

Chaplais, P. 'The Origin and the Authenticity of the Royal Anglo-Saxon Diploma', *Journal of the Society of Archivists*, 3 (1965-9), 48-61. Repr. in *Prisca Munimenta: Studies presented to Dr A. E. J. Hollaender*, ed. F. Ranger (London, 1973), 28-42.

—— 'Some Early Anglo-Saxon Charters on Single Sheets: Originals or Copies?', *Journal of the Society of Archivists*, 3 (1965-9), 317-27.

—— 'Who introduced Charters into England? The Case for Augustine', *Journal of the Society of Archivists*, 3 (1969), 526-42. Repr. in *Prisca Munimenta*, pp. 88-107.

—— 'The Letter from Bishop Wealdhere', in *Medieval Scribes, Manuscripts and Libraries: Essays presented to N. R. Ker*, ed. M. B. Parkes and A. G. Watson (London, 1978), 3-24. A corrected version is repr. in his *Essays in Medieval Diplomacy and Administration* (London, 1981), No. 14.

Charles-Edwards, T. M., 'Kinship, Status and the Origins of the Hide', *Past and Present*, 56 (1972), 3–33.

—— 'The Foundation of Lastingham', *Ryedale Historian*, 7 (1974), 13–21.

—— 'The Social Background to Irish *Peregrinatio*', *Celtica*, 11 (1976), 43–59.

—— 'The Distinction between Land and Moveable Wealth in Anglo-Saxon England', in *Medieval Settlement*, ed. P. H. Sawyer (London, 1976), 180–7.

—— 'Bede, the Irish and the Britons', *Celtica*, 15 (1983), 42–52.

—— Review of *Gildas: New Approaches*, ed. M. Lapidge and D. Dumville, in *Cambridge Medieval Celtic Studies*, 12 (1986), 115–20.

Clapham, J. H., *English Romanesque Architecture before the Norman Conquest* (Oxford, 1930).

Clarke, R. R., *East Anglia* (Ancient Peoples and Places, 14; London, 1960).

Clemoes, P. (ed.), *The Anglo-Saxons: Studies presented to Bruce Dickins* (London, 1959).

—— *The Cult of St Oswald on the Continent* (Jarrow Lecture, 1983).

—— and Hughes, K. (eds.), *England before the Conquest: Studies in Primary Sources presented to Dorothy Whitelock* (Cambridge, 1971).

Colgrave, B., 'The Earliest Life of St Gregory the Great, written by a Whitby Monk', in *Celt and Saxon*, ed. N. K. Chadwick, pp. 119–37.

Collins, R., 'Theudebert I "Rex Magnus Francorum"', in *Ideal and Reality*, ed. P. Wormald *et al.*, pp. 7–33.

Coville, A., *Recherches sur l'histoire de Lyon* (Paris, 1928).

Cowdrey, H. E. J., 'Bede and the "English People"', *Journal of Religious History*, 11 (1981), 501–23. Repr. in his *Popes, Monks and Crusaders* (London, 1984), No. 3.

Cramp, R. J., *Northumbrian Sculpture* (Jarrow Lecture, 1965).

—— *Anglian and Viking York* (Borthwick Papers, 33; York, 1967).

—— 'Early Northumbrian Sculpture at Hexham', in *Saint Wilfrid at Hexham*, ed. D. P. Kirby, pp. 115–40.

—— 'Schools of Mercian Sculpture', in *Mercian Studies*, ed. A. Dornier, pp. 191–231.

—— *A Corpus of Anglo-Saxon Stone Sculpture*, i (Oxford, 1984).

Crépin, A., 'Bede and the Vernacular', in *Famulus Christi*, ed. G. Bonner, pp. 170–92.

Cross, J. E., 'The Ethic of War in Old English', in *England before the Conquest*, ed. P. Clemoes and K. Hughes, pp. 269–82.

Dagens, C., *Saint Grégoire le Grand: Culture et expérience chrétiennes* (Paris, 1977).

Davies, W., 'Middle Anglia and the Middle Angles', *Midland History*, 2 (1973–4), 18–20.

—— *Wales in the Early Middle Ages* (Leicester, 1982).

Davis, K. Rutherford, *Britons and Saxons: The Chiltern Region 400–700* (Chichester, 1982).

Davis, R. H. C., and J. M. Wallace-Hadrill, *The Writing of History in the Middle Ages: Essays presented to Richard William Southern* (Oxford, 1981).

Day, V., 'The Influence of the Catechetical *Narratio* on Old English and some other Medieval Narrative', *ASE* 3 (1974), 51–62.

Deanesly, M., 'The Familia at Christchurch, Canterbury, 596–832', in *Essays in Medieval History presented to Thomas Frederick Tout*, ed. A. G. Little and F. M. Powicke (Manchester, 1925), 1–13.

—— 'Roman Traditionalist Influence among the Anglo-Saxons', *EHR* 58 (1943), 129–46.

Dickins, B., 'Place-Names Formed from Animal-Head Names', appendix 1 to J. E. B. Gover, A. Mawer, and F. M. Stenton, *The Place-Names of Surrey* (EPNS 11; Cambridge, 1934), 403–6.

Diesner, H. J., 'Fragen der Macht- und Herrschaftsstruktur bei Beda', *Abhandlungen der Akademie der Wissenschaften und der Literatur in Mainz* (1980), No. 8.

—— 'Inkarnationsjahre, "Militia Christi" und anglische Königsporträts bei Beda Venerabilis', *Mittellateinisches Jahrbuch*, 16 (1981), 17–34.

Dobbie, E. Van K., *The Manuscripts of Caedmon's Hymn and Bede's Death Song* (New York, 1937).

Dornier, A. (ed.), *Mercian Studies* (Leicester, 1977).

Dumville, D. N., 'Liturgical Drama and Panegyric Responsory from the Eighth Century? A Re-examination of the Origin and Contents of the Ninth-Century Section of the Book of Cerne', *JTS* NS 23 (1972), 374–406.

—— 'A New Chronicle-Fragment of Early British History', *EHR* 88 (1973), 312–14.

—— '"Nennius" and the *Historia Brittonum*', *Studia Celtica*, 10–11 (1975–6), 78–95.

—— 'Sub-Roman Britain: History and Legend', *History*, NS 62 (1977), 173–92.

—— 'On the North British Section of the *Historia Brettonum*', *Welsh History Review*, 8 (1976–7), 345–54.

—— 'The *Ætheling*: A Study in Anglo-Saxon Constitutional History', *ASE* 8 (1979), 1–33.

—— 'Latin and Irish in the *Annals of Ulster*, A.D. 431–1050', in *Ireland in Early Mediaeval Europe*, ed. D. Whitelock *et al.*, pp. 320–41.

—— 'The Chronology of *De Excidio Britanniae*, Book I', in *Gildas: New Approaches*, ed. M. Lapidge and D. Dumville, pp. 61–84.

—— 'Late-Seventh- or Eighth-Century Evidence for the British Transmission of Pelagius', *Cambridge Medieval Celtic Studies*, 10 (1985), 39–52.

—— 'The West Saxon Genealogical Regnal List: Manuscripts and Texts', *Anglia*, 104 (1985), 1–32.

—— 'The West Saxon Genealogical Regnal List and the Chronology of Early Wessex', *Peritia*, 4 (forthcoming).

—— 'The Historical Value of the *Historia Brittonum*', *Arthurian Literature*, 6 (1986), 1–26.

Duncan, A. A. M., 'Bede, Iona, and the Picts', in *The Writing of History in the Middle Ages: Essays presented to R. W. Southern*, ed. R. H. C. Davis and J. M. Wallace-Hadrill (Oxford, 1981), 1–42.

Ekwall, E., *The Concise Oxford Dictionary of English Place-Names*, 4th edn. (Oxford, 1960).

Evison, V. I., *The Fifth-Century Invasions South of the Thames* (London, 1965).

—— (ed.), *Angles, Saxons and Jutes: Essays presented to J. N. L. Myres* (Oxford, 1981).

Ewig, E., *Trier im Merowingerreich* (Trier, 1954).

—— 'Das Bild Constantins des Grossen in den ersten Jahrhunderten des abendländischen Mittelalters', *Historisches Jahrbuch*, 75 (1956), 1–46; repr. in his *Spätantikes und fränkisches Gallien* (Beihefte d. Francia, 3; Munich, 1976), 72–113.

—— 'Das Privileg des Bischofs Berthefrid von Amiens für Corbie und der Klosterpolitik der Königin Balthild', *Francia*, 1 (1972), 62–114, repr. in *Spätantikes und fränkisches Gallien*, ii. 538–83.

—— 'Bemerkungen zu zwei merowingischen Bischofsprivilegien und einem Papstprivileg des 7. Jahrhunderts für merowingische Klöster', in *Mönchtum, Episkopat und Adel zur Gründungszeit des Klosters Reichenau*, ed. A. Borst (Vorträge und Forschungen, 20; Sigmaringen, 1974), 215–49.

Fanning, T., 'Some Field Monuments in the Townlands of Clonmelsh and Garryhundon, Co Carlow', *Peritia*, 3 (1984), 43–9.

Finberg, H. P. R., *The Early Charters of the West Midlands* (Leicester, 1961).

—— *The Early Charters of Wessex* (Leicester, 1964).

—— *Lucerna: Studies of Some Problems in the Early History of England* (London, 1964).

Finsterwalder, P. W., *Die Canones Theodori Cantuariensis und ihre Überlieferungsformen* (Weimar, 1929).

Fischer, J., *Der Hausmeier Ebroin* (Diss.; Bonn, 1954).

Fisher, H. A. L., Review of Plummer, i and ii, in *EHR* 12 (1897), 336–9.

Flower, R., *The Western Isle* (Oxford, 1944).

Folz, R., 'Tradition hagiographique et culte de Sainte Bathilde, reine de Francs', *Acad. des Inscriptions et Belles-Lettres* (1975), 369-84.

—— 'Saint Oswald roi de Northumbrie, étude d'hagiographie royale', *Anal. Boll.* 98 (1980), 49-74.

—— *Les Saint Rois du moyen âge en Occident (vi^e-xiiie siècles)* (Société des Bollandistes, Subsidia Hagiographica, 68; Brussels, 1984).

Forsberg, R., 'On OE *ād* in English Place-Names', *Namn och Bygd*, 58 (1971), 20-82.

Förster, M., *Der Flussname Themse und seine Sippe: Studien zur Anglisierung keltischer Eigennamen und zur Lautchronologie des Altbritischen (Sitzungsberichte der bayerischen Akademie der Wissenschaften*, Phil.-hist. Abteilung; Munich, 1941).

Foster, I. Ll., 'The Emergence of Wales', in *Prehistoric and Early Wales*, ed. I. Ll. Foster and Glyn Daniel (London, 1965), 213-35.

Fouracre, P., 'The Merovingians, the Mayors of the Palace and the Notion of a Low-Born Ebroin', *Bulletin of the Institute of Historical Research*, 57 (1984), 1-14.

Franklin, C. V., and P. Meyvaert, 'Has Bede's Version of the "Passio S. Anastasii" come down to us in "BHL" 408?', *Anal. Boll.* 100 (1982): *Mélanges offerts à Baudouin de Gaiffier et François Halkin*, 373-400.

Frantzen, A. J., 'The Tradition of Penitentials in Anglo-Saxon England', *ASE* 11 (1983), 23-56.

Frend, W. H. C., 'The Christianization of Roman Britain', *Christianity in Britain 300-700*, ed. M. W. Barley and R. P. C. Hanson (Leicester, 1968), 37-50.

—— '*Ecclesia Britannica*: Prelude or Dead End?', *JEH* 30 (1979), 129-44.

Frere, S. S., *Britannia*, revised edn. (London, 1978).

Frickel, Dom Michael, *Deus totus ubique simul: Untersuchungen zur allgemeinen Gottgegenwart im Rahmen der Gotteslehre Gregors des Grossen* (Freiburger theol. Studien, 69; Freiburg, 1956).

Fritze, W., 'Zur Entstehungsgeschichte des Bistums Utrecht: Franken und Friesen 690-734', *Rheinische Vierteljahrsblätter*, 35 (1971), 107-51.

Fry, D. K., 'The Art of Bede: Edwin's Council', *Saints, Scholars*, i. 191-207.

Fuhrmann, H., *Einfluss und Verbreitung der pseudoisidorischen Fälschungen*, i (Stuttgart, 1982).

Gelling, M., 'Place-Names and Anglo-Saxon Paganism', *University of Birmingham Historical Journal*, 8 (1961-2), 7-25.

Gibbon, E., *The History of the Decline and Fall of the Roman Empire*, ed. J. B. Bury (7 vols., London, 1896-1900).

Godfrey, J., 'The Place of the Double Monastery in the Anglo-Saxon Minster System', *Famulus Christi*, ed. G. Bonner, pp. 344-50.

Godman, P, 'The Anglo-Latin *Opus Geminatum*, from Aldhelm to Alcuin', *Medium Aevum*, 50 (1981), 215–29.

Goetzinger, N. (ed.), *Willibrordus: Echternacher Festschrift zur XII. Jahrhunderfeier des Todes des heiligen Willibrord* (Luxemburg, 1940).

Goffart, W., 'From Roman Taxation to Mediaeval Seigneurie', *Speculum*, 47 (1972), 165–87, 373–94.

Gougaud, Dom Louis, *Les Saints irlandais hors d'Irlande* (Louvain, 1936).

Gover, J. E. B., A. Mawer, and F. M. Stenton, *The Place Names of Surrey* (EPNS 11; Cambridge, 1934).

Graus, F., *Volk, Herrscher und Heiliger im Reich der Merowinger: Studien zur Hagiographie der Merowingerzeit* (Prague, 1965).

Green, D. H., *The Carolingian Lord* (Cambridge, 1965).

Grosjean, Père Paul, 'Notes d'hagiographie celtique, 28. La seconde visite de Saint Germain d'Auxerre en Grande-Bretagne', *Anal. Boll.* 75 (1957), 174–80.

—— 'La Date du colloque de Whitby', *Anal. Boll.* 78 (1960), 233–74.

Gruffydd, R. G., 'Canu Cadwallon ap Cadfan', *Astudiaethau ar yr Hengerdd/Studies in Old Welsh Poetry*, ed. R. Bromwich and R. Brinley Jones (Cardiff, 1978), 25–43.

Hamilton Thompson, A., 'Northumbrian Monasticism', *BLTW*, pp. 60–101.

Hammer, J., 'An Unrecorded *Epitaphium Caedwallae*', *Speculum*, 6 (1931), 607–8.

Hanning, R. W., *The Vision of History in Early Britain* (New York, 1966).

Hanson, R. P. C., *St Patrick: His Origins and Careeer* (Oxford, 1968).

Harrison, K., 'Early Wessex Annals in the Anglo-Saxon Chronicle', *EHR* 86 (1971), 527–33.

—— 'The Reign of King Ecgfrith of Northumbria', *Yorkshire Archaeological Journal*, 43 (1971), 79–84.

—— 'The Synod of Whitby and the Beginning of the Christian Era in England', *Yorkshire Archaeological Journal*, 45 (1973), 108–14.

—— 'The Beginning of the Year in England, c.500–900', *ASE* 2 (1973), 51–70.

—— 'The *Annus Domini* in Some Early Charters', *Journal of the Society of Archivists*, 4 (1973), 551–7.

—— *The Framework of Anglo-Saxon History to A.D. 900* (Cambridge, 1976).

—— 'Easter Cycles and the Equinox in the British Isles', *ASE* 7 (1978), 1–8.

—— 'A Letter from Rome to the Irish Clergy, AD 640', *Peritia*, 3 (1984), 222–9.

Hart, C. R., *The Early Charters of Eastern England* (Leicester, 1966).

Hawkes, S. Chadwick, with G. C. Dunning, 'Soldiers and Settlers in

Britain, Fourth to Fifth Century', *Medieval Archaeology*, 5 (1961), 1–70.

—— Review of V. I. Evison, *The Fifth-Century Invasions South of the Thames* in *Antiquity*, 40 (1966), 322–3.

Henderson, G., *Bede and the Visual Arts* (Jarrow Lecture, 1980).

Henry, F., 'Irish Enamels of the Dark Ages and their Relation to Cloisonné Techniques', in *Dark Age Britain: Studies presented to E. T. Leeds*, ed. D. B. Harden (London, 1956), 71–88.

Higgitt, J., 'The Dedication Inscription at Jarrow and its Context', *Antiquaries Journal*, 59 (1979), ii. 343–74.

Hill, R. M. T., and C. N. L. Brooke, 'Fron 627 until the Early Thirteenth Century', in *A History of York Minster*, ed. G. E. Aylmer and R. Cant (1977), 1–43.

Hodgkin, R. H., *A History of the Anglo-Saxons*, 3rd edn. (Oxford, 1952).

Holdsworth, C., and T. P. Wiseman (eds.), *The Inheritance of Historiography 350–900* (Exeter Studies in History, 12; Exeter, 1986).

Hope-Taylor, B., *Yeavering: An Anglo-British Centre of Early Northumbria* (London, 1977).

Hughes, K., 'The Distribution of Irish Scriptoria and Centres of Learning from 730 to 1111', in *Studies in the Early British Church*, ed. N. K. Chadwick, pp. 243–72.

—— *The Church in Early Irish Society* (London, 1966).

—— *Early Christianity in Pictland* (Jarrow Lecture, 1970). Repr. in her *Celtic Britain in the Early Middle Ages: Studies in Scottish and Welsh Sources*, ed. D. Dumville (Studies in Celtic History, 2; Woodbridge, 1980), 38–52.

—— 'Evidence for Contacts between the Churches of the Irish and the English from the Synod of Whitby to the Viking Age', in *England before the Conquest*, ed. P. Clemoes and K. Hughes, pp. 49–68.

Hunter Blair, P., 'The Northumbrians and their Southern Frontier', *Archaeologia Aeliana*, 4th ser. 26 (1948), 98–106. Repr. in his *Anglo-Saxon Northumbria*, ed. M. Lapidge and P. Hunter-Blair (London, 1984), No. 3.

—— 'The *Moore Memoranda* on Northumbrian History' in *The Early Cultures of North-West Europe*, ed. C. Fox and B. Dickins (Cambridge, 1950), 245–57. Repr. in his *Anglo-Saxon Northumbria*, No. 6.

—— 'Bede's Ecclesiastical History of the English Nation and its Importance Today' (Jarrow Lecture, 1959). Repr. in his *Anglo-Saxon Northumbria*, No. 7.

—— 'The Bernicians and their Northern Frontier', in *Studies in Early British History*, ed. N. K. Chadwick, pp. 137–72. Repr. in his *Anglo-Saxon Northumbria*, No. 8.

—— 'Some Observations on the *Historia Regum* attributed to Symeon of

Durham', in *Celt and Saxon*, pp. 63-118. Repr. in his *Anglo-Saxon Northumbria*, No. 9.
— *The World of Bede* (London, 1970).
— 'The Historical Writings of Bede', *Spoleto*, 17 (1970), 197-221. Repr. in his *Anglo-Saxon Northumbria*, No. 10.
— 'The Letters of Pope Boniface V and the Mission of Paulinus to Northumbria', *England before the Conquest*, ed. P. Clemoes and K. Hughes, pp. 5-13. Repr. in his *Anglo-Saxon Northumbria*, No. 11.
— 'From Bede to Alcuin', in *Famulus Christi*, ed. G. Bonner, pp. 239-60. Repr. in his *Anglo-Saxon Northumbria*, No. 12.
— 'Whitby as a Centre of Learning in the Seventh Century', in *Learning and Literature in Anglo-Saxon England: Studies presented to Peter Clemoes*, ed. M. Lapidge and H. Gneuss, pp. 3-32.
Isenberg, G., *Die Würdigung Wilfrieds von York in der Historia Ecclesiastica Gentis Anglorum Bedas und der Vita Wilfridi des Eddius* (Diss., Münster, 1978).
Jackson, K. H., *Language and History in Early Britain* (Edinburgh, 1953).
— 'The British Language during the Period of the English Settlements', in *Studies in Early British History*, ed. N. K. Chadwick, pp. 61-82.
— 'The Pictish Language', in *The Problem of the Picts*, ed. F. T. Wainwright, ch. 6.
— 'Edinburgh and the Anglian Occupation of Lothian', in *The Anglo-Saxons: Studies presented to Bruce Dickins*, ed. P. Clemoes, pp. 35-47.
— 'On the Northern British Section in Nennius', in *Celt and Saxon*, pp. 20-62.
— Review of L. Alcock, *Arthur's Britain*, in *Antiquity*, 47 (1973), 80-1.
— '*Varia* I. Bede's *Urbs Giudi*: Stirling or Cramond?', *Cambridge Medieval Celtic Studies*, 2 (1981), 1-8.
James, E., 'Ireland and Western Gaul', in *Ireland in Early Mediaeval Europe*, ed. D. Whitelock *et al.*, pp. 362-86.
— 'Bede and the Tonsure Question', *Peritia*, 3 (1984), 85-98.
Jenkins, C., 'Bede as Exegete and Theologian', *BLTW*, pp. 152-200.
John, E., *Land Tenure in Early England* (Leicester, 1960).
— *Orbis Britanniae* (Leicester, 1966).
— 'Social and Political Problems of the Early English Church', in *Land, Church and People: Essays presented to H. P. R. Finberg*, ed. J. Thirsk = supplement to *Agricultural History Review*, 18 (1971), 39-63.
Jones, C. W., *Bedae Pseudepigrapha: Scientific Writings Falsely Attributed to Bede* (Ithaca, 1939).
— 'Bede as Early Medieval Historian', *Medievalia et Humanistica*, 4 (1946), 26-36.

—— 'Bede's Place in Medieval Schools', in *Famulus Christi*, ed. G. Bonner, pp. 261–85.

—— *Saints' Lives and Chronicles* (Ithaca, 1947).

Jones, P. F., 'The Gregorian Mission and English Education', *Speculum*, 3 (1928), 335–48.

—— *A Concordance to the Historia Ecclesiastica of Bede* (Medieval Academy of American Publication, 2; Cambridge, Mass., 1929).

Kantorowicz, E., '*Pro Patria Mori* in Medieval Political Thought', *Selected Studies* (Locust Valley, 1965), 308–24.

Kelly, J. F., 'Pelagius, Pelagianism and the Early Irish Church', *Medievalia*, 4 (1978), 99–124.

Kendall, C. B., 'Imitation and the Venerable Bede's *Historia Ecclesiastica*', in *Saints, Scholars*, i. 161–90.

Kendrick, T. D. *et al.*, *Evangeliorum Quattuor Codex Lindisfarnensis* (2 vols.; Olten and Lausanne, 1956–60).

King, M. H., 'Grammatica Mystica: A Study of Bede's Grammatical Curriculum', in *Saints, Scholars and Heroes*, ed. M. H. King and W. M. Stevens, i. 145–59.

—— and W. M. Stevens (eds.), *Saints, Scholars and Heroes: Studies in Medieval Culture in Honour of Charles W. Jones* (2 vols.; Collegeville, Minn., 1979).

Kirby, D. P., 'Bede and Northumbrian Chronology', *EHR* 78 (1963), 514–27.

—— 'Problems of Early West Saxon History', *EHR* 80 (1965), 10–29.

—— 'Bede's Native Sources for the *Historia Ecclesiastica*', *BJRL* 48 (1965–6), 341–71.

—— (ed.), *Saint Wilfrid at Hexham* (Newcastle upon Tyne, 1974).

—— '... per universas Pictorum provincias', *Famulus Christi*, pp. 286–324.

—— 'King Ceolwulf of Northumbria and the *Historia Ecclesiastica*', *Studia Celtica*, 14–15 (1979–80), 168–73.

—— 'Bede, Eddius Stephanus and the Life of Wilfrid', *EHR* 98 (1983), 101–14.

Kottje, R., *Studien zum Einfluss des Alten Testamentes auf Recht und Liturgie des frühen Mittelalters*, 2nd edn. (Bonn, 1970).

Krüger, K. H., *Königsgrabkirchen der Franken, Angelsachsen und Langobarden bis zur Mitte des 8 Jahrhunderts* (Münstersche Mittelalter-Schriften, 4; Munich, 1971).

Laistner, M. L. W., *Thought and Letters in Western Europe*, 2nd edn. (London, 1957).

—— and H. H. King, *A Hand-List of Bede Manuscripts* (New York, 1943).

Lapidge, M., 'Some Remains of Bede's Lost *Liber Epigrammatum*', *EHR* 90 (1975), 798–820.

— Appendix to R. W. Hunt, 'Manuscript Evidence for Knowledge of the Poems of Venantius Fortunatus in Late Anglo-Saxon England', *ASE* 8 (1979), 287–95.

— 'The School of Theodore and Hadrian', *ASE* 15 (1986), 45–72.

— and D. Dumville, (eds.), *Gildas: New Approaches* (Studies in Celtic History, 5; Woodbridge, 1984).

— and H. Gneuss (eds.), *Learning and Literature in Anglo-Saxon England: Studies presented to Peter Clemoes* (Cambridge, 1985).

Lasko, P., 'The Comb', in *The Relics of Saint Cuthbert*, ed. C. F. Battiscombe (1956), 336–55.

— 'Prelude to Empire: The Frankish Kingdom from the Merovingians to Pepin', in *The Dark Ages*, ed. D. Talbot Rice (London, 1965), 197–218.

Lauer, P., and C. Samaran, *Les Diplômes originaux des mérovingiens* (Paris, 1908).

Leeds, E. T., 'The Early Saxon Penetration of the Upper Thames Area', *Antiquaries Journal*, 13 (1933), 229–51.

Lehmann, P., 'Wert und Echtheit einer Beda abgesprochenen Schrift', *Sitzungsberichte der bayerischen Akademie der Wissenschaften*, Phil.-hist. Kl. (1919), Heft 4, pp. 101–20.

Leonardi, C., 'Il venerabile Beda e la cultura del secolo VIII', *Spoleto*, 20 (1973), 603–58.

Lesne, E., *L'Hiérarchie épiscopale: Provinces, métropolitains, primats en Gaule et Germanie, 742–882* (Mémoires et travaux de la faculté catholique de Lille, 1; Lille, 1905).

Levison, W., 'Bede as Historian', *BLTW*, pp. 111–51.

— *England and the Continent in the Eighth Century* (Oxford, 1946).

— *Aus rheinischer und fränkischer Frühzeit* (Collected Papers; Düsseldorf, 1948).

Lohaus, A., *Die Merowinger und England* (Münchener Beiträge zur Mediävistik und Renaissance-Forschung; Munich, 1974).

Lowe, E. A., *Codices Latini Antiquiores: A Palaeographical Guide to Latin Manuscripts prior to the Ninth Century* (11 vols. and suppl.; Oxford, 1934–71). Vol. ii, 2nd edn. (1972).

Löwe, H., 'Entstehungszeit und Quellenwert der Vita Lebuini', *DA* 21 (1965), 347–70.

— (ed.), *Die Iren und Europa im frühen Mittelalter* (2 vols., Veröffentlichungen des Europa Zentrums Tübingen, Kulturwissenschaftliche Reihe, Stuttgart, 1982).

Loyn, H. E., *Anglo-Saxon England and the Norman Conquest* (London, 1962).

— 'Gesiths and Thegns in Anglo-Saxon England from the Seventh to the Tenth Century', *EHR* 70 (1955), 529–49.

McClure, J., 'Bede's Old Testament Kings', *Ideal and Reality*, ed. P. Wormald *et al.*, pp. 76–98.

—— 'Bede and the Life of Ceolfrid', *Peritia*, 3 (1984), 71–84.

Mac Eoin, G., 'On the Irish Legend of the Origin of the Picts', *Studia Hibernica*, 4 (1964), 138–54.

Mackay, T., 'Bede's Hagiographical Method: His Knowledge and Use of Paulinus of Nola', in *Famulus Christi*, ed. G. Bonner, pp. 77–92.

Maillé, Marquise de, *Les Cryptes de Jouarre* (Paris, 1971).

Markus, R. A., 'The Chronology of the Gregorian Mission to England: Bede's Narrative and Gregory's Correspondence', *JEH* 14 (1963), 16–30. Repr. in his *From Augustine to Gregory the Great: History and Christianity in Late Antiquity* (London, 1983), No. 10.

—— *Saeculum: History and Society in the Theology of St Augustine* (Cambridge, 1970).

—— 'Gregory the Great and a Papal Missionary Strategy', in *The Mission of the Church and the Propagation of the Faith*, ed. D. Baker, *Studies in Church History*, 6 (1970), 29–38. Repr. in his *From Augustine to Gregory the Great*, No. 11.

—— 'Church History and Early Christian Historians', in *Materials, Sources and Methods of Ecclesiastical History*, ed. D. Baker, *Studies in Church History*, 11 (1975), 1–17. Repr. in his *From Augustine to Gregory the Great*, No. 2.

—— *Bede and the Tradition of Ecclesiastical Historiography* (Jarrow Lecture, 1975). Repr. in his *From Augustine to Gregory the Great*, No. 3.

—— Review-article on E. A. Thompson, *Saint Germanus of Auxerre and the End of Roman Britain*, in *Nottingham Medieval Studies*, 29 (1985), 118–22.

—— 'Pelagianism: Britain and the Continent', *JEH* 37 (1986), 191–204.

Mathisen, R. W., 'The Last Year of Germanus of Auxerre', *Anal. Boll.* 99 (1981), 151–9.

Matthews, J. F., 'Macsen, Maximus, and Constantine', *Welsh History Review*, 11 (1982–3), 431–48.

Mawer, A. (ed.), *The Chief Elements Used in English Place-Names* (EPNS i/2; Cambridge, 1924).

Mayr-Harting, H. M. R. E., *The Coming of Christianity to Anglo-Saxon England* (London, 1972).

—— *The Venerable Bede, the Rule of St. Benedict, and Social Class* (Jarrow Lecture, 1976).

—— 'St Wilfrid in Sussex', in *Studies in Sussex Church History*, ed. M. J. Kitch (London, 1981), 1–17.

Meyvaert, P., 'Diversity within Unity: A Gregorian Theme', *Heythrop Journal*, 4 (1963), 141–62. Repr. in his *Benedict, Gregory, Bede and Others* (London, 1977). No. 6.

—— *Bede and Gregory the Great* (Jarrow Lecture, 1964). Repr. in *Benedict, Gregory, Bede and Others*, No. 8.

—— 'The Registrum of Gregory the Great and Bede', *RB* 80 (1970), 162-6. Repr. in *Benedict, Gregory, Bede and Others*, No. 11.

—— 'Bede's Text of the *Libellus Responsionum* of Gregory the Great to Augustine of Canterbury', *England before the Conquest*, pp. 15-33. Repr. in *Benedict, Gregory, Bede and Others*, No. 10.

—— 'Bede the Scholar', *Famulus Christi*, pp. 40-69. Repr. in *Benedict, Gregory, Bede and Others*, No. 16.

—— 'Bede and the Church Paintings at Wearmouth-Jarrow', *ASE* 8 (1979), 63-77.

Miller, M., 'Bede's Roman Dates', *Classica et Mediaevalia*, 31 (1970), 239-57.

—— 'Relative and Absolute Publication Dates of Gildas's *De Excidio* in Medieval Scholarship', *Bulletin of the Board of Celtic Studies*, 26 (1974-6), 169-74.

—— 'Bede's Use of Gildas', *EHR* 90 (1975), 241-61.

—— 'The Dates of Deira', *ASE* 8 (1979), 35-61.

—— 'Matriliny by Treaty: The Pictish Foundation Legend', in *Ireland in Early Mediaeval Europe*, ed. D. Whitelock *et al.*, pp. 133-61.

Moisl, H., 'The Bernician Royal Dynasty and the Irish in the Seventh Century', *Peritia*, 2 (1983), 103-26.

Morris, C., 'The Plague in Britain', *Historical Journal*, 14 (1971), 205-15.

Morris, J. R., 'The Literary Evidence', *Christianity in Britain 200-700*, ed. M. W. Barley and R. P. C. Hanson, pp. 55-74.

—— 'Pelagian Literature', *JTS* NS 16 (1965), 26-60.

Mozley, J. H., 'Notes de lecture 86. Bede, Hist. Evang. [*sic*] bk. V, ch. 2', *Latomus*, 19 (1960), 578.

Myres, J. N. L., 'The Teutonic Settlement of Northern Britain', *History*, NS 20 (1935), 250-62.

—— Review of *Studies in the Early British Church*, ed. N. K. Chadwick, in *EHR* 70 (1955), 90-4.

—— 'Pelagius and the End of Roman Rule in Britain', *JRS* 50 (1960), 21-36.

—— Review of V. I. Evison, *The Fifth-Century Invasions South of the Thames*, in *EHR* 81 (1966), 340-5.

—— *Anglo-Saxon Pottery and the Settlement of England* (Oxford, 1969).

—— 'The Angles, the Saxons and the Jutes', *PBA* 56 (1970), 145-74.

—— *The English Settlements* (Oxford, 1986).

Nelson, J., 'Queens as Jezebels: The Careers of Brunhild and Balthild in Merovingian History', in *Medieval Women: Essays presented to Rosalind Hill*, ed. D. Baker (Oxford, 1978), 31-77.

Newton, R. R., *Medieval Chronicles and the Rotation of the Earth* (Baltimore, 1972).

Norberg, D., *In Registrum Gregorii Magni Studia Critica* (2 vols.; Uppsala, 1937–9).

Ó Cróinín, D., 'A Seventh-Century Irish Computus from the Circle of Cummianus', *Proc. Roy. Irish Acad.* 82 C (1982), No. 11, pp. 405–30.

—— 'Pride and Prejudice', *Peritia*, 1 (1982), 352–62.

—— 'The Irish Provenance of Bede's Computus', *Peritia*, 2 (1983), 229–47.

—— 'Rath Melsigi, Willibrord, and the Earliest Echternach Manuscripts', *Peritia*, 3 (1984), 17–42.

—— '"New Heresy for Old": Pelagianism in Ireland and the Papal Letter of 640', *Speculum*, 60 (1985), 505–16.

O'Loughlin, J. L. N., 'Sutton Hoo—the Evidence of the Documents', *Medieval Archaeology*, 8 (1964), 1–19.

O'Rahilly, T. F., *Early Irish History and Mythology* (Dublin, 1946).

Padel, O. J., *Cornish Place-Name Elements* (EPNS 56–7; 1985).

Page, R. I., 'Anglo-Saxon Runes and Magic', *Journal of the British Archaeological Association*, 3rd ser. 27 (1964), 14–31.

Picard, J.-M., 'Bede, Adomnán and the Writing of History', *Peritia*, 3 (1984), 50–70.

Poole, R. L., *Studies in Chronology and History* (Oxford, 1934).

Prestwich, J. O., 'King Æthelhere and the Battle of the Winwæd', *EHR* 83 (1968), 89–95.

Prinz, F., *Frühes Mönchtum im Frankenreich* (Munich, 1965).

Puniet, P. de, *The Roman Pontifical*, tr. M. V. Harcourt (London, 1932).

Quentin, Dom H., *Les Martyrologes historiques du moyen âge* (Paris, 1908).

Raby, F. J. E., *A History of Secular Latin Poetry in the Middle Ages* (2 vols., Oxford, 1934).

Ray, R. D., 'Bede the Exegete as Historian', *Famulus Christi*, pp. 125–40.

—— 'Bede's *vera lex historiae*', *Speculum*, 55 (1980), 1–21.

—— 'The Triumph of Greco-Roman Rhetorical Assumptions in Pre-Carolingian Historiography', in *The Inheritance of Historiography 350–900*, ed. C. Holdsworth and T. P. Wiseman, pp. 67–84.

Reynolds, L. D. (ed.), *Texts and Transmission: A Survey of the Latin Classics* (Oxford, 1983).

Riché, P., *Education et culture dans l'occident barbare, vi^e–viiie siècles*, 3rd edn. (Paris, 1962). Engl. tr. by J. J. Contreni, *Education and Culture in the Barbarian West*, 2nd edn. (Columbia, SC, 1978).

—— 'La Magie à l'époque carolingienne', *Académie des Inscriptions et Belles-Lettres* (1973), 127–38.

Rigold, S. E., 'The Supposed See of Dunwich', *Journ. Brit. Arch. Assoc.* 3rd ser. 24 (1961), 55–9.
—— 'The "Double Minsters" of Kent and their Analogies', *Journ. Brit. Arch. Assoc.* 3rd ser. 31 (1968), 27–37.
—— 'Further Evidence about the Site of "Dommoc"', *Journ. Brit. Arch. Assoc.* 3rd ser. 37 (1974), 97–102.
Rollason, D. W., 'Lists of Saints' Resting-Places in Anglo-Saxon England', *ASE* 7 (1978), 61–94.
—— *The Mildrith Legend: A Study in Early Medieval Hagiography in England* (Leicester, 1982).
—— 'The Cults of Murdered Royal Saints in Anglo-Saxon England', *ASE* 11 (1983), 1–22.
Roper, M., 'Wilfred's Landholdings in Northumbria', in *Saint Wilfrid at Hexham*, ed. D. P. Kirby, pp. 61–80.
Rutherford, I., ' *Giudi* Revisited', *Bulletin of the Board of Celtic Studies*, 26 (1974–6), 440–4.
Saint German d'Auxerre et son temps: Communications présentées à l'occasion du XIe-X^e congrès de l'Association bourguignonne des sociétés savantes, 29 juillet-2 août 1948 (Société des sci. hist. et nat. de l'Yonne; Auxerre, 1950).
Sawyer, P. H., *Anglo-Saxon Charters: An Annotated List and Bibliography* (Royal Historical Society Guides and Handbooks, 8; London, 1968).
—— (ed.), *Medieval Settlements: Continuity and Change* (London, 1976), 181–3.
Scharer, A., *Die angelsächsische Königsurkunde im 7. und 8. Jahrhundert* (Vienna, 1982).
Sharpe, R., 'Some Problems concerning the Organisation of the Church in Early Medieval Ireland', *Peritia*, 3 (1984), 230–70.
Sims-Williams, P., 'Continental Influence at Bath Monastery in the Seventh Century', *ASE* 4 (1975), 1–10.
—— 'Gildas and the Anglo-Saxons', *Cambridge Medieval Celtic Studies*, 6 (1983), 1–30.
—— 'The Settlement of England in Bede and the *Chronicle*', *ASE* 12 (1983), 1–42.
—— 'William of Malmesbury and the *Silloge Epigrafica di Cambridge*', *Archivum Historiae Pontificiae*, 21 (1983), 9–33.
Smalley, B., 'L'Exégèse biblique dans la littérature latine', *Spoleto*, 10 (1963), 631–55.
Smith, A. H., *The Place-Names of the East Riding of Yorkshire and York* (EPNS 14; Cambridge, 1937).
—— *English Place-Name Elements* (2 parts, EPNS 25–6; 1970).
Smyth, A. P., *Warlords and Holy Men* (London, 1984).

Southern, R. W., 'Bede', in his *Medieval Humanism and Other Studies*
(Oxford, 1970), 1–8.
—— 'Aspects of the European Tradition of Historical Writing: 3.
History as Prophecy', *TRHS* 5th ser. 22 (1972), 159–80.
Sprandel, R., *Der merowingische Adel und die Gebiete östlich des Rheins*
(Forschungen zur oberrheinischen Landesgeschichte, 5; Freiburg i.
Br., 1957).
Stafford, P. A., *The East Midlands in the Early Middle Ages* (Leicester,
1985).
Stancliffe, C., 'Kings and Conversion', *Frühmittelalterliche Studien*, 14
(1980), 59–94.
—— 'Kings Who Opted Out', in *Ideal and Reality*, ed. P. Wormald *et al.*,
pp. 154–76.
Steinen, W. von den, *Chlodwigs Übergang zum Christentum: ein quellen-
kritische Studie*, 3rd edn. (Darmstadt, 1968).
Stengel, E. E., 'Kaisertitel und Souveränitätsidee', *DA* 3 (1939), 1–56.
Repr. in his *Abhandlungen und Untersuchungen zur Geschichte des
Kaisergedankens im Mittelalter* (Cologne, 1965), 239–86.
—— 'Imperator und Imperium bei den Angelsachsen', *DA* 16 (1960),
15–72. Repr. in his *Abhandlungen und Untersuchungen*, pp. 287–338.
Stenton, F. M., *Latin Charters of the Anglo-Saxon Period* (Oxford, 1955).
—— 'The East Anglian Kings of the Seventh Century', in *The Anglo-
Saxons: Essays presented to Bruce Dickins*, ed. P. Clemoes, pp. 43–62.
Repr. in his *Preparatory to Anglo-Saxon England*, pp. 394–402.
—— *Preparatory to Anglo-Saxon England: Being the Collected Papers of Frank
Merry Stenton*, ed. D. M. Stenton (Oxford, 1970).
—— *Anglo-Saxon England*, 3rd edn. (Oxford, 1971).
Stevens, C. E., 'Gildas Sapiens', *EHR* 56 (1941), 353–73.
Stroheker, K. F., *Germanentum und Spätantike* (Zürich and Stuttgart,
1965).
Svennung, J., *Jordanes und Scandia: Kritisch-exegetische Studien* (Stock-
holm, 1967).
Taylor, H. M., 'Structural Criticism: A Plea for a More Systematic
Study of Anglo-Saxon Buildings', *ASE* 1 (1972), 259–72.
—— and J. Taylor, *Anglo-Saxon Architecture* (3 vols.; Cambridge, 1965–
78).
Thacker, A., 'Bede's Ideal of Reform', *Ideal and Reality*, ed. P. Wormald
et al., pp. 130–53.
Thomas, A. C., 'The Evidence from North Britain', in *Christianity in
Britain, 300–700*, ed. M. W. Barley and R. P. C. Hanson, pp. 93–121.
—— *The Early Christian Archaeology of North Britain* (Oxford, 1971).
—— *Bede, Archaeology, and the Cult of Relics* (Jarrow Lecture, 1973).
—— *Christianity in Roman Britain to A.D. 500* (London, 1981).

Thompson, E. A., 'Gildas and the History of Britain', *Britannia* 10 (1979), 203–26, and 11 (1980), 344.
—— 'St. Patrick and Coroticus', *JTS* NS 31 (1980), 12–27.
—— *Saint Germanus of Auxerre and the End of Roman Britain* (Studies in Celtic History, 6; Woodbridge, 1984).
Todd, M., '*Famosa Pestis* and Britain in the Fifth Century', *Britannia*, 8 (1977), 319–25.
Tolkien, J. R. R. (ed. A. Bliss), *Finn and Hengest: The Fragment and the Episode* (London, 1982).
Traube, L., *Perrona Scottorum* (*Sitzungsberichte d. phil.-hist. Kl. d. K. Akad. d. Wiss. zu München, 1900*; Munich, 1901), 477–94. Repr. in his *Vorlesungen und Abhandlungen*, ed. F. Boll (Munich, 1920), iii. 95–119.
Tugène, G., 'L'Histoire "ecclésiastique" du peuple anglais: réflexions sur le particularisme et l'universalisme chez Bède', *Recherches Augustiniennes*, 17 (1982), 129–72.
Turville-Petre, J. E., 'Hengist and Horsa', *Saga-Book of the Viking Society*, 14 (1953–7), iv. 273–90.
Väänänen, V., *Introduction au latin vulgaire* (Paris, 1967).
Vierck, H., 'La "Chemise de Sainte-Balthilde" à Chelles et l'influence byzantine sur l'art de cour mérovingien au VIIe siècle', in *Centénaire de l'abbé Cochet, 1975: Actes du colloque international d'archéologie* (Rouen, 1978).
Vollrath-Reichelt, H., *Königsgedanke und Königtum bei den Angelsachsen* (Kolner Historische Abhandlungen, 19; Cologne and Vienna, 1971).
Wade-Evans, A. W., *The Emergence of England and Wales*, 2nd edn. (Cambridge, 1959).
Wainwright, F. T. (ed.), *The Problem of the Picts* (London and Edinburgh, 1955).
Wallace-Hadrill, J. M., *Bede's Europe* (Jarrow Lecture, 1962). Repr. in J. M. Wallace-Hadrill, *Early Medieval History* (Oxford, 1975), 60–75.
—— *The Long-Haired Kings and Other Studies in Frankish History* (London, 1962).
—— *Early Germanic Kingship in England and on the Continent* (Oxford, 1971).
—— *The Frankish Church* (Oxford, 1983).
Wampach, C., *Geschichte der Grundherrschaft Echternach: Untersuchungen über die Person des Gründers, über die Kloster- und Wirtschaftsgeschichte auf Grund des Liber Aureus Epternacensis (698–1222)* (2 vols.; Luxemburg, 1929–30).
Ward, B., 'Miracles and History: A Reconsideration of the Miracle Stories used by Bede', in *Famulus Christi*, ed. G. Bonner, pp. 70–6.
Werner, K., *Beda der Ehrwürdiger und seine Zeit* (Vienna, 1881).

Wheeler, G. H., 'The Genealogy of the Early West Saxon Kings', *EHR* 36 (1921), 161–71.

—— 'Gildas De Excidio Britanniae, Chapter 26', *EHR* 41 (1926), 497–503.

Whitelock, D. (ed.), *English Historical Documents*, c.*500–1042* (English Historical Documents, London, 1955).

—— 'The Pre-Viking Church in East Anglia', *ASE* 1 (1972), 1–22.

—— 'Bede and his Teachers and Friends', in *Famulus Christi*, ed. G. Bonner, pp. 19–39.

—— R. McKitterick, and D. Dumville (eds.), *Ireland in Early Mediaeval Europe: Studies in Memory of Kathleen Hughes* (Cambridge, 1982).

Wilson, D. (ed.), *The Archaeology of Anglo-Saxon England* (London, 1976).

Wilson, P. A., 'The Cult of St Martin in the British Isles', *Innes Review*, 19 (1968), 129–43.

Winterbottom, M., 'Columbanus and Gildas', *Vigiliae Christianae*, 30 (1976), 310–17.

—— 'Aldhelm's Prose Style and its Origins', *ASE* 6 (1977), 39–76.

Wolfram, H., *Intitulatio*, i–ii, *Mitteilungen d. Inst. f. österreich. Geschichtsforschung*, suppl. to vols. 21 and 24 (1967 and 1973).

Wood, I., *The Merovingian North Sea* (Occasional Papers on Medieval Topics; Alingsås, 1983).

—— 'The *Vita Columbani* and Merovingian Hagiography', *Peritia*, 1 (1982), 63–80.

—— 'The End of Roman Britain: Continental Evidence and Parallels', *Gildas: New Approaches*, ed. M. Lapidge and D. Dumville, pp. 1–26.

Wood, S., 'Bede's Northumbrian Dates again', *EHR* 98 (1983), 280–96.

Wormald, F., *Collected Writings*, i, ed. J. J. G. Alexander, T. J. Brown, and J. Gibbs (London, 1984).

Wormald, P. 'Bede and Benedict Biscop', in *Famulus Christi*, ed. G. Bonner, pp. 141–69.

—— 'The Uses of Literacy in Anglo-Saxon England and its Neighbours', *TRHS* 5th ser. 27 (1977), 95–114.

—— 'Bede, "Beowulf" and the Conversion of the Anglo-Saxon Aristocracy', in *Bede and Anglo-Saxon England: Papers in Honour of the 1300th Anniversary of the Birth of Bede, given at Cornell University in 1973 and 1974*, ed. R. T. Farrell (British Archaeological Reports, 46; Oxford, 1978).

—— 'Bede, the *Bretwaldas* and the Origins of the *Gens Anglorum*', in *Ideal and Reality*, ed. P. Wormald *et al.*, pp. 99–129.

—— *Bede and the Conversion of England: The Charter Evidence* (Jarrow Lecture, 1984).

—— with D. Bullough and R. Collins (eds.), *Ideal and Reality in Frankish* and *Anglo-Saxon Society: Studies presented to J. M. Wallace-Hadrill* (Oxford, 1983).

Wrenn, C. L., 'The Poetry of Caedmon', *PBA* 32 (1946), 277–95.

Wright, C. E., *The Cultivation of Saga in Anglo-Saxon England* (Edinburgh, 1939).

Wright, N., 'Bede and Vergil', *Romanobarbarica*, 6 (1981–2), 361–79.

—— 'Gildas's Prose Style and its Origins', in *Gildas: New Approaches*, ed. M. Lapidge and D. Dumville, pp. 107–28.

—— 'Gildas's Geographical Perspective: Some Problems', in *Gildas: New Approaches*, ed. M. Lapidge and D. Dumville, pp. 85–106.

—— 'Did Gildas read Orosius?', *Cambridge Medieval Celtic Studies*, 9 (1985), 31–42.

Yorke, B., 'The Kingdom of the East Saxons', *ASE* 14 (1985), 1–36.

INDEX